Peterson's®

MASTER THE™
GRE®
GENERAL TEST
2019

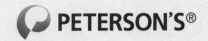
PETERSON'S®

About Peterson's

Peterson's® has been your trusted educational publisher for over 50 years. It's a milestone we're quite proud of, as we continue to offer the most accurate, dependable, high-quality educational content in the field, providing you with everything you need to succeed. No matter where you are on your academic or professional path, you can rely on Peterson's for its books, online information, expert test-prep tools, the most up-to-date education exploration data, and the highest quality career success resources—everything you need to achieve your education goals. For our complete line of products, visit www.petersons.com.

For more information about Peterson's range of educational products, contact Peterson's, 8740 Lucent Blvd., Suite 400, Highlands Ranch, CO 80129, 800-338-3282 Ext. 54229; or find us online at www.petersons.com.

ISBN-13: 978-0-7689-4248-4

Printed in the United States of America

10 9 8 7 6 5 4 3 2 1   20 19 18

Twenty-fifth Edition

Petersonspublishing.com/publishing updates

Check out our website at www.petersonspublishing.com/publishingupdates to see if there is any new information regarding the test and any revisions or corrections to the content of this book. We've made sure the information in this book is accurate and up-to-date; however, the test format or content may have changed since the time of publication.

Access 3 Practice Tests for the GRE® General Test

http://www.petersonspublishing.com/gre

Enter your email address, and Peterson's will email you an activation code and the link needed to access online practice tests for the GRE® General Test.

Contents

PART I   ABOUT THE GRE® GENERAL TEST

PART II   DIAGNOSING STRENGTHS AND WEAKNESSES

PART III ANALYTICAL WRITING

PART IV VERBAL REASONING

PART V   QUANTITATIVE REASONING

PART VI   THREE PRACTICE TESTS

APPENDIXES

Before You Begin

Master the™ GRE® General Test 2019 is your guidebook for navigating the GRE® General Test. The GRE® General Test is designed to effectively predict test takers' overall performance in graduate school. Its emphasis is on the test takers' ability to think. You'll see that in the design of questions.

You'll find reading comprehension questions that ask you to critique the validity of an author's argument or ask you to identify information that supports an author's argument. Other questions in the Verbal Reasoning section ask you to select the best word choice based on analyzing the context of a sentence or passage. In the Analytical Writing section, you'll be asked to evaluate someone else's argument and to develop an argument of your own. To de-emphasize computation and emphasize the thought processes used to arrive at answers in the Quantitative Reasoning section, you will find an on-screen calculator for the computer-delivered version. If you are taking the paper-delivered test, you will be given a calculator.

You needn't begin to hyperventilate at this information. *Master the™ GRE® General Test 2019* will

- walk you through the parts of the test.
- give you strategies to use for each type of question.
- explain how to avoid some common writing problems.
- review basic arithmetic, algebra, geometry, and data analysis.
- help you develop your vocabulary for word-choice questions.
- provide simulated practice with four practice tests.

HOW THIS BOOK IS ORGANIZED

Master the™ GRE® General Test 2019 is divided into six parts to facilitate your study:

- **Part I** explains basic information about the GRE® General Test and provides an overview with examples of the different question types you'll find on the test.

- **Part II** offers a diagnostic test to help you identify your areas of strength and those areas where you will need to spend more time in your review sessions.

- **Part III** explores the Analytical Writing section of the test and offers strategies for developing well-supported and coherent responses to the types of tasks that you will be required to answer.

- **Part IV** goes into detail about the different question formats that you will find in the Verbal Reasoning section and offers strategies for answering each question type.

- **Part V** describes the different question formats in the Quantitative Reasoning section of the test and offers strategies to help you figure out answers to the math questions.

- **Part VI** has three more tests that provide you with simulated practice in taking the GRE® General Test under timed conditions.

- The **Appendixes** offer two additional chapters to help you improve your writing. "Appendix A: Common Errors in Grammar and Mechanics," can help you avoid such mistakes as sentence faults, misplaced modifiers, subject-verb agreement issues, and pronoun problems. If misspelled words are a problem for you, check out "Appendix B: Often Confused and Confusing Words." Here, you'll find a list of commonly misspelled words—words that sound somewhat similar but have completely different meanings and if used incorrectly could lower your score.

Each chapter in Parts IV and V contains practice sections to help you review what you have just learned.

SPECIAL STUDY FEATURES

Master the™ GRE® General Test 2019 has several features that will help you get the most from your study time.

Overview

Each chapter begins with a listing of the major topics in that chapter, followed by an introduction that explains what you will be reviewing.

Summing It Up

Each chapter ends with a point-by-point summary of the main points of the chapter. It can be a handy last-minute guide to review before the test.

Bonus Information

You will find three types of notes in the margin of this book to alert you to important information.

Note

Margin notes marked "Note" highlight information about the test structure itself.

Tip

A note marked "Tip" points out valuable advice for taking the GRE® General Test.

Alert

An "Alert" identifies pitfalls in the testing format or question types that can lead test takers to make mistakes when selecting answers.

USING THIS BOOK TO PREPARE FOR THE COMPUTER-DELIVERED GRE® GENERAL TEST

There are several important things to remember as you work through this book. When taking the computer-delivered GRE® General Test, you'll be entering answers by typing on a keyboard or using a mouse. The Analytical Writing section requires that you compose short responses by typing words, sentences, and paragraphs. The numeric entry questions from the Quantitative Reasoning section require that you enter numbers into boxes. Other sections require that you select choices by clicking on them with your mouse. Since you can't answer in this fashion in a book, you'll have to fill in your answers by hand when taking the tests and completing the exercises. Also, bear in mind that some questions may appear in a slightly different form due to the limitations of print. For instance, answer options will appear with letters before each of them (A, B, C, etc.) in this guide.

On the actual exam, the answer options may appear as ovals or squares. However, all of the question content is similar to that found on the GRE® General Test.

ACCESS ONLINE PRACTICE TESTS FOR THE GRE® GENERAL TEST

Peterson's provides you with access to three additional online practice tests for the GRE® General Test. The testing content on these three practice tests was created by the test-prep experts at Peterson's. The Peterson's online testing experience resembles the testing experience you will encounter on the actual GRE® General Test. You can access these three practice tests at **http://www.petersons publishing.com/gre**. You will be asked to enter your email address, and Peterson's will email you an activation code and the link needed to access the GRE® online practice tests.

YOU ARE WELL ON YOUR WAY TO SUCCESS

You have made the decision to apply to graduate school and have taken a very important step in that process. *Master the™ GRE® General Test 2019* will help you score high on the exam and prepare you for everything you'll need to know on the day of your exam. Good luck!

GIVE US YOUR FEEDBACK

Peterson's publishes a full line of books—test prep, career preparation, education exploration, and financial aid. Peterson's publications can be found at high school guidance offices, college libraries and career centers, your local bookstore and library, and at www.petersonsbooks.com.

We welcome any comments or suggestions you may have about this publication. Your feedback will help us make educational dreams possible for you—and others like you.

STRATEGIES FOR ANSWERING DIFFERENT QUESTION TYPES ON THE GRE® GENERAL TEST

The GRE® General Test has three areas of assessment: Analytical Writing, Verbal Comprehension, and Quantitative Reasoning. This section lists in one convenient place the various test-taking strategies that are discussed in this book and that will help you master the GRE® General Test. As you read through the list, put a star next to items that you already know. Draw lines to connect those that are the same between test areas. Pay particular attention to them. The strategies for the two writing tasks are just good writing strategies; there is no mystery about them.

As you work your way through the chapters, practice exercises, and practice tests, be sure to practice the following strategies, so that on test day, the right strategy for the question type will come naturally to you.

Analytical Writing

The Analytical Writing section is divided into two tasks: an issue with which you must agree or disagree and an argument that you must analyze.

The Issue Task

- State a thesis, and state it early.
- Use a standard pattern of organization.
- Order paragraphs effectively.
- Use a standard pattern of organization.
- Develop each paragraph fully.
- Consider style, tone, and person.
- As time permits, add extras:
  - Interest-grabbing opening
  - Apt word choice
  - Varied sentence structure
- Create your writing plan:
  - Prewriting
  - Drafting
  - Writing
  - Proofreading

The Argument Task

- Look for:
  - Unreliable opinion polls, surveys, questionnaires
  - Faulty cause-and-effect relationships
  - False generalizations

- o   False analogies
- o   Either-or thinking
- o   Assumptions
- Create your writing plan:
  - o   Prewriting
  - o   Drafting
  - o   Writing
  - o   Proofreading

Verbal Reasoning

The Verbal Reasoning section is made up of three areas: Reading Comprehension, Text Completion, and Sentence Equivalence.

Strategies for Reading Comprehension Questions

Before you begin answering questions, use active reading to:

- identify the topic, main idea, thesis, or proposition of the passage.
- clarify your understanding of the content.
- summarize the passage.

Then, you can apply the following general strategies for:

- Multiple-Choice Questions
  - o   Try answering the questions before you read the answer choices.
  - o   Read all the answers before you choose.
  - o   Compare answer choices to each other and the question.
  - o   Avoid selecting an answer you don't fully understand.
  - o   Choose the *BEST* answer.
  - o   Pay attention to structure and structural clues.
  - o   Don't select an answer just because it's true.
  - o   Substitute answer choices in word meaning questions.
  - o   Choose the answer that *doesn't* fit in the EXCEPT questions.
  - o   Choose an answer that answers the question on its own.
- Select-in-Passage Questions
  - o   Match the sentence to the information.

Strategies for Text Completion Questions

- Try answering the questions before you read the answer choices.
- Focus on only one blank at a time.
- If there is more than one blank, complete the blanks in the order that makes sense to you.

- Check your answer(s) in place.
- Use structural clues:
  - Restatement
  - Cause and effect
  - Comparison or similarity
  - Main idea and details
  - Tone and style
  - Grammar and usage
- Avoid selecting the word or phrase you don't fully understand if it's unfamiliar.

Strategies for Sentence Equivalence Questions

- Read the stem first.
- Come up with your own answer.
- Check your answers in place.
- Use signal words and structural clues.
- Avoid leaping at the first likely pair of synonyms.
- Examine connotations.
- Consider grammar and usage.

Quantitative Reasoning

Quantitative Reasoning has three different types of questions: Multiple-Choice (includes Data Interpretation Sets), Numeric Entry, and Quantitative Comparison.

Multiple-Choice Questions

- Pick and plug numbers.
- Work backward from answer choices.
- Turn verbose or abstract language into concise and concrete wording.
- Calculate the least and greatest possible values.
- Make sure you're answering the correct question.
- Think through data sufficiency questions.

Special Strategies for Data Interpretation Sets

- Quickly scan the data.
- Make sure you're answering the correct question.
- Estimate.

Numeric Entry Questions

- Turn verbose or abstract language into concise and concrete wording.
- Make sure you're answering the correct question.
- Round correctly.

Quantitative Comparison Questions

- Pick and plug numbers.
- Consider when to use pick-and-plug numbers and when not to use them.
- Simplify the quantities.
- Eliminate terms when simplifying quantities.
- Avoid unnecessary calculations.
- Estimate.
- Redraw the figure.
- Recognize when an answer cannot be determined.

PART I

ABOUT THE GRE® GENERAL TEST

The Basics of the GRE® General Test

OVERVIEW

- **Test Organization**
- **Test Time Limits**
- **Test Tools**
- **Scoring the Test**
- **Test Day**
- **General Test-Taking Strategies to Remember**
- **Summing It Up**

Can a standardized test be "test taker friendly"? The Educational Testing Service (ETS), the makers of the GRE® General Test, thinks so. As proof, ETS points to the maneuverability and functionality of the computer-delivered GRE® General Test that was introduced in 2011. Within each timed section of the test, test takers can edit and change their work, skip questions, and then return to the questions before timing out of that section, which is more like a pencil-and-paper test.

However, the Quantitative Reasoning and Verbal Reasoning sections are also computer-adaptive to a degree. The questions for the second Quantitative Reasoning and Verbal Reasoning sections are based on how well you perform on the first sections of questions. Two other test-friendly functions are the on-screen calculator for doing computation and a word processing program for completing the two Analytical Writing tasks.

According to ETS, the question types introduced in 2011 better mirror the reasoning skills that test takers are called on to use in graduate and business school. The topics in the Analytical Writing section, the problems in the Quantitative Reasoning sections, and the passages used as the basis for questions in the Verbal Reasoning sections simulate the real-world issues and situations that students encounter in their course work for advanced degrees. The scores that result from the current GRE® General Test are considered by ETS to be "more reliable" than any previous test.

Chapter 1

TEST ORGANIZATION

The GRE® General Test is divided into three areas of assessment: Analytical Writing, Verbal Reasoning, and Quantitative Reasoning. The first section will always be Analytical Writing. The other sections may appear in any order.

Analytical Writing

Analytical Writing assesses your ability to think critically and transfer your ideas into well-developed, well-reasoned, and well-supported writing. There are two tasks for this section of the test: the Analyze an Argument task and the Analyze an Issue task. The first requires that you analyze someone else's argument and the second that you build your own argument either in support of or in disagreement with an opinion, policy, recommendation, or claim. Thus, the GRE® General Test assesses your ability to develop and support your own ideas and your ability to analyze another's argument and his or her supporting evidence. In addition, you will also be expected to sustain well-focused and coherent writing and control the elements of Standard Written English.

In addition, the tasks are specific but do not require prior knowledge of the subject. Completing them successfully relies only on your ability to think critically and write analytically.

Verbal Reasoning

The Verbal Reasoning sections of the GRE® General Test assess your ability to understand, analyze, and apply information found in the types of reading you'll be doing in graduate school. Among the questions you'll find are ones that ask you to reason from incomplete data; analyze and draw conclusions; identify authors' assumptions and perspectives; distinguish major and minor points; understand the structure of a text; understand the meaning of words, sentences, and passages; and understand multiple levels of meaning.

Three types of questions appear in the Verbal Reasoning section:

1. Reading comprehension
2. Text completion
3. Sentence equivalence

The reading comprehension questions are further divided into multiple-choice questions, which may require you to select only one answer choice or to pick one or more correct choices, and select-in-passage questions that require you to highlight a sentence that fits a description in a given passage.

Quantitative Reasoning

According to ETS, Quantitative Reasoning sections on the GRE® General Test measure your ability to understand, interpret, and analyze quantitative information; use mathematical models to solve problems; and apply basic mathematical knowledge and skills. The Quantitative Reasoning section requires basic knowledge in arithmetic, algebra, geometry, and data analysis. On the GRE® General Test, the subject matter of the questions will emphasize real-world scenarios and data interpretation.

NOTE

According to ETS, thousands of MBA programs worldwide now accept the GRE® General Test as an alternative to the Graduate Management Admissions Test (GMAT®).

The purpose of the on-screen calculator is to de-emphasize computation and emphasize the thought processes used to determine what the question is asking and how to go about finding the answer. While you'll find that the traditional multiple-choice question is the format used for the majority of questions, some multiple-choice questions will ask you to select one or more answers, and the numeric entry questions provide no answer options from which to choose.

The Quantitative Reasoning section consists of four types of questions:

1. Multiple-choice questions—select one answer choice
2. Multiple-choice questions—select one or more answer choices
3. Quantitative comparison questions
4. Numeric entry questions

With the exception of quantitative comparison questions, the questions in the Quantitative Reasoning sections may also appear as part of a data interpretation set: a group of questions that refer to the same tables, graphs, or other data presentation.

Number of Questions

The computer version of the GRE® General Test is divided into five scored sections and one additional section that may be an unidentified unscored section or an identified research section. The unidentified unscored section may be either a Verbal Reasoning or a Quantitative Reasoning section and may come in any order after the Analytical Writing section, which always comes first. The research section is always the last section and may be either Verbal Reasoning or Quantitative Reasoning. You won't have both unscored sections in any given test.

The breakdown of scored sections by question is as follows:

Section	Number of Sections	Number of Questions
Analytical Writing	One	Two writing tasks
Verbal Reasoning	Two	Approximately 20 questions
Quantitative Reasoning	Two	Approximately 20 questions

Within the Verbal Reasoning and Quantitative Reasoning sections, you will find the different types of question formats mixed together. For example, you may find a sequence of three reading comprehension passages (with several different question formats), a sentence equivalence question, two text completion questions, two reading comprehension passages, and so on. The same is true of Quantitative Reasoning sections, which will mix the two types of multiple-choice questions, numeric entry, and quantitative comparison questions.

TEST TIME LIMITS

The GRE® General Test will take approximately 3 hours and 45 minutes. You will also have time for several short breaks, which are not included in the actual testing time. There will be a 10-minute break after you finish the third section. Between the other test sections, you'll be allotted breaks of 1 minute each.

The breakdown of time allotments for each section is as follows:

Section	Number of Sections	Number of Questions	Time Per Section
Analytical Writing	One	Two writing tasks	30 minutes for each writing task
Verbal Reasoning	Two	Approximately 20 questions	30 minutes per section
Quantitative Reasoning	Two	Approximately 20 questions	35 minutes per section

The unscored sections will have the same number of questions and the same time allotments as the scored sections.

TEST TOOLS

Test takers at computer testing sites will find two on-screen tools, as well as increased maneuverability and functionality. For the Quantitative Reasoning sections, you'll find an on-screen calculator with the four basic functions—addition, subtraction, multiplication, division—and a square root button. You'll also be able to enter some of the answers directly from the calculator into the answer boxes using a "Transfer" function. The calculator places more emphasis on test takers' reasoning skills than on their computational skills.

For the Analytical Writing tasks, you'll be working in an ETS-designed word processing program that will allow you to write, insert and delete text, cut and paste, and undo actions. However, the program doesn't have a spell checker or a grammar checker.

The GRE® General Test enables you to move back and forth within a section so you can:

- preview and review a section.
- mark questions within a section to return to later.
- change and edit answers within a section.

The testing experience mirrors much of the paper-delivered testing process that you've been familiar with since taking your first standardized test. As a result, many of the same strategies such as "skip and return" that you've honed through years of testing can be used with the computer-delivered test.

SCORING THE TEST

For the Verbal Reasoning and Quantitative Reasoning sections of the GRE® General Test, the scales are reported in a range of 130 to 170 in one-point increments. Analytical Writing is reported in half-point increments using a 0-to-6 range. Each writing task is evaluated separately, and an average is taken and used as the reported score based on the 0–6 scale.

TEST DAY

There are several rules and restrictions to be aware of on test day. The following bulleted lists are from the ETS website (**www.ets.org/gre/revised_general/test_day/**). You should check the website for more updates as test day approaches.

General Test Center Procedures and Regulations

The following rules apply whether the test is computer- or paper-delivered.

- Dress so that you can adapt to any room temperature.
- Friends or relatives who accompany you to the test center will not be permitted to wait in the test center or be in contact with you while you are taking the test. Except for ETS-authorized observers, visitors are not permitted in the testing room while testing is in progress.
- ID verification at the test center may include thumbprinting, photographing, videotaping, or some other form of electronic ID confirmation. If you refuse to participate, you will not be permitted to take the test, and you will forfeit your registration and test fees. This is in addition to the requirement that you must present acceptable and valid identification.
- Food, beverages, and tobacco are not allowed in the testing room.
- Weapons and firearms are not allowed in the testing center.
- If you have health-related needs that require you to bring equipment, beverages, or snacks into the testing room or to take extra or extended breaks, you need to follow the accommodations request procedures described in the *Bulletin Supplement for Test Takers with Disabilities or Health-related Needs* available at **www.ets.org/s/gre/pdf/bulletin_supplement_test_takers_with_disabilities_health_needs.pdf**.
- Do not bring cell phones, smartphones (e.g., Androids, iPhones), PDAs, or other electronic or photographic devices into the test center. All forms of watches are prohibited, including digital, analog, and smartwatches.
- Personal items other than identification documents are not allowed in the testing room. Neither ETS nor the test centers assume any responsibility whatsoever for personal items or devices that you choose to bring into the test center. All forms of jewelry except for wedding and engagement rings are prohibited, and clothing is subject to inspection by the test center administrator.
- The test administrator will assign you a seat.
- On occasion, weather conditions or other circumstances beyond the test administrator or ETS's control may require a delayed start or the rescheduling of your test appointment. In the event that a technical problem at the test center makes it necessary to cancel your

test session, or if it is later determined that your scores could not be reported, you will be offered the opportunity to schedule another test appointment free of charge or receive a full refund of the original test fee.

- You will be asked to designate your score recipients at the test center on the day of the test. If an institution is not listed, ask the test center administrator for the appropriate form to indicate unlisted institutions. Complete the form and turn it in before you leave the test center. The form will not be accepted after you leave the test center.

- If you do not select score recipients on the day of the test or if you would like to send your scores to more than four score recipients, you will need to submit an Additional Score Report request for a fee of $27 per score recipient.

For Computer-Delivered Tests Only

The following procedures and regulations apply during the entire test session, which begins at sign-in, ends at sign-out, and includes breaks.

- If you requested and received an authorization voucher from ETS, you must take it with you to the test center.

- You will be required to write and sign (not print) a confidentiality statement at the test center. If you do not complete and sign the statement, you cannot take the test and your test fees will not be refunded.

- You may be required to sign the test center log before and after the test session and any time you leave or enter the testing room.

- You will be asked to remove your watch and store it during the test administration.

- The test administrator will provide you with scratch paper for use during the test. Scratch paper is not to be used before the test or during breaks. All paper, in its entirety, must be returned to the test center administrator at the end of the testing session. If you are observed using any document or paper other than the scratch paper given to you by test center staff, it will be confiscated. You may not bring your own paper, and you may not remove any paper from the testing room at any time or write on anything other than the paper provided (e.g., computer or workstation).

- If at any time during the test you have a problem with your computer, or for any reason need the administrator, raise your hand.

- Testing premises are subject to videotaping.

- The GRE® General Test includes an optional 10-minute break after the third section and 1-minute breaks between the remaining sections of the test. These break times cannot be exceeded. You are required to remain in the test center building or in the immediate area.

- If you need to leave your seat at any time other than the break, raise your hand; timing of the section will not stop.

- You will have access to an on-screen calculator during the Quantitative Reasoning sections. Personal calculators are not permitted in the testing room.

- Because of the essay scoring process, you will not be able to view your Analytical Writing scores at the time you test.
- Test centers cannot provide printed copies of unofficial score reports.

For Paper-Delivered Tests Only

The following procedures and regulations apply during the entire test session, which begins when you are admitted to the test center, ends when you leave the test center, and includes breaks.

- Test administrators will not honor requests for schedule changes.
- Take your confirmation email and identification document(s) to the test center.
- No test taker will be admitted after test materials have been distributed.
- With the exception of your email confirmation, paper of any kind is not permitted in the testing room.
- You must have the test administrator's permission to leave the room during the test. Any time lost cannot be made up. You are required to remain in the test center building or in the immediate area.
- You may work only on the test section designated by the test center supervisor and only for the time allowed. You will not be permitted to continue the test or any part of it beyond the established time limit.
- You will write your essay responses and enter your answers to test questions in the test book, rather than on a separate answer sheet.
- You will be provided with an ETS calculator to use during the Quantitative Reasoning sections. You may not use your own personal calculator.
- At the end of the test, you will be required to return your test book to the test administrator. This material is the property of ETS.
- The GRE® General Test includes a 10-minute break after the second Analytical Writing section. This break time cannot be exceeded.
- At the end of the test, you will be given the option to cancel your scores.

ALERT!
The paper-delivered test has a multiple-choice adaptation of the select-in-passage question. All other question formats are the same.

GENERAL TEST-TAKING STRATEGIES TO REMEMBER

Not all strategies will work for all questions. But there are some strategies that will work for most, if not all, questions:

- Anticipate and use the clock.
- Skip and return to questions.
- Eliminate answer choices that you know are incorrect.
- Use educated guessing.

The more you practice these and the strategies designed to address specific question types described in this book, the easier the strategies will be to remember and to apply to the appropriate questions on test day.

Anticipate and Use the Clock

When you take the GRE® General Test, a clock icon will appear on your screen to show elapsing time. That is, you will always know exactly how much time you have remaining. To take full advantage of this on-screen device, time yourself using the practice tests in this book and figure out how much time you have per question.

Suppose you typically do the easier text completion and sentence equivalence items at the rate of 30 seconds per item, whereas the harder ones take you about a minute. Given that approximately half the questions on the Verbal Reasoning sections consist of those two types, and the total number of questions on a Verbal Reasoning section is 20 questions, you might budget about 10 minutes for those two types of questions, adding in a minute or so for review, extra-hard questions, or other issues. For the 30-minute test, that leaves approximately 20 minutes for the reading comprehension questions, or about 2 minutes a question.

ALERT!

Those taking the paper-delivered test should apply the same strategy using the clock in the room.

If you find at the halfway point for time that you're working significantly faster than is necessary, you may want to slow down and take more time with each question. If, on the other hand, you find at the halfway point you're working slower than you need to be, you may want to speed up and take less time with each question. Keep in mind, however, that you cannot speed-read passages and questions, so speed up only a bit.

Skip and Return to Questions

If at first you don't see how to answer a certain question in a reasonable amount of time, don't hesitate to skip it. If you do skip a question, make sure you click the "Mark" button so that you can find that question quickly on the "Review" screen at a later point. After you've answered all the other questions—and before your time for the section has run out—go back to any question you've left unanswered and try to solve it. Remember: There's no wrong-answer penalty, so don't leave any questions unanswered!

Eliminate Answer Choices You Know Are Incorrect

Don't overlook this time-honored strategy! It will not only help you arrive at the answer, but it can also help calm test jitters as you come closer and closer to the correct answer.

Educated Guessing

Educated guessing builds on the strategy of eliminating answer choices that you know are incorrect, but you have to know something about the question for educated guessing to be effective. The process works this way:

- Eliminate answer choices you know are incorrect.
- Discard any choices in which part of the answer is incorrect.
- Reread the remaining answer choices against each other and against the question again.
- Choose the answer that seems correct to you. More often than not, you'll be right.

SUMMING IT UP

- The GRE® General Test is considered by ETS to be a superlative measure of a test taker's success in graduate or business school.

- The computer-delivered GRE® General Test allows test takers to change and edit answers within each timed section, allowing them to skip and then return to unanswered questions before the alloted time expires. An on-screen calculator and word processing program are included.

- The GRE® has three sections: Analytical Writing, Quantitative Reasoning, and Verbal Reasoning. Analytical Writing is always first.

- Quantitative Reasoning and Verbal Reasoning have two scored sections each, which may come in any order. The computer version of the test may have an unidentified, unscored Quantitative Reasoning or Verbal Reasoning section or an identified, unscored research section of either type.

- The Analytical Writing section has two tasks: an Argument Task and an Issue Task. You'll be given one prompt for each task and will not have a choice from which to select.

- Verbal Reasoning sections have a mix of reading comprehension, text completion, and sentence equivalence questions. Each has its own question format. Questions based on reading passages may be multiple-choice—select one answer; multiple-choice—select one or more answers; or select-in-passage questions. Text completion questions may require one, two, or three responses selected from lists of multiple-choice answers. Sentence equivalence questions require two answers selected from a single list of multiple-choice options.

- Quantitative Reasoning sections have multiple-choice, quantitative comparisons, and numeric entry question formats. The numeric entry questions do not offer a list of potential answers from which to choose.

- The test takes 3 hours and 45 minutes and has the following time limits and questions:

Section	Number of Sections	Number of Questions	Time Per Section
Analytical Writing	One	Two writing tasks	30 minutes for each writing task
Verbal Reasoning	Two	Approximately 20 questions	30 minutes per section
Quantitative Reasoning	Two	Approximately 20 questions	35 minutes per section

- The scores for the Quantitative and Verbal Reasoning sections are reported on a score scale of 130 to 170 with 1-point increments. The Analytical Writing score is reported on a scale of 0 to 6 with half-point increments.

- Four general test-taking strategies will help in most situations: (1) anticipate and use the clock, (2) skip and return to questions, (3) eliminate answer choices that you know are incorrect, and (4) use educated guessing.

A Quick Look at the Question Formats

OVERVIEW

- **Analytical Writing**
- **Answer Option Differences**
- **Verbal Reasoning**
- **Quantitative Reasoning**
- **Summing It Up**

The GRE® General Test assesses three areas: (1) Analytical Writing, (2) Verbal Reasoning, and (3) Quantitative Reasoning. In the Analytical Writing section, you'll be given prompts to write two types of responses: one to evaluate an argument and another to discuss an issue. While you'll find the majority of test items are in the multiple-choice format that you're familiar with from other standardized tests, the GRE® General Test presents several additional test-item formats both in the Verbal Reasoning and Quantitative Reasoning sections. This chapter introduces each test-item format with examples and also discusses the differences between the two types of writing tasks and their requirements.

ANALYTICAL WRITING

The Analytical Writing section of the GRE® General Test tests both your ability to think critically and your ability to write analytically. The section has two writing tasks: one is called the Analyze an Argument Task and the other is the Analyze an Issue Task. You'll be given a prompt and a set of directions for each task; you won't have a choice of tasks from which to select.

The Analyze an Argument Task prompt will ask you to evaluate an argument and the evidence to support it, not to give your opinion about it. The Analyze an Issue Task prompt gives you the opportunity to examine and deliver your opinion about a claim that is presented. In this way, the GRE® General Test assesses both your ability to state a position and to support it, as well as your ability to assess another person's position and the evidence supporting it. Both types of task prompts are accompanied by specific instructions about how to respond to the prompt.

To assist you in your preparation for the GRE® General Test, ETS provides access to pools of all the Issue and Argument topics used in the Analytical Writing section. Wording on the actual test may vary slightly, but previewing these topics will give you a general idea of what to expect and a chance to consider claims pertaining to unfamiliar subject matter. To look at the topic pools, visit the following URLs:

Issue topics:

www.ets.org/gre/revised_general/prepare/analytical_writing/issue/pool

Argument topics:

www.ets.org/gre/revised_general/prepare/analytical_writing/argument/pool

Time Limits

If you're taking the computer-delivered test, you'll have 30 minutes to read each prompt, gather your ideas, and write your response. In allotting your 30 minutes, take about 5 minutes to read the prompt, decide on your point of view, and marshal your ideas; take about 20 minutes to write your response; and leave about 5 minutes to reread and edit your response. Points are not deducted for spelling and grammar mistakes, but as ETS points out: "severe and persistent errors will detract from the overall effectiveness of your writing and lower your score accordingly."

Software

The computer on which you'll be taking your test will be equipped with a word processing program developed by ETS. According to ETS, you'll be able to insert and delete text, cut and paste, and undo actions. However, the program doesn't include a spell checker or a grammar checker, so using a few minutes at the end of the writing period to edit for grammar, usage, and spelling errors can be helpful in ensuring that your response is clearly expressed.

The Scoring Rubric

Your Argument Task and Issue Task responses will be scored on a 6-point scale by two readers. These readers are your audience, and your purpose in writing your response is to earn the best score that you can. The maximum score your response can earn is 6. The scale ranges in 1-point increments from 6 to 0.

Rubric for the Issue Task

6 Points

To earn 6 points, your response should exhibit these characteristics:

- A clear, focused position on the issue, and an overall response to the specific writing task that is thorough, cogent, and sophisticated

- Fully developed, persuasive support for the position, including, but not limited to, particularly apt or well-chosen examples, facts, and other illustrations, as well as an explanation that clearly and effectively links the support to the specific requirements of the writing task

- A rhetorically effective method of organization, such as one that organizes support by order of importance and saves the most effective reasons for last; connections between and among ideas are logical and may also be as subtle as they are effective

- A formal grace that is a product primarily of well-constructed, varied sentences and exact and rhetorically effective word choices
- Adherence to almost all the conventions of Standard Written English, including grammar, usage, and mechanics; errors, if any, should be minor

5 Points

To earn 5 points, your response will likely have these characteristics, though it may exceed one or more of them yet fall short on another:

- A clear, focused position on the issue, and a thoughtful, complete response to the specific writing task
- Persuasive support for the position, including, but not limited to, examples, facts, and other illustrations, as well as an explanation that clearly links the support to the specific requirements of the writing task
- An effective method of organization with logical connections between and among all ideas
- Well-constructed, varied sentences and appropriate word choices that help create clarity as well as interest
- Adherence to almost all the conventions of Standard Written English, including grammar, usage, and mechanics; errors, if any, should be minor

4 Points

To earn 4 points, a response will have these characteristics:

- A clear position on the issue and a generally complete response to the specific writing task
- Support for the position, as well as an explanation that links the support to the specific requirements of the writing task
- A logical method of organization
- Sentences and word choices that generally create clarity
- General adherence to the conventions of Standard Written English; some errors may occur

3 Points

Your response will earn only 3 points if it has *one or more* of the following characteristics:

- A generally clear position and a response to the specific writing task that may be limited in scope or marred by occasional vagueness, extraneous detail, repetition, or other flaws
- Limited or inadequate support for the position or a limited or inadequate explanation that links the support to the specific requirements of the writing task
- Lapses in organization or confusing organization, and/or lack or misuse of transitional words and phrases
- Sentences and word choices that occasionally interfere with clarity
- One or more errors in the conventions of Standard Written English that are so significant that they obstruct meaning

2 Points

Your response will earn only 2 points if it has *one or more* of the following characteristics:

- A wandering, unclear, or limited response characterized by an unclear or not fully articulated position and a response to the specific writing task that is limited or inadequate in scope or marred by vagueness, extraneous detail, repetition, or other flaws
- Inadequate support and explanation
- Confusing organization and/or general lack or misuse of transitional words and phrases.
- Sentences and word choices that interfere with clarity
- Repeated errors in the conventions of Standard Written English that are so significant that they obstruct meaning

1 Point

Your response will earn only 1 point if it has *one or more* of the following characteristics:

- An unclear position and almost no response to, or minimal understanding of, the specific task
- A total lack of support or only illogical or flawed support for the main point or points; a total lack of explanation or only an illogical or flawed explanation of the main points of your argument in relation to the specific details of the task
- No pattern of organization or confusing organization
- Sentences and word choices that interfere with clarity
- So many errors in the conventions of Standard Written English that they obstruct meaning throughout the response

0 Points

This score is possible under the following circumstances:

- The response does not answer the task in any way.
- The response is written in a foreign language.
- The response simply copies the argument.
- The response is not legible.
- The response is nonverbal.

Rubric for the Argument Task

6 Points

To earn 6 points, your response should exhibit these characteristics:

- A logically sound, well-focused answer to the specific task that is particularly insightful, thoughtful, deep, or sophisticated
- Fully developed, persuasive support for the main point or points of your response; at this high level of response, examples and other illustrations are particularly apt or well chosen, and their relationship to the focus of your analysis is extremely clear and/or well articulated
- A method of organization that complements the main ideas of the analysis by effectively creating a flow of well-organized paragraphs and easing the reader's progress through the

paper from first word to last; connections between and among ideas are logical and may also be as subtle as they are effective

- A formal grace that is a product primarily of well-constructed, varied sentences and exact and rhetorically effective word choices
- Adherence to almost all the conventions of Standard Written English, including grammar, usage, and mechanics; errors, if any, should be minor

5 Points

To earn 5 points, your response will likely have these characteristics, though it may exceed one or more of them yet fall short on another:

- A logically sound, focused answer to the specific task that reflects insight and evidences some deep thought
- Well-developed, persuasive support for the main point or points of your response; examples and other illustrations are well chosen, and their relationship to your argument is clear
- A method of organization that complements main ideas and connects ideas clearly and in a logical order
- Well-constructed, varied sentences and appropriate word choices that help create clarity as well as interest
- Adherence to almost all the conventions of Standard Written English, including grammar, usage, and mechanics; errors, if any, should be minor

4 Points

To earn 4 points, a response will have these characteristics:

- A generally focused answer to the specific task
- Varying degrees of adequate and inadequate support
- A logical method of organization, although some linkages may be missing or unclear
- Sentences and word choices that generally create clarity, though some problems may exist with structure or usage
- General adherence to the conventions of Standard Written English; some errors may occur

3 Points

Your response will earn only 3 points if it has *one or more* of the following characteristics:

- An inadequate answer to the specific task; it may not quite respond to the task or all aspects of it, it may be limited in its scope or number of points, or it may be vague or confusing in places
- Inadequate support for the main point or points of your response or support that is illogical
- A pattern of organization that does not complement the main ideas or causes confusion for the reader
- Sentences and word choices that occasionally interfere with clarity
- One or more errors in the conventions of Standard Written English that are so significant that they obstruct meaning, or very frequent minor errors

2 Points

Your response will earn only 2 points if it has *one or more* of the following characteristics:

- An inadequate or unclear answer to the specific task; it may not quite respond to the task or all aspects of it, or it may be too vague or confusing to answer the task adequately
- Little, if any, support, or support that is illogical
- Confusing or inadequate organization
- Sentences and word choices that interfere with clarity
- Repeated errors in the conventions of Standard Written English that are so significant that they obstruct meaning

1 Point

Your response will earn only 1 point if it has *one or more* of the following characteristics:

- Almost no response to, or minimal understanding of, the specific task
- A total lack of support or only illogical or flawed support
- No pattern of organization or confusing organization
- Many sentences and word choices that interfere with clarity
- So many errors in the conventions of Standard Written English that they obstruct meaning throughout the response

0 Points

This score is possible under the following circumstances:

- The response does not answer the task in any way.
- The response is written in a foreign language.
- The response simply copies the argument.
- The response is not legible.
- The response is nonverbal.

Understanding Scoring

Both the Issue Task and the Argument Task have their own scoring rubrics. As you can see from the previous rubrics, the emphasis in evaluating your response will be placed on your ability to put together a cogent and coherent piece of writing. The position that you take is not important. What is important is that you state your position effectively and demonstrate in your response an ability to develop and support your position clearly and with pertinent evidence.

Note also that the rubrics include an assessment of writing style. Varying your sentence structure and using a precise, appropriate, and effective vocabulary can make your response clearer and more interesting and forceful. Lack of sentence variety and vague, imprecise language can lower your score. While adherence to Standard Written English conventions is part of each rubric, it's less important (according to the test makers) than your ability to craft a well-developed, well-reasoned, and well-supported piece of writing. However, remember that sloppy and incorrect grammar and spelling can get in the way of coherence and affect the clarity of your response.

Each response is evaluated and scored separately, but a single combined score is reported for Analytical Writing. The combined, or reported, score is an average of the scores for the two responses. The range for the reported score is 0 to 6 with half-point increments, that is, 6 and 5.5, 5 and 4.5, 4 and 3.5, 3 and 2.5, 2 and 1.5, and 1 and 0.5. The evaluation instrument is similar to the rubrics at each level.

The Analyze an Issue Task

The prompt for the Issue Task presents you with a very brief statement, recommendation, claim, viewpoint, or policy and asks you to agree or disagree with it. The issue will be of a general nature to which anyone could respond. No special knowledge is required. You can choose to agree or disagree with the issue, as long as you follow the set of instructions that accompany the premise that is set up in the prompt. For example, you might find the prompt and a set of instructions similar to the following wording:

> A nation should require all its citizens between the ages of 18 and 30 to serve one year in national service.
>
> *Write a response in which you discuss your viewpoint on the proposed policy and the reasons for your point of view. Take into consideration the potential consequences of implementing the policy and the extent to which these consequences influence your viewpoint in developing and supporting your response.*

There are six different sets of instructions from which the item writers may choose to state how you should respond to an Issue Task. These instructions specify the degree or conditions of your agreement or disagreement. For example, you may be asked to respond using instructions similar to the following:

1. Discuss the extent to which you agree or disagree with the statement and explain your reasoning for the position you take. In developing and supporting your position, consider ways in which the statement might or might not hold true and explain how these considerations affect your point of view.

2. Discuss how much you agree or disagree with the recommendation and describe why. Using specific examples, explain how the circumstances under which the recommendation could be adopted would or would not be advantageous. In developing and supporting your viewpoint, explain how these specific circumstances affect your point of view.

3. Discuss how much you agree or disagree with the claim and include the most compelling reasons and/or examples that someone could use to dispute your point of view.

4. While addressing both provided viewpoints, discuss which more closely aligns with your own. Explain your reasons for holding this position when providing evidence for your response. As you develop and support your position, be sure to address both viewpoints.

5. Discuss how much you agree or disagree with the claim and the reasoning used to support that claim.

6. Discuss your viewpoint on the proposed policy and the reasons for your point of view. Take into consideration the potential consequences of implementing the policy and the extent to which these consequences influence your viewpoint in developing and supporting your response.

The Analyze an Argument Task

The prompt for the Argument Task presents you with a brief argument and then states your task: to analyze the argument for its logic or reasonableness and express your analysis in a well-developed, well-reasoned, and well-supported response. To do so, you'll have to identify problems in the argument's reasoning, its evidence, the assumptions (stated or implied) on which the argument's claim is based, the conclusions drawn from the argument, or the predictions based on the argument. You may also have to point out a lack of evidence, raise questions, present alternative explanations, and consider other implications. You will not have to—nor should you—agree or disagree with the argument. Save your own views for the Issue Task response.

Like the Issue Task, the Argument Task provides a prompt and a set of instructions telling you how to craft your response. The prompt—the argument—and instructions might look like the following:

> In an effort to save money and be environmentally conscious, Philadelphia replaced all its traffic lights with red, green, and amber LED lights. The move was estimated to save the city $1 million. However, the first heavy snowfall showed a flaw in the plan. The LED lights did not throw off as much heat as the old-style bulbs, so the snow did not melt from the traffic lights, causing disruptions at major intersections. A city council member put forward a motion to replace immediately all the LED lights with the older bulbs.
>
> *Write a response in which you discuss the questions that need to be asked and answered to determine if the recommendation and the argument on which it is based are reasonable. As part of your response, describe how the answers would help in the evaluation process.*

There are eight different sets of instructions for writing your response. For example, you may have wording similar to the following:

1. Discuss the evidence needed to assess the argument. Include specific examples and an explanation of how the evidence might weaken or strengthen the argument.

2. Discuss the stated and/or unstated assumptions and explain how the argument is based on these assumptions and the implications for the argument if the assumptions are shown to be unjustified.

3. Discuss the questions that need to be asked and answered to determine if the recommendation and its argument are reasonable. As part of your response, describe how the answers would help in the evaluation process.

4. Discuss the questions that need to be asked and answered to determine if the advice and its argument are reasonable. As part of your response, explain how the answers would help in the evaluation process.

5. Discuss the questions that need to be asked and answered to determine if the recommendation is likely to result in the outcome that is projected. As part of your response, explain how the answers would help in the evaluation process.

6. Discuss the questions that need to be asked and answered to determine if the prediction and its argument are reasonable. As part of your response, explain how the answers would help in the evaluation process.

7. Presented with an explanation, discuss one or more alternative explanations that could reasonably compete with the proposed explanation. Explain how your explanation(s) account for the facts in the proposed argument.

8. Discuss the questions that need to be asked and answered to determine if the conclusion and the argument it is derived from are reasonable. As part of your response, explain how the answers would help in the evaluation process.

A Word About Numbers in Argument Prompts

ETS cautions test takers not to misinterpret the purpose of any numbers, percentages, or statistics in the prompts used for the Argument Task. They are present as evidence and should be evaluated in terms of whether they support the argument that is presented, show flaws in the argument, or are extraneous. Such information may also be evidence that you can use to buttress your own points. The following is an example similar to what you might find on the GRE® General Test:

> A recent study showed that fatal crashes were reduced by 24 percent in intersections where traffic safety cameras had been installed. The data was collected between 2006 and 2013 in 14 large cities that instituted the program during that period. The conclusion was that people were paying more attention to the lights as they got close to them because running a red light meant getting a ticket. The tickets averaged as much as $100. As a result, every major city and medium-sized city should install traffic cameras at busy intersections.

As you think through ideas to write a response, you might turn these pieces of data into questions to ask yourself such as: 24 percent seems like a lot, but is that number cumulative or an average of the 14 cities? How many fatalities in real numbers does this represent? For how many years was each city actually in the program? Is the percentage skewed downward because the majority of cities were in it for only two years, three years, and so on? The data is not meant to provide you with a math problem to solve, but as a source of questions to help you shape your response.

ANSWER OPTION DIFFERENCES

All multiple-choice questions in the computer-delivered test will have answer options preceded by either blank ovals or blank squares depending on the question type. You will use your mouse to select one or more of these options. The paper-delivered test will follow the same format of answer choices, but it will use letters instead of ovals or squares for answer choices.

For your convenience in answering questions and checking answers, this book uses letter designations (A, B, C, etc.) for answer choices. Having these letters to refer to will make it easier for you to check your answers against the answer key and explanation sections.

Numeric entry questions will have to be typed in, and Analytical Writing responses will need to be composed using a keyboard and mouse in the computer-delivered test. For this guide and the paper-and-pencil exam, you will have to handwrite all of your answers and responses.

NOTE

For your convenience in answering questions and checking answers, this book uses letter designations (A, B, C, etc.), instead of the blank ovals and squares that appear on the computer-delivered test.

VERBAL REASONING

The Verbal Reasoning section has three components and several question formats. The components are (1) Reading Comprehension, (2) Text Completion, and (3) Sentence Equivalence. While the majority of questions on the Verbal Reasoning sections will be multiple-choice and the majority of those will require choosing a single answer, you will find some nontraditional question formats.

Reading Comprehension Question Formats

Based on passages ranging from one to several paragraphs in length, the Reading Comprehension questions may be multiple-choice—select one answer choice, multiple-choice—select one or more answer choices, or a select-in-passage format. The multiple-choice questions may refer back to the passage using line or sentence numbers or by highlighting text with bold type.

Multiple-Choice—Select One Answer Choice

You are undoubtedly familiar with this question format from all the other standardized tests you've ever taken. For the GRE® General Test, you'll have a list of five answer choices from which to choose for the majority of reading comprehension questions. On the actual computer-delivered test, instead of capital letters, you'll see blank ovals. The format will look something like this:

For this question, choose only <u>one</u> answer choice.

The author of the passage would most likely agree with which of the following statements?

- ○ Professor Bates did not take into consideration the number of voters who said they would vote, but didn't.
- ○ Professor Bates did not consider the problems with accuracy inherent in exit polls.
- ● Professor Bates's sample was neither large enough nor random enough.
- ○ Professor Bates should have known that plus or minus 10 points was too large a range to be valid.
- ○ Professor Bates should not have stopped sampling 10 days before the election, considering how volatile the race was.

Multiple-Choice—Select One or More Answer Choices

The list of multiple-choice options for this question format is limited to three. The answer choices for these question types are preceded by blank squares, not ovals. (But again, we use letters to indicate answer options in our guide, which allows for easy checking against the answer key and explanation sections.) The question will indicate that you should select all answer choices that apply. You may find that only one of the answers is correct, or you may find that two are, or even all three. The format will look something like this:

For this question, consider each answer individually and choose <u>all</u> that apply.

According to the critic, what qualities were more evident in her later novels than in her earlier ones?

- ■ less social satire
- ☐ more stereotypically drawn characters
- ■ more dialogue and less description of characters' motivations

A Variation on the Standard Multiple-Choice Question

Within both of the multiple-choice question formats, you may find questions that use line numbers to refer to a particular line. Questions with line numbers are usually vocabulary questions such as "In line 4, the word *sterling* most nearly means" followed by a list of possible answers. You're probably familiar with this question type if you have taken the SAT Subject Tests™ on Literature or the AP® English Literature and Composition Exam.

A Variation on the Standard Multiple-Choice Passage

You may find a passage with bold type highlighting two parts of the passage and a question that asks you about the two parts. The arrangement might look something like the following:

… **Jones's ultimate mistake in the eyes of historians was his disregard of Turner's thesis on the closing of the frontier.** However, Jones's own theory was found to be no more penetrating nor half as well supported as he claimed Turner's was. For one thing, Jones's argument was

Line considered weak because he had not consulted the territorial records. His articles tended to

5 lack statistical support, and his conclusions overly generalized from the spotty data that he had used.

Jones's response centered on the fact that he considered his function in life to be popularizing dull and boring history for a popular audience. This won him no friends in academia, but his books about the colorful frontier made him pots of money—like the pot of gold at the

10 end of a rainbow on a rain-soaked prairie—to satirize Jones's florid prose. **Jones claimed his wealth evoked jealousy in his peers.**

How does the author of the passage use the two sentences in bold to make his point that Jones was an egotist?

Select-in-Passage Questions

Select-in-passage questions appear differently on the computer-delivered and paper-delivered GRE® General Tests. On the latter test, select-in-passage questions will be in the form of traditional multiple-choice questions. On the computer-delivered test, test takers will be asked to highlight a sentence within the passage itself.

If the passage is a single paragraph, the entire passage may be the source of the answer. If the passage has several paragraphs, only a certain portion of the passage will be relevant to the question. That portion will be called out between arrows (→). To answer the question, you will need to click on the sentence that is your answer choice. If you try to click on a sentence outside the selected area, the sentence will not be highlighted. The question and directions will be set up similarly to the following arrangement:

Line

... rather than allow for a vote on the bill, the senator chose to begin a filibuster that would last for 24 hours and 18 minutes. → Senator Thurmond was speaking against the passage of the Civil Rights Act of 1957. Because of the strong emotionalism of the opposition to civil rights for African Americans, the Senate saw another record-breaking filibuster in 1964.

5　Senator Robert Byrd and his colleagues held the Senate floor for 75 hours. Senator Byrd who came in time to renounce his opposition to civil rights legislation spoke for 14 hours and 13 minutes. ←

Filibusters against civil rights legislation continued during the 1960s as Southern senators fought to keep the status quo in place. However, the Civil Rights Movement had gained momentum and would not be silenced. . . .

Select the sentence that explains the causal relationship between filibusters and proposed civil rights legislation.

Note the arrows within the passage. The portion of the passage that is the subject of the question begins within the paragraph and ends at the end of the same paragraph.

Text Completion Questions

Text completion questions are based on a single passage. The passage may have from one to three blanks. If the passage has one blank to fill in, you will select your answer from a list of five answer choices presented in a column. If the passage has two or three blanks, you will select your answer from a list of three answer choices presented in two or three columns. Once you have decided on your answer, you click on the cell with that answer. In our guide, there will be letters next to the word choices. The format will look something like the following:

For this question, choose <u>one</u> answer for each blank. Select from the appropriate column for each blank. Choose the answer that best completes the sense of the text.

A major issue that may slow the (i) _____ of electric cars is the difficulty of charging the engines. Until or unless local (ii) _____ legislate the installation of charging stations in new construction, at train stations, and in parking lots, (iii) _____ of electric cars say that the general public will not embrace these environmentally friendly vehicles.

Blank (i)	Blank (ii)	Blank (iii)
A. manufacturing	D. municipalities	G. opponents
B. proliferation	E. companies	H. advocates
C. building	F. people	I. lovers

If you're interested, the answers are proliferation (choice B), municipalities (choice D), and advocates (choice H).

Sentence Equivalence Questions

Sentence equivalence questions differ from traditional multiple-choice questions in two significant ways. First, there are six answer choices rather than the usual four or five. Second, you have to choose two answers from the list to complete the one answer blank. That is, sentence equivalence questions ask you to complete a sentence using two different words that are similar, or equivalent, in meaning. Both completed versions of the sentence must convey a similar meaning. To receive credit for your answer, both answer choices must be correct. The answer choices are preceded by blank squares, not ovals. No partial credit is given if only one of the words is correct.

The direction line for all sentence equivalence questions is the same and is worded something like the following:

For this question, choose <u>two</u> answers that best fit the meaning of each sentence and that result in completed sentences with the same or nearly the same meaning.

The art expert, hired by the potential buyer, was unable to _____ the painting as being from the school of Rembrandt.

- ■ authenticate
- ☐ place
- ☐ authorize
- ■ verify
- ☐ depose
- ☐ approve

Some Advice About Checking Answers

As you work through the practice test, you should get an idea of how long a text completion item takes you. As you increase your proficiency with these items, you may find that a simple text completion, or a text completion with just one blank, takes perhaps 20 to 30 seconds, while the longer two-blank and three-blank text completion items may run 45 seconds to a minute or more to complete.

For this reason, if you come to the end of a Verbal Reasoning section, and you have a minute or two left, your wisest use of time might be to double-check text completion or sentence equivalence items. Every one of them counts just as much as a reading comprehension answer. So, with a remaining 60 seconds, you may be able to skim and, conceivably, correct two text completion items, or 8 percent of the test, whereas 60 seconds spent on a reading comprehension question might not get you through a rereading of a passage and question.

QUANTITATIVE REASONING

The Quantitative Reasoning sections of the test intersperse multiple-choice, quantitative comparison, and numeric entry questions. The multiple-choice questions will be in two formats: the traditional "select one answer choice" and the newer "select one or more answer choices." The majority of questions will be the multiple-choice format, and the majority of those will be the traditional "select one answer choice."

Those taking the computer-delivered GRE® General Test will have an on-screen calculator to use. It will allow you to add, subtract, multiply, divide, and find square roots. It will look something like this:

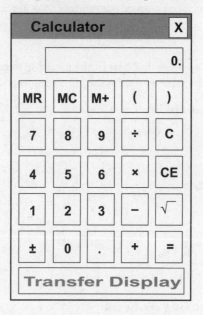

Don't bring your own calculator because you won't be allowed to use it.

Multiple-Choice—Select One Answer Choice

All questions using the multiple-choice—select one answer choice format list five possible answer choices, only one of which is correct. The choices are preceded by an oval to click to select your answer. The question will look something like the following:

For this question, choose <u>one</u> answer choice.

If $y = (x + 8)^2$, then $(-3x - 24)^2$ must equal which of the following?

  ○ $-9y^2$

  ○ $-3y^2$

  ○ $-9y$

  ○ $3y$

  ● $9y$

Multiple-Choice—Select One or More Answer Choices

This format may have, as the name states, one, two, three, or more correct answers. Unlike reading comprehension test items that use the multiple-choice—select one or more answers format, questions using this format in the Quantitative Reasoning section may have up to eight answer options. However, there will always be at least three answer choices listed and they will all have blank squares in front of them.

In most instances, the direction line with one of these questions will tell you to "indicate all that apply." However, the direction line may specify the number that you should choose. The following example provides a typical direction line for such a question:

For this question, indicate <u>all</u> the answers that apply.

Which two of the following integers give you a product of less than –54?

- ■ –9
- ☐ –5
- ☐ 6
- ■ 9
- ☐ 4
- ☐ –6
- ☐ 5
- ☐ 1

In order to gain credit for multiple-choice—select one or more answer questions, you need to select the correct number of answers, and the answers you choose must all be correct. There is no partial credit for partially correct answers.

Quantitative Comparison Questions

Quantitative comparison questions present you with two quantities, A and B. The objective is to compare the two quantities and choose one of the following answers, which always appear in this order:

- ○ Quantity A is greater.
- ○ Quantity B is greater.
- ○ The two quantities are equal.
- ○ The relationship cannot be determined from the information given.

Some quantitative comparison questions will have additional information centered above the two columns. This information will help you determine the relationship between the two quantities. Any symbol that appears more than once in a question has the same meaning throughout the question; for example, a symbol in the centered information and in Quantity A.

NOTE

The correct answers are –9 and 9. You need to look at numbers that when multiplied together result in a negative number. So, –9 × 6 = –54, which is not less than –54. Next, look at –9 × 9 = –81, which is less, so there is no need to do more.

TIP

To save time on the test, memorize the answer choices so that you don't have to read them each time you come across a quantitative comparison question.

A quantitative comparison question will look like the following:

For this question, compare Quantity A and Quantity B. This question has additional information above the two quantities to use in determining your answer.

1 kilo = 2.2 pounds

Quantity A	Quantity B
1 kilo of gold	2.2 pounds of flour

○ Quantity A is greater.

○ Quantity B is greater.

● The two quantities are equal.

○ The relationship cannot be determined from the information given.

NOTE

The two quantities are equal. Since it's stated that a kilo is equal to 2.2 pounds, Quantity A and Quantity B are equal.

Numeric Entry Questions

Unlike the other Quantitative Reasoning question formats, numeric entry questions don't have a list of answer choices from which to choose your answer. Instead, you're given a question and one or two answer boxes. If the answer is an integer or decimal, there will be one answer box. If the answer is a fraction, you'll see two answer boxes, one over the other with a line between them. You'll enter the numerator in the top box and the denominator in the bottom box.

To solve the problem, you'll use the on-screen calculator. If the answer is an integer or decimal, you can use the "Transfer Display" function to enter your answer in the box. If the answer is a fraction, you'll need to type your answer into the two boxes using the keypad.

A numeric entry question will look like the following:

For this question, enter your answer in the box.

If x and y are integers, what is the absolute value of y if $y = -6x + 32$ and $x = -4$?

NOTE

The correct answer is 56. Solve the equation for y using the value -4 for x, so

$y = -6(-4) + 32$

$y = 24 + 32$

$y = 56$

Data Interpretation Sets

In addition to the different types of question formats, you'll probably also find at least one group of questions revolving around the same table, graph, or other data representation. These are known as data interpretation sets. All that means is that to answer the two or three questions related to the data on the graphic, you will need to refer to the graphic.

SUMMING IT UP

- The GRE® General Test assesses three areas: (1) Analytical Writing, (2) Verbal Reasoning, and (3) Quantitative Reasoning.

- The Analytical Writing section requires two writing assignments: an Issue Task and an Argument Task. The Issue Task asks you to give your opinion about an issue, whereas the Argument Task asks you to evaluate an argument and the evidence used to support it.

- Each writing prompt is accompanied by a set of instructions indicating how you should respond to the issue or argument. Finished writing tasks are evaluated against a 6-point rubric. The rubrics are different for the two kinds of writing.

- The Verbal Reasoning section has three components: (1) reading comprehension, (2) text completion, and (3) sentence equivalence.

- Reading comprehension questions may be multiple-choice—select one answer choice; multiple-choice—select one or more answer choices; and select-in-passage questions. The last requires test takers using the computer-delivered test to highlight a sentence within the subject passage as the answer. For the paper-delivered test, the select-in-passage format has been converted to a multiple-choice—select one answer choice question.

    o Multiple-choice—select one answer choice questions that use the traditional one-answer multiple-choice format present a list of five answer choices preceded by ovals.

    o The multiple-choice—select one or more answer choices format presents only three possible answers preceded by squares. All three options may be correct, or only one, or only two.

- Text completion questions present a passage with from one to three blanks that must be completed by choosing from a list of possible answers. If the question has only one blank, then five possible choices are provided. If the question has two or three blanks to fill in, there will be a list of only three possible answers for each blank.

- Sentence equivalence questions provide six possible answers, but only one blank to complete. To answer the question, you must use two words from the list that will complete the sentence so that both versions are similar, or equivalent, in meaning.

- Quantitative Reasoning questions may take the form of multiple-choice—select one answer choice; multiple-choice—select one or more answer choices; quantitative comparison; and numeric entry formats.

    o Multiple-choice—select one answer choice is the traditional multiple-choice format and lists five possible answer choices preceded by ovals.

    o Multiple-choice—select one or more answer choices lists at least three answer choices, but may have as many as eight possible answers. The direction line usually says simply to "indicate all that apply." However, some questions may indicate an exact number to select.

    o Quantitative Comparison questions are set up as two columns, Quantity A and Quantity B, which you must compare and decide if one is greater than the other, they are equal, or the relationship can't be determined from the information. Some questions may provide additional information above the quantities to help you determine your answer.

- o Numeric entry questions don't list answer choices. You must calculate your answer using the on-screen calculator and enter it on-screen.
- For questions that require more than one answer, credit is given only if all answer choices are correct.

PART II

DIAGNOSING STRENGTHS AND WEAKNESSES

CHAPTER 3   Practice Test 1: Diagnostic

Practice Test 1: Diagnostic

DIRECTIONS FOR TAKING THE DIAGNOSTIC TEST

The test begins with general information about the number of sections on the test (six for the computer-delivered test, including the unidentified unscored section or an identified research section, and five for the paper-delivered test) and the timing of the test (approximately 3 hours and 45 minutes, including one 10-minute break after Section 3, 1-minute breaks after the other sections for the computer-delivered test, and 3 hours and 30 minutes for the paper-delivered test with similar breaks). The following practice test contains the five scored sections.

Each section has its own time allocation and during that time period, you may work on only that section.

Next, you will read ETS's (Educational Testing Service) policy on scoring the Analytical Writing responses. Each response is read by experienced readers and ETS may cancel any test scores that show evidence of unacknowledged use of sources, unacknowledged collaboration with others, preparation of the response by another person, and language that is "substantially" similar to the language in one or more other test responses.

Each section has specific instructions for that section.

You will be told when to begin.

ANSWER SHEET: PRACTICE TEST 1 DIAGNOSTIC TEST

Section 1: Analytical Writing

Analyze an Issue

FOR PLANNING

answer sheet

Analyze an Issue Response

_____

_____

_____

_____

_____

_____

_____

_____

_____

_____

_____

_____

_____

_____

_____

_____

_____

_____

_____

_____

_____

_____

_____

Analyze an Issue Response

_____

_____

_____

_____

_____

_____

_____

_____

_____

_____

_____

_____

_____

_____

_____

_____

_____

_____

_____

_____

answer sheet

Analyze an Issue Response

_____

_____

_____

_____

_____

_____

_____

_____

_____

_____

_____

_____

_____

_____

_____

_____

_____

_____

_____

_____

_____

_____

_____

_____

Analyze an Issue Response

Analyze an Argument

FOR PLANNING

Analyze an Argument Response

_____

_____

_____

_____

_____

_____

_____

_____

_____

_____

_____

_____

_____

_____

_____

_____

_____

_____

_____

_____

_____

_____

_____

answer sheet

Analyze an Argument Response

_____

_____

_____

_____

_____

_____

_____

_____

_____

_____

_____

_____

_____

_____

_____

_____

_____

_____

_____

_____

_____

_____

_____

_____

Analyze an Argument Response

_____

_____

_____

_____

_____

_____

_____

_____

_____

_____

_____

_____

_____

_____

_____

_____

_____

_____

_____

_____

answer sheet

Analyze an Argument Response

Section 2: Verbal Reasoning

1. Ⓐ Ⓑ Ⓒ Ⓓ Ⓔ
2. Ⓐ Ⓑ Ⓒ Ⓓ Ⓔ Ⓕ
3. Ⓐ Ⓑ Ⓒ Ⓓ Ⓔ Ⓕ
4. Ⓐ Ⓑ Ⓒ Ⓓ Ⓔ Ⓕ Ⓖ Ⓗ Ⓘ
5. Ⓐ Ⓑ Ⓒ
6. Ⓐ Ⓑ Ⓒ Ⓓ Ⓔ
7. Ⓐ Ⓑ Ⓒ Ⓓ Ⓔ

8. Ⓐ Ⓑ Ⓒ
9. Ⓐ Ⓑ Ⓒ Ⓓ Ⓔ
10. Ⓐ Ⓑ Ⓒ Ⓓ Ⓔ
11. Ⓐ Ⓑ Ⓒ Ⓓ Ⓔ
12. Ⓐ Ⓑ Ⓒ Ⓓ Ⓔ
13. Ⓐ Ⓑ Ⓒ
14. Ⓐ Ⓑ Ⓒ

15. Ⓐ Ⓑ Ⓒ Ⓓ Ⓔ
16. Ⓐ Ⓑ Ⓒ Ⓓ Ⓔ Ⓕ
17. Ⓐ Ⓑ Ⓒ Ⓓ Ⓔ Ⓕ
18. Ⓐ Ⓑ Ⓒ Ⓓ Ⓔ Ⓕ
19. Ⓐ Ⓑ Ⓒ Ⓓ Ⓔ Ⓕ
20. Ⓐ Ⓑ Ⓒ Ⓓ Ⓔ

Section 3: Verbal Reasoning

1. Ⓐ Ⓑ Ⓒ Ⓓ Ⓔ
2. Ⓐ Ⓑ Ⓒ Ⓓ Ⓔ
3. Ⓐ Ⓑ Ⓒ Ⓓ Ⓔ Ⓕ
4. Ⓐ Ⓑ Ⓒ Ⓓ Ⓔ Ⓕ Ⓖ Ⓗ Ⓘ
5. Ⓐ Ⓑ Ⓒ Ⓓ Ⓔ Ⓕ Ⓖ Ⓗ Ⓘ
6. Ⓐ Ⓑ Ⓒ Ⓓ Ⓔ
7. Ⓐ Ⓑ Ⓒ

8. Ⓐ Ⓑ Ⓒ Ⓓ Ⓔ
9. Ⓐ Ⓑ Ⓒ
10. Ⓐ Ⓑ Ⓒ Ⓓ Ⓔ
11. Ⓐ Ⓑ Ⓒ Ⓓ Ⓔ
12. Ⓐ Ⓑ Ⓒ Ⓓ Ⓔ
13. Ⓐ Ⓑ Ⓒ Ⓓ Ⓔ Ⓕ
14. Ⓐ Ⓑ Ⓒ Ⓓ Ⓔ Ⓕ

15. Ⓐ Ⓑ Ⓒ Ⓓ Ⓔ
16. Ⓐ Ⓑ Ⓒ Ⓓ Ⓔ
17. Ⓐ Ⓑ Ⓒ Ⓓ Ⓔ
18. Ⓐ Ⓑ Ⓒ
19. Ⓐ Ⓑ Ⓒ Ⓓ Ⓔ
20. Ⓐ Ⓑ Ⓒ Ⓓ Ⓔ

Section 4: Quantitative Reasoning

1. Ⓐ Ⓑ Ⓒ Ⓓ
2. Ⓐ Ⓑ Ⓒ Ⓓ
3. Ⓐ Ⓑ Ⓒ Ⓓ
4. Ⓐ Ⓑ Ⓒ Ⓓ
5. Ⓐ Ⓑ Ⓒ Ⓓ
6. Ⓐ Ⓑ Ⓒ Ⓓ
7. Ⓐ Ⓑ Ⓒ Ⓓ

8. Ⓐ Ⓑ Ⓒ Ⓓ
9. Ⓐ Ⓑ Ⓒ Ⓓ Ⓔ
10. Ⓐ Ⓑ Ⓒ Ⓓ Ⓔ
11. Ⓐ Ⓑ Ⓒ Ⓓ Ⓔ Ⓕ Ⓖ Ⓗ
12. Ⓐ Ⓑ Ⓒ Ⓓ Ⓔ
13. Ⓐ Ⓑ Ⓒ Ⓓ Ⓔ
14. Ⓐ Ⓑ Ⓒ Ⓓ Ⓔ

15. Ⓐ Ⓑ Ⓒ Ⓓ Ⓔ Ⓕ Ⓖ Ⓗ
16. Ⓐ Ⓑ Ⓒ Ⓓ Ⓔ
17. Ⓐ Ⓑ Ⓒ Ⓓ Ⓔ
18. Ⓐ Ⓑ Ⓒ Ⓓ Ⓔ
19. [ ]
20. Ⓐ Ⓑ Ⓒ Ⓓ Ⓔ

Section 5: Quantitative Reasoning

1. Ⓐ Ⓑ Ⓒ Ⓓ
2. Ⓐ Ⓑ Ⓒ Ⓓ
3. Ⓐ Ⓑ Ⓒ Ⓓ
4. Ⓐ Ⓑ Ⓒ Ⓓ
5. Ⓐ Ⓑ Ⓒ Ⓓ
6. Ⓐ Ⓑ Ⓒ Ⓓ
7. Ⓐ Ⓑ Ⓒ Ⓓ
8. Ⓐ Ⓑ Ⓒ Ⓓ

9. Ⓐ Ⓑ Ⓒ Ⓓ Ⓔ
10. Ⓐ Ⓑ Ⓒ Ⓓ Ⓔ
11. Ⓐ Ⓑ Ⓒ Ⓓ Ⓔ
12. Ⓐ Ⓑ Ⓒ Ⓓ Ⓔ
13. [ ]
14. Ⓐ Ⓑ Ⓒ Ⓓ Ⓔ
15. Ⓐ Ⓑ Ⓒ Ⓓ Ⓔ

16. Ⓐ Ⓑ Ⓒ Ⓓ Ⓔ
17. Ⓐ Ⓑ Ⓒ Ⓓ Ⓔ
18. Ⓐ Ⓑ Ⓒ Ⓓ Ⓔ
19. Ⓐ Ⓑ Ⓒ Ⓓ Ⓔ Ⓕ
20.

SECTION 1: ANALYTICAL WRITING

Analyze an Issue

30 minutes

The time for this task is 30 minutes. You must plan and draft a response that evaluates the issue given below. If you do not respond to the specific issue, your score will be zero. Your response must be based on the accompanying instructions, and you must provide evidence for your position. You may use support from reading, experience, observations, and/or course work.

High schools should eliminate their art and music programs to make room for more extensive studies in mathematics and English. Test scores in mathematics and English are of paramount interest to the colleges most students wish to attend, while art and music classes are mere electives of little use to students who do not intend to pursue careers in such creative fields.

Write a response that expresses the degree to which you agree or disagree with the claim and the reason or reasons that underlie the claim.

Your response will be read by experienced readers who will assess your ability to:

- follow the set of task instructions.
- analyze the complexities involved.
- organize, develop, and explain ideas.
- use pertinent reasons and/or illustrations to support ideas.
- adhere to the conventions of Standard Written English.

You will be advised to take some time to plan your response and to leave time to reread it before the time is over. Those taking the paper-delivered GRE® General Test will find a blank page in their answer booklet for making notes and then four ruled pages for writing their actual response. Those taking the computer-delivered test will be given scrap paper for making notes.

STOP!
IF YOU FINISH BEFORE THE TIME IS UP,
YOU MAY CHECK YOUR WORK IN THIS SECTION ONLY.

Analyze an Argument

30 minutes

The time for this task is 30 minutes. You must plan and draft a response that evaluates the argument given below. If you do not respond to the given argument, your score will be zero. Your response must be based on the accompanying instructions, and you must provide evidence in support of your analysis.

You should not present your views on the subject of the argument, but on the strength or weakness of the argument.

Skybold and Associates has seen a remarkable surge in productivity since it instituted its policy of allowing its creative staff to work from home for as many as two workdays (16 hours) per week. Results of this policy have included employees taking fewer sick and personal days as well as greater employee satisfaction and enhanced employee loyalty. In addition, Skybold envisions in the not so distant future a reduced need for office space as fewer offices and cubicles will be needed to accommodate a smaller in-house staff. This will result in dramatic savings for the company. Skybold's new telecommunicating policy is clearly a win-win situation.

Write a response that identifies questions to be answered before deciding whether the conclusion and the argument on which it is based are reasonable. Explain how the answers would help you determine whether the argument's conclusion is logical.

Your response will be read by experienced readers who will assess your ability to:

- follow the set of task instructions.
- analyze the complexities involved.
- organize, develop, and explain ideas.
- use pertinent reasons and/or illustrations to support ideas.
- adhere to the conventions of Standard Written English.

You will be advised to take some time to plan your response and to leave time to reread it before the time is over. Those taking the paper-delivered GRE® General Test will find a blank page in their answer booklet for making notes and then four ruled pages for writing their actual response. Those taking the computer-delivered test will be given scrap paper for making notes.

STOP!
IF YOU FINISH BEFORE THE TIME IS UP,
YOU MAY CHECK YOUR WORK IN THIS SECTION ONLY.

INSTRUCTIONS FOR THE VERBAL REASONING AND QUANTITATIVE REASONING SECTIONS

You will find information here on the question formats for the Verbal Reasoning and Quantitative Reasoning sections, as well as information about how to use the software program, or, if you're taking the paper-delivered test, how to mark your answers in the answer booklet.

Perhaps the most important information is a reminder about how these two sections are scored. Every correct answer earns a point, but points are not subtracted for incorrect answers. The advice from ETS is to guess if you aren't sure of an answer. ETS says that this is better than not answering a question.

All multiple-choice questions on the computer-delivered test will have answer options preceded by either blank ovals or blank squares, depending on the question type. The paper-delivered test will follow the same format for answer choices, but use letters instead of ovals or squares for answer choices.

For your convenience in answering questions and checking answers in this book, we use A, B, C, etc. By using letters, you will find it easy to check your answers against the answer key and explanation sections.

SECTION 2: VERBAL REASONING

30 minutes • 20 questions

(The paper-delivered test will have 25 questions to be completed in 35 minutes.)

For each question, follow the specific directions and choose the best answer.

For Questions 1–4, choose <u>one</u> answer for each blank. Select from the appropriate column for each blank. Choose the answer that best completes the sense of the text.

1. Russian author Leo Tolstoy wrote *War and Peace* from an _____ point of view because he wanted to convey what each of his characters was thinking and feeling.

A. accomplished
B. enormous
C. ensemble
D. omniscient
E. acrimonious

2. That Jane Austen's satiric wit is lost on some readers is (i) _____ because it is so (ii) _____ as to become caricature; for example, consider the Rev. Collins in *Pride and Prejudice*.

Blank (i)	Blank (ii)
A. logical	**D.** flashy
B. understandable	**E.** showy
C. inexplicable	**F.** overdrawn

3. One of the most (i) _____ and respected members of our community is giving a speech about some (ii) _____ issues affecting our local government at the town hall meeting this Friday.

Blank (i)	Blank (ii)
A. malevolent	**D.** crucial
B. eminent	**E.** incandescent
C. marginal	**F.** heterogeneous

4. One consequence of the desire among modern playwrights to bring (i) _____ to the theater has been the diminution of poetry as a dramatic language. On the other hand, realism in language has brought a (ii) _____ end to rant and rhetoric upon the stage. As one critic wrote, modern playwrights have been pushed to develop plays that are (iii) _____ and convincing when they could no longer rely on "verbal pyrotechnics."

Blank (i)	Blank (ii)	Blank (iii)
A. vibrancy	**D.** welcome	**G.** more forceful
B. verisimilitude	**E.** final	**H.** more cerebral
C. resemblance	**F.** limited	**I.** more believable

For Questions 5–20, choose only one answer choice unless otherwise indicated.

Questions 5–7 are based on the following passage.

The *New York Times* has boldly declared the end of the car culture in the United States. It based its claim on a few salient facts. The number of miles driven dropped steadily between 2005 and 2013. Over an even more extended period, rates of automobile ownership declined.
Line The *Times* also charted changing attitudes toward driving and car ownership by young people,
5 quoting one study that showed a 23-percent decrease in driving among young people. Car sharing, bikes, and public transit were among the reasons cited for this decrease.

But is the automobility of American culture actually over, or is it just in the slow lane? It is true that the era of massive road building projects not only seems to be over, but also actually peaked as long ago as 1980. It is also true that environmental and social factors, as well as
10 the overcrowding of our roads and highways, are shaping new attitudes across all segments of society. During the past two decades, public transportation use has grown at a far faster rate than the population. Another significant factor in the declining number of miles driven has to do with our aging population; over many years, the number of miles driven has been shown to decline by age 45. Vehicle costs as a percentage of income have also been rising
15 since the mid-90s. While all of these data do not prove the end of cars, they may point to the end of the driving boom that characterized twentieth-century America.

For Question 5, consider each answer individually and choose all that apply.

5. The passage suggests that the decline in driving is authenticated by which of the following?

   A. A 23-percent decline in car ownership among young people

   B. The end of the era of massive road building projects

   C. The steady drop in the number of miles driven

6. It can be inferred from the passage that the author most likely thinks that the *Times* writer used the term "the end of car culture" because it

   A. offered the clearest wording to contradict the phrase "automobility of American culture."

   B. generalized the facts about U.S. driving trends in the most succinct and appropriate way.

   C. created a new and appropriate catchphrase for referring to changes in driving.

   D. summarized a number of recent studies and elucidated their results accurately.

   E. reflected some current data and employed enough hyperbole to create interest.

7. In the second paragraph, the author is primarily concerned with

   A. mitigating the *Times*'s assertion that car culture is at an end.

   B. explaining why the number of miles driven has declined recently.

   C. presenting reasons for a changing demographic of car ownership.

   D. disputing the claim that car ownership is in significant decline.

   E. offering further proof for the *Times*'s claim that the car culture is over.

Questions 8–9 are based on the following passage.

Obesity results when a person consumes significantly more calories than energy burned over a long period of time, though at this point scientists cannot point to a single cause of obesity. In a large majority of obesity cases, the causes are related to genetic factors that

Line influence the metabolism of fat and that regulate the hormones and proteins that control

5 appetite. A person's appetite is determined by different processes that occur both in the brain and the digestive system. **During digestion, carbohydrates break down into different types of sugar molecules, including glucose.** Immediately after eating, blood glucose levels rise, which triggers the release of insulin, a hormone that helps change glucose into energy. As the insulin pours into the bloodstream, it pushes the glucose into cells. Insulin is a significant

10 factor in terms of obesity because it helps determine which nutrients will be burned for energy and which will be stored in cells for future use. Recent studies have found that the faster a cell processes insulin, the more fat it stores. This might be one cause of obesity, though there may be other factors to consider, and to date no one theory has been determined to be conclusive.

For Question 8, consider each answer individually and choose <u>all</u> that apply.

8. What function might a medication perform to decrease the obesity of the user?

   A. It could help the user process insulin more quickly.

   B. It could cause the user to produce more insulin.

   C. It could slow the rate at which cells process insulin.

9. Which of the following best characterizes the function of the boldfaced sentence in lines 6–7 of the passage?

    A. It provides evidence on which a theory is based.

    B. It summarizes a theory with which the author agrees.

    C. It restates a point made earlier in the passage.

    D. It disproves a commonly accepted theory.

    E. It presents a specific application of a general concept.

Questions 10–12 are based on the following passage.

    Dutch artist M.C. Escher's work covers a variety of subjects, though he is probably best known for the pieces that he drew from unusual perspectives, which result in enigmatic effects. During the course of his life, Escher adopted a highly mathematical approach, using special *Line* notations that he invented himself, including a system for categorizing shapes, colors, and 5 symmetrical properties. Looking at his work, you can see clearly that mathematics played an important role in the development of his distinctive style, yet though he studied and admired various mathematical theories over the years, Escher did not consider himself a mathematician. However, this lack of formal training allowed him to explore mathematics in a unique way, without having to adhere to any set rules or restrictions. In 1958, he wrote: 10 "In mathematical quarters, the regular division of the plane has been considered theoretically . . . . [Mathematicians] have opened the gate leading to an extensive domain, but they have not entered this domain themselves. By their very nature they are more interested in the way in which the gate is opened than in the garden lying behind it."

10. The passage suggests that the enigmatic effects of M.C. Esher's work are caused by which of the following?

    A. The fact that Escher's work covers a variety of subjects

    B. Escher's decision to draw rather than paint his work

    C. The mathematical approach Escher took to his work

    D. The way Escher used a system to categorize his shapes

    E. The unusual perspectives Escher used in his work

11. From the passage, what is Escher's view of mathematicians?

    A. They do not grasp how mathematics and art are interconnected.

    B. They will never have the ability to appreciate Escher's art.

    C. They cannot translate their theories into their own personalized notations.

    D. They will never be able to translate their theories into art.

    E. They cannot see the beauty that is inherent in their theories.

12. In the passage, "distinctive" (line 6) means

    A. disturbing.

    B. honorable.

    C. characteristic.

    D. maladjusted.

    E. macabre.

Questions 13–15 are based on the following passage.

      The fire at the Triangle Shirtwaist Factory in New York City in 1911 was one of the worst industrial disasters in U.S. history. The fire killed 146 people, many of them young immigrant women. The Triangle Shirtwaist Factory produced women's blouses, or "shirtwaists," and took up the eighth, ninth, and tenth floors of a building in New York's Greenwich Village.
    5 The fire started near closing time on March 25, 1911, on the eighth floor of the building. Most of the workers could not escape because the supervisors had locked the doors to the stairwells and exits from the outside to prevent the workers from leaving early or removing materials. Many women died from being trapped inside the building or jumped to their deaths from the top floors because ladders could not reach them. This devastating tragedy
  10 brought to light for many Americans the inhumane working conditions of sweatshops and it had a huge impact on U.S. workers. It galvanized many to push for improved factory safety standards and led to the rapid growth of the International Ladies' Garment Workers' Union, which fought for better and safer working conditions in the garment industry. New York State created a commission to investigate factory conditions, and in 1915, the state
  15 legislature enacted new measures to protect factory workers from just such tragedies as the Triangle Shirtwaist Factory fire.

For Questions 13–14, consider each answer individually and choose <u>all</u> that apply.

13. According to the passage, what was it about the Triangle Shirtwaist fire that evidently caused so great an impact on public opinion?

    A. The fire killed many people, many of whom were young women.

    B. The workers could not escape during the fire because supervisors had locked the doors to the stairwells and exits.

    C. The fire resulted in a strengthened labor movement and new labor laws.

14. Select the sentence in the passage that does NOT add to the support for the main idea of the passage.

    A. This devastating tragedy brought to light for many Americans the inhumane working conditions of sweatshops and it had a huge impact on U.S. workers.

    B. The fire started near closing time on March 25, 1911, on the eighth floor of the building.

    C. Many women died from being trapped inside the building or jumped to their deaths from the top floors because ladders could not reach them.

15. In the passage, "galvanized" (line 11) most nearly means

    A. impeded.

    B. increased.

    C. hurtled.

    D. angered.

    E. incited.

For Questions 16–19, choose the <u>two</u> answers that best fit the meaning of the sentence as a whole and result in two completed sentences that are alike in meaning.

16. In shuttering programs to reduce costs, the new CFO was _____ toward employees and refused to listen to their concerns and alternative suggestions.

    A. arrogant

    B. unkind

    C. uncharitable

    D. dismissive

    E. contentious

    F. confrontational

17. Green building, that is, the construction of new buildings and the renovation of existing ones to make them eco-friendly, is a fast-growing segment of the construction industry and one that ALLIED Builders hopes to _____ according to its five-year business plan.

    A. promote

    B. advance

    C. capitalize on

    D. upgrade

    E. exploit

    F. endorse

18. The original intention in creating NASA was to explore space, but many of the products people take for granted today, such as cordless power tools and sunglasses with polarized lenses, resulted from _____ research that NASA conducted for the space program.

    A. far-reaching

    B. wide-ranging

    C. innovative

    D. unusual

    E. cutting-edge

    F. conventional

19. Many researchers believe that _____ bacteria keep harmful bacteria from invading humans by using the material that harmful bacteria need to live.

    A. helpful

    B. malignant

    C. pathogenic

    D. benign

    E. benevolent

    F. beneficial

Question 20 is based on the following passage.

Emily Dickinson, a poet virtually unknown in her lifetime, wrote some of the most memorable lines in American poetry. Her poems are instantly recognizable for their brevity (they are often no longer than 20 lines) and their quirky punctuation and capitalization. Her *Line* frequent and often idiosyncratic use of the dash serves to emphasize many of her recurrent 5 topics. A great number of Dickinson's almost 1,800 poems deal with the themes of death and immortality, though her poems are also filled with joy and hope. Because of its unusual syntax and use of figurative language—imagery, metaphor, personification—Dickinson's poetry can seem to the uninitiated reader something of a puzzle. Present-day readers would do well to renounce a literal way of reading in order to truly appreciate Dickinson's poetry.

20. What does the author imply by the last statement in the passage?

   A. Readers should not try to find literal meaning in Dickinson's poetry.

   B. Readers of poetry today are not used to so much figurative language.

   C. Readers should try to figure out what themes were most important to Dickinson.

   D. Readers who try to unlock the mysteries of Dickinson's figurative language are doing themselves a disservice.

   E. Readers of poetry today need to consider the context in which Dickinson's poetry was written.

STOP!
IF YOU FINISH BEFORE THE TIME IS UP,
YOU MAY CHECK YOUR WORK IN THIS SECTION ONLY.

SECTION 3: VERBAL REASONING

30 minutes • 20 questions

(The paper-delivered test will have 25 questions to be completed in 35 minutes.)

For each question, follow the specific directions and choose the best answer.

For Questions 1–5, choose <u>one</u> answer for each blank. Select from the appropriate column for each blank. Choose the answer that best completes the sense of the text.

1. Social networking is a marketing tool that many companies are harnessing to sell their products; however, it must be used _____ because the hard sell risks offending potential customers.

A. with ease
B. actively
C. judiciously
D. expeditiously
E. efficiently

2. My dog Candy's lethargic behavior was initially _____, but it made sense after I took her to the veterinarian and learned that Candy is pregnant.

A. unambiguous
B. ineluctable
C. circumspect
D. cantankerous
E. inexplicable

3. Garraty states that the problems faced by private colleges in the 1820s and 1830s were of their own making to a degree. Many cities and towns wanted the (i) _____ of hosting a college, but the supply of colleges soon (ii) _____ the demand, that is, the number of potential students.

   Blank (i)

A. honor
B. admiration
C. character

   Blank (ii)

D. outperformed
E. outstripped
F. outshone

4. Because the queen is in (i) _____ health, the prince might have to (ii) _____ the role of king if his mother's health forces her to (iii) _____ the throne.

Blank (i)	Blank (ii)	Blank (iii)
A. robust	**D.** convey	**G.** abdicate
B. feeble	**E.** assume	**H.** nullify
C. cautionary	**F.** furnish	**I.** arbitrate

5. To (i) _____ with the (ii) _____ of questions that greeted her vague comment during the lecture, the professor restated her comment to (iii) _____ her intent.

Blank (i)	Blank (ii)	Blank (iii)
A. amalgamate	**D.** onslaught	**G.** elucidate
B. orient	**E.** paucity	**H.** obfuscate
C. contend	**F.** compilation	**I.** categorize

For Questions 6–20, choose only one answer choice unless otherwise indicated.

Questions 6–7 are based on the following passage.

Access to clean drinking water and sanitation systems are crucial global goals. This access constitutes a fundamental health and human dignity issue. Expanding sewage systems will also reduce contamination of soil, rivers, and oceans, thereby promoting biodiversity and
Line decreasing land degradation. Furthermore, access to clean water will reduce geopolitical
5 conflict centered on water rights. In addition, commitment to clean water goals promotes investment in new technologies, such as desalination and water reuse.

Even though the United Nations reported that between 1990 and 2010, more than "2 billion people gained access to improved water sources, and 1.8 billion gained access to improved sanitation," a more recent global assessment warns that significant problems con-
10 tinue to plague the world. Despite well-coordinated global initiatives, the latest U.N. report discusses factors that slow the progress toward clean water goals. These include the failure of some countries to set national hygiene standards, inadequate funding or poor absorption of existing funding, lack of skilled labor to implement change, and lack of political will. Only 80% of nations recognize the right to water; only some 50% recognize the right to sanitation.

6. Based on the passage, which of the following is NOT a factor that is delaying progress toward clean water goals?

    A. Failure of some nations to set national hygiene standards

    B. Inability to manage skilled labor resources at water sites

    C. Inadequate funding for global water initiatives

    D. Failure to properly use all available water funding

    E. Reluctance of some nations to consider water as a right

For Question 7, consider each answer individually and choose <u>all</u> that apply.

7. Select the sentence in the passage that is NOT a supporting detail for a central idea.

    A. This access constitutes a fundamental health and human dignity issue.

    B. Expanding sewage systems will also reduce contamination of soil, rivers, and oceans, thereby promoting biodiversity and decreasing land degradation.

    C. Despite well-coordinated global initiatives, the latest U.N. report discusses factors that slow the progress toward clean water goals.

Questions 8–9 are based on the following passage.

During World War II, the U.S. system of rationing did not work as planned, not only because it conflicted with personal needs and wants (which had grown during the previous years of deprivation because of the Great Depression and its aftermath), but because it went
Line against the national character of the American people. This was a nation based on the principle
5 that as long as you have money to spend, nothing is off limits. By limiting each individual's purchasing power, the government had imposed a new economic system that attacked this principle. The emergence of the illegal black market, on the other hand, supported this basic principle of acquisition, or consumerism, for Americans. This is not to deny that many who ran or even patronized the black market were actually motivated by greed, but it does suggest
10 that the individualistic (and frontier) spirit of Americans had not been lost.

8. Select the statement that restates the premise of the author's argument.

    A. Normally law-abiding citizens will break the law to satisfy what they consider to be their basic needs and wants.

    B. Americans during World War II acted unlawfully due to circumstances out of their control.

    C. The American system of rationing did not work because Americans circumvented its principles through the practice of the black market.

    D. As long as Americans have enough money to spend, they will spend it however they can.

    E. If the Great Depression had not deprived so many Americans of basic needs and wants, they would not have patronized the black market during World War II.

For Question 9, consider each answer individually and choose <u>all</u> that apply.

9. Which of the following, if it were true, would weaken the author's argument?

    A. During the Great Depression, many Americans found ways to circumvent the law in order to provide for their families.

    B. The majority of American citizens are law abiding and will not break the law under any circumstances.

    C. Many Americans continued to patronize the black market after rationing ended.

Questions 10–12 are based on the following passage.

The increasing awareness of lighting inefficiency and the billions of dollars of potential annual energy savings that can be achieved by switching to LED lighting has resulted in many government-funded research initiatives around the world. In addition, governments in the
Line United States, Canada, Europe, and Australia have responded to the growing need for energy
5 conservation by passing legislation that regulates or eliminates the sale of incandescent and halogen light bulbs by a certain date. However, though increasing consumers' awareness of the inefficiency of other light sources can help increase the adoption of LED lighting, regulations that focus on enforcing energy-efficient lighting are likely to work better. One example is California's Energy Efficiency Standards for Residential and Nonresidential Buildings, or
10 Title 24, that provides a set of mandatory regulations covering all aspects of new building construction. The Residential Lighting section of Title 24 requires that a high-efficiency light source be used in several areas of the home, including the kitchen and bathrooms, and that all outdoor light fixtures must either use energy-efficient bulbs or be controlled by light and motion sensors.

10. This passage achieves all of the following purposes EXCEPT it

    A. implies that LED lighting will become a necessity of the future.

    B. explains one way governments are forcing people to switch to LED lighting.

    C. cites a regulation that enforces the use of high-efficiency light sources.

    D. describes how LED lighting is more energy efficient than incandescent lighting.

    E. implies that government-funded research on energy efficiency is essential.

11. The author lists several countries and continents in line 4 in order to

    A. show the places that have been most affected by lighting inefficiency.

    B. imply that most countries do not take lighting inefficiency seriously enough.

    C. explain that only a minority of governments believe that lighting inefficiency is a problem.

    D. prove that legislation to control lighting inefficiency is extremely effective.

    E. indicate the governments that have taken initiatives to conserve energy.

12. "Mandatory" (line 10) most nearly means

    A. provisional.

    B. permanent.

    C. predetermined.

    D. discretionary.

    E. obligatory.

For Questions 13–15, choose the <u>two</u> answers that best fit the meaning of the sentence as a whole and result in two completed sentences that are alike in meaning.

13. If life did exist on other planets, scientists theorize that it would not _____ life on Earth. For example, depending on the wavelengths of life given off by the plant, plants could be red, yellow, or green.

    A. epitomize

    B. mimic

    C. illustrate

    D. typify

    E. imitate

    F. reflect

14. Scientists believe that unlocking the genome is _____; it will forever change the way we diagnose, treat, and someday even prevent disease.

    A. modernization

    B. reforming

    C. revolutionary

    D. transformative

    E. huge

    F. corrective

15. Most of the dishes served during the feast were underdone or overcooked, but at least the soup was very _____.

    A. thorough

    B. palatable

    C. vehement

    D. edible

    E. baroque

Questions 16–17 are based on the following passage.

Among people who want to make informed choices about what they eat, the issue of whether to buy local or organic food is often debated. The most popular reasons cited for buying organic are to avoid pesticides that harm your health and damage ecosystems, to
Line support a system of agriculture that uses natural fertilizers, and to support more humane
5 animal husbandry practices. The reasons cited for buying local food include supporting the local economy and also buying food that is fresher, has less packaging, and has fewer "food miles," or the distance food has to travel from source to end user. It turns out to be a complicated question, one that can sometimes lead to additional questions that must be answered in order to make a choice. Sometimes the questions are personal ones, such as:
10 What food tastes better? But larger questions can arise, too, such as: How do the choices we make about our food affect the planet?

16. What is the author's opinion about whether to buy organic or local food?

    A. We can never really know which is better.

    B. We should try to answer important questions before trying to make that decision.

    C. We should figure out which food tastes better.

    D. We should try to find other ways to support the local economy.

    E. We should buy the food that has the fewest "food miles."

17. Which of the following statements does the passage most clearly support?

    A. Buying local or organic food is better than buying food from a big chain supermarket.

    B. Buying organic food does not support the local economy.

    C. The distance food has to travel is an important consideration when deciding where to buy your food.

    D. Animals raised on organic farms are treated more humanely.

    E. Food from local farms may have been sprayed with pesticides.

For Question 18, consider each of the three choices individually and choose <u>all</u> that apply.

18. What function does "the distance food has to travel from source to end user" (line 7) serve in the passage?

    A. It is support for the argument for buying local food.

    B. It defines the term "food miles."

    C. It is support for the larger question about how food choices affect the planet.

Questions 19–20 are based on the following passage.

Voter opinion polls are often disparaged because they are seen as inaccurate or misused by network news shows eager to boost ratings. However, those who want to discredit voter opinion polling for elections overlook a few facts. First, the last week or two before an election
Line is notoriously volatile. Voters finally decide whether or not to vote, and undecided voters
5 make up their minds about the candidates for whom they will vote. This means that polls taken too far in advance of an election cannot possibly forecast with precision the outcome of that election. Second, exit polls differ from most other types of scientific polling, mainly because dispersed polling places preclude exit pollsters from using normal sampling methods. However, debating whether voter polls are accurate or not misses the point. Voter polls
10 are not intended to forecast winners and losers. They are designed to describe the broad spectrum of public opinion and to elucidate what voters are really thinking and what policies are most important to them. In fact, most of what we know about voter behavior and policy preferences comes from past opinion polls about elections. Understood in this context, we should not dismiss polling outright, but instead consider how to improve polling and to use
15 it to its best advantage.

19. "Elucidate" (line 11) most nearly means

    A. confound.

    B. elevate.

    C. vanquish.

    D. illuminate.

    E. predict.

20. Which of the following expresses the author's thesis about voter opinion polls?

    A. They can never predict the results of an election.

    B. They can help us get a sense of the general trend in an election.

    C. They can help undecided voters make up their minds.

    D. They are misused by the news media.

    E. They are highly unpredictable.

STOP!
IF YOU FINISH BEFORE THE TIME IS UP, YOU MAY CHECK YOUR WORK IN THIS SECTION ONLY.

SECTION 4: QUANTITATIVE REASONING

35 minutes • 20 questions

(The paper-delivered test will have 25 questions to be completed in 40 minutes.)

For each question, follow the specific directions and choose the best answer.

The test maker provides the following information that applies to all questions in the Quantitative Reasoning section of the GRE® General Test:

- All numbers used are real numbers.
- All figures are assumed to lie in a plane unless otherwise indicated.
- Geometric figures, such as lines, circles, triangles, and quadrilaterals, *are not necessarily* drawn to scale. That is, you should *not* assume that quantities such as lengths and angle measures are as they appear in a figure. You should assume, however, that lines shown as straight are actually straight, points on a line are in the order shown, and more generally, all geometric objects are in the relative positions shown. For questions with geometric figures, you should base your answers on geometric reasoning, not on estimating or comparing quantities by sight or by measurement.
- Coordinate systems, such as *xy*-planes and number lines, *are* drawn to scale. Therefore, you can read, estimate, or compare quantities in such figures by sight or by measurement.
- Graphical data presentations, such as bar graphs, circle graphs, and line graphs, *are* drawn to scale. Therefore, you can read, estimate, or compare data values by sight or by measurement.

For Questions 1–8, compare Quantity A and Quantity B. Some questions will have additional information above the two quantities to use in determining your answer.

1.   Quantity A   Quantity B

$$6\frac{7}{8} \qquad\qquad\qquad 3.42(2)$$

    A. Quantity A is greater.

    B. Quantity B is greater.

    C. The two quantities are equal.

    D. The relationship cannot be determined from the information given.

Questions 2–4 refer to the diagram below.

2.

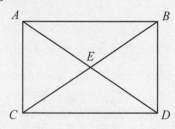

ABCD is a rectangle.

E is the intersection of *AD* and *BC*.

Quantity A	Quantity B
the area of △*CED*	the area of △*AEC*

A. Quantity A is greater.

B. Quantity B is greater.

C. The two quantities are equal.

D. The relationship cannot be determined from the information given.

3.

Quantity A	Quantity B
m∠*ACD* + m∠*CDB*	m∠*AEC* + m∠*CED*

A. Quantity A is greater.

B. Quantity B is greater.

C. The two quantities are equal.

D. The relationship cannot be determined from the information given.

4.

Quantity A	Quantity B
$(AB)^2 + (BD)^2$	*AD*

A. Quantity A is greater.

B. Quantity B is greater.

C. The two quantities are equal.

D. The relationship cannot be determined from the information given.

5.

$$y < x < 0$$

Quantity A	Quantity B
$|x|$	$|y|$

A. Quantity A is greater.

B. Quantity B is greater.

C. The two quantities are equal.

D. The relationship cannot be determined from the information given.

6.

Assume a and b are two different integers.

Quantity A	Quantity B
$(a + b)^2$	$(a + b)^3$

A. Quantity A is greater.

B. Quantity B is greater.

C. The two quantities are equal.

D. The relationship cannot be determined from the information given.

7.

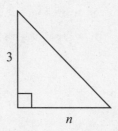

The area of the triangle is 15.

Quantity A	Quantity B
n	12

A. Quantity A is greater.

B. Quantity B is greater.

C. The two quantities are equal.

D. The relationship cannot be determined from the information given.

8. $x^2 = 9$

Quantity A   Quantity B
     x -3

A. Quantity A is greater.

B. Quantity B is greater.

C. The two quantities are equal.

D. The relationship cannot be determined from the information given.

Questions 9–20 have several formats. Unless the directions state otherwise, choose one answer choice. For Numeric Entry questions, follow the instructions below.

Numeric Entry Questions

The following items are the same for both the computer-delivered version and the paper-delivered version of the test. However, those taking the computer-delivered version will have additional information about entering answers in decimal and fraction boxes on the computer screen. Those taking the paper-delivered version will have information about entering answers on answer grids.

- Your answer may be an integer, a decimal, or a fraction, and it may be negative.

- If a question asks for a fraction, there will be two boxes. One box will be for the numerator and one will be for the denominator.

- Equivalent forms of the correct answer, such as 2.5 and 2.50, are all correct.

- Enter the exact answer unless the question asks you to round your answers.

9. A grocery store is having a sale on cherries. Usually, the cost is $6.99 per pound for cherries. This week, the price is 30% less. How much does a customer save if he purchases 2.5 pounds of cherries this week?

SHOW YOUR WORK HERE

A. $2.10

B. $5.25

C. $4.89

D. $17.48

E. $4.20

10. A regular, six-sided die is rolled three times. What is the probability that each of the three rolls will produce an odd number?

    A. $\dfrac{1}{2}$

    B. $\dfrac{1}{3}$

    C. $\dfrac{1}{6}$

    D. $\dfrac{1}{8}$

    E. $\dfrac{1}{216}$

SHOW YOUR WORK HERE

For Question 11, indicate <u>all</u> the answers that apply.

11. Find the next 3 numbers in the sequence.
    1, 1, 2, 3, 5, 8, ….

    A. 12

    B. 13

    C. 14

    D. 21

    E. 22

    F. 33

    G. 34

    H. 55

12. Let $f(x) = -3x^2(1 - x)$. Find $f(-2)$.

    A. 108

    B. 36

    C. 12

    D. −12

    E. −36

13. Solve for z: $-2(4z-2)+3z=1-z$

    A. $\dfrac{3}{4}$

    B. $-\dfrac{3}{4}$

    C. $\dfrac{4}{3}$

    D. $-\dfrac{4}{3}$

    E. $-\dfrac{5}{6}$

14. Find the value of x.

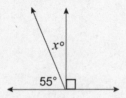

    A. 55°

    B. 35°

    C. 90°

    D. 145°

    E. 125°

For Question 15, indicate all the answers that apply.

15. Which of the following are factors of 1,200?

    A. 8

    B. 14

    C. 15

    D. 75

    E. 85

    F. 160

    G. 250

    H. 300

Questions 16–18 are based on the following data.

Annual State Budgets (in millions of dollars)

	2011	2012	2013	2014	2015	2016, est
State A	53.0	75.9	85.5	101.6	131.2	142.1
State B	14.4	14.5	20.0	19.0	39.2	43.5

16. What is the ratio of the total (State A + State B) estimated budget of 2016 to 2011's budget?

    A. 33.7 : 92.8

    B. 142.1 : 53.0

    C. 43.5 : 14.4

    D. 14.4 : 43.5

    E. 92.8 : 33.7

17. What is the total budget for State A for 2011, 2012, and 2015?

    A. 68.1

    B. 260.1

    C. 268

    D. 276.4

    E. 308.7

18. What year had the biggest percentage increase from the previous year in State B, and what was the percentage increase?

    A. 2013, 138%

    B. 2015, 206%

    C. 2014, 37%

    D. 2015, 106%

    E. 2016, 11%

SHOW YOUR WORK HERE

For Question 19, enter your answer in the box.

SHOW YOUR WORK HERE

19. Mary went to the convenience store with $20. She wanted to buy a newspaper for $1.25, a magazine for $6.50, a soda for $1.75, and then spend the rest of her $20 on dime candy. How many pieces would she get?

```
┌──────────┐
│          │
└──────────┘
```

20. If p is the greatest prime number that is a factor of 51, and q is the smallest prime number that is a factor of 58, then

    $p + q =$

    A. 5

    B. 17

    C. 19

    D. 32

    E. 46

STOP!
IF YOU FINISH BEFORE THE TIME IS UP,
YOU MAY CHECK YOUR WORK IN THIS SECTION ONLY.

SECTION 5: QUANTITATIVE REASONING

35 minutes • 20 questions

(The paper-delivered test will have 25 questions to be completed in 40 minutes.)

For each question, follow the specific directions and choose the best answer.

The test maker provides the following information that applies to all questions in the Quantitative Reasoning section of the GRE® General Test:

- All numbers used are real numbers.

- All figures are assumed to lie in a plane unless otherwise indicated.

- Geometric figures, such as lines, circles, triangles, and quadrilaterals, *are not necessarily* drawn to scale. That is, you should *not* assume that quantities such as lengths and angle measures are as they appear in a figure. You should assume, however, that lines shown as straight are actually straight, points on a line are in the order shown, and more generally, all geometric objects are in the relative positions shown. For questions with geometric figures, you should base your answers on geometric reasoning, not on estimating or comparing quantities by sight or by measurement.

- Coordinate systems, such as *xy*-planes and number lines, *are* drawn to scale. Therefore, you can read, estimate, or compare quantities in such figures by sight or by measurement.

- Graphical data presentations, such as bar graphs, circle graphs, and line graphs, *are* drawn to scale. Therefore, you can read, estimate, or compare data values by sight or by measurement.

For Questions 1–8, compare Quantity A and Quantity B. Some questions will have additional information above the two quantities to use in determining your answer.

1.

Quantity A	Quantity B
0.324875	$\dfrac{10}{31}$

- **A.** Quantity A is greater.
- **B.** Quantity B is greater.
- **C.** The two quantities are equal.
- **D.** The relationship cannot be determined from the information given.

2. Let $0 < x < 1$.

Quantity A	Quantity B
x^2	x^3

    A. Quantity A is greater.

    B. Quantity B is greater.

    C. The two quantities are equal.

    D. The relationship cannot be determined from the information given.

3. Mary is twice as old as Stephen. Stephen is 5 years older than Joe. Joe is $\frac{1}{4}$ of Mary's age. All three were born in the twenty-first century.

Quantity A	Quantity B
Mary's birth year	Joe's birth year

    A. Quantity A is greater.

    B. Quantity B is greater.

    C. The two quantities are equal.

    D. The relationship cannot be determined from the information given.

4. A try is worth 5 points. A conversion is worth 2 points. A penalty goal is worth 3 points.

Quantity A	Quantity B
3 tries, 2 conversions, 1 penalty	24

    A. Quantity A is greater.

    B. Quantity B is greater.

    C. The two quantities are equal.

    D. The relationship cannot be determined from the information given.

5.

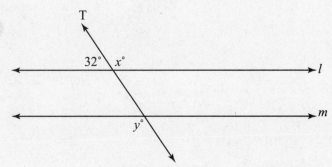

Assume lines *l* and *m* are parallel.

<u>Quantity A</u>   <u>Quantity B</u>

x   *y*

A. Quantity A is greater.

B. Quantity B is greater.

C. The two quantities are equal.

D. The relationship cannot be determined from the information given.

6.   <u>Quantity A</u>   <u>Quantity B</u>

$-\dfrac{15}{16}$ $-\dfrac{16}{15}$

A. Quantity A is greater.

B. Quantity B is greater.

C. The two quantities are equal.

D. The relationship cannot be determined from the information given.

7.   There are 15 players on Team 1. There are 22 players on Team 2.
There are more offensive players than defensive players on each team.

<u>Quantity A</u>   <u>Quantity B</u>

Number of goalies on Team 1   Number of goalies on Team 2

A. Quantity A is greater.

B. Quantity B is greater.

C. The two quantities are equal.

D. The relationship cannot be determined from the information given.

8.

$$\frac{y}{x} = 3$$

$$x, y \neq 0$$

Quantity A	Quantity B
x	y

A. Quantity A is greater.

B. Quantity B is greater.

C. The two quantities are equal.

D. The relationship cannot be determined from the information given.

Questions 9–20 have several formats. Unless the directions state otherwise, choose one answer choice. For Numeric Entry questions, follow the instructions below.

Numeric Entry Questions

The following items are the same for both the computer-delivered version and the paper-delivered version of the test. However, those taking the computer-delivered version will have additional information about entering answers in decimal and fraction boxes on the computer screen. Those taking the paper-delivered version will have information about entering answers on answer grids.

- Your answer may be an integer, a decimal, or a fraction, and it may be negative.

- If a question asks for a fraction, there will be two boxes. One box will be for the numerator and one will be for the denominator.

- Equivalent forms of the correct answer, such as 2.5 and 2.50, are all correct.

- Enter the exact answer unless the question asks you to round your answers.

9. Evaluate the function **SHOW YOUR WORK HERE**
   $f(x) = 5x^3 + 4x^2 + 8x + 1$, when $x = 2$.

   A. 73

   B. −11

   C. 183

   D. 117

   E. −73

10. If $2x - y = -1$ and $3x + 2y = 16$, what is x?   **SHOW YOUR WORK HERE**

    A. 5

    B. 2

    C. $\dfrac{15}{7}$

    D. $\dfrac{1}{2}$

    E. $\dfrac{7}{15}$

11. If $\dfrac{3}{x-1} = \dfrac{6}{3x+6}$, then $x =$

    A. −8

    B. −1

    C. 0

    D. 1

    E. 8

12. A new model hybrid car gets 45 miles per gallon for city driving and 20% more for highway driving. How many miles per gallon does the hybrid get for highway driving?

    A. 34

    B. 46

    C. 51

    D. 54

    E. 58

For Question 13, enter your answer in the box.

13. Find the area of the parallelogram.

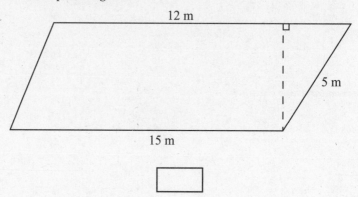

Questions 14–16 refer to the table below.

Number of Children per Family in a Neighborhood

Number of Children	Number of Families
1	19
2	36
3	21
4+	9
0	15

14. What is the total number of families that have no more than two children?

SHOW YOUR WORK HERE

A. 19

B. 36

C. 55

D. 70

E. 81

15. What is the percentage of families who have no children?

A. 9%

B. 12%

C. 15%

D. 18%

E. 21%

16. What percentage of the families has 6 children?

    A. 19

    B. 9

    C. 15

    D. 12

    E. unknown

17. In the xy-plane, what is the slope of a line that is perpendicular to the line whose equation is $x + 2y = 5$?

    A. -2

    B. $-\dfrac{1}{2}$

    C. $\dfrac{1}{2}$

    D. 2

    E. 5

18. What is the x-coordinate of the point at which the graphs of the equations $x + 2y = 4$ and $y - x = 2$ intersect?

    A. -8

    B. -2

    C. 0

    D. 2

    E. 16

SHOW YOUR WORK HERE

diagnostic test

For Question 19, choose <u>all</u> the answers that apply.

SHOW YOUR WORK HERE

19. In triangle ABC, the length of side $\overline{AB}$ is 4 cm and the length of side $\overline{BC}$ is 8 cm. Which of the following could be the length of side $\overline{AC}$?

    A. 2 cm

    B. 4 cm

    C. 6 cm

    D. 8 cm

    E. 10 cm

    F. 12 cm

For Question 20, enter your answer in the boxes.

20. Suppose that the concentric circles below share the same center. What is the ratio of the circumference of the smaller circle to the larger one?

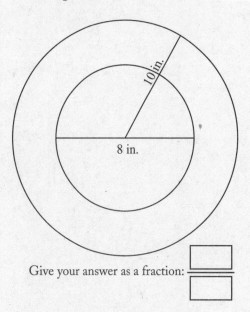

Give your answer as a fraction: ▭/▭

STOP!
IF YOU FINISH BEFORE THE TIME IS UP,
YOU MAY CHECK YOUR WORK IN THIS SECTION ONLY.

ANSWER KEYS AND EXPLANATIONS

Section 1: Analytical Writing

Analyze an Issue

Model: 6 points out of 6

Attending a good college is the primary goal of most high school students. Without a doubt, strong scores on tests that emphasize math and English skills are keys to acceptance into the colleges of these students' choice. However, high school is not a mere stepping stone to the next level of education, and proposals to cut high school art and music programs are symptomatic of a very limited view of both education and human development.

Art and music programs in a number of high schools are currently in danger because of the current emphasis on English and math scores. Such electives are considered to be superfluous because some school administrators view them as inessential to college acceptance and a waste of valuable class time that could be spent on more intensive math and English studies. Granted, performance in art and music classes may only interest colleges if the students in question plan to pursue degrees in the arts. Nevertheless, these classes have value beyond higher education. Appreciating and understanding the arts is essential to forming well-rounded human beings, which should also be a goal of high schools. I know that music classes made my own high school experience richer and more rewarding despite the fact that I am not pursuing a creative career. I also feel as though such classes have helped me to become a more sensitive and cultured person.

For those who still do not appreciate the value of creative classes, there might also be a more practical reason for retaining them. Picking up a paintbrush or instrument in the classroom may lead students to join an extracurricular art or music group. Having such extracurricular activities on their transcripts may be deciding factors in whether or not students are accepted to certain colleges. There is also the matter of how creative classes may overlap with those "essential" subjects. After all, math plays a prominent role in the reading and writing of music. To once again reference my own personal experiences, I believe that being allowed to have a creative outlet during the school day helped me to sit through the more rigorous form of learning common to the math and English classroom. Frankly, art and music classes gave me something to look forward to during the school day and improved my overall attitude toward attending school. The benefits of that positive attitude extended to all of my classes.

So I believe that high school administrators should not make hasty decisions to eliminate their creative programs for shortsighted reasons. No one is arguing that math and English classes are unimportant. Yet there is more to life than calculating and reading comprehension, and high school administrators should take this, as well as the more educational and goal-oriented benefits of keeping art and music alive in the classroom, into consideration.

This response scores 6 out of 6 for the following reasons:

- **It answers the task.** It clearly describes the extent to which it disagrees with the claim (that high schools should eliminate art and music classes), and it competently disputes the reason on which it is based (that such classes have both educational and personal benefits for students).

- **It is well supported.** The response offers specific, accurate examples of what one might know about the value of art and music classes, as well as persuasive examples of how such classes personally impacted the writer. Throughout the response, support and development are abundant, clear, and convincing.

- **It is well organized.** Paragraph 1 leads smoothly into the main attack on the claim; paragraphs 2 and 3 effectively refute the reason for the claims, thereby refuting the claim itself. Each paragraph is a well organized, discrete, and unified unit, with the final paragraph leading smoothly to closure. Several transitional words and phrases help create coherence.

- **It is fluid, precise, and graceful.** Sentences are varied throughout, with many effective uses of questions. Words are precise and varied.

- **It observes the conventions of Standard Written English.**

Model: 1 point out of 6

I totally disagree. Art and music classes are really important to high school. My high school didn't even have art and music classes. I wish it did. I love drawing in my spare time and playing guitar in my spare time. I've been for years taking private lessons in them. I think I've gotten really good at both.

I think I would enjoy playing guitar in class. A lot more than studying math. It has always been my worst subject. Even when I was in elementary school I could barely handle long division. High school math is way harder. I've never understood calculus or trigonometry even. When would you even use those in real life? I never.

I need music though. It makes me happy and creative and I like art too. I would love to be a professional musician or artist one day!

This response scores 1 out of 6 for the following reasons:

- **It answers only part of the task and reflects little or no insight.** It conveys the extent to which it disagrees with the claim (high schools should not cut their art and music programs because the essay writer personally enjoys them), but it offers little or no meaningful insight into the more consequential benefits of creative programs.

- **It is poorly supported.** The response is seriously limited and flawed in terms of support. In fact, it does not support claims. Rather, it supplies simple, illogical, or unsubstantiated support. For example, the writer undermines the idea that music and art should be taught in high schools by describing how he or she is able to study them in private classes outside of class time. Asides about his or her own creative abilities have no bearing on the writer's refutation of the claim. Paragraph 2 suggests that the writer is advocating the elimination of high school math programs, which is not a matter in the claim.

- **It is not organized well.** While paragraph 1 deals with the claim on a rudimentary level, paragraphs 2 and 3 stray from the topic with irrelevant personal opinions and experiences. Paragraph does not wrap up the writer's argument as a strong concluding paragraph should.

- **It has poorly constructed sentences.** There is little variety in sentence structure and many sentences begin with "I."

- **It has some major and minor errors in the conventions of Standard Written English.** Despite these problems, the low score does not result mainly from problems with conventions; rather, it results mainly from lack of insight and development; most fundamentally, the response lacks content.

Analyze an Argument

Model: 6 points out of 6

Upbeat and affirmative, Skybold (or its representative) appears to want to sound as visionary, decisive, and forward-looking in this argument as its name suggests. Certainly, it presents and "envisions" ideas that many readers could wish were true. What company would not want to institute a policy with such desirable and money-saving benefits? Yet, many questions must be answered in order to evaluate the conclusion that "Skybold's new telecommunicating policy is clearly a win-win situation."

First among questions to be addressed are those that probe the exact statistics about fewer sick days and personal days. By what precise number or percent have the number of sick and personal days diminished? Could that diminishment be due to factors other than the new work-at-home policy? Furthermore, over what span of time has this diminishment been measured? For example, if the policy has been in place for three months, and the absenteeism rate has truly dropped significantly over that period of time, could that not be accounted for by the fact that the policy is new? Once it is in place for a year or several years, will the same rates hold true? For the claims to have logical weight, the results surely should have held true for some long span of time, such as a year or more. These answers would help evaluate the conclusion that the policy is a "win" for Skybold.

Specific questions must also be asked in order to interpret the fabulous, though unsubstantiated, claims of greater employee satisfaction and enhanced employee loyalty. Have employees completed questionnaires about greater satisfaction? How many employees are actually more satisfied? Exactly how was the assertion of greater employee loyalty arrived at? Or does Skybold just assume this to be true? Is there any quantifiable data that exists to substantiate these claims? Finally, even if the claims are true, one must consider the dampening effects on satisfaction and loyalty should an employee have his or her desk removed at work and, consequently, be forced to share a space, or use someone else's space, on those days when he or she does not telecommute. Would he or she experience "greater employee satisfaction" then? The answers to all the questions raised in this paragraph would help evaluate the conclusion that the policy is a "win" for employees.

Perhaps the most important questions of all have to do with the writer's motivation and point of view. Was this argument written by the person who instituted the policy, perhaps as a bit of self-aggrandizement? What is the purpose, and just exactly who is the audience for this seeming self-congratulation? The answers to these questions might help peel away the outer layers of argument to expose a propagandistic core.

This response scores 6 out of 6 for the following reasons:

- **It answers the task.** With sophistication and perceptiveness, the response raises questions that would have to be answered in order to evaluate the conclusion and the reasons on which it is based. The questions are not only apt, but they are offered in abundance.

- **It is well supported.** In this case, the support is the questions, as well as the way in which they are introduced, explained, and related back to the writer's evaluative purpose. Although there are many other questions that could be asked, the ones that appear here are logically sound and presented with clarity and rhetorical effect.

- **It is well organized.** The response is a tour de force of good organization, with its attention-provoking opening that not only draws the reader in, but clearly states the claim of the argument. The three remaining paragraphs offer discrete, well-developed analyses of major points and concerns and lead skillfully to the final "most important" issues of author, purpose, and audience.

- **It is fluid, precise, and graceful.** Sentences are varied throughout, with many effective uses of questions. The response is a trove of particularly well-chosen words and phrases, from "visionary," "institute," and "probe" to the "propagandistic core" and its accompanying metaphor.

- **It observes the conventions of Standard Written English.**

Model: 2 points out of 6

Many questions must be asked about the many claims made in this argument. The first about if there was a remarkable surge in productivity. This being an interesting claim that is not explained. In order to evaluate if there was a remarkable surge in productivity, you should ask how much the production of the creative staff people had went up and basing that on the before and after figures of production of those workers, so that you would know if productivity doubled, or if it went up by 50% or if it went up by .05%, the exact amount being crucial to knowing if the policy resulted in a remarkable surge in productivity. Other questions you must ask and answer being about why Skybold brought about its new policy, after all, if the employees were upset that they couldn't ever telecommute, as so many employees do these days, then it only stands to reason that they were happier when they could finally get to telecommute. This would also help you evaluate the claim that there was a remarkable surge in productivity because the telecommuters now felt better about getting to telecommute after not being let to work from there homes before.

This response scores 2 out of 6 for the following reasons:

- **It does not fully answer the task.** This response never evaluates the conclusion that Skybold's new telecommuting policy is a win-win situation. While it does begin to raise and support interesting and logical questions about the reasons on which that conclusion is based, it falls well short of presenting a full analysis.

- **It lacks organization.** This single paragraph lacks one clear focus. The response fails to divide main ideas into separate, cogent units of discourse.

- **It has poorly constructed sentences.** Sentences are convoluted, lacking punctuation and subordination that result in meaningless jumbles of words.

- **It contains major errors in the conventions of Standard Written English.** Some of these errors are serious enough to obstruct meaning.

Section 2: Verbal Reasoning

1. D	**6.** E	**11.** E	**16.** A, D
2. B, F	**7.** A	**12.** C	**17.** C, E
3. B, D	**8.** C	**13.** A, B	**18.** C, E
4. B, D, G	**9.** A	**14.** B	**19.** A, F
5. B, C	**10.** E	**15.** E	**20.** B

1. **The correct answer is D.** In literature, an "omniscient" point of view is one that features a narrator who has total knowledge of the feelings and thoughts of all characters in the story. *Accomplished* (choice A) means "skillful," and while that word does make grammatical sense in this context, it is not as specific a choice as *omniscient*. The novel in question may have an enormous number of characters, but there is no such thing as an "enormous point of view" in literature, so choice B is not the best answer. *Ensemble* (choice C) seems to make sense in this context because the author could be dealing with an ensemble of characters, but a point of view that conveys the feelings and thoughts of all characters is called an "omniscient" point of view, not an "ensemble" point of view. *Acrimonious* (choice E) means "bitter or spiteful" and does not make any sense in this context.

2. **The correct answers are B and F.** Answer Blank (i): *Understandable* (choice B) is the best answer choice because it means "capable of being understood." *Logical* (choice A) means "capable of reasoning in a clear and consistent manner," and while it may seem correct, the writer is not reasoning something out but stating his/her opinion, so it is not the best answer choice in the context of the sentence. *Inexplicable* (choice C) is incorrect because it means "impossible to explain, incomprehensible," and is the opposite of *understandable*.

   Answer Blank (ii): In choosing answers for text completion items, consider the style and tone of the text. *Overdrawn* means "exaggerated," which fits the meaning and the tone of the sentence. *Flashy* and *showy* (choices D and E) do not match the style and tone.

3. **The correct answers are B and D.** Answer Blank (i): *Eminent* (choice B) means "well-known," and someone who is eminent is likely to be respected by a community and allowed to give a speech at a town hall meeting. *Malevolent* (choice A) means "wicked," and such a person is not likely to be respected. *Marginal* (choice C) means "unimportant," and such a person would not likely be respected or allowed to give a speech at a town hall meeting either.

Answer Blank (ii): *Crucial* (choice D) means "very important," and it is most likely that issues of great importance would be discussed at a town hall meeting. *Incandescent* (choice E) means "very bright," and *heterogeneous* (choice F) means "assorted or diverse." Neither of these words makes sense in the context of this sentence.

4. **The correct answers are B, D, and G.** Answer Blank (i): Context will help you complete this blank. This is also an instance when you might find it easier to begin by filling in one of the other blanks. *Vibrancy* (choice A) doesn't make sense in the context because poetry would add vibrancy to the theater, but the sentence says that the position of poetry has been diminished in modern plays. Choices B and C are somewhat similar in meaning, but *resemblance* (choice C) doesn't make sense if you read it in the sentence. *Verisimilitude* (choice B), which means "something that has the appearance of being real," is the correct answer by process of elimination.

Answer Blank (ii): *Final* (choice E) is redundant; an end is final. *Limited* (choice F) doesn't make sense; how can you have a limited end? *Welcome* (choice D) is the correct answer by the process of elimination, but more importantly because it means "giving pleasure."

Answer Blank (iii): The phrase that you're looking for needs to balance with the word *convincing*. In this case, *more forceful* (choice G) means "effective" and is therefore the best choice. *More believable* (choice I) is similar to *more convincing*, so choosing it would be redundant. There is nothing in the passage to indicate that modern plays should be *more cerebral* (choice H) because playwrights can't use rant and rhetoric.

5. **The correct answers are B and C.** The passage explicitly states that the era of massive road-building projects peaked in 1980 and has been in decline since then, so choice B is correct. The author also explicitly presents a steady drop in the number of miles driven in recent years, so choice C is also correct. Choice A is incorrect because the passage says that there is a 23-percent drop in driving, not car ownership, among young people.

6. **The correct answer is E.** The author's contention is most likely that car culture isn't over, but rather that the twentieth-century boom in driving is over. Nevertheless, the author is not discrediting the *Times*'s facts; instead, the author is suggesting that the conclusions drawn from them are overblown. The reader might also infer that a dramatic phrase such as "the end of car culture" was meant to attract attention. Choice A is incorrect because nothing in the passage suggests or implies it. Choice B could be true, but does not explain the sensational phrase "end of the car culture." Choice C is not supported by passage facts. Choice D is tempting because the data presented by the *Times* sounds reasonable enough, but it is incorrect because such information does not justify the term "end of the car culture."

7. **The correct answer is A.** The author begins the paragraph with a question and ends it with an assertion about the end of the twentieth-century boom in driving, rather than the end of the car culture. In between, the author offers many facts about the decline, rather than the end, of the automobile. Choices B, C, and D are all incorrect because the paragraph does not elucidate any single point presented by the *Times*. Instead, it offers new facts about the decline of the automobile. Choice E is tempting because the paragraph does offer further proof; nevertheless, all the proof it offers is bracketed by sentences that suggest that the *Times*'s conclusion about the end of the automobile needs to be mitigated, moderated, or softened.

8. **The correct answer is C.** According to the passage, "Recent studies have found that the faster a cell processes insulin, the more fat it stores," which "might be one cause of obesity…." Therefore, it makes sense to conclude that a medication that slows the rate at which cells process insulin might decrease the obesity of the medication's user. This conclusion contradicts choice A, which is the opposite of choice C. Choice B does not make sense because the passage does not imply that producing more insulin is a way to combat obesity.

9. **The correct answer is A.** An explanation of the ways in which carbohydrates break down to become sugars constitutes evidence to support the theory about the functions of insulin. Choices B and C are incorrect because the sentence neither summarizes a theory nor restates an earlier point. The sentence supports a theory rather than disproves one, so choice D would also be incorrect. Choice E is incorrect because the sentence describes a very specific process, not an application of a concept.

10. **The correct answer is E.** The answer to this question is expressed in the opening sentence of the passage, which states that Escher is "best known for the pieces that he drew from unusual perspectives, which result in enigmatic effects." While Escher's work did cover a variety of subjects, as choice A indicates, and it was drawn rather than painted, as choice B shows, the passage does not indicate that these were factors in the enigmatic effect of his work. Escher's mathematical approach (choice C) and system of categorizing shapes (choice D) are not noted or described as factors in his work's enigmatic nature, either.

11. **The correct answer is E.** By saying that mathematicians are interested only in the way the gate is opened but not the garden lying behind it, Escher is pointing out that they are interested only in how their theories work but not in the beauty "lying behind" the gate. Choices A and B are incorrect because even if they might be true of some mathematicians, Escher does not imply this in the quote. Choice C is incorrect because Escher never addresses the personalized notations of other mathematicians. Choice D is incorrect because although Escher believes that mathematical theories can be expressed artistically, he does not imply that mathematicians need to do this, just that they are not interested in doing so.

answers diagnostic test

12. **The correct answer is C.** The passage emphasizes that Escher's style was unique and unusual, so it makes sense that his work had a style with a particular character, so choice C is the best answer. The passage does not imply that his style was necessarily *disturbing* (choice A), which means "upsetting." *Honorable* (choice B) is an odd word to use to describe an artistic style. *Maladjusted* (choice D) means "alienated," and there is no indication in the passage that this word applies to Escher's style. *Macabre* (choice E) means "gruesome," and there is no indication that this word applies to Escher's work either.

13. **The correct answers are A and B.** The fire had a huge impact on public opinion because of the tragic death of so many young people, mostly women, and the exposure of the unsafe working conditions in the factory, implied in choice B. Choice C is incorrect because the strengthening of the labor movement and the passage of new labor laws were both results of heightened public opinion, not causes.

14. **The correct answer is B.** The time and place of the fire are minor details that aren't absolutely necessary in order to understand the main idea. Choices A and C are true, but incorrect answers because these are important details that clearly support the main idea of the passage. Remember that to answer a "NOT" question, like an "EXCEPT" question, you need to find the answer that *doesn't* match the information.

15. **The correct answer is E.** In this passage, *galvanized* means "incited or spurred on." *Impeded* (choice A) means "hindered," which is the opposite of what occurred. While the word *increased* (choice B) may seem correct, it doesn't match the strong quality implied in the word *galvanized*. *Hurdled* (choice C) means "jumped over," which doesn't make sense. *Angered* (choice D), while likely true, doesn't mean the same as "incited."

16. **The correct answers are A and D.** *Arrogant* (choice A) means "displaying an exaggerated opinion of one's self-worth; being self-important," and *dismissive* (choice D) means "showing disregard, being disdainful of others." Both fit the context of the sentence. *Unkind* and *uncharitable* (choices B and C) are also synonym pairs, and while the new CFO was undoubtedly unkind and uncharitable toward employees, the word *refused* in the sentence indicates that these two words are not strong enough; they also aren't typically used to describe business dealings. *Contentious* and *confrontational* (choices E and F) are also synonym pairs, but the word *refused* indicates that the CFO cut off communication so that there was no occasion for being either contentious or confrontational, both of which mean "argumentative and quarrelsome."

17. **The correct answers are C and E.** *Capitalize on* and *exploit* mean "take advantage of, make the most of." *Promote* and *advance* (choices A and B) both mean "to put forward, to aid the growth of." In the context of a business plan, the pair don't fit the sense. *Upgrade* (choice D) means "to improve," and *endorse* (choice E) means "to approve." These answer choices are not synonyms, and neither is a synonym of the other words in the list.

18. **The correct answers are C and E.** Although you may be confused because the answer choices contain three synonyms: *innovative*, *unusual*, and *cutting-edge* (choices C, D, and E), you can eliminate choice D because the characteristic of being unusual is not as strong as being either innovative or cutting edge. *Far-reaching* (choice A) and *wide-ranging* (choice B) are synonyms, but the implication from the first part of the sentence is that NASA conducted research related to the space program so that it wasn't doing research over a wide number of fields of study. You can eliminate *conventional* (choice F) because NASA, by the nature of its program, wouldn't be conducting conventional research.

19. **The correct answers are A and F.** The blank that you need to complete must be the opposite of the word *harmful*, and both *malignant* (choice B) and *pathogenic* (choice C) are considered harmful and are therefore incorrect. *Benevolent* (choice D) means "doing good, showing goodwill" and refers to people and organizations. *Benign* (choice F) is incorrect because it means "harmless, having little or no effect, showing mildness." The context requires two words that have a positive effect, and both *helpful* (choice A) and *beneficial* (choice F) are the best fit within the meaning of the sentence.

20. **The correct answer is B.** Choice B most closely describes what the author implies: modern readers are not used to figurative language and could have a difficult time making sense of Dickinson's work. Choice A is incorrect because the author doesn't suggest that modern readers should not look for literal meaning in Dickinson's work, just that it might be a little difficult to do so. The author would likely agree with choice C, but it doesn't reflect the last statement in the passage. Choice D contradicts what the author is implying in the last sentence. Choice E doesn't relate to anything in the passage.

Section 3: Verbal Reasoning

1. C	**6.** B	**11.** E	**16.** B
2. E	**7.** C	**12.** E	**17.** C
3. A, E	**8.** A	**13.** B, E	**18.** B
4. B, E, G	**9.** B, C	**14.** C, D	**19.** D
5. C, D, G	**10.** D	**15.** B, D	**20.** B

1. **The correct answer is C.** The clue to the correct answer is the phrase "hard sell"; the context of the sentence indicates that you need to find the word that indicates some opposite action. *Judiciously* (choice C) means "showing good judgment, being prudent," and matches the sense. *With ease* (choice A) doesn't quite fit the sense; you can do a hard sell easily. The same problem occurs with *actively* (choice B). *Expeditiously* (choice D) means "efficiently and quickly" and is incorrect because doing a hard sell efficiently and quickly doesn't make it any more palatable to the consumer, nor does being simply efficient (choice E).

2. **The correct answer is E.** The sentence describes a situation in which something is initially unknown or mysterious but becomes clear after a visit to the veterinarian, and *inexplicable* means "mysterious." *Unambiguous* (choice A) means the opposite of *inexplicable*. *Ineluctable* (choice B) means "inescapable," which does not make sense in this context. *Circumspect* (choice C) means "cautious," which is not as strong of an answer as *inexplicable*, considering the initially mysterious nature of the dog's behavior. *Cantankerous* (choice D) means "bad tempered," and since the passage does not indicate that this kind of behavior is symptomatic of pregnancy in dogs, it is not as strong of an answer as choice E is.

3. **The correct answers are A and E.** Answer Blank (i): *Honor* means "respect, distinction, privilege" and fits the sense of the sentence. *Admiration* (choice B) means "a feeling of pleasure or approval," but doesn't fit in the sentence because the context usually references the source of the admiration, that is, "towns wanted the admiration of other cities for hosting a college." In the sentence, however, it's the college that admires the town, which makes no sense. Choice C is incorrect because none of the many meanings of *character* fits the sense.

   Answer Blank (ii): *Outstripped* (choice E) means "to surpass, to grow greater or faster and leave behind," which fits the sense. Choice D is incorrect because *outperform* means "to perform better," and the sense of the discussion of supply and demand requires a quantitative response. The same reason makes *outshone* (choice F) incorrect.

4. **The correct answers are B, E, and G.** Answer Blank (i): The sentence indicates that the queen might be forced to give up her position to her son because of her health, so it makes sense that her health is in poor condition. *Feeble* (choice B) means "poor." *Robust* (choice A) is the opposite of *feeble*. *Cautionary* (choice C) means "warning" and does not make sense in this context.

Answer Blank (ii): To take on the role of king is to assume it, so choice E is the best answer. *Convey* (choice D) means "express," and *furnish* (choice F) means "supply." Neither of these words makes sense in this context.

Answer Blank (iii): To "abdicate" a throne is to give it up, which is possibly what the queen will have to do because of her health. *Nullify* (choice H) means "abolish," and it is unlikely she would do away with the throne completely because she was no longer fit to occupy it. *Arbitrate* (choice I) means "judge," which does not make sense.

5. **The correct answers are C, D, and G.**
   Answer Blank (i): In the sentence, the professor receives so many questions about a vague comment that she must restate that comment, so you're looking for a word that indicates she must deal with those comments in some way. The word *contend* (choice C) means "deal." *Amalgamate* (choice A) means "combine" and does not make sense in this context. *Orient* (choice B) means "situate" and does not make sense either.

   Answer Blank (ii): The professor received so many questions, she was forced to restate her comment, so the correct answer should indicate an onset or veritable assault of questions. *Onslaught* (choice D) conveys this well. *Paucity* (choice E) means "lack," which is the opposite of what the correct answer should convey. *Compilation* (choice F) means "collection," and it does not make as much sense in this context as *onslaught* does.

   Answer Blank (iii): The professor had to restate a vague comment to make it clearer, and *elucidate* means "clarify." *Obfuscate* (choice H) means the opposite of *clarify*. *Categorize* (choice I) means "classify," which does not make much sense in this context.

6. **The correct answer is B.** Choices A, C, D, and E are all mentioned in the passage as factors that are delaying progress toward clean water goals. The passage mentions that not enough skilled labor is available, not that there is a problem in managing skilled labor. Remember: for "NOT" questions, you're looking for the answer choice that *doesn't* fit.

7. **The correct answer is C.** This information, while important, is not a detail; it's actually a main idea and the topic sentence of the second paragraph. Choices A and B are both important points that support the topic sentence of the first paragraph: access to clean water and sanitation are crucial global goals.

8. **The correct answer is A.** The author's argument is that during the time of rationing, people who wouldn't ordinarily have broken the law did so because they were frustrated at not being able to have the goods they believed they deserved. The author never states choice B in the passage. Choice C restates the facts of what happened, but it doesn't address the author's argument of why it happened. Choice D might seem to be true, but it is not so close a reading of the author's argument as choice A. Choice E might be true, but this is a conclusion based on the facts, and the author never draws this conclusion in the passage.

9. **The correct answers are B and C.** If most Americans are law abiding and would not break the law under any circumstances, then the black market would not exist. Therefore, choice B would weaken the author's argument because the majority of Americans would not participate in the black market under any circumstances. Furthermore, if most Americans patronized the black market after rationing ended (choice C), that would weaken the argument that Americans only did it as a direct response to rationing. Choice A is incorrect because it would strengthen the argument that Americans will break the law if special circumstances leave them no choice.

10. **The correct answer is D.** The passage doesn't describe how LED lighting works and what makes it more energy efficient than incandescent lighting, so choice D is the correct answer. Choices A, B, C, and E are all achieved in the passage.

11. **The correct answer is E.** The author includes the list of countries and continents in line 4 only to indicate the governments that have taken initiatives to conserve energy by passing legislation to regulate or eliminate the sale of incandescent and halogen light bulbs. Choice A is not a strong answer because there is no indication that these particular places were more affected by lighting inefficiency than others. Choice B is not the best answer either because the author had a different reason for listing the places in line 4 than implying that most countries do not take lighting inefficiency seriously enough. Choice C basically restates the same conclusion in choice B and both are incorrect. The list of places does not indicate whether or not the legislation has been effective, so choice D does not make much sense.

12. **The correct answer is E.** The word *mandatory* means about the same as *obligatory*, meaning "compulsory or required." Choice A is incorrect because *provisional* means "temporary," which is not the same as *required*. *Permanent* (choice B) means "fixed," which is also not the same as *required*. *Predetermined* (choice C) means "determine in advance or to influence in a certain way," which doesn't fit the context. *Discretionary* (choice D) means "optional," which is the opposite of mandatory.

13. **The correct answers are B and E.** *Mimic* and *imitate* are synonyms that mean "to copy, to resemble." The words *epitomize* and *typify* (choices A and D) are a synonym pair, meaning "to be a typical example of," which is not exactly the same as *imitating*, which fits the sense better. *Illustrate* (choice C) means "to clarify, to present an example" and doesn't fit the sense, nor does it have a synonym among the answer choices. *Reflect* (choice F), which means "to make apparent or show an image of," has no synonym in the list nor does it fit the sense.

14. **The correct answers are C and D.** The phrase "forever change" in the second part of the sentence is the clue that identifies *revolutionary* and *transformative* (choices C and D). Both indicate radical change. *Modernization* (choice A) is also a form of change, but this doesn't fit the context. *Reforming* (choice B) may seem correct because it means "to change for the better," but it doesn't have the connotation of radical change that is implied in the sentence. *Huge* (choice E) is a vague word that doesn't indicate the nature of the change. Choice F is incorrect because *corrective* implies that something was wrong and needed to be fixed, and that's not implied in the passage.

15. **The correct answers are B and D.** The sentence draws a distinction between the underdone and overcooked dishes served during the feast and the soup. Since dishes that are underdone and overcooked are likely to be unpleasant or difficult to eat, the correct answers should suggest food that is pleasant and easy to eat. *Palatable* (choice B) and *edible* (choice D) both mean "easy and pleasant to eat." *Thorough* (choice A) means "complete," which does not make much sense in this context. *Vehement* (choice C) means "passionate," and it does not make sense to describe soup this way. *Baroque* (choice E) means "intricate," which is not really the opposite of something that is unpleasant and difficult to eat. *Unappetizing* (choice F) actually means "unpleasant and difficult to eat," so it is not the right word to use to describe the soup.

16. **The correct answer is B.** The author suggests at the end of the passage that the answer is not simple, but that we should ask ourselves questions that could help us make the decision. Choice A seems like the correct choice, except that the fact of asking ourselves questions is a closer reading of what the author seems to be implying. Choices C and E are incorrect because according to the author there are more than just these factors we should consider. Choice D is incorrect because this statement is neither stated nor implied in the passage.

17. **The correct answer is C.** Distance is clearly stated in the passage as one of the the things to consider when deciding whether to buy organic or local food (assuming they are not one and the same). Choice A might seem correct, but it is possible to buy organic and local food at big chain supermarkets; therefore, this statement isn't entirely supported by the passage. Choice B makes an assumption that is not necessarily true and is never addressed in the passage. Choice D might be correct in some cases, but animals raised on local nonorganic farms might be treated more humanely than those raised on organic farms, and thus the passage does not support this. Choice E might also be correct in some cases, but once again, the passage does not support this entirely.

18. **The correct answer is B.** The parenthetical clause defines the term *food miles* and this is its only function in the sentence. The discussion of food miles is one piece of evidence used to support buying locally grown food (choice A), but that's not the function of the definitional clause. Choice C is incorrect for the same reason.

19. **The correct answer is D.** *Elucidate* means about the same as the word *illuminate* or "to make clear." *Confound* (choice A) means "to mystify," which is the opposite of *elucidate*. *Elevate* (choice B) means "to raise," which has nothing to do with making something clear. *Vanquish* (choice C) means "to conquer," which also has nothing to do with making something clear. *Predict* (choice E) means "to forecast," which is not the same as "making clear."

20. **The correct answer is B.** The author clearly states that voter opinion polls help us identify what voters are thinking about issues. Choice A may seem correct because the author states that polls can be inaccurate, but the author doesn't explicitly state that polling can never predict the results of an election, and so this cannot be assumed. Choice C is incorrect because the author states that during the last week or two before an election, undecided voters make up their minds, but doesn't imply that polls help them make up their minds. Choice D is true in that the author states this, but this is not his thesis in the passage. Choice E is incorrect because the unpredictability of polls is neither stated nor implied.

Section 4: Quantitative Reasoning

1. A	**6.** D	**11.** B, D, G	**16.** E
2. C	**7.** B	**12.** E	**17.** B
3. C	**8.** D	**13.** A	**18.** D
4. D	**9.** B	**14.** B	**19.** 105
5. B	**10.** D	**15.** A, C, D, H	**20.** C

1. **The correct answer is A.**

$$6\frac{7}{8} = 6.875$$

$$3.42(2) = 6.84$$

Quantity A is greater.

2. **The correct answer is C.** Any values that are assigned to the side lengths of the figure will result in the two areas being equal. This is true for both whole and fractional values.

3. **The correct answer is C.** Angles in the corners of rectangles are equal to 90°, so any two added together will equal 180°. Angles formed by the bisection of a line by another line equal 180°, so Quantity A is equal to Quantity B.

4. **The correct answer is D.** If whole number values are assigned to the side lengths of this right triangle, then answer choice A would be correct. If fractional or decimal values (less than 1) are assigned to the side lengths of this right triangle, then answer choice B would be correct. Therefore, the correct answer is D.

5. **The correct answer is B.** Since y is less than x which is less than 0, when we take the absolute value of x and y, y will always be greater than x.

6. **The correct answer is D.** If a and b are both positive, then Quantity B is larger, while if they are both negative, Quantity A is larger. Since the signs of a and b are not indicated, it cannot be determined which is greater.

7. **The correct answer is B.** The area of a triangle is $\frac{1}{2}b \times h$, so using the working backwards strategy:

$$\frac{1}{2}(3)(n) = 15, \text{ so } n = 10$$

8. **The correct answer is D.**

$$x^2 = 9$$
$$x^2 - 9 = 0$$
$$(x + 3)(x - 3) = 0$$
$$x = 3, -3$$

Since x can be either 3 or −3, Quantity A can be both equal to and greater than Quantity B.

9. **The correct answer is B.** 30% of $6.99 is $6.99(0.30) = $2.10. He saves $2.10(2.5) = $5.25 this week.

10. **The correct answer is D.** Three of the die's six sides feature odd numbers, so the probability that any given roll will produce an odd number is $\frac{3}{6}$, or $\frac{1}{2}$. Each roll of the die is independent of the others, so the probability that each of the three rolls will produce an odd number is $\frac{1}{2} \times \frac{1}{2} \times \frac{1}{2}$, or $\frac{1}{8}$.

11. **The correct answers are B, D, and G.** You can find the next number by adding the last two numbers in the sequence.

$$5 + 8 = 13$$
$$8 + 13 = 21$$
$$13 + 21 = 34$$

12. **The correct answer is E.** To evaluate the function $f(x) = -3x^2(1 - x)$ for $f(-2)$:

$$f(-2) = -3(-2)^2(1 - (-2)) = -3(4)(3) = -36$$

13. **The correct answer is A.** Solve the equation:

$$-2(4z - 2) + 3z = 1 - z.$$
$$-2(4z - 2) + 3z = 1 - z$$
$$-8z + 4 + 3z = 1 - z$$
$$-5z + 4 = 1 - z$$
$$-4z = -3$$
$$z = \frac{3}{4}$$

14. **The correct answer is B.**

$$90 = 55 + x$$
$$35 = x$$

15. **The correct answers are A, C, D, and H.** The prime factorization of 1,200 is 2 × 2 × 2 × 2 × 3 × 5 × 5. Any portion of this product produces a factor of 1,200. Since 8 = 2 × 2 × 2; 15 = 3 × 5; 75 = 3 × 5 × 5; and 300 = 2 × 2 × 3 × 5 × 5, these are all factors. The other choices are not products of only the prime factors of 1,200, so they are not factors of 1,200.

16. **The correct answer is E.**

$$142.1 + 43.5 = 185.6$$
$$53.0 + 14.4 = 67.4$$
$$\frac{185.6}{67.4} = \frac{92.8}{33.7} = 92.8 : 33.7$$

17. **The correct answer is B.**

$$53.0 + 75.9 + 131.2 = 260.1$$

18. **The correct answer is D.** Estimate the difference from year to year, and then calculate the percentage. The difference between 2014 and 2015 is more than double and none of the other amounts is even close, so 2015 is the year.

$$39.2 - 19.0 = 20.2$$
$$20.2 \div 19.0 = 106\%$$

19. **The correct answer is 105.**

$20 - (1.25 + 6.50 + 1.75) =$ amount spent on candy

$$20 - (9.50) = 10.50$$
$$10.50 \div 0.10 = 105$$

20. **The correct answer is C.** The factors of 51 are 1, 3, 17, and 51, so the greatest prime number that is a factor of 51 is 17. Next, the smallest prime number that is a factor of 58 is 2 because 58 is an even number. The sum of 17 and 2 is 19.

Section 5: Quantitative Reasoning

1. A	**6.** A	**11.** A	**16.** E
2. A	**7.** D	**12.** D	**17.** D
3. B	**8.** D	**13.** 60 m^2	**18.** C
4. B	**9.** A	**14.** D	**19.** C, D, E
5. C	**10.** B	**15.** C	**20.** $\dfrac{2}{5}$

1. **The correct answer is A.** Change $\dfrac{10}{31}$ into a decimal: 0.32258, which is less than 0.324875.

2. **The correct answer is A.** Raising a number between 0 and 1 to a positive integer power results in a smaller number. For instance, $\left(\dfrac{1}{2}\right)^2 = \dfrac{1}{4}$ and $\left(\dfrac{1}{2}\right)^3 = \dfrac{1}{8}$. So Quantity A is greater.

3. **The correct answer is B.** Because Mary is the oldest, she will have a birth year that is less than either Joe or Stephen.

4. **The correct answer is B.** Evaluate each quantity:

   $3(5) + 2(2) + 3 = 15 + 4 + 3 = 22$

   22 is less than 24.

5. **The correct answer is C.** Vertical angles are congruent, so $x = 148$. Since l and m are parallel, corresponding angles are congruent. So y is also 148.

6. **The correct answer is A.** $-\dfrac{15}{16}$ is greater than -1 and $-\dfrac{16}{15}$ is less than -1.

7. **The correct answer is D.** There is no way to know the number of goalies on each team.

8. **The correct answer is D.** Pick some numbers and evaluate:

   If $y = 12$, then $x = 4$. If $y = -12$, then $x = -4$

9. **The correct answer is A.** Evaluate the function:

   $$f(x) = 5x^3 + 4x^2 + 8x + 1$$
   $$f(2) = 5(8) + 4(4) + 8(2) + 1$$
   $$f(2) = 40 + 16 + 16 + 1$$
   $$f(2) = 73$$

10. **The correct answer is B.** Multiply the first equation by 2: $4x - 2y = -2$. Add this to the second equation to get $7x = 14$. Therefore, the answer is $x = 2$.

11. **The correct answer is A.** Solve for x:

    $$\frac{3}{x-1} = \frac{6}{3x+6}$$
    $$3(3x + 6) = 6(x - 1)$$
    $$9x + 18 = 6x - 6$$
    $$3x = -24$$
    $$x = -8$$

    Or, work backwards from the answer choices:

    $$\frac{3}{x-1} = \frac{6}{3x+6}$$
    $$\frac{3}{-8-1} = \frac{6}{-24+6}$$
    $$\frac{3}{-9} = \frac{6}{-18}$$
    $$-\frac{1}{3} = -\frac{1}{3}$$

12. **The correct answer is D.** Turn the verbose language into concise and concrete terms to help you solve this problem.

    $$45(0.20) = 9$$
    $$45 + 9 = 54$$

13. **The correct answer is 60 m².** The base is 15 m. To find the height, note that the base of the right triangle is 3 m (since opposite sides of a parallelogram are congruent). Using the Pythagorean theorem shows that the height is 4 m. So, the area is (15 m)(4 m) = 60 square meters.

14. **The correct answer is D.** Using the information from the table, add the families having 0, 1, and 2 children:

$$19 + 36 + 15 = 70$$

15. **The correct answer is C.** Using the information from the table, there are $19 + 36 + 21 + 9 + 15 = 100$ total families and there are 15 families with no children, so $\frac{15}{100} = 0.15$, or 15%.

16. **The correct answer is E.** There is no information given on the number of families with 6 children.

17. **The correct answer is D.** Since the lines are perpendicular, the product of their slopes must equal –1.

First, rewrite the given equation in slope-intercept form:

$$x + 2y = 5$$
$$2y = -x + 5$$
$$y = -\frac{1}{2}x + \frac{5}{2}$$

The given equation's slope is $-\frac{1}{2}$, the coefficient of x. Therefore, the slope you're looking for is 2.

18. **The correct answer is C.** The point at which the two lines intersect lies on the graph of both equations. Therefore, you have a system of two linear equations, and you're looking for the value of x in the solution to the system. First, solve the second equation for y: $y - x = 2 \Rightarrow y = x + 2$. Now substitute this expression of y into the first equation:

$$x + 2y = 4$$
$$x + 2(x + 2) = 4$$
$$x + 2x + 4 = 4$$
$$3x = 0$$
$$x = 0$$

19. **The correct answers are C, D, and E.** Let x be the length of side $\overline{AC}$. According to the triangle inequality, x is greater than (and not equal to) the positive difference of the lengths of the other two sides, and it is less than (and not equal to) the sum of the lengths of the other two sides:

$$8 - 4 < x < 8 + 4$$
$$4 < x < 12$$

20. **The correct answer is $\frac{2}{5}$.** The larger circle has radius 10 inches, so its circumference is $2\pi(10) = 20\pi$ inches. The smaller circle has diameter 8 inches, so its radius is 4 inches. So its circumference is $2\pi(4) = 8\pi$ inches. Therefore, the desired ratio is $\frac{8\pi}{20\pi} = \frac{2}{5}$.

PART III
ANALYTICAL WRITING

The Issue Task

OVERVIEW

The Analytical Writing section of the GRE® General Test measures both your ability to think and your ability to write in response to two kinds of prompts: the Issue Task and the Argument Task. The Issue Task assesses how well you can develop and support your own position on an issue, and the Argument Task evaluates how well you can analyze someone else's argument. This chapter will focus on the Issue Task.

To respond to the Issue Task, you'll need to take a position either agreeing or disagreeing with an issue and defend your position with evidence. As part of that defense, you may be required to counter potential arguments of others.

The Issue Task prompt presents you with a brief statement of a general issue and sets the conditions under which you can respond to it. That is, you may agree or disagree with the statement, but you must discuss certain aspects of the issue based on the accompanying instructions. The issue will be one that anyone can respond to, such as whether or not it's morally justifiable to spend resources on a pet.

This chapter describes the Issue Task and the possible instructions that may accompany it as well as reviewing the components of a successful Issue Task response. The chapter ends with a sample Issue Task and six models that are analyzed and scored using a rubric based on the GRE® General Test rubric for the Issue Task.

Chapter 4

BASIC INFORMATION ABOUT THE ISSUE TASK

The Analytical Writing section is always first in any administration of the GRE® General Test. For many test takers, it is probably a relief to have it out of the way early so they no longer have to worry about it. However, reviewing the basics of the Issue Task, as well as the basic organization and development of a response, will help your confidence and your score.

Type of Question

The Issue Task presents you with one issue that you may agree or disagree with, but you must do one or the other. You can't be neutral, and you will have no choice of issues. The purpose of the Issue Task is to measure how well you can stake out a position and develop your reasoning to support it. That support has to be developed according to certain conditions contained in a set of instructions that accompany the prompt. The instructions, which are described in more detail later in this chapter, may require you to

- explain how the issue might or might not hold true in some cases.
- examine examples that could be used to challenge your position on an issue.
- discuss why you disagree with a claim and the reasoning that underpins the claim.

Typically, the Issue Task statement is very short compared to the Argument Task topic. The issue is usually stated in a single sentence, and it's always of a general nature that anyone could respond to. No special knowledge is required. ETS states that the claim made in the Issue Task statement is one that can be discussed "from various perspectives" and applied "to many different situations or conditions."

Time Limit and Software

The Issue Task has a time limit of 30 minutes. This is the same for both the computer- and paper-delivered versions.

The word processing program on the computer-delivered version allows the test taker to insert and delete text, cut and paste text, and undo actions. A spell checker and grammar checker are not included. Similarly, those taking the paper-delivered version will not have access to dictionaries or grammar handbooks during the test.

Scoring

The Issue Task has its own rubric. You'll work through this rubric later in this chapter. Issue Tasks are scored on a scale from 0 to 6. The average of the two scores is taken to arrive at a combined score from 0 to 6 in half-point increments. This is the score that is reported to graduate and business schools.

UNDERSTAND THE PROMPT: THE ISSUE

The Issue Task prompt has two parts with a line of space probably appearing between the two parts. The first part of the Issue Task prompt states one side of an issue. For example, it might suggest that everyone start paying entrance fees to the public museums and institutions that are currently free in Washington, D.C. The issue will be stated briefly and simply, most likely in just one sentence.

UNDERSTAND THE PROMPT: THE WRITING INSTRUCTIONS

The second part of the prompt outlines the instructions that set the conditions for your response. It begins with the words "Write a response. . . ." The instructions will ask you (1) to take a position, qualifying it, as you want to or need to, by extent or degree, and (2) to explain and support your position. The prompt may also ask you to explain your position in relation to one of the following:

- Conditions/circumstances under which the statement of your position might not be true
- Circumstances when the recommendation would not have the intended results
- Likely and major challenges to your position
- Views both for and against your position
- The "reasoning" on which the claim is based
- The possible consequences of taking action based on your position

The actual wording of the sets of instructions will be somewhat similar to the following:

- Discuss how much you agree or disagree with the statement and why, as well as considering how the statement might or might not always be true and how these considerations affect your point of view.
- Discuss how much you agree or disagree with the recommendation and why. Using specific examples, explain how the circumstances under which the recommendation could be adopted would or would not be advantageous. In developing and supporting your viewpoint, explain how these specific circumstances affect your point of view.
- Discuss how much you agree or disagree with the claim and include the most compelling reasons and/or examples that someone could use to dispute your point of view.
- While addressing both viewpoints provided, discuss which more closely aligns with your own. Explain your reasoning for holding this position in developing and providing evidence for your response.
- Discuss how much you agree or disagree with the claim and the reasoning used to support that claim.
- Discuss your viewpoint on the proposed policy and the reasons for your point of view. Take into consideration the potential consequences of implementing the policy and the extent to which these consequences influence your viewpoint in developing and supporting your response.

When composing your response, you must take care to focus on the specific requirements in the instructions. You could present a well-reasoned and well-supported position, but if you fail to present views both for and against your position as the prompt asks, you won't earn a high score.

UNDERSTAND THE SCORING RUBRIC

Before we go any further, let's look at the scoring rubric for the issue task against which your response will be evaluated. Your Issue Task response will be scored on a 6-point scale by two readers. These readers are your audience, and your purpose in writing this response is to earn the best score that you can. Six is the maximum score your response can earn. The scale ranges in 1-point increments from 6 to 0.

6 Points

To earn 6 points, your response should exhibit these characteristics:

- A clear, focused position on the issue, and an overall response to the specific writing task that is thorough, cogent, and sophisticated
- Fully developed, persuasive support for the position, including, but not limited to, particularly apt or well-chosen examples, facts, and other illustrations, as well as an explanation that clearly and effectively links the support to the specific requirements of the writing task
- A rhetorically effective method of organization, such as one that organizes support by order of importance and saves the most effective reasons for last; connections between and among ideas are logical and may also be as subtle as they are effective
- A formal grace that is a product primarily of well-constructed, varied sentences and exact and rhetorically effective word choices
- Adherence to almost all the conventions of Standard Written English, including grammar, usage, and mechanics; errors, if any, should be minor

5 Points

To earn 5 points, your response will likely have these characteristics, though it may exceed one or more of them yet fall short on another:

- A clear, focused position on the issue, and a thoughtful, complete response to the specific writing task
- Persuasive support for the position, including, but not limited to, examples, facts, and other illustrations, as well as an explanation that clearly links the support to the specific requirements of the writing task
- An effective method of organization with logical connections between and among all ideas
- Well-constructed, varied sentences and appropriate word choices that help create clarity as well as interest
- Adherence to almost all the conventions of Standard Written English, including grammar, usage, and mechanics; errors, if any, should be minor

4 Points

To earn 4 points, a response will have these characteristics:

- A clear position on the issue, and a generally complete response to the specific writing task
- Support for the position, as well as an explanation that links the support to the specific requirements of the writing task
- A logical method of organization

- Sentences and word choices that generally create clarity
- General adherence to the conventions of Standard Written English; some errors may occur

3 Points

Your response will earn only 3 points if it has *one or more* of the following characteristics:

- A generally clear position and a response to the specific writing task that may be limited in scope or marred by occasional vagueness, extraneous detail, repetition, or other flaws
- Limited or inadequate support for the position or a limited or inadequate explanation that links the support to the specific requirements of the writing task
- Lapses in organization or confusing organization, and/or lack or misuse of transitional words and phrases
- Sentences and word choices that occasionally interfere with clarity
- One or more errors in the conventions of Standard Written English that are so significant that they obstruct meaning

2 Points

Your response will earn only 2 points if it has *one or more* of the following characteristics:

- A wandering, unclear, or limited response characterized by an unclear or not fully articulated position and a response to the specific writing task that is limited or inadequate in scope or marred by vagueness, extraneous detail, repetition, or other flaws
- Inadequate support and explanation
- Confusing organization, and/or general lack or misuse of transitional words and phrases
- Sentences and word choices that interfere with clarity
- Repeated errors in the conventions of Standard Written English that are so significant that they obstruct meaning

1 Point

Your response will earn only 1 point if it has *one or more* of the following characteristics:

- An unclear position and almost no response to, or minimal understanding of, the specific task
- A total lack of support or only illogical or flawed support for the main point or points; a total lack of explanation or only illogical or flawed explanation of the main points of your argument in relation to the specific details of the task
- No pattern of organization or confusing organization
- Sentences and word choices that interfere with clarity
- So many errors in the conventions of Standard Written English that they obstruct meaning throughout the response

0 Points

This score is possible under the following circumstances:

- The response does not answer the task in any way.
- The response is written in a foreign language.
- The response simply copies the argument.

TIP

Much of the advice
in this section can be
applied to writing an
argument response
as well.

- The response is not legible.
- The response is nonverbal.

From these criteria, you can draw or reaffirm the following four conclusions about your task:

1. You must meet the requirements stated in the prompt completely.

2. You need a clear statement of your position; substantial, thoughtful support; and explanations that link your support to the specific task requirements.

3. You can make minor errors in grammar, usage, and mechanics without seriously jeopardizing your score, but remember that errors in these areas can affect the clarity of your writing, so be sloppy at your own peril.

4. The length of your response is in no way a deciding factor in your score. But don't assume that brevity is a virtue. According to the rubric, you'll have to produce a response of sufficient length to support your position in adequate, if not dense, detail. Although there is no magic number for success, aim to make at least three points in favor of your position—and aim to elaborate them fully.

TIP

If you're taking the
paper-delivered test
and there is enough
space on the sheets
of paper, write on
every other line. That
will leave you space
to insert additions
and neatly make
deletions. If your
handwriting isn't
legible, try printing,
but practice ahead
of time so that you
can print quickly
and legibly.

REVIEW THE ANATOMY OF AN ISSUE TASK RESPONSE

In addition to keeping track of time—and using it wisely—there are some priorities that you can set and skills you can review and practice to help you write a successful response. Obviously, it takes time to develop superior—6-point—writing skills; however, staying focused on a few simple guidelines can add a point or more to your score. Think about putting these recommendations to work for you.

State a Thesis, and State It Early

Don't make your reader guess what side of the issue you're on. There is nothing to be gained by being timid or staying on the middle of the fence. A thesis statement that makes your view on the issue absolutely unmistakable should appear somewhere in the first paragraph. Don't worry about being too obvious or even leading off with your thesis. You can, in fact, score a 6 if you state your point of view in the very first sentence. Of course, you must be sure that the thesis is clear and that it adequately reflects the content that follows.

Use a Standard Pattern of Organization

ETS makes it clear that test takers don't need to employ a standard pattern of organization to succeed. But think critically about that advice. That doesn't mean that standard patterns of organization won't succeed for either the issue or the argument response. A standard pattern of organization helps to lead your reader smoothly from point to point. In addition, such patterns help create fluency.

Order Paragraphs Effectively

Now you've got your overall structure, but how do you hang your ideas on that structure so that your paragraphs flow in logical order? Possibly the best organizational model for the issue response (and the argument response, too) is order of importance. You could order the paragraphs in the body of your response either from the most important reason to the least important reason, or from the least important reason to the most important reason. The latter is the more effective technique. It often results in a strong or memorable ending.

In crafting your paragraphs, don't begin the first two body paragraphs with something like "The first reason in support of my thesis is…" and "The second reason in support of my thesis is…." Similarly, don't end with "In conclusion" or "As I have said." Use transitional words and phrases. They can provide a smooth link from one paragraph to another—and from one sentence to another—by identifying and emphasizing the relationships between ideas. In its analysis of the scoring of sample papers, as well as in its rubrics, ETS stresses the value of transitional words and phrases. In addition to helping you create coherence, transitions can help you vary the beginnings of your sentences.

TIP

Using a standard pattern of organization has an added benefit. If you decide ahead of time how to set up your response, you can save time when faced with writing the actual response on test day.

TRANSITIONS

Review the following lists of transitional words and phrases and use them as you practice writing responses to the tasks in the practice tests. Then they will come more easily as you write the actual response.

Transitions That Introduce or Link Opinions and Reasons

because	*evidently*	*indeed*
besides	*for this reason*	*on the other hand*
by comparison	*furthermore*	*since*
consequently	*however*	*therefore*

Transitions That Introduce or Link Examples

for example	*in this case*	*one type*
for instance	*in this situation*	*to illustrate this point*

Transitions That Create Emphasis or Add Information

after all	*furthermore*	*more important*
again	*in addition*	*moreover*
besides	*indeed*	*similarly*
certainly	*in fact*	*what's more*

Transitions That Introduce Opposing Views

although this may be true	*naturally*	*on the other hand*
even though	*nevertheless*	*undeniably*
evidently	*notwithstanding*	*unquestionably*
it may be said	*of course*	*without a doubt*

Use a Standard Pattern of Paragraphing

Try a traditional structure for developing the paragraphs within the body of your response.

Topic Sentence: The topic sentence states the main idea of the paragraph. In an Issue Task response, the topic sentence of each body paragraph can state a reason that supports your point of view, or a likely "challenge," or reason, against your point of view. For example, if you're arguing that it is, in fact, a reasonable policy to insist that visitors to the nation's museums in Washington, D.C., pay an entrance fee, a topic sentence might suggest that by having to pay, people will place a greater value on their visit.

Support and Development: Once you've written the topic sentence for your paragraph, you have several choices for how to develop the meat of the paragraph. You can choose restriction (a qualification or other way of narrowing and focusing the topic sentence), explanation, and/or evidence. Your job in this part of the paragraph is to make your topic sentence convincing by developing it with supporting points. In discussing paid entry to national museums in Washington, you might talk about how families visiting for a long weekend from faraway might not come if they had to pay for two adults and several children at three museums. You could emphasize the loss of first-hand access to our nation's history for those children and how seeing, for example, the original Constitution can foster patriotism. Try to make this part of your paragraph full and dense with detail.

Final Summary or Clincher Statement: This last sentence is optional in body paragraphs, but can give a final rhetorical punch to the paragraph. You could ask a rhetorical question or restate the idea of the paragraph in a fresh way. What you want is a way to give final emphasis to the idea developed in the paragraph. If you can't think of an original and effective clincher, don't add anything to the paragraph. Go on to the next paragraph, using a transition.

If, however, this is the final paragraph in your response, search hard for a memorable final statement. You want to end your response in a way that gives closure to your thoughts and emphasizes your points. You could rephrase the thesis, summarize the main points, or direct the reader to a larger issue. The concluding paragraph should tie up all loose ends so that the reader doesn't finish with a sigh of "so what?"

Successful paragraphs can certainly deviate from this order. The important thing to keep in mind, however, is that paragraphs are themselves discrete units of discourse that require organization. It's not enough to organize the paragraphs of your essay logically. The sentences of each paragraph must be organized logically, too.

Develop Each Paragraph Fully

A huge factor in the success or relative failure of your essay will be the kinds and amount of support you provide. Never, ever write a one-sentence paragraph. If you have two-sentence paragraphs, the chances are good that they need more substance. Of course, you can't just add words for the sake of adding words, nor should you repeat yourself. What you need is more examples, illustrations, or other evidence, as well as the explanation that relates them back to the topic sentence or thesis and connects them to the next ideas. If your paragraphs lack details, ask yourself if you can add any of the following:

Facts: Facts are always the best choice for support. Statistics are one kind of fact that lend credibility to an argument. You aren't expected to pull sophisticated facts and statistics out of the air on the GRE® General Test nor should you ever make up any! But you may know some general facts such as the typical miles per gallon of an SUV versus a subcompact or a domestic car brand versus a Japanese brand if you're writing a response to a policy issue on raising emissions standards. Incorporate as many facts as you can. This is one method of appealing to your reader's reason.

Authoritative Opinions or Human Interest: You may not be able to call a quote to mind, yet you may recall a famous person's idea or point of view about your topic. For example, for a response on whether government should fund the arts, you might paraphrase the chair of the National Endowment for the Arts on the value of arts to the economy or a local restaurant owner on how much the theater down the street drives business to her establishment. This kind of support is best used sparingly, especially if the quotation or opinion appeals more to emotion than to reason. In some cases, however, appeals to emotion are as effective as appeals to reason.

Observations: Your own first-hand observations about life can be useful evidence of a point of view. In fact, since you cannot use source material on the GRE® General Test, this type of evidence is extremely helpful as it is available to you in abundance. Observations may appeal to either reason or emotion.

An Anecdote: Occasionally, a brief story not only enlivens your writing, but also adds evidence. Use an anecdote to illustrate some general truth such as how schools rely on parent volunteers. This is another technique that should be used sparingly—most likely just once in a response. Like observations, anecdotes may appeal to either reason or emotion; occasionally, they appeal to both.

Examples: Multiple examples or illustrations of an idea, such as how scandals have led to government reform, will add substance and support to a position that agrees with this claim. Use examples generously to support your points; they are usually very effective appeals to reason.

Take Care with Tone and Person

ETS makes no mention of tone in its scoring rubrics. Nevertheless, you should strive to sound reasonable. You may be forceful and impassioned at the same time, but don't cross the line into harangue or diatribe. The most successful arguments rely on valid reasoning and sophisticated support, both of which can be undercut by a shrill, overly strident, or whining voice.

Similarly, ETS makes no mention of person. Using the third person is your safest bet for both types of tasks, but there may be times when you might want to, or should, incorporate the first person (*I, me, my, myself, mine*) in your essay. It's certainly better to say *I* or *me* than to try to maintain the third person by referring to yourself as "this writer" or in any other self-conscious way. That said, refer to yourself only as necessary and don't, for example, use obvious lead-ins such as "In my humble opinion."

As Time Permits, Add Extras

Should you take time for style or craft? Yes, by all means, once you've got the substance of your ideas completely down on paper. (Of course, it's much easier for computer-delivered test takers to follow this advice than paper-delivered test takers.) Be sure, however, to view all of the following as add-ons. You can have, for example, the most interesting and well-written introduction in the

TIP

If you think you might use the first person in your response, brush up on when to use *I* (subject) versus *me* (object) and when to use *myself* appropriately (either as reflexive or intensive pronoun).

world and not do well on the task if you don't have time to develop the key points that support your opinion, or you don't have time to answer the task fully because you never deal with the key challenges to your position.

Interest-Grabbing Opening

If you have time, create an interesting lead by posing a question or offering a surprising or startling fact, or craft a formal introduction that establishes some background or context for your position. As a review of the sample essays from ETS shows, you can succeed without crafting a formal opening.

Apt Word Choice

As time permits, you should also review and revise your word choice:

- Avoid simple, overused words such as *very, really, good, bad, interesting, fun, great, awesome, incredible*, and *unbelievable*.
- Replace state of being verbs, such as *was* and *are*, with active verbs.
- Edit out clichés. (For example, don't begin an essay on dogs with "A dog is man's best friend.")
- Whenever you know a more precise, forceful, or connotatively rich word that will accurately convey your meaning, use it, BUT don't go for the big word just because it's big.

Varied Sentence Structure

If you want a 6, you have to show some style by varying your sentences. There are many ways to do this:

- Intersperse an occasional short sentence in a paragraph of long sentences.
- Vary your sentences by type by occasionally inserting a question where appropriate. (A word of caution: Avoid exclamatory sentences and exclamation points. These are almost never appropriate.)
- Vary your sentences by structure, using compound, complex, and simple sentences.
- Create sentence variation by beginning sentences in different ways, that is, make sure all sentences in a paragraph don't begin with "The" followed by the subject. Begin sentences with conjunctions, prepositions, and transitions.

A Final Word of Advice

Think of the organization for your response as the box that holds your product. Although that box is absolutely necessary, chances are you won't sell that product—no matter how good it is—in a plain cardboard box. Instead, you'll need an attractive outer layer, a packaging that says "Buy me! Buy me!" That's why you must also strive for qualities such as original and sophisticated word choice, sentence variation, and rhetorical devices in your essay. ETS readers will not give a 5 or 6 to a plain cardboard box.

CREATE YOUR WRITING PLAN

You'll have just 30 minutes to read and respond to the Issue Task prompt. But don't read the prompt and start writing. You need a plan to attack the task, and that plan has three parts: prewriting, drafting, and proofreading. Of the 30 minutes, set aside 2 to 3 minutes at the end to review and proofread your response. The bulk of the 30 minutes—say 23 or so minutes—should be spent in the actual writing of your response. The first 4 to 5 minutes should be spent in planning and prewriting.

Prewriting

The prewriting part of your writing plan has three steps that will help you focus on the task, gather your ideas, and plan the development of your response. They are tailored to the Issue Task and are slightly different from the prewriting steps for responding to the Argument Task.

Because your time is so short, you may be tempted to overlook prewriting. This is inadvisable for several reasons. First, with prewriting, you're actually testing your position to see if it will work; that is, in the few minutes you spend prewriting, you will be finding out whether you have good ideas or not. Second, organization is dependent on ideas. If you have a few ideas jotted down when you start to write, it will be much easier to order your ideas effectively. It's a trick that experienced writers use because it's much easier to start writing with a short list of ideas in front of you than no ideas at all.

Restate the Prompt: Although the issue prompt is easier to read and understand than the argument prompt, don't overlook this first step. Be sure the issue is clear to you.

Think About Reasons on Both Sides of the Issue: Understanding and being able to develop both sides of the issue are necessary in crafting a successful response. There are two main reasons for this. First, you don't need—nor are you expected—to express your truest feelings. Instead, you need to choose the side of the issue for which you can present the most convincing, well-developed argument of your own. Second, to be successful with most variations of the prompt, you need to anticipate and refute the opposing point of view.

Jot a "Quick Write": Begin by briefly identifying your position on the issue and then listing reasons that support your position. Strive for the most persuasive reasons.

If the specific instructions ask for challenges, both sides of the issue, advantages or disadvantages, or other considerations related to the opposite viewpoint, list reasons that could be given to oppose your position.

The flow of ideas won't come in any particular order, so reread your list and number the reasons in the order that you want to use them. You may also find that some ideas don't fit with the majority of your ideas, or that you have too many ideas, or some are weak. Don't be afraid to cross off ones that don't fit or are the least convincing.

TIP

Those taking the computer-delivered test will be given scrap paper for making notes, so if you're taking the computer version, consider jotting down the key requirements of the instructions. If you're taking the paper-delivered test, you may want to underline the key requirements.

Drafting

You'll actually be drafting and revising simultaneously because of the time limitation. To get the most of your actual writing time, keep these priorities in mind:

Answer the Task: Be sure that you answer the task. This may seem obvious, but in the hurry to write down your ideas, don't let your ideas take you on a line of thinking that doesn't respond to the issue and the task. Even though you have a "quick write" to work from, new ideas will come as you write. Go back to the last few lines of the prompt to be sure you aren't just agreeing or disagreeing with the issue, but also addressing both points of view, citing and refuting possible challenges, or doing whatever else the task specifically requires you to do.

Organize Your Response: The following pattern is a standard, or traditional, way to organize your overall response. It leads your reader smoothly through your response by eliminating confusion and guesswork. In addition, it helps to create fluency—or the illusion of it. If you're a writer who has trouble with organization, this pattern gives you a structure to develop your ideas around:

- Opening paragraph: Thesis or clear statement of your position
- Body paragraph 1: Reason 1 for your position, fully explained and supported
- Body paragraph 2: Reason 2 for your position, fully explained and supported
- Body paragraph 3: A statement of the most effective counterargument, an acknowledgment of its reasonableness, and your fully explained and supported response; or any other specific and developed point needed to address the writing task instructions
- Closing paragraph: Reason 3 (another key challenge or another main point) that directly responds to the specific writing instructions; support as needed; plus a detail, statement, question, or other device that delivers closure

Suppose you use this pattern of organization. How do you decide what reason to use first, second, and third? Often, the best way to organize points for an argument is by order of importance. You could choose your most significant reason to be first or last. If you use your most powerful, that is, strongest, support as the third and final point, your readers will take away from your response your most impressive piece of argument.

Provide Ample, Thoughtful, Well-Developed Support: Developing sufficient support is the key element for success on the Issue Task. The most foolproof method of organization you can use in an issue essay is to begin with a clear statement of your opinion in your opening and to develop each well-chosen point of support paragraph by paragraph.

Link Ideas Clearly: Your organization doesn't have to be traditional, or based in any way on typical instruction in college writing classes, but it does have to be logical and help to create overall coherence. Based on reviewing sample analyses, ETS values transitional words and phrases, so link paragraphs and ideas appropriately as you write. Also, don't overlook the value of a topic sentence in providing an organizational boost to your essay.

Consider Style

If you're aiming for a top score, vary your sentences and word choices. Rubric criteria specify varied, well-constructed sentences; for this test, they are an important index of your sophistication as a writer. ETS readers are also looking for appropriateness, precision, and rhetorical effectiveness in word choice.

Proofreading

When you go back over your essay in the 2 or 3 minutes you may have remaining, keep the following priorities in mind, which are based on the scoring rubric:

Check Your Thesis: Make sure you've stated it and that it's clear. Make sure it also adequately reflects the content of your essay.

Look for Omitted Words: When you're writing in a hurry, it's easy to leave out words. One omitted word can, however, destroy the sense of an entire sentence, and sentence sense is an important rubric criterion.

Check for Sentence Faults: At this stage, you want to make certain that you eliminate any ineffective fragments, run-on sentences, and fused sentences or comma splices. Because grammar counts? No, because poor grammar can obscure your meaning and bring down your score.

Don't Spend Your Time on Spelling or Commas: Keep in mind that the rubric doesn't mention spelling. It evidently has "minor error" status for the readers. Likewise, a missing comma here or there shouldn't affect your score.

A FINAL NOTE OF CAUTION

ETS wants its computer-delivered test users to know that their responses will be subjected to analysis by software that searches for similarities to published information. It warns that it will "cancel" a score if it contains any unacknowledged use of sources. In addition, ETS will cancel a response if an essay or any part of it has been prepared by another person. Finally, a score will be canceled if it includes language that is "substantially" similar to the language in one or more other test responses.

ISSUE PROMPT WITH SIX MODEL RESPONSES, SCORING, AND ANALYSES

Use this prompt as a practice opportunity and compare your response with the samples, scoring, and analyses that follow.

Time yourself and follow these 6 steps. In the real test, you will have 30 minutes.

1. Read the prompt.
2. Follow the prewriting steps.
3. Stop! Compare your "quick write" plan with the sample that follows the prompt to see different ideas (perhaps more sophisticated, perhaps less) that you might have thought of.
4. Draft your response.

NOTE

A run-on sentence consists of two independent clauses joined without punctuation; for example, *A run-on sentence looks like this it detracts from meaning.* Fix it by making the two clauses separate sentences, making one clause dependent on the other, using a semicolon, or adding a coordinating conjunction (*and, but, or*).

5. Read each model that follows the sample "quick write." Determine the positive and negative qualities of each sample response before you read its scoring analysis.

6. Score your response against the rubric on pages 104–106. Be honest in your analysis.

Issue Task

In a world filled with significant challenges, owning pets, and especially owning costly, resource-consuming dogs, is an irresponsible use of time and money.

Write a response in which you discuss how much you agree or disagree with the claim and include the most compelling reasons and/or examples that someone could use to dispute your point of view.

Sample "Quick Write"

The 6-point response to this prompt began with just 3 minutes of prewriting and planning. It looked like this:

TIP

Note how specific the "quick write" is. The writer is off to a good start for developing a response that is grounded in specific details to support any generalizations that he or she may make.

My opinion

① Dog owning not irresponsible

reasons

~~loveable~~

~~people's best friends~~

③ doing good for your town government or charitable org. by getting dog off street or out of shelter—you pay for medical, food, etc.

② homeless dogs starving

②a dogs have feelings

Challenges

④b don't take care of dogs, take care of people

~~waste of $ on such things as home-made dog treats~~

④c dogs use too many resources (time? money?)

④a dogs too pampered

Making Your Plan Work

In many ways, the success of the 6-point response based on this prewriting is due to some of the thought processes demonstrated in this plan. First, notice how the plan addresses the prompt. It has two clear parts: reasons for the position and challenges to the position. Second, notice that the writer decides not to develop all the ideas generated in the prewriting. The writer makes a judgment to develop ideas that he or she perhaps feels can be treated with deeper analysis or are less predictable answers to the prompt.

Return to this planning guide after you read the sample 6-point model below. Notice how the prewriting does not, in fact, show the eventual order of organization. Note also that there are more details than the "quick write" includes. Once the writer began to write, ideas began to flow, affirming the idea that writing is a generative process. This should be a comforting fact to remember as you prepare to take the Analytical Writing section. You don't need to list all your ideas in a "quick write"; believe that more ideas will come as you write. However, it's also important to check your "quick write" and the task instructions to make sure that your flow of ideas isn't taking you off the track of responding accurately and adequately to the task.

Furthermore, you don't want to spend the kind of time on the prewriting process that extensive planning would require. The main goal of prewriting during a timed writing test is to be sure that you've got good points to make before you begin your writing. If you don't, quickly scratch out your first plan and make another.

Model 1: 6 points out of 6

It is not irresponsible to own a dog. In fact, the truth is quite the opposite. Owning a dog is an act of generosity and compassion—as long as the dog was once homeless or most likely would have been homeless.

There is a huge overpopulation of homeless dogs in the United States. It is estimated that some 5 million dogs and cats are euthanized each year because no one has adopted them. The reality is that the number of homeless dogs is far greater than that, because many homeless animals are not identified or counted, or they spend time in, or languish in, shelters. Dogs, like other animals, are sentient beings. Dogs without homes and proper care suffer. Some starve for food; others are starved for the love and compassion on which they thrive. As many vets and animal behaviorists have explained, dogs do have emotional lives, even if those lives are different from our own.

Of course, some will counter that if we are going to relieve the suffering of the homeless, why not relieve the suffering of homeless people? That, too, is a worthy cause. I would say that those equipped with the time, money, or inclination to deal with the suffering of homeless people should devote their resources to such a cause, and those equipped to deal with the suffering of homeless dogs, even if just by adopting a single dog, should devote their resources to that cause.

Adopting a dog is not just compassionate to the dog or gratifying to its owner, it is a generous act on behalf of society. A person who adopts a dog may be taking responsibility for an animal that might otherwise roam the streets, do damage, or spread disease. After all, shelters can only accommodate so many dogs. If people do not move existing dogs out of shelters, then more animals must wait on the streets or in the wild. A person who adopts a dog from a shelter is also taking responsibility off the public for that dog's food, medical care, spaying or neutering, or, in too many cases, euthanasia and disposal. While some people might counter that saving dogs only adds to the dog population, and perhaps the very popularity of dogs as pets, every dog that is adopted is one less dog on the public or charitable dole.

In general, of course, people may argue that there are more important ways to use private or public resources than by spending them on dogs. They are correct. There are more important uses of our time and money, such as feeding the hungry. But does one worthy cause, such as feeding the hungry, invalidate all other worthy causes, such as teaching the illiterate? Cannot some people devote themselves to some worthy causes that touch or move them personally, while others devote their resources to different worthy causes? I believe we can have compassion for the least among us, including our four-footed friends, as well as for those people who do, indeed, lay a more significant moral claim upon us.

Scoring Analysis

This response scores 6 out of 6 for the following reasons:

- **It answers the task.** With care and considerable sophistication, this response not only gives cogent reasons for disagreement, but it also responds thoughtfully to the most likely and compelling challenges.

- **It is well supported.** Support for dog ownership is abundant and well explained. The writer acknowledges the validity of counterarguments, yet weakens them with provocative questions and logical reasoning or with ample and persuasive support.

- **It is well organized.** The writer uses the opening paragraph to state and qualify the position and uses subsequent, discrete, and well-constructed paragraphs to counter challenges and reinforce the position. All ideas lead logically and smoothly to a satisfying conclusion.

- **It is fluid, precise, and graceful.** The capable prose includes short sentences that are interspersed with longer ones for dramatic effect. Advanced word choices include *languish*, *sentient*, and *invalidate*. The tone and style help the reader form an opinion of the writer as objective and thoughtful.

- **It observes the conventions of Standard Written English.**

Other observations: While a different opening could create more interest, or more points could be made in support of the position, the essay nevertheless meets all the criteria for a score of 6. ETS readers do not expect perfection in 30 minutes; nor do they expect you to cover the entire waterfront of your topic. What they do expect, however, are intelligent, well-supported, well-organized, and fluent responses within the time constraints.

Write Your Observations About Model 1

Model 2: 5 points out of 6

Dogs are loveable creatures that almost no one wishes to malign. It is also true that dog owners can be responsible, morally upright human beings. Yet, it is the inescapable truth that dogs consume resources, and that we can make better use of our time, our money, and our love than by lavishing them on dogs. Coming from a family in which a pet was always like a family member, this is a statement I make with deep personal regret. Therefore, I would not go so far as to brand all dog ownership as irresponsible.

If you own a dog, you may be spending quite a lot of your time on that animal. You may exercise it two or more times a day, as well attend to its other needs to go out. You may spend time brushing it, grooming it, or taking it to be groomed, and taking it to the vet. You may have to make arrangements for it when you will be gone for a long stretch, such as more than eight hours. If you are a good dog owner, then you are also spending time training your dog and giving it the attention and love that it craves. Now think about how those hours might be spent in other ways, such as tutoring people learning English, helping an elderly person to get groceries or meet other needs, or advocating for cleaner water or air. Which is the worthiest of these causes? Of the causes mentioned, to me, the dog finishes last.

If you own a dog, you must also spend quite a bit of money on it. Sums will vary with the dog and the owner, but some dog owners report spending well over $1,000 per year on their pet. One must think about where that money could have gone, such as to homeless people, the local food pantry, or medical research aimed at finding cures for cancer. Is it really better to spend your $1,000 on Fluffy or Mitten or Max than it is to help cure cancer? I think not.

Furthermore, dogs do use up resources. The pet industry is huge in America, cranking out as it does all kinds of unnecessary items for dogs ranging from luxury dog beds to Halloween hats and costumes. Page through almost any catalog and you will find items such as luxury dog beds and designer sweaters. Furthermore, dogs soil our roads and parks. If a dog owner is responsible and cleans up, each of the nation's millions of dogs is then responsible for the use of thousands of plastic bags. A dog consumes other resources as well, such as food and water. Therefore, no matter how loveable they may be, dogs do not merit the many resources that we lavish on them.

Scoring Analysis

This response scores 5 out of 6 for the following reasons:

- **It answers the task.** Some excellent reasons are given for agreeing with the position. The response also capably addresses counterarguments, such as all the hours spent on animals that might be spent more responsibly or productively.

- **It is well supported.** For example, the final paragraph that bulwarks the writer's position offers capable, persuasive support. Other paragraphs also contain ample, detailed, and well-developed support.

- **It is generally well organized.** A few organizational missteps mar the response by failing to make the position as clear as possible from the outset and by articulating counterclaims or challenges (such as dogs being loveable) less clearly and centrally than they could have been. (Attention to topic sentences might have cured this problem.) For the most part, however, the flow of ideas is logical.

- **It is fluid.** Words and sentences are clear; some words, such as *malign, inescapable,* and *advocating* are quite sophisticated. The sentences are, in general, more serviceable than elegant. (Compare them with the sentences in the 6-point response.)

- **It observes the conventions of Standard Written English.** There are a few minor errors that do not interfere with meaning.

Other observations: In an Issue Task, be sure your position is clearly stated from the outset. If a personal statement such as the one about family might somehow obfuscate that position, leave it out. Note how the writer never really develops the qualification at the end of that final line of the first paragraph. In addition, there is no transition between that statement and the following paragraph. These failings contribute to the response scoring a 5 instead of a 6.

Write Your Observations About Model 2

_____

_____

_____

_____

_____

_____

_____

_____

_____

_____

_____

_____

_____

_____

_____

_____

_____

_____

_____

_____

_____

_____

_____

_____

_____

_____

_____

_____

_____

_____

_____

_____

_____

_____

_____

_____

Model 3: 4 points out of 6

Individuals and families who own dogs know what a financial drain it is to have such a pet. For a big dog, food costs alone can run $50 per month. In addition, there are vet bills for everything from routine vaccinations to heartworm medication to occassional illness or injury. There are leashes, bowls, collars, licences, whistles, and dog beds to buy. In addition, some people buy dog toys, dog sweaters and booties, and even high-end dog biscuits. Most people have to board their dogs at least from time to time, while others board them often, hire dog walkers, or send their dogs to day care. That means spending anywhere from approximately $1,000 per year to upwards of $10,000 per year, on their dog. Some of these owners pass by the homeless people on the street, or go through poor neighborhoods with children who are not eating right, with their purebred, just-groomed dog decked out in it's lovely new handnit sweater. This fabulous waste of money is common in our country, where dog ownership seems to be on the rise. Going hand in hand with that waste of money is the time they waste on caring for, walking, and toting around dogs when we might be involved in feeding the hungry, working for a cleaner enviroment or taking steps to end global warming, or addressing other really important challenges.

Pets, of course, are not useless, and they do bring joy into peoples' lives. Pets must be used as guide dogs for some people. They may also be important in mental or psychological healing. For example, when used to provide therapy to children or others who have experienced grave loss or other tramma. Also, a visit from a well-trained dog at a nursing home, children's ward, or other place where such companions are both welcome and useful has many beneficial affects. Indeed, a dog can be a light in the life of any lonely or sick person.

Those who feel their lives are not complete without a pet certainly have a right to one. But do they need a designer dog? Do they need doggie daycare? And do they need two dogs, or three, or five? Furthermore, could such people not also look outward at the world, and spend some of their energy on tasks that need doing, instead of so much energy on loving and pampering their dogs? In my humble opinion, it is far better to help the people of this world then to spend our presious time and resources on cute, but unnecessary, animal friends.

Scoring Analysis

This response scores 4 out of 6 for the following reasons:

- **It answers the task.** This response clearly takes a position and supports the position. It is less effective on responding to the possible challenges to that position.

- **It supports the position well but is limited in terms of explaining and countering challenges.** Examples are appropriate and various, but responses to likely challenges are not so clearly explained or developed as they should be. In fact, the writer does a better job of agreeing with the challenges than refuting them in any way.

- **It lacks strong organization.** The argument starts immediately before the position is clear; paragraph 1 needs reorganization. Paragraph 2 could also be more clearly and fluidly linked to both the paragraph that precedes it and the one that follows it.

- **It is generally clear.** Most points are clear, but paragraph 2 should also be more sharply focused to reflect and specifically refute challenges to the writer's position. The tone at times verges on the harangue.

- **It observes the conventions of Standard Written English.** There are several minor flaws, but they do not interfere with meaning. They do, however, help contribute to the score of 4.

Other observations: This response contains a wealth of insights, but the critical thinking outshines the writing. Because the reader almost has to remind herself or himself of the side of the question that he or she supports, the entire essay loses its persuasiveness. This problem is exemplified by the ending, where meaningful questions are raised and qualifying circumstances considered, but the level of clarity and focus is not such that the reader can be perfectly certain of where the writer is going with them. The "over-the-top" rhetoric also gets in the way of the seriousness of some of the writer's points. Notice, too, how much weaker the vocabulary (as evidenced by choices such as "really important") and sentences are in this essay than they are in the 5- and 6-point responses.

Write Your Observations About Model 3

Model 4: 3 points out of 6

Face it, America! Owning a dog is egotistical. An indulgence of the most selfish people for the most selfish reasons. Dogs are everywhere where a lot of people don't want them. There's always people who are ignoring leash laws or cleanup laws and letting their dogs run up to and frighten people and children who do not like dogs and never wanted them around in the first place. Letting their dogs make a mess in parks and on the streets, too, and just leaving that behind. Or letting their dogs use other peoples' lawns and killing bushes or green areas through repeated use. These people somehow think their dogs deserve rights, that their dog has the right to be on someone else's property as long as it is attached to their leash. There, however, being no bill of rights for dogs.

Plus, look at the money people spend on their dogs, and not just on the necessary things like a license and rabies shots but on crazy things like designer collars and bows and ribbons and special haircuts. People are making themselves, not there dogs, feel good with these things.

Some people will say that pets help you out when you are lonely and give you friend when you need one. I say why not a person for a friend instead of a dog.

Some people will also say that people should have dogs to help out blind people or to serve as guide dogs. I have no problem with that. But those dogs aren't pets. They are specially trained animals for a special service, not indulged, spoiled animals owned by selfish people.

Scoring Analysis

This response scores 3 out of 6 for the following reasons:

- **It answers the task in a limited way.** This response makes its position very clear, but barely touches on the challenges to the writer's position. Only one challenge is actually dealt with—that dogs can dispel loneliness or be friends—and that challenge is treated quite simplistically and ineffectively.

- **It offers inadequate support.** Support is present, especially in the first paragraph, but it could have been more effectively used in service of the writer's position had it not been presented as a laundry list of the irresponsible deeds of some dog owners. There is inadequate support to rebut the challenges to the writer's position.

- **It lacks organization.** The response would benefit from a true introductory paragraph and placing much of the current paragraph 1 in a second, well-developed paragraph as support for a clearly stated topic sentence.

- **It is fluid, but not precise.** Ideas flow in a variety of sentence structures, including sentence fragments, and the latter are effective in places, but the overall impression is a writer writing at break-neck speed to finish in 30 minutes.

- **It contains errors in the conventions of Standard Written English.** There are several consistent flaws, some of which interfere with meaning.

Other observations: Try to avoid the personal and name-calling approach taken here. It's fine to express passion for your point of view; you may even create a distinctive voice. But remember that an argument is most effective when it creates the appearance of objectivity. Edit out any name-calling, gratuitous judgments, or vitriol.

Write Your Observations About Model 4

_____

_____

_____

_____

_____

_____

_____

_____

_____

_____

_____

_____

_____

_____

_____

_____

_____

_____

_____

_____

_____

_____

_____

_____

_____

_____

_____

_____

_____

_____

Model 5: 2 points out of 6

If you want unconditional love, you need a dog. A dog will love you when no one else cares. A dog will always be there for you. A dog will help you get through the times when you are sad or lonely.

The best thing about owning a dog is coming home from a hard day and theres your dog so happy to see you and wag its tail and jump all over you like you are the greatest person in the world.

You should also own a dog because there are so many unwanted dogs in the world and some of them are going to die or be put to death in shelters and other places because no one wants them.

You should also own a dog because no animal should have to have it's life cut short when there are so many people out there who would gain so much from having a dog, even though it is expensive and takes time from you.

If someone tells you its not right to own a dog because dogs don't do anything for the world, you can tell them how much your dog does for you.

Scoring Analysis

This response scores 2 out of 6 for the following reasons:

- **It answers only part of the task.** The position is clear, and, indeed, the last point is a good one, but challenges to the position are not developed.

- **It lacks support.** The assertions are either not backed up or are backed up with extremely simple or inadequate support.

- **It is poorly written.** Most "paragraphs" are just one sentence. No single idea is explored in depth. Variety of sentence structure and word choice are not apparent.

- **It contains errors in the conventions of Standard Written English.** There are several minor grammatical errors that add to the overall impression that this piece was poorly conceived and written.

Other observations: This writer could probably have scored an extra point or more by paying more attention to structuring and developing paragraphs.

Write Your Observations About Model 5

Model 6: 1 point out of 6

If there's one thing people have a real, 100% right to in this nation, it's there property, and a dog is a kind of property. Therefore, no one has the right to take that property away or to say a person cannot own a dog.

It's fine for a person to own a dog because a dog meets that person's needs or wants in some way. The dog might make the person feel good or more loved. The dog might make the person feel like someone or something on this earth depends on him and would not be the same without him. The dog might even be trained to fetch the person's slippers for him or do some other job. There has even been times when dogs have saved their owner's lifes. It is not right for anyone without a dog to say that someone with a dog can't have that dog. No one has the right to do that.

Scoring Analysis

This response scores 1 out of 6 for the following reasons:

- **It answers only part of the task.** This response takes a clear position while failing to respond to challenges. The first paragraph is off task.
- **It lacks support.** There is almost no support; the support that appears is simple and predictable.

Other observations: In addition to other flaws that sink the response, the final two lines also present the reader with an example of circular reasoning—saying something is so because it is so. Avoid this kind of reasoning in your own response.

Write Your Observations About Model 6

SUMMING IT UP

- The Issue Task is part of the Analytical Writing section, which is always first in an administration of the GRE® General Test. The time limit for the issue task is 30 minutes.

- The Issue Task of the Analytical Writing portion of the GRE® General Test measures how well you can develop and support your own position on an issue.

- The Issue Task is of a general nature and no special knowledge is required to analyze and form an opinion about it.

- The Issue Task statement will be accompanied by a set of instructions that establishes the conditions or requirements for the response.

- You will be presented with one issue to write about. You won't have a choice of issues from which to select.

- If you're taking the computer-delivered version of the GRE® General Test, you'll use specially designed word processing software that allows the user to insert and delete text, cut and paste text, and undo actions. There is no spell or grammar checker.

- The Issue Task is scored against a rubric using a 0 to 6 range in 1-point increments. The scores for the Issue Task and the Argument Task are averaged and reported as a combined score ranging from 0 to 6 in half-point increments.

- Follow these steps when writing the issue task:
  o State the thesis early.
  o Use a standard pattern of organization, namely order of importance.
  o Order paragraphs effectively.
  o Use a standard pattern of paragraphing: topic sentence, support and development, final summary statement.
  o Develop each paragraph fully: use facts, authoritative opinions or human interest, observations, anecdote, and examples.

- While spelling is not included in the scoring rubric, transitions are, so be sure to include them as you draft your response. If time permits, you can add extras to the response such as an interest-grabbing opener, appropriate word choice, and varied sentence structure.

- Your writing plan should consist of the following steps:
  o Prewriting: restate the prompt, think about reasons on both sides of the issue, jot a quick write
  o Drafting: answer the task, organize your response, provide well-developed support, consider style, link ideas clearly, take care with tone and person
  o Proofreading: check your thesis, look for omitted words, check for sentence faults, don't spend time on spelling or commas

- While you shouldn't spend time on spelling or minor mechanical errors, remember that misspelled words and lack of punctuation or wrong punctuation can detract from meaning.

The Argument Task

OVERVIEW

- **Basic Information About the Argument Task**
- **Understand the Prompt: The Argument**
- **Understand the Prompt: The Writing Instructions**
- **Understand the Scoring Rubric**
- **Review the Basics of Argumentation**
- **Learn the Flaws in Arguments**
- **Create Your Writing Plan**
- **A Final Note of Caution**
- **Argument Prompt With Six Model Responses, Scoring, and Analyses**
- **Summing It Up**

The Analytical Writing section of the GRE® General Test measures both your ability to think and your ability to write in response to two kinds of prompts. One of these prompts is the Argument Task. It presents you with a very brief argument and then states your task. Depending on the question, you'll have one of eight sets of directions explaining how you should construct your response. This chapter describes the prompt and sets of writing instructions and walks you through strategies that will aid you in crafting a successful response. To help you put it all together, the chapter ends with a sample Argument Task and six responses complete with analyses based on the GRE® General Test rubric for Argument Tasks.

BASIC INFORMATION ABOUT THE ARGUMENT TASK

The Analytical Writing section is always first in any administration of the GRE® General Test. For many test takers, it is probably the most stressful part of the test. Evidently, the test maker slots it first so anxious test takers can get it out of the way.

Chapter 5

Type of Question

For the Argument Task, you must write a response to an argument within certain guidelines set by the instructions that accompany the argument. The task for an argument response is not to craft your own opinion about the argument, but to analyze the argument. The instructions, which are described in more detail later in this chapter, may require that you:

- explain how certain evidence would make a claim stronger or weaker.
- examine stated and unstated assumptions to explain how much the argument depends on them, as well as what the argument loses if the assumptions are not valid or correct.
- present and discuss alternative explanations that could reasonably compete with the proposed explanation.

The content of the argument will be drawn from a wide range of subject areas. You might find a prompt about funding for the fine arts, a policy to monitor employee internet use, a health study's recommendation, or a government plan for land use. Topics are drawn from the physical and social sciences, the fine arts, and the humanities. However, no special knowledge of the subject is necessary to develop a well-reasoned and well-written response. The topics are general in nature, and the goal of the exercise is to enable test takers to demonstrate "complex thinking and persuasive writing" ability.

Unlike other essay portions of standardized tests that you may have taken, there is only one prompt. You won't get a choice of arguments from which to choose to write about.

Time Limit and Software

Like the Issue Task, the Argument Task has a time limit of 30 minutes. The time limit is the same on both the computer-delivered and paper-delivered tests.

The computer-delivered test has a word processing program that allows the test taker to edit by inserting and deleting text, cutting and pasting text, and undoing actions. There is no spell checker or grammar checker. This is similar to the restrictions placed on those taking the paper-delivered test. They will have no access during the test to dictionaries or grammar handbooks.

Scoring

Both the Argument Task and the Issue Task have their own rubrics. You'll work through the rubric for the Argument Task later in this chapter. Both tasks share the same score scale, which ranges from 0 to 6. The average of the two scores is taken to arrive at a combined score from 0 to 6 in half-point increments. This is the score that is reported to graduate and business schools.

UNDERSTAND THE PROMPT: THE ARGUMENT

All the prompts in the Argument Task have two parts: the argument and the specific instructions. The first part of the prompt states a brief argument, expressed completely in just a few sentences, which may end with a conclusion, a recommendation, a bit of advice, or a prediction. For example, the argument might suggest how funds are to be spent, a new policy that should be instituted, or why things would go better if a particular plan or action were implemented.

Think about this description of the first part of the prompt. An argument expressed in just a few sentences has to lack evidence—or enough evidence. Indeed, it has to be big on assertions and small on explanation and development. In short, it has to be a flawed argument.

Don't be fooled if the prompt has numbers, percentages, or other statistics. Their function is to support the argument—or to appear to support the argument. They may actually reveal a flaw in the argument that you can build on in your own line of reasoning.

UNDERSTAND THE PROMPT: THE WRITING INSTRUCTIONS

The second part of the prompt states the task or special instructions that define your response. These instructions will begin with the words "Write a response. . ." and then explain how that response should be shaped. Typically, you'll be told to be specific in explaining your analysis, that is, you'll need to provide examples, reasons, questions to answer, or alternative explanations, depending on the prompt. The sets of instructions for responding to an argument task will have wording similar to the following:

- Discuss the evidence needed to assess the argument. Include specific examples and an explanation of how the evidence might weaken or strengthen the argument.

- Discuss the stated and/or unstated assumptions and explain how the argument is based on these assumptions and the implications for the argument if the assumptions are shown to be unjustified.

- Discuss the questions that need to be asked and answered to determine if the recommendation and its argument are reasonable. As part of your response, describe how the answers would help in the evaluation process.

- Discuss the questions that need to be asked and answered to determine if the advice and its argument are reasonable. As part of your response, explain how the answers would help in the evaluation process.

- Discuss the questions that need to be asked and answered to determine if the recommendation is likely to result in the outcome that is projected. As part of your response, explain how the answers would help in the evaluation process.

- Discuss the questions that need to be asked and answered to determine if the prediction and its argument are reasonable. As part of your response, explain how the answers would help in the evaluation process.

- Presented with an explanation, discuss one or more alternative explanations that could reasonably compete with the proposed explanation. Explain how your explanation(s) account for the facts in the argument that is proposed.

- Discuss the questions that need to be asked and answered to determine if the conclusion and the argument it is derived from are reasonable. As part of your response, explain how the answers would help in the evaluation process.

If the task asks you to raise questions, don't fail to raise them. If it asks you to provide alternative explanations, be sure you include them. And, above all, remember that you're being asked to analyze

NOTE
You can see by the writing instructions that you're being directed to respond in specific terms to the presented argument. In the words of ETS, you'll need to "support ideas with relevant reasons and examples" in "a well-focused, coherent discussion."

and evaluate a flawed or, at best, an incomplete argument. That knowledge can help you focus your thinking.

UNDERSTAND THE SCORING RUBRIC

Before we go any further, let's look at the scoring rubric for the Argument Task against which your response will be evaluated. Two readers will read and analyze your response using a six-point scale. The readers are your audience, and scoring high is your purpose. Scores range from 6 as the maximum to 0. Scores are whole numbers.

6 Points

To earn 6 points, your response should exhibit these characteristics:

- A logically sound, well-focused answer to the specific task that is particularly insightful, thoughtful, deep, or sophisticated

- Fully developed, persuasive support for the main point or points of your response; at this high level of response, examples and other illustrations are particularly apt or well chosen, and their relationship to the focus of your analysis is extremely clear and/or well articulated

- A method of organization that complements the main ideas of the analysis by effectively creating a flow of well-organized paragraphs and easing the reader's progress through the paper from first word to last; connections between and among ideas are logical and may also be as subtle as they are effective

- A formal grace that is a product primarily of well-constructed, varied sentences, and exact and rhetorically effective word choices

- Adherence to almost all the conventions of Standard Written English, including grammar, usage, and mechanics; errors, if any, are minor

5 Points

To earn 5 points, your response will likely have these characteristics, though it may exceed one or more of them yet fall short on another:

- A logically sound, focused answer to the specific task that reflects insight and evidences some deep thought

- Well-developed, persuasive support for the main point or points of your response; examples and other illustrations are well chosen, and their relationship to the focus of your analysis are clear

- A method of organization that complements main ideas and connects ideas clearly and in a logical order

- Well-constructed, varied sentences and appropriate word choices that help create clarity as well as interest

- Adherence to almost all the conventions of Standard Written English, including grammar, usage, and mechanics; errors, if any, are minor

4 Points

To earn 4 points, a response will have these characteristics:

- A generally focused answer to the specific task
- Varying degrees of adequate and inadequate support
- A logical method of organization, although some linkages may be missing or unclear
- Sentences and word choices that generally create clarity, though some problems may exist with structure or usage
- General adherence to the conventions of Standard Written English; some errors may occur

3 Points

Your response will earn only 3 points if it has *one or more* of the following characteristics:

- An inadequate answer to the specific task; it may not quite respond to the task or all aspects of it; it may be limited in its scope or number of points; or it may be vague or confusing in places
- Inadequate support for the main point or points of your response or support that is illogical
- A pattern of organization that does not complement the main ideas or causes confusion for the reader
- Sentences and word choices that occasionally interfere with clarity
- One or more errors in the conventions of Standard Written English that are so significant that they obstruct meaning, or very frequent minor errors

2 Points

Your response will earn only 2 points if it has *one or more* of the following characteristics:

- An inadequate or unclear answer to the specific task; it may not quite respond to the task or all aspects of it, or it may be too vague or confusing to answer the task adequately
- Little, if any, support, or support that is illogical
- Confusing or inadequate organization
- Sentences and word choices that interfere with clarity
- Repeated errors in the conventions of Standard Written English that are so significant that they obstruct meaning

1 Point

Your response will earn only 1 point if it has *one or more* of the following characteristics:

- Almost no response to, or minimal understanding of, the specific task
- A total lack of support or only illogical or flawed support
- No pattern of organization or confusing organization
- Many sentences and word choices that interfere with clarity
- So many errors in the conventions of Standard Written English that they obstruct meaning throughout the response

0 Points

This score is possible under the following circumstances:

- The response does not answer the task in any way.
- The response is written in a foreign language.
- The response simply copies the argument.
- The response is not legible.
- The response is nonverbal.

From these criteria, you can draw or reaffirm the following four conclusions about your task:

1. You must answer the prompt completely.
2. Your ideas, support, and analysis must be in-depth, sophisticated, and well-developed to earn the highest score.
3. To dramatically affect your score, grammar, usage, and mechanics errors must be both numerous and serious. (However, that doesn't mean you can be sloppy.)
4. The quality of your ideas is far more important than the quantity. However, in order to identify significant problems or flaws and to examine them in adequate, if not dense, detail, you'll need to write a response of some length. Although there is no magic number for success, aim for well-elaborated coverage of at least three flaws in the argument.

REVIEW THE BASICS OF ARGUMENTATION

The good news about the GRE® General Test Argument Task is that you don't need any knowledge of formal argument. You don't have to identify an argument as deductive or inductive, or worry about syllogisms. The purpose of the Argument Task, according to ETS, is to assess your analytical writing skills and your informal reasoning skills. Nevertheless, a quick review of what an argument is and what it does may prove useful in helping you tease out the assumptions, supposed facts, explanations, etc., on which an argument prompt is based.

Basic Argument Facts

The following basic facts define an argument:

An argument, or the claim or thesis at the center of the argument, can be simple or complex. In the prompts you are presented with, your job is always to find the claim, and treat it like a claim, not a fact, no matter how simple or "fact-like" it may appear.

An argument persuades. At the heart of an argument is the purpose of causing someone to think in a new way or adopt a new way of acting. Arguments may well inform, but if they don't also at least seek to persuade, they aren't arguments.

Arguments rely on evidence. Evidence can consist of everything from a simple anecdote to complex statistics. Examples, illustrations, and facts are all evidence. Evidence alone is never enough, however. The best arguments explain and interpret the evidence and successfully relate that support back to the claim. Because the arguments you will be presented with on the GRE® General Test are so brief, this kind of interpretation will be entirely missing from them. Furthermore, most arguments will lack evidence of any kind—or they will present only flawed or problematic evidence.

There is one additional fact about arguments that you won't find present in the short argument statements on the GRE® General Test, but that you can use to your advantage in writing your response:

A successful argument often depends, at least in part, on rhetorical devices to engage and sway the audience. An argument may use rhetorical devices while leading into the claim, reasserting it, or explaining the evidence that supports it. Exploiting the rich connotations of words for their emotional effect, luring the reader in through an engaging opening, or using devices such as parallelism, inversion, or figures of speech to transport the reader smoothly down the road of the argument are some of the rhetorical devices that writers use. Such devices are uncommon in Argument Tasks because they are too short. However, in developing your response, you will be framing a long analysis, which is essentially an argument for your point of view, and you can use these devices most effectively for that purpose.

Rhetorical Devices

There are a variety of rhetorical devices that you could employ in your response. The following are perhaps the most useful in this case:

- **Rhetorical question as a lead-in to your introductory paragraph:** Are libraries dead?
- **Metaphor:** A library's after-school programs are a beacon of hope for children of working parents.
- **Simile:** A library's after-school programs are like a magnet that draws the children of working parents to homework clubs and fun reading groups.
- **Understatement:** A library is home to the children of working parents.
- **Overstatement:** With fewer than 400 books a month being borrowed, the city library's circulation of books is dead.
- **Onomatopoeia:** sssssshhhh or click-click, tap, tap—which are the sounds of the modern library?
- **Parallel structure:** I came to the library, I saw its collection of DVDs and CDs, and I was captured by the possibilities of free entertainment.

The Basic Language of Argumentation

In dissecting the argument, it will be helpful if you know what you're looking for. The following is a quick review of the parts and qualities of arguments:

The Claim: The claim is the main idea, proposition, or thesis statement of the argument. As you read the argument part of the prompt, look for the claim, that is, what the argument is about.

The Conclusion: The conclusion is the idea that is reached in the argument. Ask yourself: What's the conclusion arrived at by the end of the argument?

Premise/Assumption: The reasoning process to reach the conclusion begins with premises (or statements assumed to be true). Some people use the word "premise" as a synonym for an "assumption," which is any statement set forth as true or presumed to be true and may be stated or implied. The premises, or assumptions, are the meat of the argument. They lay out the support for the claim, proposition, or thesis. Responding to them will be the major part of your writing.

Counterargument: All argument writers should expect someone to counter their ideas, or present an opinion that opposes their own. In an extended argument, a good writer will anticipate and address counterarguments. The argument prompt is too short for any extended counterarguments; in writing your Argument Task, you're in effect countering the argument made in the prompt.

Assessing an argument as sound, valid, logical: These are three terms that are standard ways to convey that a point is reasonable, logical, or substantiated.

Assessing an argument as unsound, invalid, illogical: Similarly, these are three terms that brand an argument as unreasonable or that identify it as untrue.

The perspective or point of view: As you respond to the Argument Task, consider the perspective or point of view from which the argument is made. As you analyze the premises, ask yourself if the information is one-sided, biased, or a depiction of several sides to the argument. If it's one-sided, which is likely because of space limitations and the need of item writers to provide something for test takers to write about, what is that point of view? Then, consider what some other points of view about the topic might be and who might hold those other views. That information should help you develop your response.

LEARN THE FLAWS IN ARGUMENTS

The GRE® General Test will present you with flawed arguments. Remember that it's not your job to agree or disagree with the claim, but to expose those flaws. The most common flaws you'll find will be embedded in statements of, or references to, the following:

Unreliable Opinion Polls, Surveys, Questionnaires

You can expose the potential flaws or unreliability of an opinion poll, a survey, a questionnaire, or similar instrument by asking or speculating about the following:

- How many people took part?
- Was it a representative sample?
- Was it a random sample, self-selected, or handpicked?
- What questions were asked?
- Did the wording of the question contribute to a certain answer? (Consider that some questions are leading questions. Consider, too, that some questions do not allow for the full range of possible answers.)

In addition, instruments that are intended to measure change may not account for novelty, that is, initial responses to a change or new policy may be different over time. Also, those who design and analyze surveys, opinion polls, and questionnaires can leap to conclusions that aren't borne out by the data. They overstate or overgeneralize from the data.

Faulty Cause-and-Effect Relationships

Always examine cause-and-effect relationships in the argument. Sometimes, the prompt will confuse a correlation or an association with a cause, or propose a false cause. For example, an argument might suggest that every inch of space in a building is in use; therefore, a new building is needed. But you might be able to undercut this argument by conjecturing about how the space is being used. It may be storing useless equipment or supplies that should be discarded or recycled. You could then point out that the cause is not lack of space, but bad use of space.

False Generalizations

Even if a set of evidence does logically lead to a valid conclusion, it is possible to overgeneralize. That is, it's possible to suggest the data applies to more situations or to more people than it actually does. Another term for this is *sweeping generalization*.

More common, perhaps, is the hasty generalization that bases a conclusion, a recommendation, advice, or a prediction on too small a sample or an unrepresentative sample. For example, an argument might suggest that because a few public libraries in the state are failing to keep up with technology, all public libraries have the same problem and state government should fund upgrades for all libraries in the state.

False Analogies

If two or more things are alike in one or more ways, it's illogical to suggest that, on the basis of that similarity, they are alike in other ways. For example, if the city funded a new city hall last year, a good choice that met with overwhelming approval, the argument may make a false analogy by suggesting that the new public safety building will be a similarly good choice and meet with the same overwhelming approval.

Either-Or Thinking

This line of "reasoning" suggests that if one thing is true, the other cannot be true, as in "Either we build the new public safety building now, or we act with wanton disregard for the safety of every citizen in this community." Either-or thinking may be used to argue that two courses of action cannot exist at the same time or lead as effectively to the same result at the same time.

Assumptions

ETS rolls many of the specific flaws described above, as well as others, into the blanket term "assumptions." For example, ETS calls faulty cause-and-effect, or the fact that one thing is said to cause another but didn't necessarily, a flawed assumption. Therefore, feel free to use "faulty," "incorrect," or "illogical assumption" to identify most flaws you find, or expose the flaws without naming their type.

A statement such as "One problem with the argument is . . ." is perfectly acceptable based on the models that ETS presents. What will make or break your response is not the language you use to identify flaws, but the ability to recognize flaws, explain the problems with their supposed "support" of the argument, and relate the flaws back to the specific writing instructions.

CREATE YOUR WRITING PLAN

Now that you know what to expect in an Argument Task, it's time to create a plan for attacking it. Think of it as three-pronged: prewriting, drafting, and proofreading. You'll have just 30 minutes to do all this, so you should plan to spend the bulk of that time—say 23 or so minutes—drafting. However, you need to know what you're going to write, so don't skip prewriting.

Prewriting

The prewriting part of your writing plan has these steps that will help you focus on the task, gather your ideas, and plan the development of your response:

Restate the prompt: Read the entire prompt carefully and then restate it in your own words to make certain that you understand the argument and the specific instructions.

Identify the claim/issue and any statements based on the claim: Next, find the claim. Sometimes the word "claim" is actually used in the prompt, but most of the time it is not. Remember that the claim is the main idea or proposition. Statements based on the claim may include advice, recommendations, predictions, explanations, and conclusions. Ask:

- Is the main claim true?
- Is it true in all cases?
- Under what circumstances would it not be true?

Ask some "what if" questions about situations or circumstances in which the claim would be weakened or invalidated. Then decide whether the conclusion, recommendation, prediction, explanation, or advice logically follows from the claim. Ask yourself why.

Examine the claim/issue from different perspectives: For example, a town is deciding whether it needs a new public safety building to replace its old fire and police station.

Think about this question from the point of view of:

- a person who works in the station every day.
- people who will make money from the new construction.
- people who will feel more important if a new station is built.
- taxpayers, some of whom may be burdened by high taxes, unemployment, or both.
- people who think the old building is just fine and it's better to renovate than build new.

Jot a "Quick Write": Spend 2 or 3 minutes jotting down your ideas. (Computer-delivered test takers will be able to use scrap paper that is provided for this purpose.) This isn't a full outline, but just a list of flaws in the argument, main points, and few supporting ideas for each main point. Ideas won't come in any particular order, so list them as they flow. Then cross out ideas that don't seem as though they fit, and number ideas you want to use in the order in which you want to use them.

The most sophisticated ideas earn the highest scores on the analytical writing measure; therefore, don't just plan on developing the first ideas that pop into your head! Instead, use the best, least simplistic, and most original ideas for your response, ideas that you can substantiate in meaty, persuasive ways. If possible, position your best idea at the end of your response for greatest rhetorical effect. If you can, also come up with an idea for the opening that will appeal to your audience—with drama, human interest, or vivid detail.

Some Tried-and-True Sentence Starters

You can use the basic language of analyzing an argument in sentence starters such as those on the following list. You'll find fleshed-out examples of several of these starters in the sample responses later in this chapter. These sentence starters can help bring clarity to your writing, as well as give your writing an organizational boost by providing transitions between sentences and paragraphs:

- The first problem/the most fundamental problem/an obvious flaw in this argument is . . .
- The statement/prediction/conclusion that XXX is an unjustified assumption because . . .
- A problem with this reasoning is . . .
- It is arguable that . . .
- What if . . .
- The writer/author/argument implies that . . .
- Nothing in this argument actually tells/explains/supports . . .
- This argument asserts that . . .
- This assertion is illogical because . . .

Drafting

In reality, you won't just be drafting: you'll be drafting and revising simultaneously because there's no time to do them as separate steps. To get the most out of your limited time, keep these priorities in mind as you draft:

Answer the task: Some test takers produce competent essays that fail to answer the task and, therefore, sink them. After you write your opening or first paragraph, glance briefly back at the task to be sure you are addressing it or are on track to addressing it. (Computer-delivered test takers can do this by clicking on "Question Directions" at the top of the screen.) As you answer the task, be as thoughtful and insightful as you can be. Be sure you focus on the flaws in the argument.

Organize your response: The following pattern is a standard, or traditional, way to organize your overall response. It leads your reader smoothly through your response by eliminating confusion and guesswork. In addition, it helps to create fluency—or the illusion of it. If you're a writer who has trouble with organization, this pattern gives you a structure to develop your ideas around:

- Opening paragraph: Thesis or clear statement of your position
- Body paragraph 1: Reason 1 for your position, fully explained and supported
- Body paragraph 2: Reason 2 for your position, fully explained and supported
- Body paragraph 3: A statement of the most effective counterargument, an acknowledgment of its reasonableness, and your fully explained and supported response; or any other specific and developed point needed to address the writing task instructions
- Closing paragraph: Reason 3 (another key challenge or another main point) that directly responds to the specific writing instructions; provides support as needed; plus a detail, statement, question, or other device that delivers closure to your response

TIP

Using a standard pattern of organization has an added benefit. If you decide ahead of time how to set up your response, you can save time when faced with writing the actual response on test day.

Suppose you use this pattern of organization. How do you decide what reason to use first, second, and third? Often, the best way to organize points for an argument is by order of importance. You could choose your most significant reason to be first or last. If you use your most powerful, that is, strongest, support as the third and final point, your readers will take away from your response your most impressive piece of argument.

Provide ample, thoughtful, well-developed support: As you lay out each main point of your response, be sure you support it fully with the best evidence, and be sure you explain that evidence clearly enough so that it actually does evaluate the recommendation, advice, prediction, explanation, or conclusion. All the topics are meant to be general enough that anyone can answer them. For example, a prompt may ask you to discuss the questions that would need to be asked in order to decide if a recommendation to adopt honor codes by colleges and universities is reasonable. No special knowledge is required to respond to this prompt, but if you have experience with an honor code, you could incorporate that experience. Observations, such as your own experience, facts, authoritative opinions, examples, and human interest stories can and should be used liberally to support your points.

Link ideas clearly: Your organization doesn't have to be traditional, or based in any way on typical instruction in college writing classes, but it does have to be logical and coherent. Based on reviewing sample analyses, ETS values transitional words and phrases, so link paragraphs and ideas appropriately as you write. Also, don't overlook the value of a topic sentence in providing an organizational boost to your essay.

Consider style: If you're aiming for a top score, vary your sentences and word choices. Note that transitional words and phrases not only help you create coherence, but they can help you vary the beginnings of sentences as well.

TIP

If you have enough time, look for ways to increase the style quotient of your response by making your opening more attention getting, tweaking word choice so that it's stronger or more vivid, and varying your sentences.

TRANSITIONS

Review the following lists of transitional words and phrases and use them as you practice writing responses to the tasks in the practice tests. In that way, you can integrate them into your writing style so they flow as you write your actual responses on test day.

Transitions That Introduce or Link Opinions and Reasons

because	evidently	indeed
besides	for this reason	on the other hand
by comparison	furthermore	since
consequently	however	therefore

Transitions That Introduce or Link Examples

for example	in this case	one type
for instance	in this situation	to illustrate this point

Transitions That Create Emphasis or Add Information

after all	furthermore	more important
again	in addition	moreover
besides	indeed	similarly
certainly	in fact	what's more

Transitions That Introduce Opposing Views

although this may be true	naturally	on the other hand
even though	nevertheless	undeniably
evidently	notwithstanding	unquestionably
it may be said	of course	without a doubt

Proofreading

Save 2 or 3 minutes for proofreading and fine-tuning your essay. An omitted word could invalidate a good point by making the sentence in which it appears unclear or nonsensical. Look specifically for the following:

Check your thesis: Make sure that you've stated it and stated it clearly. Make sure your response reflects this statement.

Look for omitted words: When you're writing in a hurry, it's easy to leave out what could be a crucial word.

Check for sentence faults: At this stage, you want to make certain that you eliminate any ineffective fragments, any run-on sentences, and any fused sentences or comma splices.

Don't spend time on spelling or commas: Keep in mind that the rubric doesn't mention spelling. Spelling evidently has "minor error" status for ETS readers. Likewise, ETS readers aren't concerned with errors such as a missing comma here or there.

NOTE

Correct a fused sentence by making two sentences or, if the sentences are closely related in meaning, by replacing the comma with a semicolon.

A FINAL NOTE OF CAUTION

ETS wants its computer-delivered test takers to know that their responses will be subjected to analysis by software that searches for similarities to published information. It warns that it will "cancel" a score if it contains any unacknowledged use of sources. In addition, ETS will cancel a response if an essay or any part of it has been prepared by another person. Finally, a score will be canceled if it includes language that is "substantially" similar to the language in one or more other test responses.

ARGUMENT PROMPT WITH SIX MODEL RESPONSES, SCORING, AND ANALYSES

Use this prompt as a practice opportunity and compare your response with the samples, scoring, and analyses that follow.

Time yourself; in the real test, you will have 30 minutes.

1. Read the prompt.
2. Follow the prewriting steps.
3. Stop! Compare your "quick write" plan with the sample that follows the prompt to see different ideas (perhaps more sophisticated, perhaps less) that you might have considered.
4. Draft your response.
5. Read each model that follows the sample "quick write." Determine the positive and negative qualities of each sample response before you read its scoring analysis.
6. Score your response against the rubric on pages 134–136. Be honest in your analysis.

Argument Task

A majority of Smithtown taxpayers seem to agree that our fair city's infrastructure requires great attention. Our sewer system, bridges, and roads are all in desperate need of updates and repairs. This will cost close to $2 billion in taxpayer money. Therefore, it seems unreasonable to expect taxpayers to also continue paying for the free Summer Concert Series in Warren Park. Yes, it is the taxpayers who pay for the local musicians; the upkeep of the park grounds, stage and sound system; and the crew required to run it at a cost of $100,000 per season. When essential work is needed and placing such a burden on our local economy, should mere entertainment really be at the top of our list of priorities? If people are really so eager to attend concerts in Warren Park, they should be willing to pay top-dollar for tickets the way anyone would at a privately owned venue. According to a recent poll in the *Smithtown Gazette*, 44% of Smithtown taxpayers agree.

Write a response in which you discuss the stated and/or unstated assumptions, and explain how the argument is based on these assumptions and the implications for the argument if the assumptions are shown to be unjustified.

Sample "Quick Write"

The 6-point response to this prompt began with a process like the one that follows. First, the writer identified flaws. Notice that not every flaw in the argument is recorded here. Notice also, however, that the writer found many flaws and, therefore, a firm basis for analysis.

Flaws

— cost of concert series small compared to infrastructure repair

— assumes entertainment is not important to community

— fails to address concerts may draw more people to community

— assumes people will pay "top-dollar" to see local acts

— is the concert series really "at the top" of the city's list of priorities?

— 44% is a minority of taxpayers

TIP

Note how specific the "quick write" is. The writer is off to a good start for developing a response that is grounded in specific details to support any generalizations that the writer may make.

Now look at the plan the writer quickly made:

> (1a) cost of concert series is minimal
>
> (1b) is rebuilding bridges and sewer systems really more
> important than music?
>
> (2a) series provides employment
>
> (2b) concerts may draw more people to community
>
> (2c) people probably won't pay "top-dollar" to see local acts
>
> (3) exaggerates concert series' burden on community
>
> (4) 44% is a minority

Making Your Plan Work

As you'll see when you read the 6-point response based on this prewriting activity, some of the success of the response is due directly to ideas listed here. First, notice how the plan isn't a formal outline; it doesn't need to be. There is no five-paragraph organization of introduction, body, and conclusion expressed in the quick write. Instead, the plan goes to the heart of the 30-minute argument task and reflects a great variety of evidence for exposing the flaws in the argument. You'll see in the response how this planning leads to a dense, richly supported analysis that effectively undermines the argument.

Notice how, even in the prewriting, the writer goes beyond the obvious ideas (relatively small cost of concert series and the fact that a minority of taxpayers are in favor of defunding the series) to think a little more deeply about the nature of the concert series and its implications.

When you read the resulting response, you'll also see that the writer didn't use every idea here. For example, the writer left out the idea that entertainment may be as important as rebuilding the city's infrastructure, which was probably a good choice because it was one of the less consequential kinds of support he or she could have provided.

Furthermore, there are many more ideas in the response than appear in this simple plan. Remember that fact when you make your plan. You don't have to come up with every possible idea during prewriting. Writing is a generative process; ideas come to writers as they write. Trust that they will come to you, too. The secrets to successful prewriting are mainly the following:

- Quickly generate more ideas than you think you need.
- Edit out the least significant, the simplest, or the most predictable ideas.
- Know when to stop: try not to spend more than 3 minutes on prewriting.

Model 1: 6 points out of 6

A local government is responsible for ensuring that its citizens live in a safe and clean environment. Citizens are expected to shoulder some of the burden of maintaining such essential infrastructure elements as bridges, roads, and sewer systems, and they do that with their tax dollars. However, there is more to maintaining a city than ensuring its infrastructure is in fine working order; a concept that seems lost on the argument against continuing to use tax dollars to fund the Summer Concert Series in Warren Park.

First of all, there is a serious problem regarding false equivalence. This occurs when someone makes a comparison between two essentially dissimilar things. In the case of this particular argument, the writer compares the $2 billion needed to complete the infrastructure work with the comparatively minimal cost of $100,000 to maintain the Summer Concert Series. That $100,000 would be a veritable drop in the bucket toward the infrastructure work, and it hardly seems reasonable to imply that defunding the concert series would do much to swell the infrastructure budget.

Furthermore, there is the argument's rather shortsighted refusal to recognize how a concert series of this sort may assist the local economy. The argument references the fact that part of that $100,000 goes to the musicians, sound crewmembers, and maintenance people who may rely on the series to make ends meet. There is also the matter of how local, free events such as these strengthen a community, help to give it an identity, and inspire citizens to remain members of those communities. It would be an exaggeration to suggest there would be some sort of mass exodus without the concert series, but something so relatively inexpensive that makes a community more appealing to live in can only be good for the local economy, and this is another matter the argument fails to address. Events such as these also may draw in people from other communities. Such out-of-towners would likely frequent local businesses, and may be deterred from visiting if the concerts are no longer free of cost. After all, the hard fact is that the series features local artists, which are likely not top-name performers the average person would be willing to pay "top dollar" to see.

Essentially, the argument for defunding the concert series is guilty of overstating the burden and importance of the series. As I have already stated, the cost of maintaining it is comparatively minimal. Also worth noting is the argument's seemingly exaggerated suggestion that the concert series is "at the top of (Smithville's) list of priorities." Realistically, the necessary infrastructure work is at the top of that list, so the writer is most likely merely using hyperbolic language to appeal to taxpayers in a clumsy manner.

There is also a simple fact that undermines the argument for defunding the Summer Concert Series: only a minority of Smithville citizens is in favor of defunding the program. The statistic culled from the *Smithville Gazette* concludes the argument on a note that destabilizes itself: if 44% of taxpayers are for defunding the series, then 56% are either for it or at least, undecided. The argument would be more convincing without this statistic. If nothing else, it would have been wiser to bury the statistic within the argument rather than using it as the argument's final word. However, even doing that would not have rescued an argument that commits the exaggerations, oversights, and false equivalences that this one does.

Scoring Analysis

This response scores 6 out of 6 for the following reasons:

- **It answers the task.** The writer examines several statements that form the basis of the argument for their implications and for their reasonableness. In doing so, the author probes deeply to create a thoughtful analysis of several unsubstantiated statements and their implications.

- **It is well supported.** The writer offers numerous examples of how the concert series may be good for an overburdened local economy, such as how it keeps certain locals employed and likely draws in out-of-towners who may pump dollars into the local economy. Other points are likewise well substantiated.

- **It is well organized.** There is a clear opening and an effective closing, and the body paragraphs are logically organized. All ideas lead logically from one to the next.

- **It is fluid, precise, and graceful.** Sentences and word choices (such as "false equivalence" and "hyperbolic") are varied and, at times, quite sophisticated and graceful. Statements are placed effectively at the ends of paragraphs for clincher effect. The tone and style are appropriate to the task.

- **It observes the conventions of Standard Written English.**

Other observations: Notice how this response doesn't try to refute every statement and implication—nor does it need to in order to be successful. For example, it never undermines the importance of rebuilding the city's infrastructure. Notice, too, how it thinks beyond the argument itself, not merely refuting many of the writer's arguments but also discussing points the argument may have willfully failed to make. Also, examine how rich, varied, and dense the support is for the idea that Smithville should continue to fund its Summer Concert Series.

Write Your Observations About Model 1

Model 2: 5 points out of 6

The writer of this argument makes some very strong points. He or she says that nothing is more important than rebuilding a city's infrastructure, and you can hardly argue against that. But there are some significant flaws too.

Let's get the big one out of the way first. The writer says that 44% of the people in Smithville want taxpayers to stop contributing money to the Summer Concert Series. Well, that is not most of the people in the community. What the writers is unintentionally saying here is that 56% of the taxpayers do want the concert series, and that only hurts his or her argument.

Also the writer seems to be suggesting that the $100,000 needed to fund the concert series is somehow similar to the massive $2 billion price tag of paying for all of the infrastructure work as if getting rid of that measly $100,000 cost will somehow bring that $2 billion much closer within reach. It is an unfair comparison. It is especially unfair considering the musicians and park workers who expect to get paid from that $100,000. The writer references the local economy in his or her argument but does not address how the local economy may rely on the concert series. As I've explained, local musicians and laborers may rely on it. But what if local businesses benefit from the series too? After all, ones in the vicinity of Warren Park may receive an upsurge in patronage because of the concerts. What if those businesses go bankrupt because of the elimination of the concert series? What effect will that have on the local economy?

So defunding the concert series is unlikely to affect the infrastructure budget, which is the writer's main argument, and it may even benefit the Smithville community. Significantly, most Smithville residents are against defunding the series. Therefore, there are flaws in what is and isn't included in this argument, and these flaws make for a rather unconvincing plea to defund the Summer Concert Series in Warren Park.

Scoring Analysis

This response scores 5 out of 6 for the following reasons:

- **It answers the task.** The writer examines some statements that form the basis of the argument for their implications and for their reasonableness. The analysis raises many thoughtful points.
- **It is well supported.** The writer offers competent what-if questions that expose the possible flaws in statements that form the basis of the argument. The writer also offers clear examples, although not in depth.
- **It is well organized.** The ideas lead logically from one to the next.
- **It is fluid and precise.** Sentences and word choices are varied, although many of the word choices are more serviceable than sophisticated. The tone and style are for the most part appropriate to the task.
- **It observes the conventions of Standard Written English.**

Other observations: Notice that while this response touches on many ideas, it actually examines and develops fewer statements and implications than the 6-point essay does. The opening is competent, but quite predictable. Compare the opening, as well as the body paragraphs, with the 6-point response to see differences in the quality of both the thinking and the writing.

Write Your Observations About Model 2

Model 3: 4 points out of 6

The writer of this argument clearly does not appreciate what music does for a community. I have been to many free concerts in my own local park, and I have to say that it has always been a very, very positive experience. And I'm not just talking about enjoying some great music or an entertaining show. During free concerts, the park is always packed to capacity. That means those concert goers are also working up a thirst and a hunger, and what do they do about that? They go to local business to buy food and drinks. So a free concert can be really positive for a local economy. They also need to buy gas to drive back from the concert.

So arguing that a free concert series does not draw in money is pretty flawed. What's more, the concert series the writer of this argument is talking about does not sound like much of "a burden on our local economy" in Smithville. Just think about it. OK, $100,000 does sound like a lot of money, but compare that figure to the $2 billion needed to do all that work on bridges, sewers, and roads in Smithville. It really is not that much money, so it is pretty out of line for the writer of the argument to suggest that those two things are in any way comparible. What would that $100,000 accomplish? Maybe they could but a new traffic light for one of those broken down roads, but probably not much more. Is it really fair to take the funding away from a whole concert series for something like that?

My guess is that the writer of this argument has something to gain from not making the concert series free anymore. Maybe he works for some sort of concert ticket company or something and intended to get rich from selling tickets to the series instead of allowing it to be free. Maybe he's a musician and thinks he will get paid more for putting on concerts if the park sells expensive tickets instead of letting people in just for free. The thing is that he is not going to get rich from just offering up local entertainment that most people have probably never heard of. Sure, I have seen local musicians at my local park, and some of them have been pretty amazing, but I never would have gone to those shows if I actually had to pay for my ticket. And I probably would not have had the leftover money to go to one of my local businesses to buy a bottle of soda and a few hot dogs or whatever. That's the sort of thing that keeps a local business afloat, you know. So there are a few more problems with the argumentative essay.

Really, it is ridiculous to compare spending $100,000 on a bit of entertainment to $2 billion on road and bridgework. Obviously, I'm not going to say that the city does not need that work. Cities need roads and bridges in good repair, and I'm glad that the argument at least doesn't argue that taxpayers shouldn't have to pay for those things, but there is more to la city than its roads and bridges. There are also people. People who join together at concerts get a real sense of community. I definitely feel like more of a member of my community when I'm at one of my local free concerts than I do when I'm at home by myself watching TV or playing video games or whatever. So there's that too.

Scoring Analysis

This response scores 4 out of 6 for the following reasons:

- **It generally answers the task.** That is, it probes the argument both for what it says directly and what it fails to mention. It identifies weaknesses in the argument that seriously undermine it.

- **It is supported, but often simply and repetitively.** The examples of the writer's own concert-going experiences form support, but that support is simple, weak, and tangential. Some ideas are repeated, and the assumption that the writer of the argument has "something to gain" by arguing to defund the concert series lacks realistic support.

- **It is organized.** In general, the ideas flow in an acceptable order, though some repeated ideas should have been deleted. There is no transition between the opening paragraph and the second paragraph.

- **It is sufficiently clear.** The sentences and words are mainly serviceable, though they lack sophistication. A number of sentences are convoluted and difficult to understand though they do not detract from the meaning of the paragraphs.

- **It observes the conventions of Standard Written English.** There are several errors here, but, in general, they do not interfere with meaning.

Other observations: This is an example of a very long response that doesn't succeed on the basis of its length. In fact, its length is part of its problem. The response would have been more cogent had repeated ideas and vague assertions been deleted. While ETS gives no indication in its scoring rubrics of how informal diction and a less than objective tone might undercut a score, it is probably safe to assume that the writer's choices in these regards in no way enhance this response and may well undermine it by contributing to the scorer's sense of inadequate word choice or unconventional usage in respect to the purpose, audience, and writing occasion.

Write Your Observations About Model 3

Model 4: 3 points out of 6

The main flaw with the argument is that $100,000 is an insignificant amount of money compared to $2 billion. I am not sure what difference to the infrastructure budget the author of this argument thinks defunding the Summer Concert Series in Warren Park will have, but I certainly cannot fathom it. If this is the best argument the writer can make, he or she has built his argument on a pretty creaky structure.

Now the good point the writer made was including a statistic. Statistics offer excellent support for arguments so, the detail about how 44% of people in Smithville oppose the taxpayer funding of Summer Concert Series in Warren Park makes for a very convincing argument on that point. Had the writer included more statistics like this, he or she would have made a much more convincing argument for defunding the Summer Concert Series in Warren Park.

As it stands though, the argument is not convincing enough. One statistic does not a convincing argument make. There's that money issue at the heart of the flaw of this argument to refuse taxpayer dollars to the Summer Concert Series in Warren Park. If I had written this argument, I would have found more statistics, because nothing makes an argument more convincing. I simply was not convinced that refusing to use a mere $100,000 to pay for the Summer Concert Series in Warren Park would have any positive effect on Smithville, the town in this argument. In fact it may be bad for the community of Smithville.

Scoring Analysis

This response scores 3 out of 6 for the following reasons:

- **It answers the task in a very limited way.** The first paragraph is well written, and offers a fair analysis of one of the argument's main points, but the second paragraph is weak as it places too much emphasis on the mere inclusion of statistics rather than how well those statistics support the central argument. Overall, it identifies for analysis just two ideas in the argument: the comparatively low cost of maintaining the concert series and the percentage of people in favor of defunding it.

- **It is not well supported.** All insights in this response are crammed into the first two paragraphs without much support. The final paragraph repeats the insights in the first two paragraphs pointlessly. The final sentence of the response indicates that defunding the concert series may be bad for the community without supporting this assertion in any way.

- **It lacks organization.** The response lacks an introductory paragraph. The final sentence of the passage is an observation that warrants further explanation, so it provides a weak conclusion.

- **It is fluid and precise.** Unfortunately, good word choice and sentence construction as well as appropriate style and tone do not outrate poor critical analysis.

- **It observes the conventions of Standard Written English.** Unfortunately, excellent command of the conventions of Standard Written English do not outweigh poor critical analysis.

Other observations: This is an example of how a well-written response doesn't score high because the quality (or extent) of the thinking is not on the same level as the quality of the word choice or sentence construction. The writer may have run out of ideas or out of time.

Write Your Observations About Model 4

_____

_____

_____

_____

_____

_____

_____

_____

_____

_____

_____

_____

_____

_____

_____

_____

_____

_____

_____

_____

_____

_____

_____

_____

_____

_____

_____

_____

_____

_____

_____

_____

_____

_____

_____

_____

Model 5: 2 points out of 6

The argument makes an excellent point regarding the cost of maintaining the Concert Series in Warren Park; that is that it costs $100,000 a year. That is a lot of money by any standards but only if its for one person. Still it gets broken down among a lot of different things. The musicians, the park workers, the sound crew, etc. How much money is each of those people even making; it isn't a lot of money if there are a lot of concerts in one season. So how many concerts are there? The writer of the argument is right. They should cancel the series because I doubt anyone is making much money off it. I for one think that musicians are talented people. Who deserve to be well compensated for their talents.

Scoring Analysis

This response scores 2 out of 6 for the following reasons:

- **It answers the task in a very limited way.** It identifies for analysis just one idea in the argument: the cost of maintaining the concert series. It does, however, ask good questions.

- **It is not supported.** While the writer shows some insight in the ideas selected for analysis, these ideas are, mainly, not explained and developed.

- **It lacks organization.** A single paragraph is not a response.

- **It has poorly constructed sentences.** There are fragments and awkward compound sentences.

- **It contains errors in the conventions of Standard Written English.** While not committing obvious grammatical errors, the writer shows a lack of command of sentence construction.

Write Your Observations About Model 5

Model 6: 1 point out of 6

Taxpayers should not have to pay for concerts. Even if they are free and in public parks like this one. Really public concerts in parks are a nuisance. Think about people who live buy public parks like this one. I bet they don't like them very much. They are noisy, local musicians are never as good as professional musicians, and sitting through some long, drawn-out concert is usually really boring. Why should a taxpayer have to pay for something like that?

Scoring Analysis

This response scores 1 out of 6 for the following reasons:

- **It does not answer the task.** Instead, it agrees with a premise in the prompt on a personal level.
- **It is not supported.** The writer does not explain or develop the ideas.
- **It lacks organization.** A single paragraph is not a response.

Write Your Observations About Model 6

SUMMING IT UP

- The Argument Task of the Analytical Writing portion of the GRE® General Test measures how well test takers can analyze an argument, including the evidence to support that argument, and then discuss their analysis using examples from the given argument.

- The argument will be of a general nature and no special knowledge will be required to analyze and discuss it.

- The prompt will be accompanied by a set of instructions that establishes the conditions or requirements for your response.

- You will be presented with one argument. You won't have a choice from which to select.

- The Argument Task is part of the Analytical Writing section, which is always first in an administration of the GRE® General Test. The time limit for the argument task, like the Issue Task, is 30 minutes.

- Those taking the computer version of the GRE® General Test will use specially designed word processing software that allows the user to insert and delete text, cut and paste text, and undo actions. There is no spell or grammar checker.

- Like the Issue Task, the Argument Task is scored against a rubric using a 0 to 6 range in 1-point increments. The scores for the Argument Task and the Issue Task are averaged and reported as a combined score ranging from 0 to 6 in half-point increments.

- The basic facts of argumentation are the following:
  - o An argument can be simple or complex.
  - o An argument is meant to persuade.
  - o An argument relies on evidence.
  - o A successful argument often depends on rhetorical devices to sway the audience.

- The basic language of argument is claim, conclusion, premise/assumption, counterargument, assessment of an argument (sound, valid, logical; unsound, invalid, illogical), perspective, or point of view.

- The flaws in an argument can be based on unreliable opinion polls, surveys, and questionnaires; faulty cause-and-effect relationships; false generalizations; false analogies; either-or thinking; or assumptions.

- Your writing plan should consist of the following steps:
  - o Prewriting: restate the prompt, identify the claim/issue and any statements based on it, examine the claim/issue from different perspectives, jot a quick write
  - o Drafting: answer the task, organize your response, provide well-developed support, link ideas clearly, consider style
  - o Proofreading: check your thesis, look for omitted words, check for sentence faults, don't spend time on spelling or commas

- While spelling is not included in the scoring rubric, transitions are, so be sure to include them as you draft your response.

- While you shouldn't spend time on spelling or minor mechanical errors, remember that misspelled words and lack of punctuation or wrong punctuation can detract from meaning.

PART IV
VERBAL REASONING

Strategies for Reading Comprehension Questions

OVERVIEW

- **Basic Information About Reading Comprehension Questions**
- **Active Reading**
- **General Strategies for Answering Multiple-Choice Questions**
- **Additional Strategies for Multiple-Choice Questions—Select One or More Answer Choices**
- **Strategies for Select-in-Passage Questions**
- **Practice Questions**
- **Answer Key and Explanations**
- **Summing It Up**

Chapter 6 describes the reading comprehension questions on the GRE® General Test. These questions make up about half of each Verbal Reasoning section. The majority of reading comprehension questions are multiple-choice questions—select one answer choice. However, there are two other formats for reading comprehension questions: select-in-passage questions and multiple-choice questions—select one or more answer choices. In addition to basic information about the reading comprehension section, Chapter 6 offers useful strategies to help you answer reading comprehension questions in all three formats quickly and competently.

BASIC INFORMATION ABOUT READING COMPREHENSION QUESTIONS

The reading comprehension questions on the Verbal Reasoning section of the GRE® General Test assess your ability to understand, analyze, and apply information found in the types of reading you will encounter in graduate school. About half the questions on the verbal section of the GRE® General Test are reading comprehension questions.

Chapter 6

ALERT!

All multiple-choice questions in the computer-delivered test will have answer options preceded by either blank ovals or blank squares, depending on the question type. The paper-delivered test will follow the same format of answer choices, but use letters instead of ovals or squares for answer choices. For your convenience in answering questions and checking answers in this book, the letters A, B, C, D, etc. are used for the answer choices. This way, it is easier to check your answers against the answer key and the answer explanations.

The Passages

There are approximately ten reading comprehension passages on the GRE® General Test. They are based on information found in a wide range of scholarly and everyday sources from nonfiction books to popular periodicals to scholarly journals. The arts and humanities, physical sciences, biological sciences, social sciences, and business are all content areas that may be represented in the passages.

The passages may be from one to several paragraphs in length. Most, however, will be one paragraph; only one or two will be longer. Some passages will inform. Others will analyze. Still others will argue a point and seek to persuade. As in all real-world writing, a single passage may reflect more than one mode of exposition.

Each reading comprehension question on the computer-delivered test appears on a separate screen with the passage on which it is based. If the passage is too long to display legibly on a single screen, as in the case of multi-paragraph passages, you will be able to scroll through the passage without changing screens.

Directly before the start of the passage is a statement of how many questions each passage has. For example:

Questions 1–3 are based on the following passage.

A direction line appears from time to time during the questions—not each and every time—telling you how many answers to select. For example:

> **For Questions 1–3, choose only <u>one</u> answer choice unless otherwise indicated.**

A Word to the Wise: Put Aside Your Personal Views

When it comes to the content of the passages, ETS notes that occasionally "your own views may conflict with those presented in a passage." That is, you may have a reaction to the content of a passage that runs the gamut from mild disagreement to outrage. Don't let these reactions interfere with your analysis. To succeed, temporarily shelve any feelings and get on with answering the question(s) about the passage.

Question-and-Answer Formats

Each passage is followed by one to six questions. There are three formats that questions and answers may take for reading comprehension questions:

1. Multiple-choice questions—select one answer choice
2. Multiple-choice questions—select one or more answer choices
3. Select-in-passage

Most reading comprehension questions ask you to select *one* answer from a list of five possible answer choices. The answer choices for these questions will be preceded by *ovals*.

You will find a few multiple-choice questions that ask you to select *one or more answers* from a list of three possible choices. One, two, or all three answers may be correct. You have to select all the correct possibilities to earn credit for that question. The answer choices for these questions are preceded by *squares*.

You will find only a few questions that ask you to *select a particular sentence* in the passage as your answer. To do this, you will highlight your answer choice by clicking on the sentence. If you are working with a passage of several paragraphs, the paragraph or paragraphs that the question refers to will be marked with an arrow at the beginning and end of the subject paragraphs. Clicking on a sentence in any other part of the passage will not highlight it.

For your convenience in working through this book, we are marking answer choices as A, B, C, and so on.

NOTE

If you're taking the paper-delivered version of the test, you will be asked to choose a sentence from a list of multiple-choice possibilities for the select-in-passage computer questions.

Skills

The purpose of the GRE® General Test is to predict success in graduate school. Therefore, the questions on the test are meant to assess the preparedness of potential graduate school students. You will find questions that ask you to use the skills and abilities that are expected of students in graduate school. To answer questions on the reading comprehension section, you will need to be able to:

- identify or infer the main idea, or major point, of a passage.
- distinguish between main and subordinate ideas (major and minor points, in GRE® test parlance).
- summarize information.
- reason from incomplete data to infer missing information.
- determine the relationship of ideas to one another and/or to the passage in which they appear.
- analyze a text.
- draw conclusions from information.
- identify the author's assumptions or perspective.
- identify the strengths and weaknesses of a position.
- develop and assess alternative ideas.
- determine the meaning of individual words, sentences, and paragraphs, and of longer pieces of writing.

Some questions require you to use more than one skill at a time. For example, you might need the main idea to answer a question, but to find it, you might have to distinguish between main ideas and subordinate or supporting details. Or you might have to find a relationship between ideas by both inferring information about main and subordinate ideas and using structural clues to understand meaning.

Recurring Question Types

The list of skills may seem daunting, but when put in the context of actual questions, they will seem much more familiar. For example, the question "Which of the following best restates the author's point of view?" asks for the main idea of the passage. To find it, you may need to infer it, or it may be directly stated, though probably not in a graduate-level piece of writing.

You will find that certain categories of questions recur among the reading comprehension questions. The common question types are as follows:

- **Main Idea Questions:** These questions require you to identify or infer the main idea (or major point), summarize the passage, draw conclusions from complete or incomplete information about the main idea, and infer relationships between the main idea and subordinate details. You will find this to be a common question type, both in this book and on the GRE® General Test.

  o   Which of the following does the passage most clearly support?

  o   What was the underlying cause of the financial crisis?

  o   What qualities of the painter's style most influenced the critic's view?

  o   The passage implies that the president's actions were based on…

  o   Select the sentence that restates the premise of the author's argument.

- **Supporting or Subordinate Details Questions:** These questions ask you to identify subordinate details, infer subordinate details, summarize the passage, draw conclusions about subordinate details, or infer relationships between two or more subordinate details.

  o   The passage mentions financial regulations in order to…

  o   You can infer that the president's actions were based on…

  o   The passage notes each of the following causes EXCEPT…

  o   Based on the passage, which of the following was excluded from the experiment?

  o   The passage suggests that which set of data is the more compelling?

  o   The purpose of the sentence "Yet a close look . . . continents" is to…

  o   Select the sentence that restates the author's claim.

- **Author's Perspective Questions:** To answer these questions, you may need to infer the author's attitude or tone, or deduce the author's unstated assumptions. Not every question that mentions the author—or even the author's beliefs—is a perspective question. The question may, for example, be a main idea question such as the last example under Main Idea Questions.

  o   What was the underlying cause of the financial crisis, according to the author?

  o   The author attributes the early experimental results to…

  o   It can be inferred from the passage that the author believes that…

  o   The author of the passage most likely agrees with which historian's view as described in the passage?

  o   Select the sentence that best describes the author's attitude toward critics of Darwin.

- **Application Questions:** These test items ask you to evaluate the strengths and weaknesses of an argument, develop alternative explanations, hypothesize about the relationship of new ideas to stated or implied ideas, and use structural clues to determine or infer meaning. As their name suggests, these questions will often require you to apply or build on what you have already identified or inferred about the main idea, supporting details, or the author's perspective in earlier questions in the set for a particular passage and then apply that information to a different idea or situation.

  o Which of the following, if it were true, would weaken the author's argument?

  o Select the sentence that best describes the opinions of the anthropologists who actually examined the skeleton.

  o What is the primary purpose of the two groups of words in bold type?

  o Which of the following is most similar in reasoning to the ideas expressed in the final sentence?

  o According to the passage, which is the correct sequence of events?

- **Word-Meaning Questions:** These questions are easy to spot because they're accompanied by line numbers to help you quickly pinpoint the word and the context. They require you to infer the meaning of a word from the specific context in which it appears. The phrase "specific context" is important because words have different meanings in different subject areas and as different parts of speech.

  o "Verisimilitude" (line XX) most nearly means…

  o In the passage, "obfuscate" means…

ACTIVE READING

This is a timed test, and you will—and should—feel the pressure of the clock. Nevertheless, you can't read a GRE® General Test reading comprehension passage at the same rate at which you read the back of a cereal box or the latest posting to your favorite blog. In general, adjust your reading rate so that you're reading every passage with concentration and active participation. This can be hard to do when the clock is ticking, but it's your best bet to improve your comprehension, and it is especially good advice when the content is unfamiliar to you.

Just slowing down as you read won't help you much. You need to focus on and participate actively in what you are reading. Participating actively includes the following steps:

- Identify the topic, main idea, thesis, or proposition.
- Clarify your understanding.
- Summarize what you've read.

To help you understand the process, skim the following reading comprehension passage to get an idea of its topic, main idea, and details.

TIP

If you are running out of time, you could go through remaining passages looking for word-meaning questions. To answer the sentence, read the question, the sentence referred to in the question, and the sentences immediately before and after this sentence.

Passage 1

     Sculptor Henry Moore (born 1898) achieved prominence in the 1930s with his earliest recumbent figures. An English abstractionist, Moore has also been associated with romantic feeling in the relationship of his biomorphic forms to nature. His sculptures, which often
Line consist of large flowing, rhythmic masses united by a common base, have been called universal
5 shapes by art historian Brian McAvera, who credits them with subconscious appeal to our essential humanity. Yet, this characterization is not entirely comforting, for the biomorphic figures, many of which are suggestive of the female figure, can both soothe and disturb as they evoke motherhood, sexuality, or even a surreal anxiety. Moreover, Moore can be said to have explained and celebrated the void as much as he explored the body in his sculptures,
10 which, as time marched forward and his fame grew, came to be modeled rather than carved and more the product of mass-production techniques than of exacting attention to every inch of every surface.

Identify the Topic, Main Idea, Thesis, or Proposition

The more unfamiliar the subject matter of the passage is, the more basic your approach must be. Furthermore, working step by step to find meaning can help you focus. Determine the main idea first. If you can't identify the main idea, then start by identifying the simple subject, or topic, of the passage. For example, the topic of Passage 1 is the sculptures of Henry Moore.

To get from topic or subject to thesis, main idea, or proposition, ask yourself what the author is saying about the topic or subject. If you can establish only part of that thesis, main idea, or proposition, do as much as you can. For example, you might begin identifying the thesis of Passage 1 as:

> The author is saying that Henry Moore's sculptures consist of large flowing masses, some of which are figures that both comfort and disturb.

Clarify Your Understanding

TIP

Don't forget these four test-taking strategies listed in Chapter 1: (1) anticipate and use the clock, (2) skip and return to questions, (3) eliminate answer choices that you know are incorrect, and (4) use educated guessing.

There are a variety of techniques for clarifying understanding. One is to ask and answer questions as you read. For example, you might ask yourself what a concept means or the meaning of a word in the context of the passage. As you read Passage 1 on Henry Moore, you might ask yourself what *biomorphic* means. At least one question on the reading comprehension test is almost certain to be about the meaning of a key word. Often, this word will convey a meaning that is specific to the context. Again, if you can establish only part of that meaning, do at least that much, using knowledge of word parts, context clues, or other applicable strategies. For example:

> In the passage, the term *biomorphic* seems to have a specific meaning that is related to shapes, figures, and nature. The word part *bio–* suggests humans or animals; the word part *morph–* suggests forms or shapes.

Another way to clarify understanding is by stopping to restate or paraphrase information. This usually involves rereading the previous sentence or perhaps a couple of sentences. For example, you might stop and ask yourself just exactly what the second sentence in the passage is saying. Restate whatever you can. Don't worry if you can't restate everything. Your thinking might be something like the following:

The second sentence of the test passage says that Moore's work was abstract; that is, he didn't represent things as they really are. It says his shapes are biomorphic, or forms of humans and animals. It says his sculptures had a relationship to nature.

Summarize

Quickly summarize the passage to yourself after you have read it, but before you begin answering the question(s). This strategy can also help you clarify your understanding.

GENERAL STRATEGIES FOR ANSWERING MULTIPLE-CHOICE QUESTIONS

The purposes, structures, and content of the reading comprehension passages and questions you will encounter on the GRE® General Test will vary widely, and, unfortunately, there is no single strategy and no magic bullet that can guarantee success with all. In addition to active reading, the following ten general strategies will help you answer reading comprehension multiple-choice questions, whether you need to select one answer choice or one or more answer choices:

1. Restate the question.
2. Try answering the question before you read the answer choices.
3. Read all the answers before you choose.
4. Compare answer choices to each other and the question.
5. Avoid selecting an answer you don't fully understand.
6. Choose the *best* answer.
7. Pay attention to structure and structural clues.
8. Don't select an answer just because it's true.
9. Substitute answer choices in word meaning questions.
10. Choose the answer that *doesn't* fit for EXCEPT questions.

This list may seem like a huge number of strategies to remember and use on test day, but there are two things to remember about the strategies:

1. Not all strategies will work for all questions. That said, the first three strategies will work for any question. If you've taken the SAT® or AP® Subject Tests, you've used these strategies.

2. The more you practice using the strategies as you work through this book, the easier they will be to remember, to figure out which are the appropriate strategies to use for different questions, and to apply on test day.

For the first six strategies in this section, you will focus on a single reading comprehension passage and a single question. There is an additional strategy later in the chapter for multiple-choice questions—select one or more answer choices. You will want to mark the page with the passage and the question with a sticky note or other bookmark so that you can refer to it easily.

Question 1 is based on the following passage.

Sculptor Henry Moore (born 1898) achieved prominence in the 1930s with his earliest recumbent figures. An English abstractionist, Moore has also been associated with romantic feeling in the relationship of his biomorphic forms to nature. His sculptures, which often
Line consist of large flowing, rhythmic masses united by a common base, have been called universal
5 shapes by art historian Brian McAvera, who credits them with subconscious appeal to our essential humanity. Yet, this characterization is not entirely comforting, for the biomorphic figures, many of which are suggestive of the female figure, can both soothe and disturb as they evoke motherhood, sexuality, or even a surreal anxiety. Moreover, Moore can be said to have explained and celebrated the void as much as he explored the body in his sculptures,
10 which, as time marched forward and his fame grew, came to be modeled rather than carved and more the product of mass-production techniques than of exacting attention to every inch of every surface.

For Question 1, choose only <u>one</u> answer choice.

1. The passage suggests that the main quality of Moore's work is most nearly which of the following?

    A. A romantic presentation of human or animal forms

    B. An attempt to reinvent abstraction as a mirror of nature

    C. A soothing evocation of the often recumbent female figure

    D. A blend of artisan craft and mass production techniques

    E. A use of flowing forms with universal appeal but diverse response

Time Out for Some Advice on Unfamiliar Material

If you come across a passage like this that is totally unfamiliar to you—whether it is about fine arts, political geography, or any other subject—don't leap to the conclusion that the passage is too difficult for you. Instead, master your emotions and proceed logically by using your strategies. As the GRE® website says, "Do not be discouraged if you encounter unfamiliar material; all the questions can be answered on the basis of the information provided in the passage."

You may be tempted to "mark" a passage like this to come back to later without giving it an active reading. Although the format of the test makes it easy to mark a question and return to it, use this strategy only if you are still stumped after having given the passage a purposeful, focused reading and have at least attempted to answer one or more of the questions. This is especially true when a reading comprehension passage is accompanied by more than one question.

Think about it. If you save for later a passage with three questions, and you are doing a typical test with 20 questions, you have just delayed answering approximately 15 percent of the test. Putting off large chunks of the test until later can lead to increased anxiety. Saving, returning, and, most of all, rereading also eats into your precious time. Sometimes you may have no choice, but give the passage and its questions a good try first.

Restate the Question

Here again is the question that accompanies the passage on Henry Moore.

For Question 1, choose only <u>one</u> answer choice.

1. The passage suggests that the main quality of Moore's work is most nearly which of the following?

   A. A romantic presentation of human or animal forms

   B. An attempt to reinvent abstraction as a mirror of nature

   C. A soothing evocation of the often recumbent female figure

   D. A blend of artisan craft and mass production techniques

   E. A use of flowing forms with universal appeal but diverse response

Read the direction line and the question. What does the direction line ask you to do?

> The direction line says to select one answer. On the computer version of the test, the ovals that precede the answer choices convey the same information.

In addition to verifying what you must select, paraphrase or restate the question to be sure that you know what you are being asked to find:

- The question asks which is the most important quality of Moore's work, according to the author?

- You need to find and weigh all the characteristics of Moore's work that are presented in the passage and decide which is most important. Although this strategy may seem to involve looking for supporting details, you're actually really looking for the main idea, or topic, of the passage.

Try Answering the Question Before You Read the Answer Choices

This strategy is especially useful when you feel confident that you understand the passage. But it is also a useful strategy when you feel unsure of your understanding. By trying to answer the question in your own words first, you can get part of the way toward the correct answer. When you check the answers, you'll either find an answer that's the same as your idea, but in different words, or no answer that is even close to yours, so you know you've missed the point. Coming up with your own answer or a partial answer is, in fact, a way to clarify your understanding in relation to the specific question you have to answer.

Again, returning to Question 1, come up with the best answer you can before you begin to eliminate choices. For example, you might come up with this answer:

> The passage emphasizes forms and shapes that suggest humans or animals and their effects on the viewer. The viewer has an immediate recognition because the shapes are "universal," but recognition doesn't always mean comfort or a good feeling.

ALERT!

Don't rely on outside information to answer questions. Base your answers solely on the information in the passage. You may know that mannerism was a Renaissance art style, but in this passage mannerism is used in its twentieth-century sense.

Read All the Answers Before You Choose

After you've developed some idea of the correct answer, read all the answer choices listed. Don't read the first one and, if it seems correct, choose it and go on to the next question. Keep in mind that a well-constructed test will have answers that are close approximations of the correct answer.

For example, you might jump to the conclusion that the right answer to the question about the main quality of Moore's work is choice A. Reading carefully through all the answers, and eliminating them one by one, however, may lead you to a different choice.

Compare Answer Choices to Each Other and the Question

Suppose you eliminate three answer choices, but cannot eliminate one of the two remaining choices. If you are crunched for time, you can make your best guess at this point. If you have time, however, don't guess before you try this strategy: Compare the choices to each other and to the question. The following is based on Question 1 and assumes that you've eliminated choices B, C, and D:

- Choice A is very different from choice E. Choice A does get to the heart of Moore's work by mentioning human or animal, or biomorphic, forms. Yet it calls them "romantic," an idea that a later detail about mass production seems to refute. In comparison, choice E also presents the fundamental idea of forms while incorporating more of the fundamental facts: first, that the forms are universal, and second, that they evoke diverse responses, which the passage explains can range from soothing to disturbing.

- The question asks for a main quality. Choice E encompasses the notion of universal appeal; of abstract, flowing forms; and of "diverse" responses of the viewer. In comparison, the key word in choice A seems to be "romantic," which, in the context of the passage, is a less important quality that is not developed, or perhaps even contradicted or limited, by the author. Therefore, choice E is the best answer. **The correct answer is E.**

Avoid Selecting an Answer You Don't Fully Understand

Again, suppose you have eliminated three choices, but you're at a loss to eliminate one of the two remaining answers. As you reread the choices, avoid selecting the one that is more confusing or unintelligible to you. You might work your way through your dilemma something like this:

- Choice A is hard to understand. The passage implies that a romantic feeling is evoked by Moore's forms, but the term *romantic* isn't really ever defined in the passage, and it seems to relate to only some of his work.

- Choice E is easier to understand and also clearly sums up more of the ideas in the paragraph. Therefore, choice E is more likely to be correct.

Choose the *Best* Answer

Once again, suppose you have been able to eliminate three choices, but are having trouble eliminating one of the two remaining answers. As you try to choose, remember that your goal is to select the *best* answer. Therefore, if both answers appear reasonable or possibly correct to you, your task is to choose the better—more reasonable—of the two.

- Choice E sums up the ideas in the paragraph. It summarizes essential or main qualities of Moore's work: universality, abstract forms, and diverse response.

- On the other hand, choice A seems as if it could possibly be correct, but it definitely doesn't sum up most of the main ideas that the passage's author attributes to Moore.

- You're looking for the main idea of the passage, so choice E is more likely to be correct (because it encompasses more key information).

For the next four strategies, you will focus on a multiparagraph passage and four questions to learn to apply the strategies. Once again, it is probably wise to mark the passage for easy reference as you try out the various strategies.

Passage 2 differs in three significant ways from the first passage you read. First, it has four paragraphs. While most passages you encounter on the test will be a single paragraph in length, at least one passage is likely to be longer. Second, notice also that this passage contains some information in bold type. Figure that this must be important information to pay close attention to as you read. Finally, note that the passage contains two arrows. These arrows relate to the select-in-passage question type covered later in this chapter.

For Questions 2-6, choose only <u>one</u> answer choice unless otherwise indicated.

Questions 2–6 are based on the following passage.

Americans take a profound interest in wildlife, as long as that wildlife is in other people's backyards. American Audubon societies strive mightily to save Central America's jaguar, while schoolchildren across the nation focus on China's endangered panda and the African
Line elephant. But when it comes to America's own most pressing wildlife problem, deer, the
5 public is curiously—and dangerously—somnolent.

Adaptable to a wide range of habitats, including the paved roads and manicured, pesticide-rich lots of suburban America, white-tailed deer live in at least part of every state except for, possibly, Hawaii, Alaska, and Utah. And just about everywhere, as their numbers increase yet their habitat decreases, the animals are wreaking havoc: **destroying public and**
10 **private landscape; eating row crops and nursery stock; and, most significantly, carrying with increasingly alarming frequency tick-borne pathogens that cause Lyme disease, babesiosis, and other newly emerging diseases.**

While states pretend to deal with these animals by establishing hunting seasons to harvest populations, as well as by offering information on control, the problem escalates. One reason
15 for this may be that deer populations were endangered in the 1930s and brought back, leading wildlife agencies to trumpet the success of "sustainable hunting." Another more disturbing reason may be that Americans think deer are cute. Called "charismatic" animals on at least one website, tick-infested deer are seemingly beloved for their fluffy white tails; their large, dark eyes; their lithe and graceful prancing motions; and, perhaps, most of all, their reticence
20 for retreat in the face of human contact.

But what are the economics of cuteness? Just a few annual costs include $2 billion borne by U.S. farmers and 150 human fatalities plus $3.8 billion in insurance payouts to drivers who hit deer. Additionally, there's the approximately $11,000 per case of Lyme disease—and all of these costs will rise dramatically as deer populations grow. These costs alone show **the**
25 **necessity of stopping deer in their tracks.**

Now, read Question 2.

2. What function do the two groups of words in bold type serve in this argument?

    A. The first anticipates the argument's conclusion; the second provides support for that conclusion.

    B. The first supports the proposition or opinion; the second states the proposition or opinion.

    C. The first presents the proposition or opinion; the second presents the final support for the proposition or opinion.

    D. The first serves as an intermediate conclusion; the second serves as a definitive conclusion.

    E. The first presents the argument; the second restates and reinforces the argument.

Pay Attention to Structure and to Structural Clues

When you read actively, you should be drawing a conclusion about the author's purpose. Many passages inform, but the purpose of this particular passage is to persuade. As part of reading actively, you should also be looking for the main idea, proposition, or thesis of the passage. The point of view of this passage is that more has to be done to stop the problems caused by deer. Once you know you are reading a persuasive piece—an argument, in other words—and once you determine the thesis or proposition, begin the work of tracing the argument's development and separating claims from evidence, opinions, and judgments.

- The first segment in bold type presents a series of effects caused by deer; these facts support the opinion that strong measures are necessary to stop the problems caused by deer.

- The second segment in bold type states an opinion.

Persuasive writing is often organized inductively in order to lead the reader through a process of reasoning. With this method of organization, the conclusion often presents the opinion for the first time; it may also draw a final conclusion or present a clincher statement that reinforces the opinion or proposition. Therefore, while a proposition, or thesis, may be stated at the beginning of an argument both for clarity and clout, stating it at the end of an argument, as if it were the most logical conclusion possible, is also rhetorically effective.

- The first segment in bold type presents facts about the dangerous and costly effects of deer as supporting evidence for the idea that stronger measures for controlling deer are necessary.

- The intermediate claim "the animals are wreaking havoc," which leads up to the facts and signals a list with its closing colon, suggests that support for the claim will follow.

- The factual claims about land destruction, crop damage, and disease are evidence that supports the intermediate claim as well as the conclusion drawn by the final sentence, and the final sentence clearly states the proposition, or argument. Therefore, choice B is correct. **The correct answer is B.**

Sometimes, structural clues reveal the writer's thinking over the course of an entire paragraph. For example, a passage from the GRE® General Test online sample questions reveals the following structure, and clues to meaning, embedded in it:

- Sentence 1: "According to …"
- Sentence 2: "In this view …"
- Sentence 3: "… however …"

These clues tell you that you're reading one view—stated and explained in sentences 1 and 2. In sentence 3, you're reading its rebuttal or some significant qualification of it (beginning with *however*) in the remainder of the paragraph.

In another sample passage, there are no structural clues until the passage's midway point. These structural clues follow:

- Sentence 4: "It follows that …"
- Sentence 6: "Therefore, …"

These clues tell you that you're most likely reading an argument.

To give you more practice with argument questions, try Question 3, which is based on the same passage as Question 2. The GRE® General Test showcases the following type of question more than once in its practice materials.

3. Which of the following, if it were true, would most seriously weaken the argument?

   A. Expenditures for landscape damages include losses of plantings and foundations, as well as costs of fencing, netting, and repellants.

   B. Controversial deer culling proposals tend to elicit organized resistance from anti-hunting constituencies.

   C. The highest cost of automobile accidents involving deer is reported by the states of Pennsylvania and Michigan, with annual price tags of $343 and $339 million respectively.

   D. In its most recent report, the CDC states that 95% of all cases of Lyme disease originated in just thirteen states.

   E. Hunting in the United States, mainly deer, generates some $67 billion in business revenues and creates approximately 1 million jobs annually.

This question asks you to find the relationship between a hypothetical or an alternative idea and the ideas in the passage. This is an application question because you're applying information from one situation to other situations. You will use a variety of reading comprehension skills to answer the question, including making inferences, drawing conclusions, and evaluating hypotheses.

Try answering Question 3 on your own before you read the following answer rationale:

The argument is that stronger measures are needed to stop the problems presented by the white-tailed deer in America.

- You can eliminate choice A because this information supports the idea that damage to the landscape from deer is significant and costly.

- You can eliminate choice B because it neither weakens nor strengthens the argument; instead, it heads off in a new direction by anticipating, but not countering, opposition to the thesis.

- Choice C is incorrect because it adds increased specificity to the costs of crashes with deer, which is already reported in paragraph 4 and strengthened by this information.

- Choice D is tempting, but also incorrect, because this fact does not necessarily clash in any way with facts in the passage that point to the increasing incidence and cost of Lyme disease.

- Choice E shows the great economic benefit of deer. This idea contradicts the thesis, or controlling opinion. Therefore, choice E is correct. **The correct answer is E.**

Don't Select an Answer Just Because It's True

You want to choose an answer because it answers the question. Some answers may be true, but that doesn't mean that they answer the question. With a question like the following, restating the question is especially useful. It will help you to anchor your thoughts before you dive into the verbiage of the answer choices.

4. The passage suggests which of the following as a cause of American insensitivity to the problems created by white-tailed deer?

   A. White-tailed deer thrive even in conditions that are seemingly hostile to them.

   B. Americans prefer to focus on the wildlife issues of other countries and continents.

   C. Hunting has proven to be an inadequate means of controlling the deer population.

   D. A self-congratulatory stance derived from past wildlife management efforts prevails.

   E. The white-tailed deer does not pose equal threats in every state in the nation.

Try answering this question on your own first. Remember to read all the answer choices before you choose one.

- Choice A is true, but the author does not suggest it as a cause of insensitivity.

- Even though this statement is used to open the argument, the author never states a cause-effect relationship between this focus and insensitivity to the problems posed by deer. Instead, the author suggests the irony of the two co-existing attitudes, so choice B is incorrect.

- While the author implies the truth of choice C, that hunting has been an inadequate means of control, hunting is not given as a reason for insensitivity.

- Paragraph 3 presents two key reasons why the deer problem escalates, and, by implication, goes unsolved. Choice D is true, but keep reading to the end of the answer choices.

- While passage facts permit the reader to infer the truth of choice E (How can states without deer be as threatened by them as states with them?), it does not suggest this as a reason for failure to deal with the problems presented by deer.

Each of the five answers has some truth to it. But only choice D correctly answers the question of cause. Choice D is true, and it's the best answer because it's consistent with the cause-effect relationships stated or implied by the passage. **The correct answer is D.**

Substitute Answer Choices in Word Meaning Questions

Word meaning questions may appear more than once on the GRE® General Test. The context in which the word is used will help you choose the correct answers. Reading the answer choices may not be enough to get you to the correct answer because often a word will have several meanings and you need to find the meaning of the word as it is used in the passage. To do this, substitute each answer choice for the word in the passage.

5. In the passage, "lithe" (line 19) most nearly means

   A. light.

   B. supple.

   C. alacritous.

   D. labored.

   E. ambulatory.

You may already know that *lithe* means "nimble, supple, or graceful," choice B. If you don't know its meaning, however, you could substitute each answer choice in the sentence: "Called 'charismatic' animals on at least one website, tick-infested deer are seemingly beloved for their fluffy white tails; their large, dark eyes; their _____ and graceful prancing motions; and, perhaps, most of all, their reticence or retreat in the face of human contact."

-   While lithe movements might appear light, this is not the full, exact, or correct meaning of *lithe*, so choice A is incorrect.

-   Neither were the movements described as quick, so choice C doesn't work.

-   The context suggests movements that are the opposite of labored, so you can eliminate choice D.

-   Choice E doesn't work because *ambulatory* means "capable of movement" and does not describe the movement itself. **The correct answer is B.**

Choose the Answer That Doesn't Fit for EXCEPT Questions

You may find one or two EXCEPT questions. These questions ask you to find the answer choice that doesn't fit with the other answer choices. That is, you're looking for the wrong answer as your right answer. If you took the SAT® or any AP® Subject Tests, you'll remember this question type.

6. All of the following support the claim of "cute," likable, or endearing deer EXCEPT their:

   A. association with nursery stock.

   B. physiognomy.

   C. agility.

   D. seeming shyness.

   E. avoidance of human beings.

The article mentions damage to nursery stock as evidence of the problems caused by deer, so choice A does not support the claim of cuteness. Choices B, C, D, and E are developed with details about the appearance and behavior of deer. Physiognomy, or facial appearance, is touched on with details about the deer's eyes, agility is implied by descriptive details about movement, and shyness and avoidance are expressed by the passage details of "reticence" and "retreat." Only choice A fails to support the claim. **The correct answer is A.**

NOTE

Remember to use other strategies for multiple-choice questions, such as restating the questions and trying to come up with answers on your own.

ADDITIONAL STRATEGIES FOR MULTIPLE-CHOICE QUESTIONS—SELECT ONE OR MORE ANSWER CHOICES

You will find a few multiple-choice questions on the GRE® General Test that may require one or more answers to be correct. We say "may" because only one answer may be correct, or two, or all three choices. The direction for the question will state that you are to choose "all that apply." If you choose only choice A, and choice C is also correct, you won't get credit for the question. To get credit, you need to select "all that apply."

The multiple-choice questions—select one or more answer choices questions have only three choices listed as possible answers. Each choice is preceded by a square rather than an oval. For your convenience in checking answers, we have used A, B, and C to signal the answer choices.

The major strategy that you need to remember for answering questions that use the format of multiple-choice questions—select one or more answer choices is *to choose an answer that answers the question on its own.*

Choose an Answer That Answers the Question on Its Own

Each answer choice has to answer the question on its own. Don't make the mistake of thinking that because there may be more than one answer, combining partial answer choices gives you a complete answer. Always assess each answer as a standalone. Is it accurate? Is it complete? Then move on to the next answer and ask yourself the same questions.

Question 7 is based on the following passage.

Telematics, a science that will, conceivably, by the year 2025, allow every car to be connected to the internet, should be used to stop or significantly reduce the 1.48 million crashes now estimated to result from texting or other cellphone use while driving. Through a combination
Line of GPS and knowledge of individual drivers' habits and their typical locations during the day
5 gathered in part from mobile carriers, telematics has the potential both to block handheld use of phones and texting, as well as to shut down a driver's phone when a text or call comes in. While insurance companies as well as many mobile carriers have become ardent opponents of texting while driving, a network-level technology solution, not to mention the Big Brother-style encroachment on civil rights, gives significant pause. Will millions of lives hang in the
10 balance, then, until the self-driving car makes the issue moot?

For Question 7, consider each answer individually and choose all that apply.

7. The second-to-last sentence "While insurance . . . significant pause." (lines 7–9) serves which of the following purposes in the passage?

   A. It counters the argument expressed in the first sentence.

   B. It provides evidence for the positive effect of telematics.

   C. It suggests the limitation of freedom imposed by telematics.

The first sentence argues that telematics should be employed to cut the accident rate resulting from cellphone use and texting. Although the second-to-last sentence begins with a kind of reassertion of the thesis, that sentence mainly brings up a problem with telematics, or the "network-level solution" involving mobile carriers: drivers being monitored and controlled "Big Brother" style. Therefore, the second-to-last sentence counters, or raises a point in opposition to, the first sentence, so choice A is correct. Choice B is incorrect because the next-to-the-last sentence does not supply evidence and is mainly about a negative consequence. However, choice C is correct because ultimately, the use of telematics described here is a surveillance system that curtails the freedom of the driver. **The correct answers are A and C.**

STRATEGIES FOR SELECT-IN-PASSAGE QUESTIONS

Select-in-passage questions ask you to choose a sentence within a passage as the correct answer. You will have a direction line, but no listing of multiple-choice answers (unless you're taking the paper-delivered test). For a passage that is a single paragraph, any sentence in the entire paragraph is fair game for the answer. For multiparagraph passages, arrows [→] mark the beginning and end of the text from which you should select the sentence. To make your choice, click on any part of the sentence that you determine to be the answer. If you click on a sentence that is not between the arrows, it will not be highlighted and will not register as an answer.

This may seem silly, but don't lose track of where a marked section begins and ends. You don't want to waste time analyzing sentences in a part of the passage that isn't the subject of the question. If you try to click on a sentence in the unmarked portion of the passage, it won't highlight, so your answer won't be wrong, but you will have wasted precious time.

Similar to answering questions with the multiple-choice questions—select one or more answer choices format, you need to assess each sentence in the marked section of a passage as a stand-alone sentence.

The special strategy that applies to select-in-passage questions is *match the sentence to the information*.

Match the Sentence to the Information

The GRE® General Test information materials about the test note two facts about select-in-passage questions. First, a select-in-passage question contains the description of a sentence—content, tone, purpose, author's perspective, or similar aspect. In answering the question, you must look for the sentence that contains that information. However, you should not select a sentence if any part of the information in the sentence doesn't match the question.

NOTE

International students taking the paper-delivered test will encounter both multiple-choice and select one answer question types in the select-in-passage portion of the test.

This relates to the second caveat for select-in-passage questions: A question may not necessarily describe all aspects of the sentence for the sentence to be the correct answer. Sentences in the passages may be long and complicated. A question may focus on one or two aspects of a sentence. The sentence you choose just can't *contradict* the description in the question.

Question 8 is based on the following passage.

Fareed Zakaria notes in *The Post-American World* that there really is no such thing as Asia; he calls Asia a Western cultural construct. In other words, Zakaria suggests that Asia isn't really a continent, which calls for an examination of the term *continent*. If continents are defined
Line as discrete landmasses separated by large bodies of water, then North and South America
5   should be one American continent, as the canal that separates them is neither a large nor a natural body of water. Furthermore, if continents are described as large landmasses separated by large bodies of water, then Greenland, one of Earth's largest islands, is rather arbitrarily defined as an island instead of a continent.

Other problems with the historical and cultural constructs that underlie the classification
10 of continents include the classification of smaller islands, especially those located beyond the continental shelf of their so-called "continent," such as Hawaii. Clearly, political constructs also affect historical classification. Indeed, a close look at how the word *continent* is applied proves Zakaria's point and shows that the meaning of the word has more to do with the conventions long established to identify the somewhat agreed-upon number of continents
15 on Earth than it has to do with strict geographical or other criteria.

For Question 8, choose only <u>one</u> answer choice.

8. In which sentence does the author state the main idea of the paragraph?

    A. The first sentence ("Fareed Zakaria … construct")

    B. The second sentence ("In other words, . . . *continent*")

    C. The fifth sentence ("Other problems . . . Hawaii")

    D. The sixth sentence ("Clearly . . . classification")

    E. The last sentence ("Indeed, a close . . . criteria")

Zakaria's assertion that Asia is not a discrete or unified continent leads into the topic of continents and how they are defined. Therefore, the first sentence is not a main idea, and choice A should be eliminated. Whereas the second sentence does clarify the first, it doesn't yet get to the central focus of the entire passage, which goes beyond the example of Asia, so choice B is also incorrect. Choice C is incorrect because it's an example that supports the main idea. Choice D must also be eliminated because it supports the main idea rather than states it. Choice E alone provides an overview idea that encapsulates the many ideas of the paragraph. Therefore, choice E is the correct answer. Notice how choice E does a bit more than state the main idea. It also affirms Zakaria's idea. Although Zakaria's point about Asia is a minor rather than major one, the remainder of the sentence does state the main idea. **The correct answer is E.**

PRACTICE QUESTIONS

For Questions 1–15, choose <u>one</u> answer choice unless otherwise directed.

Question 1 is based on the following passage.

Prosopagnosia, or face blindness, was lately given a boost in long-overdue recognition as a genetic disorder when the distinguished professor of neurology and best-selling author Oliver Sacks described his own affliction with the disease. Like other prosopagnosiacs, Sacks
Line has a fundamental inability to recognize faces, and not just the faces of random strangers or
5 people he met for the first time last week. One index to the profundity of Sacks's problem is reflected in a study that found that prosopagnosiacs who looked at photos of their own family members were unable to recognize 30% of the faces. Sacks himself admits that he often does not recognize a person whom he has met just five minutes before.

1. The passage achieves all of the following purposes EXCEPT:

   A. explain why prosopagnosia was given recognition as a genetic disorder.

   B. tell or imply how prosopagnosia manifests itself.

   C. cite research that helps define the challenges faced by prosopagnosiacs.

   D. personalize and humanize the disorder known as prosopagnosia.

   E. imply the severity of the challenges faced by prosopagnosiacs.

Questions 2–4 are based on the following passage.

Was ideology the leading actor in the unfinished drama that we call the Cold War? This question is endlessly disputed, often by attributing to the Soviets, as George F. Kennan was among the first to do, and to do at great length (in what became known as the "long
Line telegram"), a messianic impulse in terms of communism. Similarly, the centrality of antipathy
5 to capitalism in Soviet policy is usually emphasized. At the same time, no such messianic impulse is routinely attributed to the United States in terms of capitalism, and if antipathy to socialism is mentioned at all, it is couched in "necessary evil" rhetoric—or the necessary evil is implied. Almost as often, the argument does not pit economic systems, but instead presents the ideological struggle as one between democracy (the forces of good) and com-
10 munism (the forces of evil).

A more reasoned way of evaluating ideology as a principal actor is to concede that ideology only partially explains the origins of the Cold War. It was, then, only contributory to the lasting struggle between U.S. and Soviet interests that continues to this day, despite the collective historical agreement that the curtain fell on the final act of the Cold War with the
15 breakup of the Soviet Union.

All such arguments, however, no matter how they express the antagonism between the United States and the Soviet Union, focus on how one or both sides concentrated its resources on a triumph over the competing ideology. Yet, this is a myopic view, as it discounts the fundamental nature and priorities of powerful states. As Mary Hampton points out in
20 a point-counterpoint on this topic, the vital interests of every state, powerful or relatively

powerless, are not defined by ideology but by national security. Furthermore, a state will always seek to preserve its security, which might involve an internal shift in policy or new or shifting alliances; it will act, first and foremost, in accordance with its own power and the power distribution among states with which it is allied.

For Questions 2–4, consider each answer individually and choose all that apply.

2. Which is the first sentence in this passage to clearly reflect the author's perspective on a question posed earlier in the passage?

   A. Sentence 5 ("Almost as often … the forces of evil.")

   B. Sentence 8 ("All such arguments … competing ideology.")

   C. Sentence 10 ("As Mary Hampton … by national security.")

3. It can be inferred from the passage that the author believes that Mary Hampton

   A. has a limited understanding of the Cold War.

   B. is an authority on the topic of the Cold War.

   C. is correct in her belief that national security defines a country's ideology.

4. In the passage, "concentrated" (line 17) most nearly means

   A. thought hard about.

   B. reduced.

   C. thickened.

   D. focused.

   E. purified.

NOTE

In the computer-delivered version of the GRE® General Test, Question 2 would be a select-in-passage question rather than multiple-choice.

Questions 5–7 are based on the following passage.

The precipitate rise in the incidence of type 1, or juvenile, diabetes, as well as the startling decrease in average age at onset, has led to a nearly commensurate rise in causation hypotheses. The single factor that scientists have most commonly and consistently linked with the rise of
Line   cases of type 1 diabetes is weight gain, and, indeed, children's weights are increasing generation
  5   by generation, and the greater BMI (body mass index), the younger the child is likely to be at the age of onset. Other factors linked to this rise in incidence and decrease in average of age of onset and tracked with varying degrees of success in recent studies include psychological stress, the increased wealth of the homes in which the children reside, the increased levels of hygiene in the homes in which the children reside, and nourishment by infant formula during
 10   the first six months of life. Some of these theories have garnered more academic support than others, but, no matter how much support they have received, correlation is not causation.

5. The writer mentions greater BMI at earlier ages in this paragraph in order to

   A. introduce a common causation hypothesis.

   B. provide support for an implied argument.

   C. reinforce the importance of a healthful diet for children.

   D. provide a possible explanation for the confusion of cause and correlation.

   E. cast doubt on studies that collect data on wealth and hygiene.

6. Which of the following, if it were true, would most seriously weaken the import of a specific data set suggesting a correlation?

   A. The average age at onset of type 1 diabetes decreased by one year over a period of just five years.

   B. Nourishment by baby formula has not been correlated to a rise in BMI.

   C. Among stress factors, only poor performance in school and divorce have been shown to correlate with increased incidence of type 1 diabetes.

   D. The incidence of type 1 diabetes is rising at a slower rate among children who are not overweight.

   E. There is a higher rate of type 1 diabetes in households with incomes of more than $80,000 than in households with lower incomes.

For Question 7, consider each answer individually and choose all that apply.

7. The sentence "Some of these theories…correlation is not causation" (lines 10–11) serves which of the following purposes in the passage?

   A. It provides evidence for an argument against the conclusions previously stated in the passage.

   B. It makes an assertion that supports the conclusions previously stated in the passage.

   C. It questions the conclusions previously stated in the passage.

Questions 8–9 are based on the following passage.

Robert Frost is often categorized as an anti-Romantic writer, that is, as a poet whose poetry contradicts the ideals of Romanticism as embodied in the works of Wordsworth, Keats, Shelley, and others. **Simultaneously, he is categorized as an anti-modernist, a poet who**
Line **has little in common with his contemporaries, Eliot, Pound, Joyce, Woolf, and others.**
5 Nevertheless, because modernists declared that modernism was, among other things, the rejection of Romanticism, there can be only partial validity in the claim that Frost was both anti-Romantic and anti-modernist. **Instead, as the poems bear out, Frost was at once neither and a bit of both, and one does not have to look far in the poems for substantiation.** Whether the reader is "Stopping by Woods" or out among the "Birches," nature and wildness
10 are the gateways to introspection and imagination, even if emotion receives short shrift. At the same time, modernism asserts itself—albeit in traditional poetic form—in poems such

as "After Apple Picking," with its evocation of a transitional state of consciousness; and in "The Death of the Hired Man," "Desert Places," and "Acquainted with the Night" with their experience of alienation, loss, and despair.

8. It can be inferred that the author judges which of the following characteristics as most clearly defining or epitomizing Romanticism?

   A. The reliance on traditional poetic forms

   B. The rejection of modernism

   C. Nature and wildness as the gateway to introspection and imagination

   D. Poems such as "Stopping by Woods" and "Birches"

   E. Poems that evoke a transitional state of consciousness

9. In the passage, what is the primary purpose of the two groups of words in boldface type?

   A. The first provides contrast to the sentence that precedes it; the second expands upon and elucidates the sentence that precedes it.

   B. The first provides background information that leads up to the argument; the second presents the argument.

   C. The first reinforces the argument through contrast; the second explains the argument through explanation and expansion.

   D. The first states a position that the argument as a whole contradicts; the second presents the argument.

   E. The first provides contrast to the sentence that precedes it; the second provides evidence that supports the argument.

Questions 10–11 are based on the following passage.

When explaining the issues of urbanization in Africa of the late twentieth century, some textbooks conflate effects of the phenomenon with effects of urbanization in the newly industrialized cities of England in the early nineteenth century. That is, some historians
Line restrict their analysis to the problems of overcrowding, lack of sanitation, and inadequate
5 housing that occur in the wake of rapid mass movement from rural to urban areas. Their analysis ignores arguments, such as those put forth by the 1996 UN Habitat II conference, suggesting that economies of scale are preferable for the delivery of health care, clean water, electricity, and other needs. It further overlooks the freedoms available to women in the cities, where they may escape tribal or religious practices, or find fulfillment in both traditional and
10 nontraditional roles.

10. The author of the passage would most likely consider which of the following ideas most similar to the reasoning of historians mentioned in lines 3–5?

    A. Economies of scale is a relatively recent economic concept that suggests, not entirely accurately, that bigger is always better.

    B. The problems of overcrowding, lack of sanitation, and inadequate housing also occurred in major U.S. cities during the Industrial Revolution.

    C. The increased disparity in economic class in today's Mumbai cannot be attributed to globalization alone.

    D. Urbanization has a negative effect on traditional social mores and usually proves disruptive to cultural unity.

    E. The recent economic crises in Ireland may best be explained by examining financial crises in the United States in the late nineteenth century.

11. Which of the following, if it were true, most seriously undermines the support that the final sentence provides for the claim?

    A. Urban women are more likely than men to have to deal directly with the problems of lack of sanitation.

    B. Women in large urban centers often achieve a higher level of education than they achieve in rural areas.

    C. Many rural women find fulfillment through local tribal and religious practices.

    D. Inadequate housing in the cities often offers more advantages than adequate housing in rural areas.

    E. Women in large urban centers often work in the marketplace.

Questions 12–14 are based on the following passage.

Andrew Dickson White famously asserted that Darwin's *On the Origin of Species* came "into the theological world like a plough into an ant-hill." At all costs, the anthill had to be rebuilt with some ants reconstructing the same structure and others making only slight alterations
Line to it. Among the many ants rebuilding the hill was Teilhard de Chardin, who, among other
5 things, posited (without so much as a wink!) that the descent of man was actually the ascent of man. His new anthill took shape in *The Phenomenon of Man*, which Julian Huxley would subsequently hail as the synthesis of the "whole of knowable reality" and a triumph of human significance. Yet, the phrase "whole of knowable reality" is, along, of course, with Teilhard's fatuous scientific arguments, a clue to just how scientifically unpalatable this particular
10 philosophically respected, yet scientifically incoherent reconstruction of the anthill was. For example, P. B. Medawar found such flowery, unscientific, and abstract language "suffocating"— and the very obfuscation of sense.

12. Which of the following statements does the passage most clearly support?

A. The author believes that Teilhard de Chardin made at least one strong point about *On the Origin of Species.*

B. *The Phenomenon of Man* is a triumph of human significance.

C. The author of the passage agrees with the judgments of P. B. Medawar.

D. Andrew Dickson White is the foremost authority on Darwin's work.

E. *On the Origin of Species* is an influential but highly flawed work.

13. It can be inferred that P. B. Medawar took issue with all of the following aspects of *The Phenomenon of Man* EXCEPT the

A. blurring of scientific fact.

B. attempt to rebuild the anthill.

C. lack of concreteness and specificity.

D. rebuttal of Darwin's ideas in poetic language.

E. obfuscation of sense.

14. In the passage, "fatuous" (line 9) means

A. sensible.

B. sarcastic.

C. overweight.

D. famous.

E. foolish.

Question 15 is based on the following passage.

The pivotal considerations affecting the design of any stationary robotic arm are the central tasks and workspace, which will, in turn, affect the desired degrees of freedom (DOF). A relatively simple design might have just 3 DOFs—not counting any additional DOFs on the end effector or gripper. When designers create an FBD (free body diagram) for a new robotic arm, other considerations reflected in that diagram will include the limitations of each DOF, which should be accounted for in the FBD by annotations showing maximum joint angles and exact arm link lengths. Engineers commonly use a coordinate system known as the Denavit-Hartenberg (D-H) Convention for this purpose.

Line

5

15. According to the information in this passage, in what order would these steps in the design of a robotic arm most likely take place?

   A. Determine DOFs, plan for D-H, draw FBD.

   B. Determine maximum joint angles, draw FBD, add end effector or gripper.

   C. Draw FBD, annotate joints according to D-H system, determine DOFs.

   D. Identify robotic task(s), determine DOFs, create FBD with D-H.

   E. Create FBD, determine DOFs, add end effector DOF.

ANSWER KEY AND EXPLANATIONS

1. A	**6.** D	**11.** C
2. C	**7.** C	**12.** C
3. B, C	**8.** C	**13.** B
4. D	**9.** B	**14.** E
5. A	**10.** E	**15.** D

Passage Summary for Question 1: The passage introduces the phenomenon of prosopagnosia to the general reader through the lens of Oliver Sacks's experience of the disease. It briefly explains what prosopagnosia, or face blindness, is.

1. **The correct answer is A.** This question involves main idea and supporting details. The passage briefly tells how prosopagnosia manifests itself through the inability to recognize faces (choice B), cites research (choice C), personalizes and humanizes the issue by attaching a famous name to it (choice D), and suggests the severity of the disease (choice E) by suggesting that subjects don't recognize their own family members or people they've met five minutes earlier. Therefore, choices B, C, D, and E are incorrect answers to the question. What the passage doesn't tell is why the disease received attention as a genetic disorder (choice A).

Passage Summary for Questions 2–4: The passage argues that ideology was not a cause of the Cold War. The ideological argument, the writer explains, typically asserts that the Soviet Union alone was messianic, and that its system, unlike the capitalist system, was evil. The author acknowledges in the second paragraph that it is more rational to think of ideology as one cause, not the leading cause, of the Cold War, but then, in the third paragraph, the author calls any argument for ideology myopic, or short-sighted. Instead, the writer suggests that the Cold War occurred not because states were acting to preserve their ideology, but because states were acting to preserve their national security.

2. **The correct answer is C.** This question asks about author's perspective. The only question posed in the passage is whether ideology was a leading cause of the Cold War. Sentence 5 doesn't answer that question; instead, it helps explain the typical ideological argument, so eliminate choice A. Sentence 8 makes a summary statement about the ideological arguments, but doesn't answer the question, so eliminate choice B. Sentence 10 (choice C) most clearly implies the answer, which is that ideology was not the main cause; the vital interest of national security was.

3. **The correct answers are B and C.** The author refers to Mary Hampton's conclusion about the Cold War without contradicting or questioning it, which implies that the author accepts her as an authority on the topic of the Cold War and agrees with her conclusion, which is that national security defines a country's ideology. These correct choices contradict choice A, which incorrectly implies that the author does not accept Hampton as an authority on the Cold War and disagrees with her conclusion regarding national security. Remember to read the sentences around the sentence in question for its context. Substituting the answer choices in the sentence may also help.

4. **The correct answer is D.** Each answer choice could be used as a synonym for *concentrated*, but choice D is the only one that makes sense in this particular context. The United States and the Soviet Union did more than think hard about their resources, so choice A is not the most logical definition. If they had reduced their resources, they would have been defeating their own efforts, so choice B is incorrect. It is odd to say that a country "thickened its resources," so choice C is not the best answer. Similarly, a country would not purify its resources, so choice E does not make sense.

Passage Summary for Questions 5–7: This passage mentions various theories, or causation hypotheses, for the rise in incidence, or decrease in age of onset of type 1 diabetes. It begins with what has been shown to be the most common and consistent correlation with the rise of the disease, weight gain; it also presents the correlation between BMI and early onset. The writer goes on to mention other correlations, some of which have more support than others: psychological stress, household wealth, household cleanliness, and infant formula. Yet, the author warns, none of these correlations is necessarily a cause.

5. **The correct answer is A.** Like many of the questions on the GRE® General Test, this question is about main idea and supporting details. The passage implies that scientists have most consistently explored weight gain as a cause of type 1 diabetes; weight gain is most commonly and consistently linked with the rise in incidence. While scientists have found that the increased incidence correlates with this rise, not that it causes the disease, this idea nevertheless constitutes a causation hypothesis (choice A). Choice B can be eliminated because this paragraph is informational; there is no implied argument. The passage does not state or imply anything about a healthful diet, so choice C is incorrect. Choice D is also incorrect because the passage clearly states that psychological stress, increased wealth, increased levels of hygiene, and infant formula have all been linked either to the rise in incidence or to the decrease in average age of onset of the disease. The passage does not cast doubt on any studies, so choice E is also incorrect.

6. **The correct answer is D.** This is an application question. Both choices A and E would strengthen the correlation, so they should be eliminated. Choice B should also be eliminated because, among other reasons, the question refers to a single data set. Choice C is also incorrect because the cited forms of stress do fall under the category of psychological stress. Even though the incidence of type 1 diabetes is rising at a slower rate among children who are not overweight, it is still rising; therefore, choice D undercuts or weakens the correlation between being overweight and developing the disease. Remember, the phrase "if it were true" signals that you're looking for an answer that *isn't* true. Think of it as another kind of "EXCEPT" or "NOT" question.

7. **The correct answer is C.** The sentence makes a general statement that questions the logic of how the conclusions previously stated in the passage were reached. It is not specific enough to serve as evidence to actually argue against those conclusions, so choice A is not the best answer. It also does not support those conclusions, so choice B is incorrect.

Passage Summary for Questions 8 and 9: The author argues that while some people call Frost anti-Romantic and others call him anti-modern, both labels can apply—and both labels don't apply. The author then provides evidence to show that Frost was Romantic, at least in one sense, while admitting that the poems cited are not true to all aspects of Romanticism. The writer also provides evidence that Frost was modern, at least in one sense, while also admitting that Frost was traditional in terms of poetic form.

8. **The correct answer is C.** This question asks only about supporting details. Choices D and E can be eliminated because poems are not characteristics. The phrase about "traditional poetic forms" is couched in the discussion of what modernism is "not," so choice A is unlikely to be the answer. Nothing in the passage suggests that Romanticism is the rejection of modernism, so choice B is incorrect. The answer to this question appears in the third sentence. Here, the author is explaining why Frost "was at once neither and a bit of both." Since the second of the two sentences that follow is about modernism, it can be inferred that the first is about Romanticism. That is where the words about nature and wildness appear.

9. **The correct answer is B.** Did you notice that the question is asking you to apply information to come up with your answer? While choice A provides an accurate description of what the sentences do in the passage, it doesn't describe the primary purpose of the two groups of words in bold type. You can also eliminate choices C, D, and E because they don't accurately explain the purpose of the word groups. Choice B is the best answer—the most accurate answer—but only reading through all the answer choices will assure you of this.

Passage Summary for Questions 10 and 11: The passage says that some textbooks mistakenly merge the issues of urbanization in late twentieth-century Africa with the issues of urbanization in the industrialized cities of England during the early nineteenth century. That is, they explain a contemporary or recent problem by providing the same explanations that have been given for a much different time and place. According to the author, these historians ignore twentieth-century ideas such as economies of scale and the changed and changing status of women.

10. **The correct answer is E.** This is another application question. The passage makes it clear that historians don't take into account the notion of economies of scale, so choice A is incorrect. Choices B, C, and D take the ideas of the passage off into entirely new directions, unrelated to the reasoning specified in the question, so they should be eliminated. Only choice E suggests a line of reasoning in which the problems of today are explained by the events of the past.

11. **The correct answer is C.** How did you do with this application question? The claim is that some textbooks erroneously suggest that urbanization in Africa today leads to the same problems as it did, or is much the same phenomenon as it was, during the Industrial Revolution. The final sentence of the paragraph supports that claim by suggesting that women in particular benefit from urbanization (that is, it's not necessarily the nineteenth-century England industrial scourge) because their movement from rural areas to the cities can liberate women from tribal and religious practices, which, the passage implies, can oppress them or diminish their sphere of influence. Therefore, to undermine the claim, the correct answer has to say something about how women are not diminished by tribal life, or that city life oppresses them. Choice D can be immediately eliminated because it doesn't relate to women. Choices A and E neither support nor weaken the claim, whereas choice B strengthens it. Choice C is then the only correct answer because it claims that many rural women are fulfilled through local tribal and religious practices.

Passage Summary for Questions 12–14: The passage begins with White's famous response to Darwin's On the Origin of Species, *which suggests that Darwin's huge, new, powerful ideas completely upset the little world of ants—that is, people who were used to thinking a certain way and simply could not accept the fundamental shift in worldview that Darwin presented. The implied claim is that ants began rebuilding the anthill, or that "little" people with little ideas began to refute Darwin's colossal ideas. One philosopher the passage maligns for "rebuilding," and, therefore, misreading or subverting Darwin, is Pierre Teilhard de Chardin. The passage also mentions responses to Teilhard de Chardin: there was Julian Huxley who lavishly praised the work, and P.B. Medawar who disliked it immensely, in large part because of Teilhard de Chardin's flowery language.*

12. **The correct answer is C.** The author is extremely dismissive of the beliefs and judgments of Teilhard de Chardin and Julian Huxley, and so is P. B. Medawar. The author also refers to Medawar's judgments unquestioningly and uncritically, which implies agreement with those judgments. There is no evidence to support choice A in the passage; the author is completely dismissive of Teilhard. Choice B is the conclusion of Julian Huxley, not the author, who is completely dismissive of both Huxley and *The Phenomenon of Man*. Although the author quotes Andrew Dickson White's comment about Darwin's work in the passage, there is not enough evidence to reach the extreme conclusion in choice D. The author never implies that *Origin of Species* really needed to be rebuilt, so there is not enough support for the statement in choice E.

13. **The correct answer is B.** Supporting details are the subject of this EXCEPT question. The passage states directly that Teilhard de Chardin's *The Phenomenon of Man* contains absurd scientific arguments and is also scientifically unpalatable because of the very "flowery" way in which the work is written. When the author calls Teilhard's work an "incoherent reconstruction," he or she is stating that it lacked sense. Medawar also takes issue with how the book obfuscates sense. Eliminate both choices A and E. Medawar's complaint about the flowery language eliminates choices C and D as well. Medawar does not, however, object to Teilhard de Chardin's or anyone else's attempt to "rebuild the anthill"—or rebut Darwin, so choice B is correct.

14. **The correct answer is E.** The author mocks Teilhard de Chardin's arguments throughout the passage, so choice E makes the most sense. Choice A is the opposite of *fatuous*. Choice B seems to mistake *fatuous* for *facetious*, which means "sarcastic." Choice C seems to mistakenly conclude that *fat* is a root word in *fatuous*. Choice D has a somewhat similar spelling to that of *fatuous*, but the two words are not synonyms.

Passage Summary for Question 15: The passage presents a few of the basic concepts in the design of a robotic arm, including identifying the central tasks and the workspace, determining the degrees of freedom, making a diagram, and labeling that diagram with coordinates.

15. **The correct answer is D.** To give you more practice, here is another application question. The passage implies that the first considerations in this design are the central tasks and the workspace; these must be known in order to determine the degrees of freedom (DOF) that the robotic arm must have. Although it may not be clear on first reading, the order of information in the paragraph is basically sequential; therefore, since choices A, B, C, and E do not follow the paragraph order, they must be eliminated.

SUMMING IT UP

- There are approximately ten reading comprehension passages on the Verbal Reasoning sections of the GRE® General Test.

- Most passages will be one paragraph in length, though you will find one or two passages that have multiple paragraphs.

- Passages may be informational, analytical, or persuasive.

- There are three formats for questions: (1) multiple-choice—select one answer choice, (2) multiple-choice—select one or more answer choices, and (3) select-in-passage.

- The select-in-passage questions on the computer-delivered test will require students to choose a sentence within the passage to highlight as the answer. For international students taking the paper-delivered version, the select-in-passage questions will be in the form of multiple-choice questions—select one answer questions.

- Computer-delivered versions of the GRE® General Test will have approximately 20 questions for each of the two Verbal Reasoning sections, of which perhaps more than half will be reading comprehension questions. The time limit is 30 minutes. Students taking the paper-delivered version will have 25 questions to be completed in 35 minutes.

- Multiple-choice questions—select one answer questions are preceded by ovals. Multiple-choice questions—select one or more answer choices are preceded by squares.

- Multiple-choice questions—select one answer questions are followed by a list of five possible answer options. Multiple-choice questions—select one or more answer choices are followed by a list of only three answers.

- Answer all questions based only on the information contained in the passage. Don't use anything from your own experience or outside knowledge.

- Don't allow your own opinions to enter into your selection of an answer.

- You will find that certain types of questions recur among the reading comprehension questions: main idea (major point), supporting details (minor points), author's perspective, application, and word meaning.

- Remember to use the following active reading strategies when reading the passages:
  o Identify the topic, main idea, thesis, or proposition.
  o Clarify your understanding.
  o Summarize what you've read.

- The following strategies can be helpful for both kinds of multiple-choice questions:
  o Restate the question.
  o Try answering the question before you read the answer choices.
  o Read all the answers before you choose.
  o Compare answer choices to each other and the question.
  o Avoid selecting an answer you don't fully understand.
  o Choose the *best* answer.
  o Pay attention to structure and structural clues.

- o   Don't select an answer just because it's true.
- o   Substitute answer choices in word meaning questions.
- o   Choose the answer that *doesn't* fit for EXCEPT questions.

- The following strategy applies to multiple-choice—select one or more answer choices questions: *choose an answer that answers the question on its own.*

- In addition to choosing an answer that stands on its own, the following strategy can be helpful for answering select-in-passage questions: *match the sentence to the information.*

Strategies for Text Completion Questions

OVERVIEW

- **Basic Information About Text Completion Questions**
- **Strategies for Text Completion**
- **Practice Questions**
- **Answer Key and Explanations**
- **Summing It Up**

The GRE® General Test has at least two Verbal Reasoning sections. Reading comprehension, text completion, and sentence equivalence questions are all included within the Verbal Reasoning sections. This chapter describes the question formats for text completion test items and also provides a discussion of strategies to help you answer this question type.

BASIC INFORMATION ABOUT TEXT COMPLETION QUESTIONS

The text completion questions on the GRE® General Test assess your ability not only to actively interpret and evaluate what you read, but also to supply words and phrases whose meaning is consistent with the ideas that are presented. You will complete text by choosing among three to five options to fill in one, two, or three blanks in a passage. You can expect around one quarter to one third of the questions on each Verbal Reasoning section to be text completion questions, that is, five to seven questions.

The text completion items (as well as the sentence equivalence items) test your vocabulary. (In some ways, they take the place of the antonyms and analogies questions that used to be on the GRE® test.) To do well on these questions, you need to know "big" words—words such as *refulgent, dissimulation,* and *deleterious.* Not all the words are a test of the size of your vocabulary, however. Some items will involve words that are close in meaning or ones that represent an unusual meaning of a familiar word.

As you will see in reading this chapter, the text completion items are not just about vocabulary. They also test your reading comprehension skills. Furthermore, you may also have to apply your knowledge of grammar and usage in order to choose the best answers.

Regardless of the number of blanks, each question is worth one point. All the blanks for a test item must be answered correctly in order to earn a point for that question.

Chapter 7

Passages and Question Formats

Unlike the reading comprehension questions, the text completion items offer a predictable sameness of format. Overall, the text completion passages are much less intimidating. Generally speaking, you will need to spend less time with a text completion passage than with a reading comprehension passage. Of course, the shorter length of a text completion passage, compared to the typical reading comprehension passage, also contributes significantly to greater ease of reading.

Text completion questions are fill-in-the-blank questions. The blanks are embedded in passages of different lengths, ranging from one sentence to approximately five sentences.

- In single sentences, you will typically be required to fill in just one blank. There are, however, exceptions.
- In passages that consist of multiple sentences, you will most likely be required to fill in two or three blanks.

Text completion items are interspersed with the other test items in the Verbal Reasoning sections. Each text completion question appears on a separate screen. In the computer-delivered test, all passages are short enough to display on a single screen; you won't need to scroll or change screens to answer a text completion question.

The Direction Line and Answer Choices

Text completion items have only one type of direction line, worded something like the following:

For Questions 1–10, choose <u>one</u> answer for each blank. Select from the appropriate column for each blank. Choose the answer that best completes the sense of the text.

In most cases, you will be selecting a single word for each blank. Occasionally, you will be presented with a list of phrases or group of words from which to select the answer.

- If the sentence or passage contains only *one blank*, there will be five answer choices listed in a single column.
- If the sentence or passage contains *two blanks*, you will choose the first answer from a column of three choices (Blank (i)) and the second from a second column of three choices (Blank (ii)).
- If the sentence or passage contains *three blanks*, you will choose each answer from one of three columns—Blank (i), Blank (ii), Blank (iii)—with three choices each.

To select an answer in the computer-delivered test, click on the cell that contains your answer choice. If you change your mind, clicking on another cell will change your answer. In the paper-delivered test, simply fill in the appropriate answer choice.

STRATEGIES FOR TEXT COMPLETION

Text completion questions lend themselves to a variety of specific strategies. As you read through the following strategies, note that the first four are really commonsense reminders.

1. Try answering the question before you read the answer choice(s).
2. Focus on one blank at a time.
3. If there is more than one blank, complete the blanks in the order that makes sense to you.
4. Check your answer(s) in place.

The last four strategies ask you to make use of what you learned in English composition classes.

1. Use structural clues.
2. Consider tone and style.
3. Consider grammar and usage.
4. Avoid selecting a word or phrase that you don't fully understand or is unfamiliar.

In addition, remember to apply the four test-taking strategies discussed in Chapter 1.

1. Anticipate and use the clock.
2. Skip and return to questions.
3. Eliminate answer choices you know are incorrect.
4. Use educated guessing.

Try Answering the Question Before You Read the Answer Choice(s)

As you read a passage, try to get a clear sense of what the passage is about. Then, before you read the answer choices, fill in the answer blank(s) in your own words. What you come up with doesn't need to be sophisticated or polysyllabic. It just needs to be a word or words that capture the meaning of the sentence. With your answer in mind, check the list of answers and choose the one that seems to best match your idea.

Try this now with Question 1 below.

For Question 1, choose <u>one</u> answer for the blank. Choose the answer that best completes the sense of the text.

1. Emerging African democracies of the 1960s and 1970s faced insurmountable problems that ranged from lack of infrastructure to borders that ignored ethnic conflict: in fact, these _____ governments were destined to fail.

A. despotic
B. ephemeral
C. incompetent
D. deteriorating
E. fledgling

TIP

Remember that there is no penalty for wrong answers. If you absolutely cannot decide on an answer even through the process of elimination, make your best guess based on what you do know.

ALERT!

If you find test time running out and you still have a number of questions to answer, go quickly through the test looking for text completion and sentence equivalence questions. They're quicker to answer than reading comprehension questions, and a point is a point, no matter what question you answer to earn it.

If you try to fill the blank before you read the answers, you might come up with either the word *new* or *democratic*. You can safely eliminate *democratic* because it's highly unlikely that ETS is going to make the answer that simple. That is, the test-item writer isn't going to repeat a word, or form of a word, that already appears in the passage as the correct answer. Your next step, then, is to look for a word in the list that means the same as, or close to the same as, *new*. *Fledgling* means "young and inexperienced," which suggests the meaning of *new*. *Fledgling* is most often applied to birds leaving the nest and trying their wings for the first time, just as the new democracies referred to in the passage were beginning to grow, develop, or "take flight" in a metaphorical sense. **The correct answer is E.**

Focus on Only One Blank at a Time

The majority of the text completion items will present you with either two blanks or three blanks to fill. When you have multiple blanks to fill, it is best to arrive at the answers by concentrating on just one blank at a time. Try out this strategy as you read the following two-blank item.

For Question 2, choose one answer for each blank. Select from the appropriate column for each blank. Choose the answer that best completes the sense of the text.

2. A major part of the body's immune system, the lymphatic system is responsible for producing, maintaining, and distributing lymphocytes (white blood cells that attack bacteria in blood and take the form of T cells and B cells) in the body, as well as for defending the body against pathogens. Besides removing waste, dead blood cells, and toxins from cells and the tissues between them, the lymphatic system also works in concert with the circulatory system to deliver oxygen, nutrients, and hormones from the blood to the cells. The (i) _____ role of the lymphatic system in fighting disease and maintaining homeostasis (ii) _____.

Blank (i)	Blank (ii)
A. pivotal	D. must not be trivial
B. autonomous	E. cannot be gainsaid
C. hypothetical	F. will not be equivocated

Starting with the first blank might lead you to a word that conveys the importance or centrality of the lymphatic system. You might, for example, come up with the words *key*, *major*, *necessary*, or *central*. Reading down the list of answers for Blank (i), you find choice A, *pivotal*, which means *key* or *essential*, so this is the answer for Blank (i). But read all the answer choices for Blank (i) just to be sure *pivotal* is the best choice. Once the first blank is filled, it can be easier to come up with the second answer. For example, it makes no sense to say that "the pivotal role must not be trivial." Neither does it make sense to say that "the pivotal role will not be equivocated," meaning "using vague language." Therefore, the correct answer for the second blank is choice E, "cannot be gainsaid." *Gainsaid* means "denied." **The correct answers are A and E.**

If There Is More Than One Blank, Complete the Blanks in the Order That Makes Sense to You

Don't assume that you need to fill the first blank first, the second blank second, and the third blank third. Begin by filling in the blank that is easiest or most obvious to you. Try this strategy now with the following three-blank item.

For Question 3, choose one answer for each blank. Select from the appropriate column for each blank. Choose the answer that best completes the sense of the text.

3. Those calling for the regulation of commodities trading are, at best, uninformed. Instead of (i) _____ traders for spikes in prices of wheat, oil, and metals, as well as for the bubbles, legislators would be wiser to consider how speculators help to create (ii) _____ by injecting cash into markets—which contributes to market efficiency. Furthermore, legislators who are gung-ho to rein in traders might bother to note that speculators have little or no effect on the production, and only (iii) _____ effect on the consumption, of goods.

Blank (i)	Blank (ii)	Blank (iii)
A. regulating	**D.** liquidity	**G.** minimal
B. scapegoating	**E.** activity	**H.** negative
C. castigating	**F.** inventory	**I.** lasting

Suppose you read the passage and know that injecting, or moving, cash into markets creates liquidity, so you mark choice D for Blank (ii). With *liquidity* in place for Blank (ii), you can now move back to Blank (i) or on to Blank (iii). In either case, you can use the concept of liquidity to help you make sense of the rest of the passage. The more words you fill in, the easier it will be for you to come up with the answer that is most difficult for you. For the record, the correct answer for Blank (i) is choice B, *scapegoating*. *Scapegoating* means "blaming unfairly." The correct answer for Blank (iii) is choice G, *minimal*. **The correct answers are B, D, and G.**

You will revisit Question 3 and read a more detailed analysis later in this chapter.

Check Your Answer(s) in Place

When you've chosen your answer(s), it's a good idea to reread the question quickly with the answers in place. All the words together should create a unified whole. That is, the meanings should all work together; everything should be grammatically correct; and the tone and style should be consistent.

Use Structural Clues

Many text completion items will take the form of organizational structures for writing that are familiar to you and that you can use to help you determine the correct answer. These structures include sentences and paragraphs that compare, contrast, restate, show causes and/or effects, and present main idea and supporting details. Some of these passages will contain what the test maker calls "signposts," that is, trigger, signal, or transitional words and phrases to help you understand the meaning of the passage—more specifically, the relationship of ideas in that passage.

You can use the following types of structural clues to help you determine meaning and fill in the blanks of many text completion questions. As you work through various examples, you will note that, in some cases, a single sentence or passage may contain more than one type of structure and structural clue. The following clues can help you identify answers:

- Restatement
- Cause and effect
- Contrast
- Comparison or similarity structure
- Main idea and details

Restatement

Restatement is a presentation of an idea in words other than those used the first time the idea is presented; an amplification or clarification of an idea; or the presentation of an example of the idea. A sentence or passage that uses restatement will most often have two independent clauses joined by a colon, a semicolon, or a correlative conjunction such as *moreover*. Or, a restatement might take the form of two sentences, the second of which begins with a signal word for restatement. (See the box on the following page for signal words.)

Depending on the restatement structure used, one of the following will be apparent:

- Sentence 2 or clause 2 presents in other words the meaning of sentence 1 or clause 1.
- Sentence 2 or clause 2 amplifies or clarifies sentence 1 or clause 1. This is a more likely combination than mere repetition of an idea in other words.
- Sentence 2 or clause 2 exemplifies sentence 1 or clause 1. That is, sentence 2 or clause 2 provides a single example or illustration.

Signals for Restatement

Among the words and phrases that can signal restatement relationships are the following:

for example	*in other words*	*that is*
for instance	*in short*	*this means*
in fact	*namely*	*thus*

Often, you may have to infer the words and phrases that signal restatement, amplification, clarification, or illustration. For an example of restatement, we'll look again at Question 1. You should be able to identify a restatement signal before you read the analysis that follows the question.

For Question 1, choose <u>one</u> answer for the blank. Choose the answer that best completes the sense of the text.

1. Emerging African democracies of the 1960s and 1970s faced insurmountable problems that ranged from lack of infrastructure to borders that ignored ethnic conflict: in fact, these _____ governments were destined to fail.

A. despotic
B. ephemeral
C. incompetent
D. deteriorating
E. fledgling

A thought process to work through Question 1 might go something like this:

- Note that the signal phrase "in fact," along with the second clause more or less restating or amplifying the first, signals a restatement.

- Knowing that you're working with restatement, next restate, paraphrase, or summarize the item. Focus on only the parts of the passage that reflect the restatement you want to zero in on. Eliminate extraneous wording. For this passage, you would concentrate on the two main clauses and eliminate the clause that begins with "that ranged from . . . ." You might arrive at this summary: "New African governments faced huge problems; these _____ governments could do nothing but fail."

- The omission of extra words helps make it clear that the word that fits the blank must be a synonym for emerging or new, or it must in some way express a similar or close meaning.

- To arrive at the correct answer, use the process of elimination. The first four choices are not synonyms for new, nor do they evoke something new. Therefore, the correct answer is choice E, *fledgling*.

Go back to Question 1 above and drop out the words "in fact." Reread the passage without those words and you'll see that you're still dealing with restatement, even though it's not quite so apparent. **The correct answer is E.**

Cause and Effect

A sentence or passage with a cause-and-effect structure expresses the reason(s) someone did something or something occurred, or expresses the result(s) of an action or event. A cause-and-effect relationship can be expressed in one sentence or in a longer passage.

Cause-and-Effect Signals

Cause-and-effect relationships may or may not include signal words. Among the words and phrases that can signal cause-and-effect relationships are the following:

as a result	*in order to*	*so that*
because	*reason why*	*therefore*
consequently	*since*	*thus*
for	*so*	*why*

Sometimes, you will have to infer cause-and-effect relationships. For example, Question 4 below begins with the infinitive phrase "To defeat the English,…." You can and should reasonably infer that this phrase means "[In order to] defeat the English,…" or "[Because he wanted to] defeat the English,…." This is your first step.

For Question 4, choose <u>one</u> answer for the blank. Choose the answer that best completes the sense of the text.

4. To defeat the English, Metacomet, whom the English called King Philip, knew he had to bring disparate and sometimes warring groups together into a _____.

A. battalion
B. community
C. legation
D. confederation
E. hierarchy

An analysis of Question 4 could take this shape:

- Once you know that you're working with cause and effect, begin by restating, paraphrasing, or summarizing the item in a way that reflects your understanding of the cause-and-effect relationship. For example, you might arrive at this loose paraphrase or summary: "In order to defeat the English, Metacomet had to bring together different and warring groups into a _____."

- This summary, which leaves out the clause "whom the English called King Philip," which is extraneous to the cause-and-effect relationship, makes it clear that the reason, or cause, for bringing together the groups was defeat of the English. So the word that goes into the blank must be one that names a group that can defeat someone or something. That immediately leaves out the all-too-peaceable or scientific sounding "community," as well as the diplomatic and also peaceful "legation." It also leaves out *hierarchy*: a hierarchy alone wouldn't accomplish the job of defeating someone.

- Using cause-and-effect clues in this case quickly narrows down the possible choices to *battalion* (choice A) and *confederation* (choice D).

- To reach the correct answer, try a general strategy, such as comparing two answers against each other and against the passage. A confederation brings many different groups together, which is the point of the sentence. **The correct answer is D.**

Contrast

A sentence or passage with a contrast structure expresses differences. This commonly used structure is probably very familiar to you.

Contrast Signals

Like other structures, contrasts of information may or may not include signal words. Among the words and phrases that can be used to signal contrasts are the following:

although	*however*	*on the contrary*
as opposed to	*in contrast*	*on the other hand*
but	*in spite of*	*otherwise*
by contrast	*instead*	*still*
conversely	*nevertheless*	*unlike*
despite	*nonetheless*	*yet*

Most often, you will have to infer contrasts or the words and phrases that signal them. Question 5, however, does contain a contrast word.

For Question 5, choose <u>one</u> answer for the blank. Choose the answer that best completes the sense of the text.

5. Judging by the various glances exchanged, the statistics Mai offered during the meeting struck everyone in attendance as _____; later, however, she managed to authenticate most of them in her expansive written analysis.

A. valid
B. inconsequential
C. spurious
D. unexpurgated
E. superfluous

An analysis of the contrast relationship in Question 5 could look something like this:

- Once you have identified the structure as a contrast, restate, paraphrase, or summarize the item in a way that reflects your understanding of the contrast relationship. For example, you might arrive at this paraphrase: "The glances showed people thought Mai's statistics were _____; later, her analysis showed they were authentic."

- This loose paraphrase makes it clear that the answer must express the opposite, or near opposite, of "authentic."

- Through the process of elimination, choices A, B, D, and E should all be ruled out because they don't show or suggest the opposite of authentic. *Valid* (choice A) means "just, producing the desired results, or legally binding," which is somewhat similar to *authentic*. *Inconsequential* (choice B) is incorrect because it isn't the opposite of *authentic*. Choice D is incorrect because *unexpurgated* refers to removing offensive material from something. Choice E is incorrect because *superfluous* means "unnecessary, more than what is required." Therefore, *spurious* (choice C), meaning "false," is the correct answer.

Try rereading the passage after eliminating the signal word *however* to help familiarize yourself with an alternative way in which a contrast passage might appear. **The correct answer is C.**

Comparison or Similarity Structure

Like a sentence or passage expressing contrasting ideas, a sentence or passage expressing a comparison or similarity should also be familiar to you. Such a structure expresses how two or more things are alike.

Comparison Signals

Among the words and phrases that can signal a comparison are the following:

also	*in comparison*	*moreover*
and	*in the same way*	*same*
another	*like*	*similarly*
as	*likewise*	*too*
by the same token		

For Question 6, choose <u>one</u> answer for the blank. Choose the answer that best completes the sense of the text.

6. Debussy is regarded as the germinal musical impressionist who created color through the use of individual instruments in the orchestra; by the same token, Monet's use of blocks of color, in lieu of line, was a(n) _____ influence on impressionism in art. There, however, the similarity between the two "impressionists" ends.

A. imperative
B. seminal
C. discernable
D. super
E. formidable

An analysis of the comparison in Question 6 could look something like this:

- Note that the signal phrase "by the same token" along with the word *similarity* indicate a comparison.

- The next step is to restate, paraphrase, or summarize the item in a way that reflects your understanding of the comparison relationship, or structure. For example, you might arrive at this summary: "Debussy had great influence in music because of his use of color; likewise, Monet was a _____ influence in art because of how he used color."

- This summary significantly reduces the original in order to focus on the comparison. It makes clear that the word that belongs in the blank must be an adjective that suggests great influence.

- At this point, you might use the process of elimination. Choice A should be eliminated because *imperative* means "absolutely necessary." Choice C is also incorrect because the similarity suggests that Monet had more than a discernable, or noticeable, influence on art; he had a great influence. Choice D is likewise incorrect because *super*, which can mean "particularly excellent," is too informal for this passage. Finally, choice E is incorrect because *formidable*, while suggesting a meaning that fits, does not exactly match the meaning expressed by the first clause. The context makes it clear that the effect of each artist on his discipline was not only huge or formidable, it was also influential. *Seminal* (choice B) is the only word that conveys something formative or something that shaped, influenced, or decided what was to come. **The correct answer is B.**

Now try analyzing Question 6 without the signal words in the passage.

If you look back at Question 1, you'll see that it could also be approached as a comparison, but without any signal words. Structures can be combined or overlapped in a single sentence or passage. Your task is not to identify the "right" structure, but to identify and use structures that will best help you find the answer.

Main Idea and Details

Main ideas and details as an organizing structure consist of more than one sentence. The main idea may be stated at the beginning of the passage, in the middle, or at the end. The main idea may also be implied through the details in the passage. Although passages may occasionally contain signal words and phrases such as "for example" to help you identify details, you will most likely have to infer the main idea based on the content of the passage.

Take a look again at Question 2. See if you can identify its main ideas and details before you read the analysis.

For Question 2, choose <u>one</u> answer for each blank. Select from the appropriate column for each blank. Choose the answer that best completes the sense of the text.

2. A major part of the body's immune system, the lymphatic system is responsible for producing, maintaining, and distributing lymphocytes (white blood cells that attack bacteria in blood and take the form of T cells and B cells) in the body, as well as for defending the body against pathogens. Besides removing waste, dead blood cells, and toxins from cells and the tissues between them, the lymphatic system also works in concert with the circulatory system to deliver oxygen, nutrients, and hormones from the blood to the cells. The (i) _____ role of the lymphatic system in fighting disease and maintaining homeostasis (ii) _____.

Blank (i)	Blank (ii)
A. pivotal	**D.** must not be trivial
B. autonomous	**E.** cannot be gainsaid
C. hypothetical	**F.** will not be equivocated

To help you answer a text completion question, consider this analysis of the main idea and supporting details in the passage for Question 2:

- Begin by finding the main idea (the last sentence) and the details that support it (everything that precedes the last sentence).

- Then, once again, restate, paraphrase, or summarize the part or parts of the passage containing the blank or blanks you must fill in. For example, you might arrive at this summary: "The _____ part played by the lymphatic system in the body _____."

- This summary depends, of course, on the details for correct completion, so now reread the details. The details inform you of the various and important roles the lymphatic system plays in the body. Therefore, the first blank must have to do with importance, or being essential.

- The word that comes closest in meaning to important is *pivotal*. *Pivotal* (choice A) is the correct answer for Blank (i).

- To complete Blank (ii), work with the more complete version of your summary: "The pivotal part played by the lymphatic system in the body _____." If you come up with your own answer for this blank, you might say "cannot be (or must not be or will not be) denied." Therefore, look for the answer choice that means "denied." In this case, choice E.

If you don't know the meaning of all the words—or even if you do—remember to use the process of elimination. *Trivial* doesn't mean "denied." Neither does *equivocated*. So while you may not know that *gainsaid* (choice E) means "denied," by the process of elimination, it must be the correct answer. **The correct answers are A and E.**

Consider Tone and Style

Although this strategy won't apply to every passage, some passages will carry a distinctive tone that you can use as a clue to meaning. For example, the author's attitude may be sympathetic, indignant, questioning, mournful, celebratory, or praising. If there is an obvious tone, don't overlook it as a clue to the words that belong in the blanks. Look again at Question 3 and see if you can identify the tone of the passage for Blanks (i) and (ii).

For Question 3, choose <u>one</u> answer for each blank. Select from the appropriate column for each blank. Choose the answer that best completes the sense of the text.

3. Those calling for the regulation of commodities trading are, at best, uninformed. Instead of (i) _____ traders for spikes in prices of wheat, oil, and metals, as well as for the bubbles, legislators would be wiser to consider how speculators help to create (ii) _____ by injecting cash into markets—which contributes to market efficiency. Furthermore, legislators who are gung-ho to rein in traders might bother to note that speculators have little or no effect on the production, and only (iii) _____ effect on the consumption, of goods.

Blank (i)	Blank (ii)	Blank (iii)
A. regulating	D. liquidity	G. minimal
B. scapegoating	E. activity	H. negative
C. castigating	F. inventory	I. lasting

An analysis of the question based on tone would be something like this:

- The critical, almost indignant, tone of this passage is signaled by two groups of words that denigrate legislators: "at best, uninformed" and "legislators who are gung-ho to rein in traders . . ."

- This critical tone tells you that the author is not going to make particularly moderate or measured word choices. Instead, at least some of the words that are most consistent with the message will be words with strong negative connotations. Of all the answer choices, *scapegoating* (choice B) has the most negative connotations. It is, in fact, the correct answer for Blank (i).

- Based on this assessment of the tone and sense of the passage, the best choice for the second blank is *liquidity* (choice D).

Similarly, considering the author's style might help you arrive at a correct answer. **The correct answers are B and D.**

Read Question 6 again, but this time pay attention to the writer's style.

For Question 6, choose one answer for the blank. Choose the answer that best completes the sense of the text.

6. Debussy is regarded as the germinal musical impressionist who created color through the use of individual instruments in the orchestra; by the same token, Monet's use of blocks of color, in lieu of line, was a _____ influence on impressionism in art. There, however, the similarity between the two "impressionists" ends.

A. imperative
B. seminal
C. discernable
D. super
E. formidable

The style of the passage is formal and academic; therefore, the word that fits in the blank must be the same in order to work with that style. A quick read-through of the answer choices comes across *super*. Though it means "particularly excellent" and might at first appear to be correct, *super* is an informal word appropriate to an informal context. It doesn't fit the style of this passage, so choice D can be eliminated. That leaves you four other choices with which to use the process of elimination.

Use Grammar and Usage

You will be able to eliminate some answer choices because they violate the rules of grammar or do not match the customary way in which a word or phrase is used. For example, look again at Question 3, Blank (iii):

For Question 3, choose <u>one</u> answer for each blank. Select from the appropriate column for each blank. Choose the answer that best completes the sense of the text.

3. Those calling for the regulation of commodities trading are, at best, uninformed. Instead of (i) _____ traders for spikes in prices of wheat, oil, and metals, as well as for the bubbles, legislators would be wiser to consider how speculators help to create (ii) _____ by injecting cash into markets—which contributes to market efficiency. Furthermore, legislators who are gung-ho to rein in traders might bother to note that speculators have little or no effect on the production, and only (iii) _____ effect on the consumption, of goods.

Blank (i)	Blank (ii)	Blank (iii)
A. regulating	**D.** liquidity	**G.** minimal
B. scapegoating	**E.** activity	**H.** negative
C. castigating	**F.** inventory	**I.** lasting

Notice that both *negative* and *lasting* actually require the article *a* before them. Only *minimal* fits in the space as it is worded. Therefore, *negative* (choice H) and *lasting* (choice I) must both be eliminated. **The correct answer is G.**

Avoid Selecting the Word or Phrase You Don't Fully Understand or Is Unfamiliar

Look again at Question 4 and its answer choices.

For Question 4, choose <u>one</u> answer for the blank. Choose the answer that best completes the sense of the text.

4. To defeat the English, Metacomet, whom the English called King Philip, knew he had to bring disparate and sometimes warring groups together into a _____.

A. battalion
B. community
C. legation
D. confederation
E. hierarchy

Suppose you have no idea what *legation* means. In most cases, you should not leap to choose this word or any other unfamiliar word. *Legation*, which means "a permanent diplomatic mission," is incorrect in the context of Question 4. Of course, if you have clearly eliminated every other choice, then an unfamiliar word may be correct.

PRACTICE QUESTIONS

For Questions 1–10, choose <u>one</u> answer for each blank. Select from the appropriate column for each blank. Choose the answer that best completes the sense of the text.

1. The governor exercised tremendous _____ when she kept herself from being drawn into the childish bout of name calling her political opponent attempted to initiate.

A. insight
B. tenacity
C. vicissitude
D. temperance
E. loquaciousness

2. Even though they have the power to create any outlandish situations they can imagine, fantasy writers often set themselves very strict rules and guidelines for what is possible in their stories. Without doing so, their work will lack any _____ of reality and be nearly impossible for readers to accept.

A. participation
B. moral
C. implement
D. hierarchy
E. semblance

3. Architects and sound engineers routinely use sound-absorbing materials on ceilings and walls. In addition, they have sometimes tried to create optimal acoustics by building the ceilings and walls of concert halls with rippled or (i) _____ surfaces, so that the sound is reflected and (ii) _____ at many angles.

Blank (i)	Blank (ii)
A. invariably rigid	**D.** distorted
B. highly polished	**E.** diffused
C. slightly undulating	**F.** auditory

4. Physics is one of the least (i) _____ defined sciences, as it (ii) _____ with such other research areas as quantum chemistry and biophysics.

Blank (i)	Blank (ii)
A. consciously	**D.** overlaps
B. rigidly	**E.** contributes
C. comprehensibly	**F.** eradicates

5. The investigative panel was nothing short of outraged by the bus driver's negligence and lack of remorse. It determined that the driver had failed to follow the established (i) _____. As a result, she had compromised the safety of the passengers. More fundamentally, however, she had actually and effectively (ii) _____ at least two of her riders' rights.

Blank (i)	Blank (ii)
A. code of conduct	**D.** abrogated
B. rules of engagement	**E.** renounced
C. terms of use	**F.** negated

6. The playwright created atmosphere in part through the (i) _____ afternoon on which he set the scene. The cloying humidity seemed at once to (ii) _____ the characters' physical energy and play devil's advocate to their sense of morality.

Blank (i)	Blank (ii)
A. sultry	**D.** sap
B. unsettled	**E.** beguile
C. bone-chilling	**F.** intensify

7. Even as technology and even government initiatives seek to (i) ____ our privacy when using the Internet, there are measures that can be taken to (ii) ____ a degree of privacy while using the Internet. One can choose an Internet Service Provider that promises to protect its customers' privacy, use the privacy-friendly HTTPS browser extension whenever websites offer it as an option, and use a trustworthy VPN or Virtual Privacy Network to filter out invasive advertising and (iii) _____ the collection of personal data.

Blank (i)	Blank (ii)	Blank (iii)
A. safeguard	**D.** sustain	**G.** spur
B. befuddle	**E.** imply	**H.** thwart
C. undermine	**F.** instigate	**I.** scrutinize

8. Is understanding your stature in relation to the universe ultimately a psychic (i) _____ of your sense of self? On the one hand, gauging your own experience of space and time in relation to the space and time of galaxies can make you feel (ii) _____ small. On the other hand, sensing you are one with this great universe, or even knowing that its cosmic rays pass through you, may in some ways (iii) _____ that sense of smallness.

Blank (i)	Blank (ii)	Blank (iii)
A. raveling	**D.** antithetically	**G.** mitigate
B. diminution	**E.** debilitatingly	**H.** expropriate
C. misappropriation	**F.** infinitesimally	**I.** enervate

9. The peasants portrayed in Pieter Brueghel the Elder's renowned paintings performed physical labor from sunup to sundown and lived grim, short lives. In *The Wedding Dance*, Pieter Brueghel depicts a nearly frenzied release from that daily round of (i) _____ and (ii) _____ in which peasants dance and (iii) _____ to the music of the bagpipes.

Blank (i)	Blank (ii)	Blank (iii)
A. employment	**D.** inanity	**G.** unwind
B. privation	**E.** woe	**H.** carouse
C. mediocrity	**F.** striving	**I.** sing

10. Despite being (i) _____ for twisting the English language in wonderfully nonsensical ways and creating fantastical creatures such as Horton the Elephant, Yertel the Turtle, and the Lorax, Theodore "Dr. Seuss" Geisel often had decidedly (ii) _____ ideas in mind when composing these tongue-twisting tales for toddlers. By Seuss' own admission, *Horton Hears a Who!* is a metaphor for the way the Japanese of Hiroshima and Nagasaki suffered amidst the atomic bombing that ended World War II, and the title character of *Yertel the Turtle and Other Stories* represents no less a villain than Adolph Hitler. Meanwhile, *The Lorax* is a very sober and moving (iii) ____ to protect our natural environment.

Blank (i)	Blank (ii)	Blank (iii)
A. disavowed	**D.** figurative	**G.** entreaty
B. reputed	**E.** grandiose	**H.** condemnation
C. lionized	**F.** exuberant	**I.** scripture

ANSWER KEY AND EXPLANATIONS

1. D	**6.** A, D
2. E	**7.** C, D, H
3. C, E	**8.** B, F, G
4. B, D	**9.** B, E, H
5. A, F	**10.** B, E, G

1. **The correct answer is D.** The sentence implies the governor restrained herself from being drawn into the bout of name calling, and *temperance* means "restraint." *Insight* (choice A) means "keen understanding," which does not fit the context of this sentence as well as choice D does. Neither does *tenacity* (choice B), which means "stubbornness" or "persistence." *Vicissitude* (choice C) means "a change of circumstances," which does not make sense in this context at all. *Loquaciousness* (choice E) means "a tendency to talk a lot," which is the opposite of how the governor is characterized in this sentence.

2. **The correct answer is E.** Based on the context, you can conclude that fantasy writers adhere to guidelines and rules so that their work is not completely unrealistic and unacceptable to readers. This means they want to maintain a certain appearance of reality, and *semblance* means "appearance." *Participation* (choice A) does not work well in this context since reality does not really participate in anything. *Moral* (choice B) means "lesson," which does not make sense in this context. *Implement* (choice C) means "tool," which does not make sense either. *Hierarchy* (choice D) means "a system arranged according to importance or power," which does not make sense in this context.

3. **The correct answers are C and E.** For the first blank, the phrase with the closest meaning to *rippled* is what you're looking for. In this case, choice A can be eliminated because *invariably rigid* means the opposite of *rippled*. *Highly polished* (choice B) can also be eliminated because the phrase makes no sense in the sentence. For the second blank, choice E is correct because a rippled surface would diffuse the sound "at many angles" to create the desired effect. *Distortion* is the opposite of the desired effect, so choice D is incorrect. Choice F should also be eliminated because *auditory* means "related to the process of hearing," not "able to be heard" or *audible*.

4. **The correct answers are B and D.** The sentence implies that physics shares traits with other sciences such as quantum chemistry and biophysics, and this suggests that physics is not a firmly or "rigidly" defined science. *Consciously* (choice A) means "knowingly," which does not make as much sense in this context as choice B does. Choice C implies that the definition of physics is incomprehensible or impossible to understand, which is too extreme. For Blank (ii), the best answer is choice D, since the implication that physics shares traits with other sciences indicates that it overlaps with other sciences. Choices E and F simply do not make sense in this context; *contributes* means "adds to" and *eradicates* means "erases."

5. **The correct answers are A and F.** Choice A is correct for Blank (i) because a "code of conduct" is a set of principles and practices outlined for an individual, group, or organization. Choices B and C are incorrect because "rules of engagement" (choice B) generally outline when and how force should be used, and "terms of use" (choice C) often establish a relationship between a company's product and its user. For Blank (ii), choice F is correct because this blank requires a synonym or near synonym for *denied*. *Abrogated* (choice D) can be eliminated because an abrogation is an official or legislative annulment or cancellation. Choice E can also be eliminated because *renounced* makes no sense in this context.

6. **The correct answers are A and D.** *Sultry* means "excessively hot or humid," which matches the "cloying humidity" mentioned in Sentence 2; therefore, choice A is correct. You can eliminate choices B and C, because neither "unsettled" nor "bone-chilling" suggests excessive humidity. Choice D is the correct answer for the second blank, as *sap* means "to exhaust" or "to deplete." This is the only answer that makes sense in the context of lessening physical energy or moral fortitude. Choices E and F, *beguile* and *intensify*, make no sense.

7. **The correct answers are C, D, and H.** For the first blank, choice C is correct because the context implies that technology and the government want to prevent our internet privacy, and *undermine* is a synonym of "prevent." *Safeguard* (choice A) is the opposite of "prevent." *Befuddle* (choice B) means "confuse," so it is not the best word for this particular context. For the second blank,

choice D is the best answer since the paragraph offers ways to maintain privacy on the internet and *sustain* means "maintain." *Imply* (choice E), which means "suggest," and *instigate* (choice F), which means "stimulate," do not make sense in this context. For the third blank, the word *thwart* (choice H) makes the most sense since the paragraph is offering ways to prevent the collection of one's personal data, and to "thwart" is to "prevent." *Spur* (choice G) is the opposite of "prevent." *Scrutinize* (choice I) means "examine," which does not make sense.

8. **The correct answers are B, F, and G.** For the first blank, choice B is correct because the context implies some kind of a reduction or diminishment. Choice A can be eliminated because *raveling* suggests an undoing rather than a decrease in size, as is clearly conveyed by Sentence 2. *Misappropriation* (choice C) makes no sense and can be eliminated. For the second blank, choice F is correct because *infinitesimally* conveys the sense of extreme smallness. *Antithetically* (choice D) which means "in direct opposition," is incorrect because it makes no sense. *Debilitatingly* suggests weakening rather than diminishment, so choice E is also incorrect. For Blank (iii), choice G is the correct because, as the signal phrase "on the other hand" suggests, this blank calls for a word that suggests a decrease or lessening of the sense of smallness. This means that both choices H and I can be eliminated because *expropriate* means "to deprive someone of something" and *enervate* means "to weaken or destroy strength." Neither suggest a decrease or reduction as mitigate does.

9. **The correct answers are B, E, and H.** To restate the grim daily round of physical labor from sunup to sundown, *privation* (choice B) is the best choice for Blank (i) and *woe* (choice E) is the best choice for Blank (ii). For Blank (i), the words *employment* and *mediocrity* (choices A and C) are not only inaccurate, but they're also not negative enough. For Blank (ii), *inanity* and *striving* (choices D and F) are similarly insufficiently negative as well as inaccurate. For Blank (iii), *carouse* (choice H) is correct because the passage says the peasants are depicted as in "a nearly frenzied release." Neither *unwind* (choice G) or *sing* (choice I) express the meaning conveyed by *carouse*, which is "to engage in noisy, drunken, boisterous, or even riotous merrymaking."

10. **The correct answers are B, E, and G.** *Reputed* (choice B) is the correct answer for Blank (i) because the opening sentence of the paragraph describes for what Dr. Seuss is best known, and *reputed* means "known." *Disavowed* (choice A) means "denied," which does not make much sense in this context. *Lionized* (choice C) means "glorified," which is too extreme for this context.

For Blank (ii), *grandiose* (choice E) is correct because the author is implying that Dr. Seuss had grander goals than merely twisting the English language and creating fantastical creatures; he was actually commenting on world events and the environmental crisis. *Figurative* (choice D) means "indirect," and while this may describe his approach to creating stories, it does not describe his actual ideas when creating them. *Exuberant* (choice F) means "excitedly joyful," and considering the grim ideas behind many of his stories, this word is hardly appropriate here.

Choice G is the correct answer for Blank (iii) since a writer as socially and politically conscious as Dr. Seuss has been established to be in the paragraph would likely make a plea to protect the natural environment, and *entreaty* means "plea." *Condemnation* (choice H) is the opposite of a plea and it does not make grammatical sense in this context. *Scripture* (choice I) is a Biblical verse, which does not make sense either.

SUMMING IT UP

- Text completion questions assess your ability to interpret and evaluate what you read and supply words or phrases whose meaning is consistent with the ideas presented.

- Text completion questions have from one to three blanks to be filled in.

- Test items that have one blank offer a list of five options. Test items with two or three blanks offer lists of three options for each blank.

- Some test items will revolve around words that are close in meaning or ask for an unusual meaning of a familiar word. Some items may involve less familiar words.

- Passages for the text completion test items tend to have lighter concept loads than those for reading comprehension questions on the GRE® General Test.

- The following strategies for answering text completion questions involve both common sense and knowledge gained in English composition classes:

  o Try answering the questions before you read the answer choice(s).

  o Focus on only one blank at a time.

  o If there is more than one blank, complete the blanks in the order that makes sense to you.

  o Check your answer(s) in place.

  o Use structural clues: restatement, cause and effect, contrast, comparison, main idea, and details.

  o Consider tone and style.

  o Consider grammar and usage.

  o Avoid selecting a word or phrase that you don't fully understand or is unfamiliar.

- General test-taking strategies that are also helpful include:

  o Anticipate and use the clock.

  o Skip and return to questions.

  o Eliminate answer choices you know are incorrect.

  o Use educated guessing.

Strategies for Sentence Equivalence Questions

OVERVIEW

- **Basic Information About Sentence Equivalence Questions**
- **Strategies for Sentence Equivalence Questions**
- **Practice Questions**
- **Answer Keys and Explanations**
- **Summing It Up**

Sentence equivalence questions ask you to determine how a sentence should be completed—in two ways. You will need to pick two words that are close in meaning. This chapter describes the purpose of the sentence equivalence test items and offers strategies to help you do well on these questions.

BASIC INFORMATION ABOUT SENTENCE EQUIVALENCE QUESTIONS

Like text completion items, sentence equivalence questions on the GRE® General Test assess your ability both to interpret what you read and to supply words whose meanings are consistent with the ideas presented in the test items. Unlike text completion items, however, sentence equivalence items place more emphasis on the meaning of the completed sentence.

Also, like text completion items, sentence equivalence items test your vocabulary. Therefore, knowing "big" words—such as *dichotomous* and *prescient*—can help you do well, but that's not the only way to score points. Learning and using a few key strategies can help you as well.

Question Format

Each sentence equivalence question is a single sentence with one blank followed by six answer choices. This is the simplest of the verbal formats and is the same each and every time. From the list of six options, you must choose two answers for each question. You have to choose two answers that have similar (equivalent) meaning so that they both complete the sentence with a similar (equivalent) meaning.

Chapter 8

There is only one type of direction line for the text completion items. It will be worded something like this:

For Questions 1–2, choose the <u>two</u> answers that best fit the meaning of the sentence as a whole and result in two completed sentences that are alike in meaning.

You can expect perhaps one quarter or fewer—maybe 5 or 6—of the items on the Verbal Reasoning section to be sentence equivalence items. These items are interspersed with the other items on each of the two scored verbal sections of the test.

Each sentence equivalence item appears on a separate screen. All passages are short enough to display on a single screen, so you won't need to scroll or change screens. In fact, these short items require the least from you of any of the verbal items and should be finished the most quickly.

Selecting Answers

When you have decided on an answer to a question, click on your choice. The oval preceding your selection will completely darken. Remember for sentence equivalence test items to click on two choices. Once you are satisfied with your two answers, hit the "Next" button.

To earn credit for a sentence equivalence test item, you must choose both correct answers. Choosing only one correct answer of the pair will not gain you any credit.

Consider using the "Mark" option. Because the sentence equivalence questions are less time-consuming than reading comprehension items, they are easier to revisit. When you mark a sentence equivalence item, you are making a commitment to revisit only approximately 4 percent of the test. This is not a huge task to put off until later and, therefore, a reasonable strategy to use with challenging items.

If you're running out of time, go through the section and look for any unanswered sentence equivalence questions. You can answer them quickly and earn credit.

STRATEGIES FOR SENTENCE EQUIVALENCE QUESTIONS

You will be using many of the same strategies for sentence equivalence items that you may use for other Verbal Reasoning questions on the test. Strategies can be grouped into two categories: those that are general commonsense ideas and those that you learned in English composition classes. The first group includes the following three strategies:

1. Read the item stem first.
2. Come up with your own answer.
3. Check your answers in place.

More specific language strategies include the following:

1. Use signal words and structural clues.
2. Avoid leaping at the first pair of synonyms.

3. Examine connotations.

4. Consider grammar and usage.

Remember to apply the following four test-taking strategies as well:

1. Anticipate and use the clock.

2. Skip and return to questions.

3. Eliminate answer choices that you know are not correct.

4. Use educated guessing.

Notice how these review strategies are integrated into the approaches for answering each of the sample items in this chapter.

Read the Item Stem First

Read through the entire sentence before you do anything else. Get a clear sense of what it's about first. The answers are deliberately structured with multiple pairs of synonyms and with close meanings that might appear correct at first glance, so you want to be sure that you understand the meaning of the incomplete sentence.

Come Up with Your Own Answer

Coming up with your own answer before you read the answer choices can be one of the most efficient methods you can use with sentence equivalence items. Try this now with Question 1 below.

For Question 1, choose the <u>two</u> answers that best fit the meaning of the sentence as a whole and result in two completed sentences that are alike in meaning.

1. Jade could not keep her negativity or aggression to herself; it seemed that everywhere she went, some kind of _____ ensued.

   A. kerfuffle

   B. insurgency

   C. insurrection

   D. rebellion

   E. demonstration

   F. disturbance

Working through the answer process might take this shape:

- Read the sentence first and try to figure out your own answer. Using this strategy, you come up with either the word *problems* or the word *difficulty*.

- Step 2 is to look for a pair of words in the list that mean the same as, or close to the same as, *problems* or *difficulty*.

ALERT!

Both the computer-delivered and paper-delivered (for international test takers) GRE® General Tests have two scored sections of Verbal Reasoning questions. Each section of the computer-delivered test will have approximately 20 questions with a time limit of 30 minutes. Each section of the paper-delivered test will consist of 25 questions with a time limit of 35 minutes.

- *Kerfuffle* means "disturbance" or "minor outburst or tumult." It is a state of commotion rather than complete uproar like choices B, C, and D. A kerfuffle is not so intense or serious as an insurgency, insurrection, or rebellion.

- In the context of the completed sentence, *disturbance* means the same thing. Therefore, the correct answers are *kerfuffle* (choice A) and *disturbance* (choice F). For the record, *demonstration* connotes a protest, usually large in nature, so choice E is incorrect also. **The correct answers are A and F.**

Check Your Answers in Place

You aren't finished when you select your two answer choices. Remember that the answers must create equivalence, so the last step in the process of completing this type of test item is an evaluation of meaning. To do this, read the item quickly twice, first with the first answer you have chosen in the blank, and the second time with the second answer in place. Ask yourself: Do the two sentences mean the same? Weigh the meaning of the completed sentences against each other before you click on the answer choices.

Use Signal Words and Structural Clues

Many sentence equivalence items will include transitions—signal words and phrases—such as *consequently, because, on the other hand, although, moreover, however,* and *in fact*. These words signal a relationship between ideas in the sentence. Pay close attention to them. They can help you decide whether the answer should show cause and effect, contrast, comparison, or restatement. Familiar signal words for different types of structures are included in the following boxes:

NOTE

Restatement is a presentation of an idea in words other than those used the first time the idea is presented, an amplification or clarification of an idea, or the presentation of an example of the idea.

Signals for Restatement

Among the words and phrases that can signal restatement relationships are the following:

for example	*in other words*	*that is*
for instance	*in short*	*this means*
in fact	*namely*	*thus*

Cause-and-Effect Signals

Cause-and-effect relationships may or may not include signal words. Among the words and phrases that can signal cause-and-effect relationships are the following:

as a result	*in order to*	*so that*
because	*reason why*	*therefore*
consequently	*since*	*thus*
for	*so*	*why*

Contrast Signals

Like other structures, contrasts of information may or may not include signal words. Among the words and phrases that can be used to signal contrasts are the following:

although	however	on the contrary
as opposed to	in contrast	on the other hand
but	in spite of	otherwise
by contrast	instead	still
conversely	nevertheless	unlike
despite	nonetheless	yet

Comparison Signals

Among the words and phrases that can signal a comparison are the following:

also	in comparison	moreover
and	in the same way	much like
another	just as	same
as	like	similarly
by the same token	likewise	too

Not all test items for sentence equivalence will have signal words and phrases. You will need to recognize clues to organizational structures such as restatement and cause and effect without the help of transitional words and phrases.

To practice identifying and using structural clues with sentence equivalence items, read Question 1 again and then read through the analysis that follows based on the sentence's restatement structure.

For Question 1, choose the two answers that best fit the meaning of the sentence as a whole and result in two completed sentences that are alike in meaning.

1. Jade could not keep her negativity or aggression to herself; it seemed that everywhere she went, some kind of _____ ensued.

   A. kerfuffle

   B. insurgency

   C. insurrection

   D. rebellion

   E. demonstration

   F. disturbance

Reading this sentence, you may decide that it has a restatement structure. The second part of the sentence (the part following the semicolon) amplifies the information in the first part of the sentence (the part preceding the semicolon). No signal word or phrase is present. Structural analysis helps you determine that the pair of words you are looking for must name something that results from negativity or aggression. Insurgency, insurrection, and rebellion are all actions that go well beyond negativity or aggression. They don't express the same minor degree of problem, commotion, or upset that is conveyed by the first part of the sentence, so eliminate choices B, C, and D. *Demonstration* (choice E) is usually used in conjunction with a large group, so it is incorrect as well. Negativity and aggression might both lead to a disturbance. The only synonym or near synonym on the list for disturbance is *kerfuffle*. Therefore, the correct answers are *kerfuffle* and *disturbance*. **The correct answers are A and F.**

It's also reasonable to think that this sentence is structured as a cause-and-effect relationship. The following is one way you might work through it looking for an effect of Jade's attitude:

- If you begin by restating the item with cause and effect in mind, you might arrive at this paraphrase: "Because Jade could not keep her negativity or aggression in check, she caused some kind of _____ everywhere she went."

- Structural analysis helps you determine that the pair of words you are looking for must name something that results from negativity or aggression.

- The rest of the analysis is the same as above, so the correct answers are *kerfuffle* (choice A) and *disturbance* (choice F).

Avoid Leaping at the First Pair of Synonyms

You might think it's a good idea just to find the pair of synonyms among the answer choices, wrap up an item at lightning speed, and move on to the next item. You would be wrong. First, many answer sets contain more than one set of synonyms. Second, as the test maker warns, even if a word is a synonym for the correct choice, it doesn't necessarily lead to the same meaning in the completed sentence. Finally, two words may be synonyms, but they may have different connotations.

Take a look at Question 1 again.

For Question 1, choose the two answers that best fit the meaning of the sentence as a whole and result in two completed sentences that are alike in meaning.

1. Jade could not keep her negativity or aggression to herself; it seemed that everywhere she went, some kind of _____ ensued.

   A. kerfuffle

   B. insurgency

   C. insurrection

   D. rebellion

   E. demonstration

   F. disturbance

The first pair of synonyms in the answer choices for Question 1 is *insurgency* and *rebellion* (choices B and C). The meaning of these words, however, suggests an outcome that would arise from problems that are far greater than negativity. Note also that choices B, C, and D are similar. If you chose two answers just by looking for synonym pairs in the list of answer choices, you would have a dilemma on your hands. Which two should you choose?

Examine Connotations

In choosing answers, think about the connotations that the words carry. As you read Question 2, for example, consider just exactly what kind of walking is meant.

For Question 2, choose the <u>two</u> answers that best fit the meaning of the sentence as a whole and result in two completed sentences that are alike in meaning.

2. Kierkegaard said that he had "walked himself into his best thoughts"; in fact, research links exercise with heightened states of _____ experience.

    A. examining
    B. pensive
    C. thoughtful
    D. meditative
    E. generative
    F. contemplative

The walking in this sentence led to thinking, so it was likely solitary and prolonged walking. That information may help you in considering the connotations of the answer choices. Even though *pensive* and *meditative* are synonyms, they don't quite result in equivalence in the sentence. *Pensive* (choice B) has to be eliminated because it suggests a deep or melancholy thoughtfulness, an inward kind of experience that would not likely yield the "best thoughts" or be generative. Similarly, *contemplative* and *thoughtful* are synonyms. *Contemplative* (choice F) carries connotations of prolonged thought, the kind of thought that might arise over the course of a long walk. However, *thoughtful* (choice C) doesn't have that connotation, so eliminate it. *Generative* (choice E) must be eliminated because there is no similar word that would result in equivalence. *Examining* (choice A) is also incorrect in terms of usage and has no twin. Through elimination, that leaves *meditative* (choice D) and *contemplative* (choice F) as synonyms that have similar connotations. **The correct answers are D and F.**

NOTE

Two words that are often confused are "connotation" and "denotation." Connotation is an idea or meaning suggested by a word. Denotation is the literal meaning of a word.

Consider Grammar and Usage

As with the text completion items, the words you select for sentence equivalence must result in correct grammar and standard usage when inserted into the sentence. Look again at Question 2 and the first answer choice.

For Question 2, choose the <u>two</u> answers that best fit the meaning of the sentence as a whole and result in two completed sentences that are alike in meaning.

2. Kierkegaard said that he had "walked himself into his best thoughts"; in fact, research links exercise with heightened states of _____ experience.

   A. examining

You can eliminate choice A because, even though the form of the word *examining* makes it appear as if it could be an adjective, it results in an ambiguous and nonstandard usage in the sentence "in fact, research links exercise with heightened states of examining experience."

PRACTICE QUESTIONS

For Questions 1–10, choose the <u>two</u> answers that best fit the meaning of the sentence as a whole and result in two completed sentences that are alike in meaning.

1. In rare instances, a person may suffer from a congenital deficiency in the glycoprotein Alpha-1 antitrypsin, and this _____ condition results in a predisposition to early-onset pulmonary emphysema even if the person in question does not smoke.

   A. atypical
   B. phenomenal
   C. unparalleled
   D. peculiar
   E. eccentric
   F. arcane

2. Even though the senator's speeches were marked by an admirable _____, he was not always able to translate his insight into legislation.

   A. alacrity
   B. acuity
   C. astuteness
   D. perspicacity
   E. ingenuity
   F. erudition

3. At first the symbols on an eye chart may appear _____ through a phoropter, but they should become significantly clearer as the optometrist switches through the device's various lens strengths.

   A. recognizable
   B. crystalline
   C. amorphous
   D. assiduous
   E. shapeless
   F. zealous

4. The appetite of the venture capitalist for a quick and lucrative killing could only be described as _____.

   A. avaricious

   B. grasping

   C. voracious

   D. unslaked

   E. indomitable

   F. rapacious

5. The textbook contained little information relevant to the topic I am researching; moreover, it is written in an extremely _____ fashion, so I might not have been able to find the information I need even if the author included it.

   A. methodical

   B. unsystematic

   C. emblematic

   D. muddled

   E. quintessential

   F. shuffled

6. The woman could scarcely have been more disparaging about her ex-husband's participation in family life and responsibilities; she accused him of both physical laziness and _____.

   A. lethargy

   B. apathy

   C. petulance

   D. decrepitude

   E. turpitude

   F. languor

7. Despite waking up with a severe cold that made him feel weak and achy, Professor Shankar still managed to work up the _____ to teach his class in his usual manner.

   A. mien

   B. vitality

   C. attentiveness

   D. resolve

   E. enervation

   F. capriciousness

8. As the play progressed, Molière could see that his tragedy was falling flat, so he moved quickly to transform the developing _____ into a farce.

   A. travail

   B. flop

   C. drudgery

   D. composition

   E. fiasco

   F. creation

9. While the ability to enact beneficial policies should be a key characteristic of any viable presidential candidate, one should not underestimate the commander-in-chief's role as a representative of his or her country, so the ideal leader is also eloquent, charismatic, and _____.

   A. sufficient

   B. domineering

   C. puissant

   D. analogous

   E. dynamic

   F. supine

10. Members of the audience practically writhed in their seats as they endured the speaker's _____.

   A. jeremiad

   B. oratory

   C. exhortation

   D. harangue

   E. declamation

   F. tirade

ANSWER KEY AND EXPLANATIONS

1. A, D	**6.** A, F
2. C, D	**7.** B, D
3. C, E	**8.** B, E
4. C, F	**9.** C, E
5. B, D	**10.** D, F

1. **The correct answers are A and D.** Your analysis of this sentence should hinge on the phrase "In rare instances," because that's what makes the "deficiency in the glycoprotein Alpha-1 antitrypsin" atypical and peculiar. Notice how similar all the choices are here; each could be used in a certain context to mean "atypical." So try the process of elimination. You can eliminate *phenomenal* and *unparalleled* (choices B and C) because they both have positive connotations that would not be used to describe a condition that puts one's health at risk. *Eccentric* (choice E) is incorrect because it is more usual to use it to describe an atypical person rather than an atypical condition. *Arcane* (choice F) suggests something that is atypical because it is exceptionally old, and there is no suggestion in the paragraph that people once suffered from Alpha-1 antitrypsin deficiency more than they do today.

2. **The correct answers are C and D.** With this question, you should be looking for a comparison or similarity to "insight." Don't be fooled by the word "not." *Astuteness* and *perspicacity* (choices C and D) can both mean "shrewdness," but they both can also mean "intellectual sharpness or keenness," depending on the context, so they are correct in this sentence. Choice A should be eliminated because *alacrity* means "eagerness, liveliness, or quickness" and doesn't make sense. Choice B is incorrect because *acuteness* refers to sensitivity, not insight. *Ingenuity* (choice E) often means "cleverness," which isn't the same as insight. Choice F can also be eliminated because *erudition* is scholarly or deep learning, which isn't the same as insight. It also has no twin in the list.

3. **The correct answers are C and E.** This item is structured as a contrast; it contains the clue "but." So you should be looking for words with the opposite meaning of "clearer," and those words are *amorphous* (choice C) and *shapeless* (choice E). *Recognizable* (choice A) has almost the same meaning as "clearer," so it is not the right word for this context. *Assiduous* (choice D) means "diligent" or "constant," and *zealous* (choice F) means "eager." Neither of these words makes any sense in this context.

4. **The correct answers are C and F.** This is a question that hinges on word usage. *Voracious* and *rapacious* both mean "having an insatiable appetite for something," so they both match the word *appetite*. Choices A and B are incorrect because even though *avaricious* and *grasping* mean "greedy," an appetite cannot be correctly described as avaricious or grasping. Choice D is incorrect because a thirst, not an appetite, is slaked (or left *unslaked*), and choice E is incorrect because *indomitable* is not applied to an appetite; furthermore, it doesn't fit the meaning of the sentence.

5. **The correct answers are B and D.** In this sentence, the second independent clause amplifies the first independent clause, which is signified by the use of the conjunctive adverb "moreover." So the correct answers should indicate that the textbook suffers from flaws in addition to its lack of relevant information. The words need to describe the way the book is written, so *unsystematic* and *muddled* are the best answers since they both imply chaotic organization. *Methodical* (choice A) has the opposite meaning. *Emblematic* and *quintessential*, (choices C and E) both mean "typical," which is too neutral for this context. *Shuffled* (choice F) has a meaning similar to that of *unsystematic* and *muddled*, but it does not convey disorganization as strongly as the correct answers do.

6. **The correct answers are A and F.** Both *lethargy* and *languor* denote an extreme lack of energy or state of physical weakness or listlessness, so they match "physical laziness." You can eliminate *apathy* (choice B), which means "lack of interest"; *petulance* (choice C), which means "irritability"; *decrepitude* (choice D), which means "a state of deterioration due to old age"; and *turpitude* (choice E), which means "baseness or depravity."

7. **The correct answers are B and D.** In this contrast item, you are looking for words that describe the opposite of the feelings of someone who feels weak and achy, and those words are *vitality* (choice B) and *resolve* (choice D). *Mien* (choice A) makes sense in this context, but it fails to provide the specific contrast that choices B and D do. *Attentiveness* (choice C) also makes sense but this word relates more to a level of interest than a level of energy, which is what this sentence most requires. *Enervation* (choice E) means "exhaustion," which is the opposite of what this sentence requires. *Capriciousness* (choice F) means "fanciful humor," which is not really necessary to teach a class.

8. **The correct answers are B and E.** Comparison or similarity clues in this item tip you off to the fact that what was "developing" was also falling flat, or failing to have the desired effect on the audience. Therefore, what was developing was a *flop* (choice B) or a *fiasco* (choice E), words that are not synonyms (a fiasco is more disastrous than a flop), but which both result in nearly the same meaning for the sentence as a whole. *Travail* and *drudgery* (choices A and C) are near synonyms but make no sense in terms of usage and don't provide the proper comparison. The third set of near synonyms or possible synonyms is *composition* and *creation* (choices D and F) and must also be eliminated because they don't convey the sense of something falling flat or failing.

9. **The correct answers are C and E.** Both cause and comparison ideas are at play in this item, whose answers are not synonyms; yet, the answers create equivalence in the completed sentence. So the correct answers should remain in step with the positive personality traits "eloquent" and "charismatic." *Puissant* and *dynamic*, which both suggest vigor and strength, are the best words for this context. *Sufficient* (choice A) is far too weak a word. *Domineering* (choice B) has a meaning somewhat similar to that of *puissant* and *dynamic*, but it also has negative connotations. *Analogous* (choice D) means "similar," which does not make sense in this context. *Supine* (choice F) implies a lack of energy, so it is the opposite of the words this sentence requires.

10. **The correct answers are D and F.** The cause in this item is the speaker's *harangue* or *tirade*, and the effect is the audience's great discomfort. Choice A isn't so likely an answer because a *jeremiad* is often mournful; it may go on and on and may look gloomily at the future, but it is much less likely to make its listeners so physically or visibly uncomfortable as a tirade or harangue would. Mere *oratory* (choice B) and *declamation* (choice E), which can be both pompous and excessively loud, would not result in such great discomfort; in fact, they could as likely be uplifting, so choices B and E are also incorrect. Similarly, *exhortation* alone, no matter how forceful, is less likely to elicit the physical response of writhing with discomfort than a harangue or tirade is, so choice C is also incorrect.

SUMMING IT UP

- Sentence equivalence test items assess your ability to interpret what you read and to supply words whose meanings are in line with the ideas presented in the test items.

- The emphasis is on the meaning of the complete sentence for sentence equivalence test items.

- Each sentence equivalence test item is a single sentence with one blank followed by six answer choices. From the six answer choices, you must select two answers for the question that will result in two sentences with a similar—equivalent—meaning.

- Both answer choices must be correct in order to earn credit for the question.

- Commonsense strategies for answering sentence equivalence questions are the following:
  o   Read the item stem first.
  o   Come up with your own answer.
  o   Check your answers in place.

- More specific language strategies are the following:
  o   Use signal words and structural clues.
  o   Avoid leaping at the first pair of synonyms.
  o   Examine connotations.
  o   Consider grammar and usage.

- General test-taking strategies that are also helpful include the following:
  o   Anticipate and use the clock.
  o   Skip and return to questions.
  o   Eliminate answer choices you know are incorrect.
  o   Use educated guessing.

PART V

QUANTITATIVE REASONING

Strategies for Multiple-Choice Questions

Chapter 9

OVERVIEW

- **Basic Information About Multiple-Choice Question Types**
- **Math Conventions**
- **Strategies for Selecting One Answer Choice**
- **Strategies for Selecting One or More Answer Choices**
- **Strategies for Multiple-Choice Questions in Data Interpretation Sets**
- **Practice Questions**
- **Answer Key and Explanations**
- **Summing It Up**

The Quantitative Reasoning section of the GRE® General Test evaluates test takers' understanding of basic math concepts in arithmetic, algebra, geometry, and data analysis and their ability to apply these concepts to analyze and interpret real-world scenarios. This may sound daunting if you haven't had math for several years, but working through the strategies and the practice questions in this and the next two chapters should reassure you that the math on the GRE® General Test is not that difficult.

In this chapter, you will find an introduction to the two types of multiple-choice questions on the GRE® General Test and to certain strategies that will help you answer these questions correctly and quickly.

BASIC INFORMATION ABOUT MULTIPLE-CHOICE QUESTION TYPES

On the GRE® General Test, there are two formats for multiple-choice questions:

- Multiple-choice questions—select one answer choice
- Multiple-choice questions—select one or more answer choices

You may find multiple-choice questions as stand-alone items, or they may be part of a group of questions that refer to the same tables, graphs, or other form of data presentation. In the latter case, they are known as data interpretation questions.

Most multiple-choice questions on the GRE® General Test are of the familiar multiple-choice questions—select one answer choice type. These questions are accompanied by five answer choices, each with an oval beside it. These questions have only one correct answer, as you would surmise from the name.

Multiple-choice questions—select one or more answer choices are accompanied by a varying number of answer choices. Each answer choice has a square beside it, which is a reminder that the question is a multiple-choice question that may have more than one correct answer, as the name suggests.

The following notes apply to "one or more answer choice" questions:

- The number of answer choices is not always the same—though typically you will see at least three choices.

- The number of correct answer choices is also not always the same. It may be that only one answer choice is correct, or two, or three, or all of them.

- Usually, the question asks you to select all correct answer choices. Sometimes, though, a question will instruct you to select a certain number of answer choices—in which case, of course, you should select exactly that number of choices.

- In order to answer a question correctly, you must select all the correct answer choices, and only those.

  o   You do not get any credit if you select some, but not all, of the correct answer choices.

  o   You do not get any credit if you select the correct number of answer choices, but not all the choices you have selected are correct. (That is, if three out of five answer choices are correct, and you select two of the correct ones as well as an incorrect one, you don't get any credit.)

Although in this book we refer to answer choices as A, B, C, and so on, the answer choices are not labeled on the actual GRE® General Test. The oval or square beside each answer choice is blank.

MATH CONVENTIONS

The test maker provides the following information that applies to all questions in the Quantitative Reasoning section of the GRE® General Test:

- All numbers used are real numbers.

- All figures are assumed to lie in a plane unless otherwise indicated.

- Geometric figures, such as lines, circles, triangles, and quadrilaterals, *are not necessarily* drawn to scale. That is, you should *not* assume that quantities such as lengths and angle measures are as they appear in a figure. You should assume, however, that lines shown as straight are actually straight, points on a line are in the order shown, and more generally, all geometric objects are in the relative positions shown. For questions with geometric figures, you should base your answers on geometric reasoning, not on estimating or comparing quantities by sight or by measurement.

- Coordinate systems, such as *xy*-planes and number lines, *are* drawn to scale. Therefore, you can read, estimate, or compare quantities in such figures by sight or by measurement.

- Graphical data presentations, such as bar graphs, circle graphs, and line graphs, *are* drawn to scale. Therefore, you can read, estimate, or compare data values by sight or by measurement.

The On-Screen Calculator

The GRE® General Test provides you with an on-screen calculator. You may use the calculator at any point during the Quantitative Reasoning sections, but you may find it particularly useful with the numeric entry questions. Before we talk about how you may use the calculator, let's discuss when you should and should not use it.

In general, you *should use* the on-screen calculator if you need to perform difficult calculations. However, most calculations on the GRE® General Test are not that complicated, so most of the time you will not need the calculator. In particular, you *should not use* it in the following cases:

- when the required calculations are simple to perform mentally or on scratch paper
- when you need to give the answer as a fraction rather than a decimal (either in numeric entry questions or in multiple-choice ones)
- when estimating will suffice (for instance, in certain quantitative comparison or data interpretation questions)

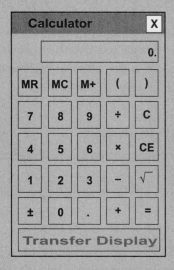

The following are a few notes on using the calculator. Learn them before test day to relieve some of the stress you may experience on that day.

- Unlike some other calculators, this one follows the order of operations. So, for instance, if you type in sequence "1", "+", "3", "×", "5", "=" the calculator will yield "16" as the answer because it will perform the multiplication of 3 by 5 first and then add 1 to the result. If, however, you need to compute $(1+3) \times 5$ instead, then you must type the following sequence: "(", "1", "+", "3", ")", "×", "5", "=". Alternatively, you may type "1", "+", "3", "=", "×", "5", "=". However, it is easy to make mistakes if you try to perform a lengthy combination of operations as a single sequence on the calculator. It may be better to perform each individual computation on its own, use your scratch paper to note intermediate results, and then perform new computations on these results. In the above example, calculate $1+3$ first, note the result ("4") on your scratch paper, clear the calculator display by pressing the "C" button, and finally calculate 4×5.

- When you click the memory sum button ("M+"), the number in the calculator display is placed in the calculator's memory bank, and the letter "M" appears to the left of the display. When you later click "M+" again, the number in the calculator's display is added to the number in the memory bank. When you click the memory recall button ("MR"), the number in the calculator's memory bank at that time appears in the display area. The memory clear button ("MC") clears the memory.

- In numeric entry questions, you may click the calculator's "Transfer Display" button in order to transfer the number displayed on the calculator to the answer box. You cannot use the "Transfer Display" feature if the answer is a fraction. Note that if you click "Transfer Display" on a question that asks you to round your answer to a certain degree of accuracy, you may need to edit the number in the answer box so that it is appropriately rounded up or down.

STRATEGIES FOR SELECTING ONE ANSWER CHOICE

TIP

Don't forget these four test-taking strategies listed in Chapter 1: (1) anticipate and use the clock, (2) skip and return to questions, (3) eliminate answer choices that you know are incorrect, and (4) use educated guessing.

Reviewing the math principles that are covered in the GRE® General Test is an important part of preparing to take the test. However, using test-specific strategies can help you move through the test more quickly and with greater confidence. The following four strategies work especially well for multiple-choice questions that require only one answer:

1. Pick and plug numbers.
2. Work backward from the answer choices.
3. Turn verbose or abstract language into concise and concrete wording.
4. Estimate.

Pick and Plug Numbers

Picking and plugging numbers can be a useful strategy if:

- a question and its answer choices contain variables, but you're not certain how to solve the question directly.

- you are dealing with a question about percents.

- you are not certain about a particular number property—such as whether the product of two odd numbers is odd or even.

Apply the strategy by:

- picking simple numbers so that calculations are reasonable.

- plugging these numbers into the answer choices.

- eliminating any choices that don't produce the desired result.

For Example 1, choose <u>one</u> answer choice.

Example 1

Susan can run $2x$ miles in y hours. In 75 minutes, how many miles will Susan run?

A. $\dfrac{5y}{8x}$

B. $\dfrac{2x}{75y}$

C. $\dfrac{150x}{y}$

D. $\dfrac{5xy}{2}$

E. $\dfrac{5x}{2y}$

You can solve this question directly: if Susan runs $2x$ miles in y hours, then she runs $\dfrac{2x}{y}$ miles per hour. Thus, in 75 minutes, that is, in $\dfrac{5}{4}$ hours, she will run $\dfrac{2x}{y} \times \dfrac{5}{4} = \dfrac{5x}{2y}$ miles. If you don't feel comfortable solving directly, you have an alternative.

Let $x = 4$ and $y = 1$.

Susan can run 8 miles in 1 hour (60 minutes), so in 75 minutes Susan will run 10 miles: one-and-a-quarter as many miles as she can run in 1 hour. Now, plug the values $x = 4$ and $y = 1$ into the answer choices and see which of them yield(s) 10.

A. $\dfrac{5 \times 1}{8 \times 4} = \dfrac{5}{32}$ Eliminate.

B. $\dfrac{2 \times 4}{75 \times 1} = \dfrac{8}{75}$ Eliminate.

C. $\dfrac{150 \times 4}{1} = 600$ Eliminate.

D. $\dfrac{5 \times 4 \times 1}{2} = 10$ This option is a possibility. Hold on to it and solve option E.

E. $\dfrac{5 \times 4}{2 \times 1} = 10$ This option is also possible.

Since two answer choices produce the desired result, you need to check these choices again.

Pick different numbers—say, $x = 6$ and $y = 2$. Susan runs 12 miles every 2 hours, or 6 miles per hour. Therefore, in 75 minutes, Susan will run 7.5 miles.

D. $\dfrac{5 \times 6 \times 2}{2} = 30$ Eliminate.

E. $\dfrac{5 \times 6}{2 \times 2} = 7.5$ Correct.

The correct answer is E.

Picking numbers can be a useful back-up tool if you're not confident that you can solve a question directly. However, when it comes to percentage increase/decrease problems, it is not only a good backup, but an excellent way to find the right answer even more quickly than if you were solving directly. Consider the following example:

For Example 2, choose <u>one</u> answer choice.

Example 2

    Mary sold her biology textbook to her friend John for a 40% discount compared with the price she paid to buy it. After completing his class, John sold the book on the internet for 20% more than the price he paid Mary for the book. The price for which John sold the book is what percent of the price that Mary paid?

    A. 40

    B. 60

    C. 72

    D. 80

    E. 120

Pick the number $100 to represent the amount that Mary paid to buy the book. She then sold the book to John for a 40% discount of $100, or $100 − 40 = $60. John sold it for 20% more than the $60 he paid, so he sold it for $72.

What percent of $100 (the price Mary paid to buy the book) is $72 (the price John got when he sold it)?

$$\frac{72}{100} = \frac{x}{100} \Rightarrow x = 72$$

The correct answer is C.

Work Backward from the Answer Choices

In some cases, if there are numbers in the answer choices, and if, in order to solve directly, you may have to work through some complicated equations, you may choose to work backward from the answer choices.

For Example 3, choose <u>one</u> answer choice.

Example 3

In city X, the first $30,000 of someone's annual income are taxed at the rate of 5%, while any income over $30,000 is taxed at the rate of 10%. If in a certain year Betty paid $2,100 in city X taxes, what was her income that year?

  A. $32,000

  B. $33,000

  C. $34,000

  D. $35,000

  E. $36,000

In this example, you can turn the information in the question stem into an equation, and then solve that equation directly. Or, you can go straight to the answer choices, and, since the choices are listed from least to greatest, begin with choice C, the middle one. If Betty's income had been $34,000, then she would have paid $\frac{5}{100}\$30,000 + \frac{10}{100}\$4,000 = \$1,500 + \$400 = \$1,900$.

This amount is too low also, so Betty must have earned more than $34,000. You can eliminate choices A and B in addition to choice C, because they are less than choice C. Next, check choice D.

If Betty's income had been $35,000, then she would have paid $\frac{5}{100}\$30,000 + \frac{10}{100}\$5,000 = \$2,000$.

This amount is also too low, so you can eliminate choice D. That leaves choice E. **The correct answer is E.**

Turn Verbose or Abstract Language into Concise and Concrete Wording

Sometimes it seems as though test makers are trying to confuse you with wordy questions. Don't worry! You can always turn excessive verbiage into diagrams or mathematical expressions that are easier to understand and work with.

NOTE

Turning verbose or abstract language into concise and concrete wording is an important strategy to help you answer any math question.

For Example 4, choose <u>one</u> answer choice.

Example 4

Diana prepared a certain amount of a chemical solution and stored it in 10 right-cylindrical containers, each with a diameter of 8 inches and a height of 8 inches. Alternatively, she could have stored the same amount of the solution in 40 right-cylindrical containers, all of them with the same height as one another and with a radius of 2 inches. What is the height of these containers?

A. 4

B. 8

C. 10

D. 16

E. 40

TIP

These are the two most important strategies for you to follow: (1) always read questions carefully and (2) reword confusing questions into concise and concrete language. You need to understand what a question is asking in order to answer it correctly.

Begin by writing down the given information, removing the clutter of any extraneous words. The dimensions of the first set of containers are $r = 4$ and $h = 8$. The dimensions of the second set of containers are $r' = 2$ and h'.

The volume of the solution equals 10 times the volume of each of the initial containers: $V_{total} = 10\pi r^2 h$. The volume also equals 40 times the volume of each of the alternate containers: $V_{total} = 40\pi r^2 h$. Equate these two expressions: $10\pi r^2 h = 40\pi r^2 h'$.

Next, substitute the values of r, h, and r: $10\pi 4^2 \times 8 = 40\pi 2^2 h'$. Eliminate π from both sides of the equation and calculate the two squares: $10 \times 16 \times 8 = 40 \times 4h'$. Divide both sides by 160: $h' = 8$. **The correct answer is B.**

Estimate

Estimating is a very valuable strategy for data interpretation questions as well as for quantitative comparisons. However, even in regular multiple-choice questions with a single correct answer, estimating may help, especially if you're running out of time.

For Example 5, choose <u>one</u> answer choice.

Example 5

Sixty percent of the 25 professors in a certain university's engineering department are male. If two male professors retire and two female professors are hired, what percent of the department's professors will be male? (Assume no other changes in the engineering faculty.)

A. 48

B. 52

C. 56.5

D. 60

E. 68

It's best to solve this question directly. However, you should also note that, after the changes, the engineering department will have fewer male professors than it had before, but the same total number of professors. The percentage of its faculty that's male should drop from the original 60%. Thus, you can eliminate answer choices D and E because they are greater than 60%.

For the record, to solve this directly, first find the number of male professors before the changes:
$\frac{60}{100} = \frac{x}{25} \Rightarrow x = \frac{60 \times 25}{100} \Rightarrow x = 15$

After the changes, the department still has 25 professors, but this time 13 of them are male. Set up a proportion in order to turn 13 into a percentage: $\frac{13}{25} = \frac{x}{100} \Rightarrow x = 52$. **The correct answer is B.**

STRATEGIES FOR SELECTING ONE OR MORE ANSWER CHOICES

Remember that the number of answer choices is not always the same for this multiple-choice format. You might have three answers to choose from—the basic number of choices—or as many as five or more. The number of correct answers that you can be asked to choose varies as well. If you don't choose all the correct answers, you will not get credit for the correct answers that you do choose.

Of the five strategies listed for multiple-choice questions that require only one answer, picking numbers and working backward from the answer choices are not useful strategies when you aren't told how many correct answer choices there are. Estimating can be very useful, especially in data interpretation questions, as you'll see later in this chapter. As for turning verbose language into something concise and concrete: It's always a helpful strategy in mathematics! However, the following strategies and notes are specific to multiple-choice questions with one or more correct answer choices:

- Calculate the least and greatest possible values.
- Make sure you're answering the correct question.
- Think through data sufficiency questions.

Calculate the Least and Greatest Possible Values

On some questions, it is helpful to calculate what the least and greatest possible values for the answer choices are, and then eliminate any choices that do not fit within that range.

NOTE

If you decide to skip a question, make sure you click the "Mark" button, so you can find it quickly on the "Review" screen later. Remember: There's no wrong-answer penalty, so don't leave any questions unanswered!

For Example 6, indicate all the answers that apply.

Example 6

A kiosk sells only the following snacks: cookies for $1.50 each, ice-cream bars for $2.50 each, and chips for $1.00 each. Clara bought four snacks at the kiosk. Which of the following could be the total amount that she paid?

Indicate all such amounts.

A. $3.50

B. $4.00

C. $4.50

D. $6.50

E. $8.50

F. $10.50

Start by calculating the least and greatest possible values, in order to limit your options. If Clara bought four bags of chips, the cheapest item, then she spent $4. Thus, all answer choices that are an amount less than $4 are incorrect. If she bought four ice-cream bars, the most expensive item, she spent $10. Thus, all answer choices that feature an amount greater than $10 are incorrect.

You're left with the middle four answer choices, and indeed, all four of them are possible: $4 represents a purchase of four bags of chips; $4.50 represents a purchase of three bags of chips and one cookie; $6.50 represents a purchase of two cookies, one bag of chips, and one ice-cream bar; and $8.50 represents a purchase of three ice-cream bars and one bag of chips. **The correct answers are B, C, D, and E.**

Note in which of the following questions you MUST work backward from the answer choices. Do not start by calculating all the possible amounts that Clara could have spent. The answer choices do not have to list all of these amounts, only some of them. For instance, Clara could have spent $7.50 if she had bought two ice-cream bars, one cookie, and one bag of chips. However, $7.50 is not one of the answer choices—so you don't want to waste your time making calculations that are unnecessary.

Make Sure You're Answering the Correct Question

This is always sound advice, of course, but it is of particular importance in answering questions with one or more correct answer choices. Most of these questions ask you to select all the correct answer choices. However, you may also come upon a question that asks you to select a specific number of answer choices. You have to read the questions carefully to be sure of what to do.

For Example 7, indicate all the answers that apply.

Example 7

If p is a prime number, then the product of which <u>two</u> of the following numbers must be the square of an integer?

A. $\dfrac{1}{p}$

B. $\sqrt{p}$

C. p^2

D. p^3

Since you know that the product of only two of the answer choices is a perfect square, you may not need to check all the possible combinations. When you find the two answer choices that work, you can stop and move on to the next question. In this case, if you noticed early on that the product of $\dfrac{1}{p}$ and p^3 is p^2, a perfect square, you won't have to consider any other products. **The correct answers are A and D.**

Think Through Data Sufficiency Questions

Example 8 is a data sufficiency question: a question that asks you to determine whether each answer choice is sufficient on its own to provide a definitive answer to the question. Sometimes, a data sufficiency question is of the yes/no variety (as is the case with this example). For such questions, an answer choice is sufficient

- if it provides a positive answer,

OR

- if it provides a negative answer.

For Example 8, indicate all the answers that apply.

Example 8

Angela is five years older than Melissa, who is two years younger than Heather. Which of the following statements <u>individually</u> provide(s) sufficient additional information to determine whether Heather is older than 23 years old?

Indicate <u>all</u> such statements.

A. Angela is 27 years old.

B. Melissa is younger than 21 years old.

C. Heather is twice as old as Melissa was ten years ago.

Begin by reviewing the information in the question. If Angela is five years older than Melissa, and Melissa is two years younger than Heather, then Angela is three years older than Heather. It helps to write out these relationships as equations:

$$A = M + 5$$
$$H = M + 2$$
$$A = H + 3$$

Answer choice A: If Angela is 27 years old, then Heather is 24 years old—in other words, she is older than 23 years old. Answer choice A is sufficient.

Answer choice B: This tells you that Melissa is younger than 21 years old. Since $H = M + 2$, Heather is younger than 23 years old. Answer choice B is sufficient, as well.

Answer choice C: Write out this statement as an equation:

$$H = 2(M - 10) \Rightarrow$$
$$H = 2M - 20$$

You now have two equations that relate H and M (the other one is $H = M + 2$). These two equations are distinct—that is, one is not a multiple of the other—so it is possible to solve these equations and find a unique solution for H and M. Therefore, the third answer choice is also sufficient. **The correct answers are A, B, and C.**

STRATEGIES FOR MULTIPLE-CHOICE QUESTIONS IN DATA INTERPRETATION SETS

In each Quantitative Reasoning section, you should expect to see one set of questions that are grouped together and refer to the same data presentation—such as a graph or table. The questions will be either multiple-choice (both types) or numeric entry. The following strategies are helpful in solving data interpretation sets:

- Scan the data quickly.
- Make sure you're answering the correct question.
- Estimate.

The last two are useful for all types of questions in the Quantitative Reasoning section.

Quickly Scan the Data

When you first encounter a data interpretation set, scan the data in order to get a general idea of the information presented. Just as you do when reading a Reading Comprehension passage, don't waste time on the details. There will be time for the details when you look at the actual questions. Rather, note the following:

- What kind of data—such as sales figures, population trends, etc.—are presented?
- Do the graphs/tables give actual values or percentages?
- If more than one table or graph is presented, how are they related? For instance, does one table give actual values, whereas the other gives percentages?

- What units are used (for example, millions vs. billions of dollars)?
- Are there any notes above or below the data that give additional information?

Make Sure You're Answering the Correct Question

Don't make careless mistakes when considering the questions. If a question asks about June sales figures, don't look in the July column of the table by mistake. If you're asked to find a percentage, don't look for or calculate actual values.

The following example is a straightforward bar graph. It compares enrollment by male and female students majoring in science, engineering, and mathematics. The information is presented in real numbers.

Examples 9–10 are based on the following data.

NUMBER OF STUDENTS AT UNIVERSITY K MAJORING IN SCIENCE, ENGINEERING, AND MATHEMATICS

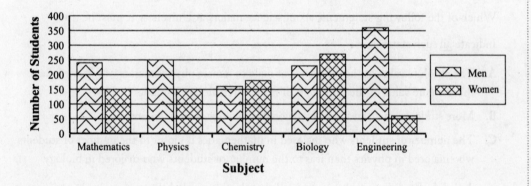

For Example 9, choose <u>one</u> answer choice.

Example 9

If a total of 12,049 students are enrolled in University K, approximately what percentage of these students is majoring in engineering?

A. 0.5

B. 3

C. 3.5

D. 17

E. 20

This question is not particularly difficult, as long as you don't make any careless mistakes. Make sure you look at the bars representing the engineering majors, not any of the other four sets of bars. Also, make sure you consider both male and female engineering majors, not just male or just female students.

The number of male engineering majors is approximately 355. The number of female engineering majors is approximately 70. Thus, the total number of engineering majors is approximately 425. Solve a proportion in order to find what percent of the total student population 425 is: $\frac{425}{12,049} = \frac{x}{100} \Rightarrow x \approx 3.53$. **The correct answer is C.**

Estimate

For some questions, you only need to find approximate values. Don't waste time performing exact calculations if you don't have to. In particular, remember that graphs are drawn to scale, so you can use them to estimate values. Consider the following:

For Example 10, indicate <u>all</u> the answers that apply.

Example 10

Which of the following statements about science majors at University K must be true?

Indicate <u>all</u> such statements.

A. The absolute value of the difference of male to female physics majors was greater than the absolute value of the difference of male to female mathematics majors.

B. More students, male and female, majored in biology than in engineering.

C. The number of students who majored in mathematics is closer to the number of students who majored in physics than it is to the number of students who majored in biology.

Answer choice A: From the graph, you can tell that there were slightly more male physics majors than male mathematics majors, but slightly fewer female physics majors than female mathematics majors. You don't need to worry about their exact numbers. The visual evidence is sufficient to tell you that when you subtract the number of female physics majors from the number of male physics majors, you get a larger number than you do when you subtract the number of female mathematics majors from the number of male mathematics majors. Answer choice A is true.

Answer choice B: The number of students who majored in biology was approximately 225 (male) + 275 (female) = 500. In example 9, you approximated the number of engineering students as 425. Again, the visual evidence is sufficient, even if your estimates are not perfect. Answer choice B is true.

Answer choice C: Once again, you can estimate from the graph that the number of students who majored in mathematics is slightly less than 400, which is similar to the number of students who majored in physics. You've already estimated the number of students who majored in biology as 500. Thus, answer choice C is true, as well.

The correct answers are A, B, and C.

PRACTICE QUESTIONS

For Questions 1–15, unless the directions state otherwise, choose <u>one</u> answer choice.

1. The sum of squares of three consecutive positive odd integers is 155. What is the largest of these three integers?

   A. 3

   B. 5

   C. 7

   D. 9

   E. 11

2. Each year between 2001 and 2011, an Italian winemaker in Montalcino used between 75% and 80% of his grapes to produce his Brunello di Montalcino wine, and the rest to produce his Rosso di Montalcino wine. If in 2011 he produced 2,500 cases of Brunello, which of the following could have been the total number of cases of wine he produced that year?

   Indicate <u>all</u> such numbers of cases.

   A. 3,128

   B. 3,153

   C. 3,241

   D. 3,308

   E. 3,334

3. If a is a positive even integer less than 10, b is a negative even integer greater than −10, and c is a positive odd integer between 2 and 10, which of the following cannot be an integer?

   A. $\dfrac{bc}{a}$

   B. $\dfrac{ac}{b}$

   C. $\dfrac{ab}{c}$

   D. $\dfrac{ab}{c^2}$

   E. $\dfrac{2ab}{c^3}$

4. What is the probability of randomly selecting a jack or a club from a standard well-shuffled 52-card deck?

   A. $\dfrac{1}{3}$

   B. $\dfrac{17}{52}$

   C. $\dfrac{4}{13}$

   D. $\dfrac{1}{4}$

   E. $\dfrac{15}{52}$

SHOW YOUR WORK HERE

5. The average (arithmetic mean) weight of a football team's offensive linemen is 320 pounds, while the average weight of the team's defensive linemen is 300 pounds. If the team has at least 50% more defensive linemen than offensive linemen, which of the following could be the average weight of all of the team's offensive and defensive linemen, combined?
Indicate <u>all</u> such weights.

A. 304

B. 305

C. 306

D. 307

E. 308

F. 309

6. The lengths of two of the sides of a triangle are 5 meters and 6 meters. Which of the following are possible lengths of the third side? Select <u>all</u> that apply.

A. 1 meter

B. 2 meters

C. 3 meters

D. 5 meters

E. 9 meters

F. 11 meters

G. 12 meters

SHOW YOUR WORK HERE

7. In a high school orchestra, 40% of the string players are violinists, 20% are violists, 25% are cellists, and 15% are bassists. If 2 violinists, 1 violist, 1 cellist, and 1 bassist are added, what will be the percentage of violinists in the orchestra? (Assume no other changes to the orchestra's string section.)

A. 30%

B. 35%

C. 40%

D. 45%

E. It cannot be determined.

8. If a and b are two of the solutions of the equation $x^3 - x^2 - 6x = 0$, with $a \neq 0$ and $a \neq b$, then which of the following could be the graph of $\dfrac{x}{a} > b$?
Indicate all such graphs.

A.

B.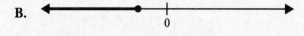

C.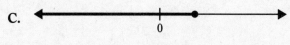

D.

9. Each of the managers of a 20-person technical support team received $3,000 as a year-end bonus, whereas each of the nonmanagers received $1,200 as a year-end bonus. If the total amount that the 20 employees received was $31,200, how many of the team's members are managers?

A. 1

B. 2

C. 3

D. 4

E. 5

SHOW YOUR WORK HERE

Questions 10–12 are based on the following data.

INCOME DATA FOR TOWN X's FOUR NEIGHBORHOODS: A, B, C, and D.

Annual Income in 2017	Percent of Neighborhood Populations			
	A	B	C	D
$0–$24,999	14%	4%	17%	13%
$25,000–$49,999	30%	19%	34%	31%
$50,000–$74,999	26%	29%	27%	32%
$75,000–$99,999	19%	28%	15%	18%
$100,000–$249,999	9%	14%	6%	5%
> $250,000	2%	6%	1%	1%

10. In the neighborhood with the smallest percentage of six-figure earners in 2017, what percent of the population earned less than $50,000 that year?

   A. 23
   B. 31
   C. 34
   D. 44
   E. 51

11. If the percentage of people who resided in neighborhood B in 2017 and earned between $0 and $24,999 was 20% less than the percentage of people who resided in neighborhood B in 2007 and earned between $0 and $24,999, and if the latter percentage was 20% less than the percentage of people who resided in neighborhood B in 1997 and earned between $0 and $24,999, what percent of the people who resided in neighborhood B in 1997 earned between $0 and $24,999 that year?

   A. 4
   B. 5
   C. 6
   D. 6.25
   E. 6.67

SHOW YOUR WORK HERE

12. Which of the following statements must be true?

Indicate all such statements.

A. In 2017, the neighborhood with the highest average income was neighborhood B.

B. In 2017, 12% of the people living in town X earned less than $25,000.

C. If in 2017 more than twice as many people lived in neighborhood A as in neighborhood B, then the number of people who lived in neighborhood A and earned $100,000 or more was greater than the number of people who lived in neighborhood B and earned $100,000 or more.

13. Which quadrant(s) in the *xy*-plane does the graph of $y = (x + 5)(x + 1)$ intersect? Select all that apply.

A. Quadrant I

B. Quadrant II

C. Quadrant III

D. Quadrant IV

14. A couple plans to install ceramic tile in their 9 × 18 foot kitchen using 9-inch square tiles. The manufacturer sells boxes of 16 tiles. How many boxes does the couple need to purchase to ensure the entire floor can be covered with tiles?

A. 12

B. 18

C. 24

D. 30

E. 36

SHOW YOUR WORK HERE

15. If x and y are integers such that $|x - y| = 1$, which of the following statements individually provide(s) sufficient additional information to determine what x is? Indicate <u>all</u> such statements.

A. x and y are the solutions of the equation $a^2 + 7a + 12 = 0$.

B. $y = 3$

C. x and y are both prime numbers, and y is odd.

SHOW YOUR WORK HERE

ANSWER KEY AND EXPLANATIONS

1. D	**9.** D	**11.** D
2. A, B, C, D	**10.** D	**12.** C
3. E	**6.** B, C, D, E	**13.** A, B, C
4. C	**7.** C	**14.** B
5. A, B, C, D, E	**8.** A, B, D	**15.** C

1. **The correct answer is D.** Let x be the smallest of the three consecutive odd integers. Then, the other two are $x + 2$ and $x + 4$. The equation relating them is $x^2 + (x + 2)^2 + (x + 4)^2 = 155$.

   Solve for x:

   $$x^2 + (x + 2)^2 + (x + 4)^2 = 155$$
   $$x^2 + x^2 + 4x + 4 + x^2 + 8x + 16 = 155$$
   $$3x^2 + 12x + 20 = 155$$
   $$3x^2 + 12x - 135 = 0$$
   $$3(x^2 + 4x - 45) = 0$$
   $$3(x + 9)(x - 5) = 0$$
   $$x = -9, 5$$

   So $x = 5$ (since the integers are assumed to be positive). The three integers, therefore, are 5, 7, and 9. The largest of them is 9.

2. **The correct answers are A, B, C, and D.** For this question, the strategy "calculate the least and greatest possible values" is the most helpful. Calculate the least and greatest values and then select all the choices that fall between them. The 2,500 cases of Brunello that the winemaker produced in 2011 are between $\frac{3}{4}$ and $\frac{4}{5}$ of his total production.

   If P is his total production that year, then

   $$\frac{3}{4}P < 2,500 < \frac{4}{5}P.$$

   The first inequality yields $P < 3,333.\overline{3}$.

   The second yields $P > 3,125$.

   Any answer choice that falls between these two numbers is correct.

3. **The correct answer is E.** "Which of the following cannot be" means that you can eliminate any answer choice for which you can find at least one example that *can* be true. In other words, it does not matter if, let's say, for choice A, the fraction $\frac{bc}{a}$ is sometimes not an integer. As long as it can be an integer at least once, then choice A is not the correct answer.

First, turn the abstract language into more concrete wording.

- If a is a positive even integer less than 10, then a may be 2, 4, 6, or 8.
- If b is a negative even integer greater than −10, then b may be −2, −4, −6, or −8.
- If c is a positive odd integer between 2 and 10, then c may be 3, 5, 7, or 9.

Next, move on to the answer choices:

A. As long as $a = 2$, then $\frac{bc}{a}$ will be an integer, no matter what the other two numbers are. Eliminate it.

B. As long as $b = -2$, then $\frac{ac}{b}$ will be an integer, no matter what the other two numbers are. Eliminate it.

C. If $c = 3$ and either $a = 6$ or $b = -6$ (or both), then $\frac{ab}{c}$ will be an integer. Eliminate it.

D. If $c = 3$, $a = 6$, and $b = -6$, then $\frac{ab}{c^2}$ will be an integer. Eliminate it.

E. Numbers 5 and 7 are not part of the prime factorization of any of the possible values that a and b may take, so if $c = 5$ or $c = 7$, $\frac{2ab}{c^3}$ cannot be an integer. If $c = 3$, raising it to the third power will produce three 3s in the denominator. At best, the numerator will have two 3s as factors (if $a = 6$ and $b = -6$), so $\frac{2ab}{c^3}$ cannot be an integer if $c = 3$. Finally, if $c = 9$, the denominator will have even more 3s. Thus, $\frac{2ab}{c^3}$ cannot be an integer.

4. **The correct answer is C.** There are 13 clubs in such a deck and 4 jacks. But, there is only one jack of clubs. To ensure you do not double-count that card, subtract one from the total, 17. Since the card is randomly selected and the deck is shuffled, all cards are equally likely to be drawn. So the probability of the desired event is $\frac{16}{52} = \frac{4}{13}$.

5. **The correct answers are A, B, C, D, and E.** Calculate the greatest possible value and then select all the choices that fall between it and 300. If the team has exactly 50% more defensive linemen than offensive linemen, then for every 3 defensive linemen there are 2 offensive linemen. In this scenario, the average of the weights is the following weighted average:

$$\frac{2 \times 320 + 3 \times 300}{5} = 308$$

If the team has more than 50% defensive linemen, then that average will be even lower.

6. **The correct answers are B, C, D, and E.** The sum of the lengths of any two sides of a triangle must be greater than the length of the third. This is true for choices B, C, D, and E, but not for the others.

7. **The correct answer is C.** This is a tricky question. Answer choice E seems correct, since you know only the starting percentages of string players, but not their exact numbers. On the other hand, choice E may be a trap. If you don't feel confident, you can skip this question and revisit it later. However, working from what you know, you can make the information more concrete, and arrive at the correct answer. Five new string players are added, and two of them are violinists. In other words, 40% of the new players are violinists. Because 40% of the original string players were violinists, and 40% of the ones added are violinists, the percentage of violinists remains unchanged.

8. **The correct answers are A, B, and D.** Begin by scanning the answer choices in order to see what type of answers to look for. Next, work out the math in the question, and see which answer choices fit your results.

   First, manipulate the equation $x^3 - x^2 - 6x = 0$. Factor out an x from each term: $x(x^2 - x - 6) = 0$

   Then factor the quadratic expression, using reverse FOIL (First, Outside, Inside, Last). Remember that $x^2 - x - 6 = (x + a)(x + b)$, where $ab = -6$ and $a + b = -1$, the coefficient of x. The numbers 2 and −3 for a and b are the only ones that qualify, so the expression becomes $x(x + 2)(x - 3) = 0$.

   Thus, the possible solutions of the equation are $x = 0$, $x = -2$, and $x = 3$. All three of these solutions are possible values for b and the possible values for a are −2 or 3.

There are four different possibilities:

1. If $a = -2$ and $b = 0$, then $x < 0$ (Remember that multiplying both sides of an inequality by a negative number reverses the direction of the inequality.) The graph of this inequality appears in answer choice A.

2. If $a = -2$ and $b = 3$, then $x < -6$. The graph of this inequality appears in choice B.

3. If $a = 3$ and $b = 0$, then $x > 0$. The graph of this inequality is not listed.

4. If $a = 3$ and $b = -2$, then $x > -6$. The graph of this inequality appears in choice D.

9. **The correct answer is D.** Work backward, starting with choice C. If there are 3 managers, then together they received $9,000. The remaining 17 employees received $20,400. These two amounts add up to $29,400, which is too low. Thus, there are more than 3 managers. Move on to choice D. If there are 4 managers, then together they received $12,000. The remaining 16 employees received $19,200. These two add up to $31,200.

10. **The correct answer is D.** Make sure you're answering the correct question. "Six-figure earners" means that you have to look at the bottom two rows, not just the bottom row. Also, "less than $50,000" means you should add the top two rows in the appropriate column. So, first, identify the neighborhood with the smallest percentage of six-figure earners: that's neighborhood D, $5 + 1 = 6\%$ of its residents earn $100,000 or more. Next, add the percentages of D residents who earned between $0 and $49,999: $13 + 31 = 44$.

11. **The correct answer is D.** First, translate English into math:

The percentage of B residents who earned between $0 and $24,999 in 2017 is 4.

20% fewer B residents earned between $0 and $24,999 in 2017 than in 2007. Hence, if X is the percentage of those folks who earned between $0 and $24,999 in 2007, then $4 = \dfrac{80}{100}X \Rightarrow X = \dfrac{400}{80}$.

20% fewer B residents earned between $0 and $24,999 in 2007 than in 1997. Hence, if Y is the percentage of those folks who earned between $0 and $24,999 in 1997, then $X = \dfrac{80}{100}Y \Rightarrow \dfrac{400}{80} = \dfrac{80}{100}Y$. Solve for Y to get $Y = 6.25$.

12. **The correct answer is C.** Do not conclude hastily that statement 1 (choice A) is true. It may be, for instance, that all of the B residents earned at the lowest end of their income range (e.g., all the $250,000 + earners actually earned $250,000), while the A residents earned at the highest end of their income range. In this scenario, the residents in neighborhood A had a higher average income than the residents in neighborhood B.

Statement 2 (choice B) takes the straight average of the percentages of residents in the four neighborhoods who earned between $0 and $24,999. However, if all four neighborhoods did not have the same number of people in 2017, you need a weighted average—and such an average may be different from 12%. Thus, statement 2 (choice B) is not necessarily true.

Finally, evaluate statement 3 (choice C). In 2017, 11% of the residents in neighborhood A earned $100,000 or more, and 20% of the B residents did also. If P_A is the total number of A residents in 2017 and P_B is the total number of B residents in 2017, then $P_A > 2P_B$. Thus, 11% of P_A is greater than 20% of P_B and statement 3 (choice C) is true.

13. The correct answers are A, B, and C. The graph of this quadratic equation crosses the x-axis at $x = -5$ and $x = -1$, opens upward since the coefficient of the squared term is positive, and has its vertex at $(-3, -4)$. Further, it intersects the y-axis at $(0, 5)$. Its graph is as follows:

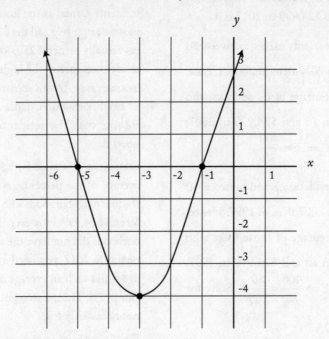

The graph does not cross into quadrant IV, but does intersect the other three.

14. The correct answer is B. The floor dimensions, in inches, are 108 by 216 (since there are 12 inches in 1 foot). You can fit 12 tiles across the shorter side (since 108 divided by 9 is 12) and 24 tiles across the longer side (since 216 divided by 9 is 24). So, all told, 12(24) = 288 square tiles are needed. Since there are 16 in one box, the couple needs to purchase $\dfrac{288}{16} = 18$ boxes of tiles.

15. The correct answer is C. This is another data sufficiency question. First, you need to understand the question stem.

If $|x - y| = 1$, then either $x - y = 1$ or $x - y = -1$.

x and y are consecutive integers (since the absolute value of their difference is 1), but otherwise, the range of possibilities for x and y is infinite. There's nothing more you can do with the question stem alone.

Step 2 is to consider the answer choice options. For choice A, factor the quadratic equation:

$a^2 + 7a + 12 = 0 \Rightarrow (a + 4)(a + 3) = 0$. The two solutions are $a = -4$ and $a = -3$. However, you do not know which of the two solutions is x and which is y, so this answer choice is not sufficient for you to determine what the value of x is. (Plug in $x = -4$ and $y = -3$, and then $x = -3$ and $y = -4$ into the absolute value equation in the question stem, and you'll see that both options work.)

Choice B pins down the value of y. However, that is still not sufficient: The absolute value equation is satisfied if $x = 4$ as well as if $x = 2$.

Moving on to choice C, because x and y are consecutive integers (as you determined above), and if both are prime, then they have to be the numbers 2 and 3. (All other prime numbers are odd, so the only way to get two consecutive integers that are both prime is if one of the two is the number 2.) Additionally, y is odd, which means that $x = 2$. This statement is sufficient.

SUMMING IT UP

- There are two types of multiple-choice questions on the Quantitative Reasoning section of the GRE® General Test:
  - multiple-choice—select one answer choice
  - multiple-choice—select one or more answer choices
- Multiple-choice questions may be structured separately or they may be part of a data interpretation set, which includes several questions built around presentation of data, such as a table or graph.
- Multiple-choice questions that require only one answer have five answer choices to select from. Each answer choice is preceded by an oval.
- Multiple-choice questions that ask for one or more answer choices are accompanied by a varying number of answer choices. These answer choices are preceded by squares, not ovals, as a signal to choose one or more answer choices.
- Strategies that are useful for all math questions are the following:
  - Make sure you're answering the correct question.
  - Skip and come back to questions—used sparingly.
- Strategies specific to multiple-choice questions—select one answer choice are the following:
  - Pick and plug numbers.
  - Work backward from the answer choices.
  - Turn verbose or abstract language into concise and concrete wording.
  - Estimate.
- Strategies specific to multiple-choice questions—select one or more answer choices are the following:
  - Calculate the least and greatest possible values.
  - Make sure you're answering the correct question.
  - Think through data sufficiency questions.
- Strategies for data interpretation sets are the following:
  - Scan the data quickly.
  - Make sure you're answering the correct question.
  - Estimate.

Strategies for Numeric Entry Questions

OVERVIEW

- **Answer Format for Numeric Entry Questions**
- **A Reminder About Using the On-Screen Calculator**
- **Strategies for Numeric Entry Questions**
- **Practice Questions**
- **Answer Key and Explanations**
- **Summing It Up**

This chapter describes the answer format for numeric entry questions and provides the following three useful strategies for solving numeric entry questions:

1. Turn verbose or abstract language into concise and concrete wording.
2. Make sure you're answering the correct question.
3. Round correctly.

Like multiple-choice questions, numeric entry questions may be stand-alone items, or they may be part of a data interpretation set: a group of questions that refer to the same tables, graphs, or other form of data presentation. Strategies for data interpretation, other than estimating, apply to numeric entry questions as well.

Finally, remember also that you can always skip a question and return to it if you find that you're having trouble figuring out what it's asking or you think it will take too long to answer.

ANSWER FORMAT FOR NUMERIC ENTRY QUESTIONS

Numeric entry questions do not offer any answer choices from which you can choose. Rather, they present you with a question and

- one answer box, if the answer is an integer or decimal.
- two answer boxes, if the answer is a fraction.

You have to use your keyboard to input your answer in the appropriate answer box. If the answer is a fraction, type the numerator in the top box and the denominator in the bottom box.

Chapter 10

Entering Answers

Here are a few instructions about entering answers that you should be familiar with before you take the test. Knowing how to enter answers will ease some of the stress you may experience on test day.

- To erase a numeral in the answer box, use the "backspace" key.

- To enter a negative sign, type a hyphen.

- To remove the negative sign, type the hyphen again.

- To enter a decimal point, type a period. Note that you cannot use decimal points in fractions.

- Equivalent forms of the answer, such as 2.5 and 2.50, are all correct.

- You do not need to reduce fractions to lowest terms.

A REMINDER ABOUT USING THE ON-SCREEN CALCULATOR

The on-screen calculator can be especially useful in answering numeric entry questions. One feature that can save you a few seconds—and keep you from making an entry mistake—is the "Transfer Display" function. You may click this button to transfer the number displayed on the calculator to the answer box. However, you cannot use the "Transfer Display" feature if the answer is a fraction.

Note that if you click "Transfer Display" on a question that asks you to round your answer to a certain degree of accuracy, you may need to edit the number in the answer box so that it is appropriately rounded up or down.

STRATEGIES FOR NUMERIC ENTRY QUESTIONS

Because numeric entry questions don't provide any answer choices, you will not be able to use some of the strategies—such as working backward from the answer choices and eliminating incorrect ones—that are helpful on multiple-choice questions. On the other hand, you will not be tempted by trap answer choices, those that are the result of using incorrect processes or faulty computations. Let's review what you can—and should—do in order to answer numeric entry questions correctly.

Turn Verbose or Abstract Language into Concise and Concrete Wording

Remember to write out equations or draw diagrams when the question does not provide any, in order to get a clearer picture. In this respect, numeric entry questions are no different from multiple-choice questions.

For Example 1, enter your answer in the box.

Example 1

> Dominic bought a pair of shoes for $90, two t-shirts for $20 each, and four pairs of socks. If he paid 8% sales tax on the entire purchase, and if the total amount of the tax he paid was $12, what was the cost of each pair of socks?
>
> $ [   ]

NOTE

For a money question, the dollar symbol will appear to the left of the answer box. Don't worry about entering it— you can't. You can only enter numbers, a decimal point, and a negative sign in the answer boxes for numeric entry questions.

Instead of trying to think this through in the abstract, write out the information you have as an equation. Let S be the cost of each pair of socks. Then, before tax, Dominic paid $\$90 + 2 \times \$20 + 4S$. The amount of tax he paid was 8% of $\$90 + 2 \times \$20 + 4S$, or $\frac{8}{100}(\$90 + 2 \times \$20 + 4S)$. Equate this to \$12 and solve for S:

$$\frac{8}{100}(\$90 + 2 \times \$20 + 4S) = \$12$$

$$\frac{2}{100}(\$90 + 2 \times \$20 + 4S) = \$3$$

$$\frac{2}{100}\$130 + \frac{2}{100}4S = \$3$$

$$\frac{2}{100}4S = \$0.4$$

$$S = \$5$$

The correct answer is \$5.

Make Sure You're Answering the Correct Question

Your worst enemy on numeric entry questions, especially if you feel you have to race against the clock, is a careless mistake—such as confusing the diameter for the radius or giving an answer in the wrong units (e.g., minutes instead of hours, or feet instead of inches). To avoid such mistakes, always read the question carefully and double-check your work.

For Example 2, enter your answer in the box.

Example 2

What is the median of the first ten positive integers?

$$\boxed{}$$

This is not a hard question, but one that invites two kinds of careless mistakes. When a question asks for the mean, median, or mode, make sure you don't mistakenly calculate the wrong one. Second, don't answer hastily. In this case, don't answer "5," thinking that the middle number among the first ten positive integers will be 5. After more reasoned thinking, you would realize that because there are ten numbers—that is, an even number of numbers—the median will be the average of the middle two numbers: 5 and 6. **The correct answer is 5.5 (or equivalent).**

For Example 3, enter your answer in the boxes.

Example 3

If 12 of the 20 members of Springfield's city council are male, what is the ratio of female council members to male council members?

Give your answer as a fraction.

Here you are asked to find a part-to-part ratio: female-to-male council members. Do not provide a part-to-whole ratio (e.g., female-to-total council members), or the wrong part-to-part ratio (male-to-female council members).

If there are 20 council members and 12 are male, the remaining 8 are female. The ratio you're looking for is $\frac{8}{12}$. Since fractions do not need to be reduced to lowest terms, you do not need to reduce $\frac{8}{12}$ to $\frac{2}{3}$. **The correct answer is $\frac{8}{12}$ (or any equivalent fraction).**

Round Correctly

Sometimes, a numeric entry question will ask you to round your answer to a certain degree of accuracy. Once you've performed the necessary calculations, don't lose sight of that instruction. For instance, if you're asked to round your answer to the nearest integer, and your calculations yield 13.6, type "14" in the answer box.

Make sure, however, that you don't round any numbers until the very end. For instance, let's say that in the process of computing the answer, you have to multiply 11.2 by 3. That product is 33.6, which, rounded to the nearest integer, is 34. However, if before performing the final calculation you had rounded 11.2 down to 11, you would have given your answer as "33," which would have been incorrect.

For Example 4, enter your answer in the box.

Example 4

In 2013, the sales of The Cranston Computer Company, a manufacturer of desktop and laptop computers, increased by 20% compared with 2012. In 2014, Cranston's sales decreased by 20% compared with 2013. Cranston's 2012 sales were what percent of its 2014 sales? Give your answer to the nearest 0.1.

Pick the number 100 to represent the company's sales in 2012.

Then, the 2013 sales were 120 and the 2014 sales were $120 - \dfrac{20}{100}(120) = 96$.

Now you need to find what percent of 96 (the 2014 sales) is 100 (the 2012 sales). Set up and solve a proportion—remembering that you need to round your answer to the nearest tenth of a percent:

$$\frac{100}{96} = \frac{x}{100} \Rightarrow x = \frac{10,000}{96} \Rightarrow x = 104.1\overline{6}$$

The correct answer is 104.2% (or equivalent).

Note that the calculator will give you the answer as 104.16667, and this is the number that will be placed into the answer box if you use the calculator's "Transfer Display" feature. In that case, you must then click onto the answer box and change "104.16667" to "104.2." If you don't, your answer will be marked incorrect.

TIP

Always read questions carefully. Doing so and turning confusing questions into concise and concrete wording may be the two most important strategies you can use. You need to understand what a question is asking in order to answer it correctly.

PRACTICE QUESTIONS

For Questions 1–10, enter your answer in the boxes.

1. The average (arithmetic mean) number of minutes it takes a contestant to complete an obstacle course is 23 minutes. If every contestant is given a 45-second reduction from their time due to a malfunctioning obstacle, what would be the resulting average completion time of the course?

   [   ] minutes [   ] seconds

2. The face of a cube has area $4\pi^{\frac{2}{3}}$ square inches and a sphere has diameter 4 inches. What is the ratio of the volume of the sphere to the volume of the cube?

   Give your answer as a fraction.

3. A concession stand on a beach boardwalk sells waffle cones for $4 and large slushies for $5. In one evening, they sell twice as many slushies as waffle cones and the total profit is $280. What is the sum of the number of waffle cones and slushies sold on this evening?

   [   ]

4. Line *m* is parallel to a line whose equation is $2x - 6y = 0$. If the point $(1,1)$ is on this line, what is its *y*-value when $x = -9$? Give your answer as a fraction.

5. For all numbers *a* and *b*, $a \lozenge b = a^2 b$. What is the value of $\left[(-2) \lozenge (-3)\right] \lozenge (-2)$?

6. Company A, a widget manufacturer, has eight stores in town X. The average (arithmetic mean) number of widgets these stores sold in March 2016 is 150. Not including the company's flagship store in town X, the average (arithmetic mean) number of widgets the remaining seven stores sold in March 2016 is 130. How many widgets did the flagship store sell in March 2016?

SHOW YOUR WORK HERE

Questions 7 and 8 are based on the following data.

SALES OF NEW CARS IN COUNTRY A, BY CATEGORY, IN 2017

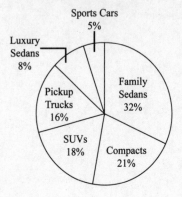

AVERAGE HIGHWAY FUEL CONSUMPTION, BY CATEGORY, FOR NEW CARS SOLD IN 2017

Category	Average Fuel Consumption
Compact Cars	32
Family Sedans	28
Luxury Sedans	24
Sports Cars	24
SUVs	23
Pickup Trucks	21

7. If in 2017 the total number of new cars that were sold across all categories was 1,621,018, how many categories of cars had sales of fewer than 250,000 cars?

8. What was the average fuel consumption on the highway for all cars sold in 2017?
   Give your answer to the nearest 0.1.

9. Working alone at its constant rate, Machine A produces 15 widgets every 90 minutes. Working alone at its constant rate, Machine B produces widgets twice as quickly as does Machine A. If the two machines work together at their respective constant rates, how many hours will it take them to produce 75 widgets?

   hours

10. Fill in the missing power: $\dfrac{m^{-2} \cdot \left(m^{3}\right)^{2}}{\left(\left(m^{2}\right)^{-2}\right)^{3}} = m^{\boxed{}}$

ANSWER KEY AND EXPLANATIONS

1. 22 minutes 15 seconds	**6.** 290
2. $\frac{4}{3}$	**7.** 2
3. 60	**8.** 26.3
4. $-\frac{7}{3}$	**9.** 2.5
5. –288	**10.** 16

1. **The correct answer is 22 minutes 15 seconds.** Since *all* contestants are given the exact same reduction, the mean will decrease by the same amount of time.

2. **The correct answer is $\frac{4}{3}$.** Since the area of a face of the cube is $4\pi^{\frac{2}{3}}$ square inches, an edge has length $\left(4\pi^{\frac{2}{3}}\right)^{\frac{1}{2}} = 2\pi^{\frac{1}{3}}$ inches. So the volume of the cube is $\left(2\pi^{\frac{1}{3}}\right)^3 = 8\pi$ cubic inches. The radius of the sphere is 2 inches, so its volume is $\frac{4}{3}\pi \cdot 2^3 = \frac{32}{3}\pi$ cubic inches. Therefore, the ratio of the volumes is $\dfrac{\frac{32}{3}\pi}{8\pi} = \frac{4}{3}$.

3. **The correct answer is 60.** Let x be the number of waffle cones sold and y the number of slushies sold. Then, $4x + 5y = 280$ and $y = 2x$. Solve this system of equations using substitution: $4x + 5(2x) = 280$, so $14x = 280$ and $x = 20$. Therefore, the concession stand sold 20 waffle cones and 40 slushies in one evening. The sum, therefore, is 60.

4. **The correct answer is $-\frac{7}{3}$.** Two lines are parallel if they have the same slope. The slope of the given line is $\frac{1}{3}$. Using point-slope formula with $m = \frac{1}{3}$ and the point $(1, 1)$ yields the equation of line m as $y - 1 = \frac{1}{3}(x - 1)$. This is equivalent to $y = \frac{1}{3}x + \frac{2}{3}$. The y-coordinate of the point when $x = -9$ is therefore $y = \frac{1}{3}(-9) + \frac{2}{3} = -3 + \frac{2}{3} = -\frac{7}{3}$.

5. **The correct answer is –288.** Here, too, you should solve carefully and double-check your work before you move on. Perform the calculations, starting with the operation in brackets to the left.

$$
\begin{aligned}
\left[(-2)\lozenge(-3)\right]\lozenge(-2) &= \left[(-2)^2 \times (-3)\right]\lozenge(-2) \\
&= \left[-4 \times (-3)\right]\lozenge(-2) \\
&= (-12)^2 \times (-2) \\
&= 144 \times (-2) \\
&= -288
\end{aligned}
$$

6. **The correct answer is 290.** Turn words into equations. The eight stores together sold $150 \times 8 = 1,200$ widgets.

The seven stores other than the flagship store averaged 130 widgets, so together they sold $130 \times 7 = 910$.

Thus, the flagship store sold $1,200 - 910 = 290$ widgets.

7. **The correct answer is 2.** Find what percent of 1,621,018 is 250,000:

$$\frac{250,000}{1,621,018} = \frac{x}{100} \Rightarrow x \approx 15.42$$

There were only two categories whose sales were less than 15.42% of the total: luxury sedans and sports cars. Make sure that you don't mistakenly answer 4, the number of categories of cars with sales of more than 15.4% of the total.

8. **The correct answer is 26.3.** For this question, you need to use the two data displays together. Additionally, in the end you must remember to round correctly. The question asks you for a weighted average. Assume there were 100 cars sold, 32 of which were family sedans, 21 of which were compact cars, and so on. Then, multiply the number of cars in each category by that category's average fuel consumption. Finally, divide this product by 100, the total number of cars sold:

$$\frac{32 \times 28 + 21 \times 32 + 18 \times 23 + 16 \times 21 + 8 \times 24 + 5 \times 24}{100} = 26.3$$

9. **The correct answer is 2.5.** Make the information in this question more concrete. You need to start by finding how many widgets each machine produces in an hour. If Machine A produces 15 widgets every 90 minutes, then it produces two-thirds of that number, or 10 widgets, every hour.

Machine B is twice as fast, so it produces $2 \times 10 = 20$ widgets every hour. Thus, the two machines working together produce $10 + 20 = 30$ widgets every hour. To find how many hours the two machines together will need in order to produce 75 widgets, set up and solve the proportion:

$$\frac{30}{1} = \frac{75}{x} \Rightarrow x = 2.5$$

10. **The correct answer is 16.** Use the exponent rules as follows:

$$\frac{m^{-2} \cdot \left(m^3\right)^2}{\left(\left(m^2\right)^{-2}\right)^3} = \frac{m^{-2} \cdot m^6}{\left(m^{-4}\right)^3} = \frac{m^4}{m^{-12}}$$

$$= \frac{m^4}{m^{-12}} = m^4 \cdot m^{12} = m^{\boxed{16}}$$

SUMMING IT UP

- Numeric entry questions do not offer lists of possible answers. Instead, you will be presented with a question and one or two answer boxes.
  - If the answer should be an integer or a decimal, there will be one answer box.
  - If the answer should be in the form of a fraction, there will be two answer boxes, one over the other for numerator and denominator.
- Some numeric entry questions may be part of a data interpretation set.
- The screen will show a calculator for you to use.
  - To erase numerals in an answer box, use the "backspace" key.
  - To enter a negative sign, type a hyphen, and to erase a negative sign, type the hyphen again.
  - To enter a decimal point, use a period.
- Equivalent forms of an answer are correct.
- Fractions don't need to be reduced to lowest terms, but some directions may instruct you to round decimals up or down.
- The three specific strategies to use for solving numeric entry questions are the following:
  - Turn verbose or abstract language into concise and concrete wording.
  - Make sure you're answering the correct question.
  - Round correctly.

Strategies for Quantitative Comparison Questions

OVERVIEW

- **Basic Information About Quantitative Comparison Questions**
- **Strategies for Quantitative Comparison Questions**
- **Practice Questions**
- **Answer Key and Explanations**
- **Summing It Up**

In this chapter, you will find an introduction to the quantitative comparison questions that you will encounter on the GRE® General Test, as well as a discussion of strategies to help you answer these questions quickly and competently. A few of these strategies will be familiar to you from the chapters on multiple-choice questions and numeric entry questions. Most, however, are specific to answering quantitative comparison questions. The strategies are:

- Pick and plug numbers.
- Simplify the quantities.
- Avoid unnecessary calculations.
- Estimate.
- Redraw the figure.
- Recognize when the answer cannot be "The relationship cannot be determined."

The one thing you won't find in the quantitative comparison section of the GRE® General Test is data sets. Each quantitative comparison question is a stand-alone item.

Chapter 11

BASIC INFORMATION ABOUT QUANTITATIVE COMPARISON QUESTIONS

Quantitative comparisons present you with two Quantities, A and B. Your task is to compare these quantities and choose one of the following answers:

- Quantity A is greater.
- Quantity B is greater.
- The two quantities are equal.
- The relationship cannot be determined from the information given.

These answer choices, *in this exact order*, appear with all quantitative comparison questions. Memorize the answers in order, so you don't waste time reading them for each question.

On the official GRE® General Test, these answer choices are not labeled A, B, and so on. They are merely listed in this order, each with an oval to its left. For your convenience in this book, we've labeled the ovals A, B, C, and D.

There are two other points of information to remember.

1. Some questions feature additional information centered above the two quantities. You should use this information to help you determine the relationship between the two quantities.

2. Any symbol that appears more than once in a question (e.g., one that appears in Quantity A and in the centered information) has the same meaning throughout the question.

STRATEGIES FOR QUANTITATIVE COMPARISON QUESTIONS

In addition to the strategies explained here, remember that you can always skip and return to a question. You have to click the "Mark" button so that you can find the question quickly in the "Review" screen when you are ready to give it another try. However, you can only go back to a question in the section you are currently working on.

Pick and Plug Numbers

Picking and plugging numbers to represent variables is a powerful strategy if you are asked to compare expressions that contain variables. You pick numbers to represent the variables, and then plug these numbers into the expressions given in Quantities A and B. Work quickly, but also thoroughly. Depending on the question, you should choose

- not only positive, but also negative numbers.
- not only integers, but also fractions (in particular fractions between 0 and 1, and 0 and –1).
- the numbers 1 and 0.

For Example 1, compare Quantity A and Quantity B. This question has additional information above the two quantities to use in determining your answer.

Example 1

$$\frac{x}{y} = 3$$

$$y \neq 0$$

Quantity A	Quantity B
x	y

A. Quantity A is greater.

B. Quantity B is greater.

C. The two quantities are equal.

D. The relationship cannot be determined from the information given.

First, rewrite the centered information as $x = 3y$, which is easier to work with.

This question features variables in both quantities, so picking numbers is likely to get you to the right answer quickly. Choose different numbers for y, and see what results you get for x, as well as what the relationship between the two quantities is. To keep track of the results, draw a table on your scratch paper.

y		x
1	<	3
2	<	6
$\frac{1}{3}$	<	1

So when y equals 1, x equals 3; when y equals 2, x equals 6; and when, y equals $\frac{1}{3}$, x equals 1. In all three cases x is greater than y, so you may be tempted to conclude that Quantity A will always be greater than Quantity B. However, you have not yet tested a sufficient variety of numbers, so you should not jump to a conclusion yet. (In fact, testing $y = 2$ in particular was a waste of time because there was no reason to think that it would have yielded a different result than did $y = 1$.) In order to be thorough, you should also test numbers that have some different properties.

y		x
−1	>	−3

In this example, picking a negative number for y results in y being greater than x. Because you have now found at least one instance in which x is greater than y, as well as at least one instance in which y is greater than x, you are finished. **The correct answer is D.**

TIP

The GRE® General Test does not penalize wrong answers, so educated guessing could raise your score.

For Example 2, compare Quantity A and Quantity B. This question has additional information above the two quantities to use in determining your answer.

Example 2

$$\frac{x}{y} = 3$$

$$y \neq 0$$

Quantity A	Quantity B
$|x|$	$|y|$

A. Quantity A is greater.

B. Quantity B is greater.

C. The two quantities are equal.

D. The relationship cannot be determined from the information given.

This question is similar to Example 1, but there is one important difference. You are now being asked to compare the absolute values of the two variables, not the variables themselves.

Again, start by rewriting the centered information in the following form: $x = 3y$

Pick numbers again.

y	x	$|y|$		$|x|$
1	3	1	<	3
-1	-3	1	<	3
$\frac{1}{6}$	$\frac{1}{2}$	$\frac{1}{6}$	<	$\frac{1}{2}$

This time, because the absolute values eliminate the minus signs, the pattern that emerges is reliable. Because x equals 3 times y and because you're asked to compare the absolute values of x and y, no matter what value you pick for y, the absolute value of x will always be greater than the absolute value of y. **The correct answer is A.**

When to Use (and Not to Use) Pick and Plug

Picking numbers is a useful strategy, but you should keep in mind that it doesn't always answer the question definitively.

- It is best used when it reveals quickly two different relationships between the quantities, in which case you have proved that the answer is choice D.

- It is also helpful if the possible values that the variables may take are few, and you are able to test them all.

However, if the possible values that the variables may take are infinite—or if they are finite, but too many for you to check in any reasonable amount of time—then you cannot use this strategy alone to answer the question. Even if you test many numbers, all of which produce the same result, it's entirely possible that some other numbers, which you have not yet tested, may produce a different result.

That said, even in such a case, picking numbers may be useful if you are stuck and do not know how to proceed. After you've picked a few numbers and examined the results, you may notice a pattern that you may not have noticed previously and that will help you compare the quantities.

Simplify the Quantities

Sometimes, test-item writers present you with expressions—either in the two quantities or in the centered information—that appear complicated, thus making your job harder. In such cases, you can help yourself by:

- simplifying each quantity in order to make it easier to evaluate it on its own.
- manipulating one quantity in such a way as to make it easier to compare it with the other quantity.
- simplifying the centered information so that you end up with a new piece of information that's easier to interpret.

For Example 3, compare Quantity A and Quantity B.

Example 3

Quantity A	Quantity B
$4x^2 - 8x + 4$	$(2x - 2)^2$

- **A.** Quantity A is greater.
- **B.** Quantity B is greater.
- **C.** The two quantities are equal.
- **D.** The relationship cannot be determined from the information given.

As written, these quantities are hard to compare. However, you can manipulate either quantity so that it resembles the other one. For instance, if you distribute Quantity B, you get:

$$(2x - 2)^2 = 4x^2 - 8x + 4$$

Thus, Quantity A is the distributed form of Quantity B, so the quantities are equal. **The correct answer is C.**

For Example 4, compare Quantity A and Quantity B. This question has additional information above the two quantities to use in determining your answer.

Example 4

$$-1 < x < y < 0$$

<u>Quantity A</u>   <u>Quantity B</u>

xy $\dfrac{x}{y}$

   A. Quantity A is greater.

   B. Quantity B is greater.

   C. The two quantities are equal.

   D. The relationship cannot be determined from the information given.

In this question, you should simplify the two quantities together in order to arrive at something that's easier to compare. Start by assuming that one quantity is larger than the other, and simplify the inequality until you arrive at a statement that you can evaluate. If that statement is correct, then your initial assumption was correct. If that statement is incorrect, your initial assumption was incorrect. Let's see this process at work.

Begin by assuming that Quantity A is larger than Quantity B:

$$xy > \frac{x}{y}$$

Next, cancel x from both sides of the inequality—that is, divide both sides by x. You can do this for two reasons: First, because $x \neq 0$, division by x is permissible; second, because $x < 0$, you know that division by x will reverse the sign of the inequality. (If you don't know whether a variable is positive or negative, you cannot multiply or divide both sides of the inequality by that variable.) So you are left with $y < \dfrac{1}{y}$.

Now evaluate whether this statement is correct or not. Since y is a fraction between 0 and −1 (such as $-\dfrac{1}{2}$), its reciprocal will also be a negative number, but one smaller than −1 (such as −2). Thus, y is greater than $\dfrac{1}{y}$, and the inequality $y < \dfrac{1}{y}$ is incorrect. This means that the initial assumption that Quantity A is larger than Quantity B was also incorrect.

Since it turns out that $y > \dfrac{1}{y}$, you should reverse the sign of the inequality for each one of the prior steps, thus arriving at $xy < \dfrac{x}{y}$. **The correct answer is B.**

Eliminating Terms When Simplifying Quantities

This example also illustrates another helpful tool you can use when you simplify two expressions together. You can eliminate any term that appears on both expressions, as long as you keep the following rules in mind:

- You can add or subtract any term to or from both quantities. For instance, if both quantities feature the term $3y$, you can subtract it from both of them.

- You can multiply or divide both quantities by any nonzero term, as long as you know whether this term is positive or negative.

Avoid Unnecessary Calculations

Remember that you do not always need to find the exact value of the two quantities in order to compare them. This will save you time.

For Example 5, compare Quantity A and Quantity B.

Example 5

<table>
<tr><td align="center">Quantity A</td><td align="center">Quantity B</td></tr>
<tr><td align="center">The average (arithmetic mean) of all odd integers between 10 and 30</td><td align="center">The average (arithmetic mean) of all even integers between 11 and 31</td></tr>
</table>

- **A.** Quantity A is greater.
- **B.** Quantity B is greater.
- **C.** The two quantities are equal.
- **D.** The relationship cannot be determined from the information given.

To answer this question, you could, of course, list all the odd integers between 10 and 30, add them up, and find their average in order to determine the exact value of Quantity A. Then you could do the same for the even integers in Quantity B. However, that would be a very time-consuming process. Luckily, you don't have to do all that.

Instead, think about what the two quantities are. Quantity A is the average of ten integers, starting with the number 11 and ending with the number 29. Quantity B is also the average of ten such integers, this time starting with 12 and ending with 30. Notice that both quantities feature the same number of terms.

Next, you should note that the smallest term in Quantity B is larger than the smallest term in Quantity A; the second smallest term in Quantity B is larger than the second smallest term in Quantity A; and so on, for each of the ten terms in the two quantities, since in both cases the numbers increase by 2.

Thus, the sum of the terms in Quantity B is larger than the sum of the terms in Quantity A, and, therefore, the average of the terms in Quantity B is also larger than the average of the terms in Quantity A. No further work is needed. **The correct answer is B.**

Estimate

One particular way to avoid unnecessary calculations is estimating.

For Example 6, compare Quantity A and Quantity B.

Example 6

Quantity A	Quantity B
$65 \times \dfrac{6}{5}$	47% of 130

    A. Quantity A is greater.

    B. Quantity B is greater.

    C. The two quantities are equal.

    D. The relationship cannot be determined from the information given.

Avoid the temptation to use the calculator. As a quantitative comparison, the question asks you to compare the two quantities, not to evaluate them fully.

First, look at Quantity A. The fraction $\dfrac{6}{5}$ is greater than 1. That means that Quantity A is greater than 65. Stop there for the moment, and move on to Quantity B.

Quantity B features a number that is less than 50% of 130. 50% of 130 is 65, so Quantity B is less than 65.

In other words, Quantity A is greater than 65, whereas Quantity B is less than 65, which means that Quantity A is greater than Quantity B. **The correct answer is A.**

Redraw the Figure

TIP

Redrawing the figure can be useful in answering other types of questions as well.

Remember that geometric figures on the GRE® General Test are not necessarily drawn to scale. When in doubt, you can always redraw a figure on your scratch paper, altering any quantities such as side lengths or angle measures that have not been defined fully. Doing so may reveal additional information about the figure that may not have been obvious from the figure that the test maker provided.

For Example 7, compare Quantity A and Quantity B. This question has additional information above the two quantities to use in determining your answer.

Example 7

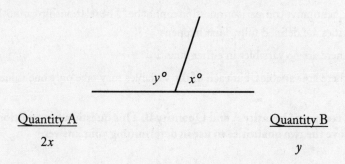

Quantity A	Quantity B
$2x$	y

   A. Quantity A is greater.

   B. Quantity B is greater.

   C. The two quantities are equal.

   D. The relationship cannot be determined from the information given.

As the figure is drawn, you may be tempted to assume that $x°$ is an acute angle and $y°$ is an obtuse angle. Further, you may be tempted to estimate the value of the two angles and try to compare the two quantities that way. Don't!

The figure is not necessarily drawn to scale, and you have no further information to help you evaluate the angles. You can redraw the figure on your scratch paper in order to see this latter point visually:

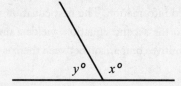

The only thing that the original figure tells you definitively is that $x°$ and $y°$ are supplementary angles—that is, that they add up to 180°. Thus, the relationship between the two quantities cannot be determined. **The correct answer is D.**

Recognize When the Answer Cannot Be "The relationship cannot be determined."

The answer in a quantitative comparison question cannot be "The relationship cannot be determined." if the two quantities are defined fully. That happens

- when there are no variables in either quantity.
- when there are variables, but each of the variables may take only one value.

For Example 8, compare Quantity A and Quantity B. This question has additional information above the two quantities to use in determining your answer.

Example 8 $x - 3 = 2$
                                                       $3y = x + 7$

<table>
<tr><td align="center">Quantity A</td><td align="center">Quantity B</td></tr>
<tr><td align="center">x</td><td align="center">y</td></tr>
</table>

- **A.** Quantity A is greater.
- **B.** Quantity B is greater.
- **C.** The two quantities are equal.
- **D.** The relationship cannot be determined from the information given.

Even though the quantities feature variables, these variables are defined absolutely because of the two equations in the centered information. The first equation yields a unique value for x, and that value, when substituted into the second equation, yields a unique value for y. Because both quantities are fully defined, a definitive comparison between them is possible. In this case, $x = 5$ and $y = 4$. **The correct answer is A.**

PRACTICE QUESTIONS

For Questions 1–15, compare Quantity A and Quantity B. Some questions will have additional information above the two quantities to use in determining your answer.

1.
$$\frac{x}{y} - 4 = 0$$

$$x \neq 0,\ y \neq 0$$

Quantity A	Quantity B
$\dfrac{1}{x}$	$\dfrac{1}{y}$

A. Quantity A is greater.

B. Quantity B is greater.

C. The two quantities are equal.

D. The relationship cannot be determined from the information given.

2.
$$x < y$$

Quantity A	Quantity B
$-x^2$	xy

A. Quantity A is greater.

B. Quantity B is greater.

C. The two quantities are equal.

D. The relationship cannot be determined from the information given.

3.   Assume $a < b < 0$ and a and b are both integers.

Quantity A	Quantity B
$a + b$	$(a + b)^3$

A. Quantity A is greater.

B. Quantity B is greater.

C. The two quantities are equal.

D. The relationship cannot be determined from the information given.

4.

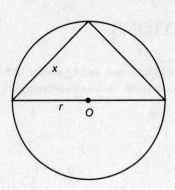

Quantity A	Quantity B
The circumference of the circle with center O and radius r	$4x$

A. Quantity A is greater.

B. Quantity B is greater.

C. The two quantities are equal.

D. The relationship cannot be determined from the information given.

5.

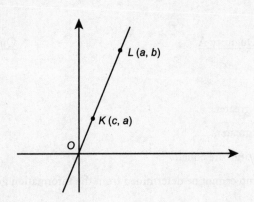

Quantity A	Quantity B
$b - a$	$c - a$

A. Quantity A is greater.

B. Quantity B is greater.

C. The two quantities are equal.

D. The relationship cannot be determined from the information given.

6.

Quantity A	Quantity B
The diameter of a circle	The circumference of the same circle

A. Quantity A is greater.

B. Quantity B is greater.

C. The two quantities are equal.

D. The relationship cannot be determined from the information given.

7.

Quantity A	Quantity B
The largest prime factor of 88	The largest even divisor of 90

A. Quantity A is greater.

B. Quantity B is greater.

C. The two quantities are equal.

D. The relationship cannot be determined from the information given.

8. Assume x and y are positive real numbers such that $x^2 + y^2 = 1$.

Quantity A	Quantity B
$\frac{x}{y} + \frac{y}{x}$	xy

A. Quantity A is greater.

B. Quantity B is greater.

C. The two quantities are equal.

D. The relationship cannot be determined from the information given.

9.

Quantity A	Quantity B
$\sqrt{230}$	The average (arithmetic mean) of all prime numbers between 10 and 20

A. Quantity A is greater.

B. Quantity B is greater.

C. The two quantities are equal.

D. The relationship cannot be determined from the information given.

10.   Quantity A   Quantity B

$$\left(\frac{14}{42}\right)^4$$ $$\frac{1}{3} \times \frac{2}{9} \times \frac{3}{(-6)} \times \frac{(-1)}{3}$$

A. Quantity A is greater.

B. Quantity B is greater.

C. The two quantities are equal.

D. The relationship cannot be determined from the information given.

11. ABC is a right triangle with legs of length $\dfrac{x}{y}$ and y.

Quantity A   Quantity B

$$\frac{x\left(5 - \sqrt{17}\right)\left(\sqrt{17} + 5\right)}{\sqrt{256}}$$ The area of
triangle ABC

A. Quantity A is greater.

B. Quantity B is greater.

C. The two quantities are equal.

D. The relationship cannot be determined from the information given.

12.   Quantity A   Quantity B

The number of prime numbers   The number of multiples of 3
between 1 and 100   between 1 and 100

A. Quantity A is greater.

B. Quantity B is greater.

C. The two quantities are equal.

D. The relationship cannot be determined from the information given.

13.

$$xy^2z^3 > 0$$

$$xyz < 0$$

Quantity A	Quantity B
y	xz

A. Quantity A is greater.

B. Quantity B is greater.

C. The two quantities are equal.

D. The relationship cannot be determined from the information given.

14. Point $P\,(a, b)$ lies in quadrant I of the rectangular coordinate system. Point $Q\,(m, n)$ is 180° rotationally symmetric to point P about the origin O.

Quantity A	Quantity B
The distance between points P and Q	$\left[\left(|a| + |n|\right)^2 - 2\,|bm|\right]^{\frac{1}{2}}$

A. Quantity A is greater.

B. Quantity B is greater.

C. The two quantities are equal.

D. The relationship cannot be determined from the information given.

15. M and N are two right cylinders, such that the height of cylinder M is 10% greater than the height of cylinder N, and the radius of cylinder M is 10% less than the radius of cylinder N.

Quantity A	Quantity B
The volume of a sphere with diameter D	The volume of a right circular cone whose height and base diameter are both D

A. Quantity A is greater.

B. Quantity B is greater.

C. The two quantities are equal.

D. The relationship cannot be determined from the information given.

ANSWER KEY AND EXPLANATIONS

1. D	**6.** B	**11.** C
2. D	**7.** B	**12.** B
3. A	**8.** D	**13.** B
4. D	**9.** A	**14.** A
5. A	**10.** C	**15.** A

1. **The correct answer is D.** Begin by manipulating the centered information:

    $$\frac{x}{y} - 4 = 0 \Rightarrow \frac{x}{y} = 4 \Rightarrow x = 4y$$

    Now pick numbers for y, and see what the relationship between the two quantities is.

y	x	$\frac{1}{x}$		$\frac{1}{y}$
1	4	$\frac{1}{4}$	<	1
-1	-4	$-\frac{1}{4}$	>	-1

    Clearly, the relationship between the two quantities cannot be determined from the information given.

2. **The correct answer is D.** You cannot simplify the two quantities any more than they already are. You might be tempted to divide both quantities by x; however, that would be wrong. If x equals 0, then division by x would not be permissible. Additionally, you don't know whether x is positive or negative, so you don't know whether dividing by x would change the direction of the inequality or not. Instead, pick numbers for x and y right away.

x	y	$-x^2$		xy
2	3	-4	<	6
0	Any positive number	0	=	0

    When $x = 2$ and $y = 3$, Quantity B is greater than Quantity A, whereas when $x = 0$ and $y =$ any number, then the two quantities are equal.

3. **The correct answer is A.** Since a and b are both negative integers, $a + b$ is a negative integer. Cubing this expression creates another negative integer further to the left along the number line. So Quantity A is larger.

4. **The correct answer is D.** Even though the triangle inscribed in the circle appears to be isosceles, don't assume that it is. The triangle is definitely a right one, since one of its sides is a diameter of the circle; however, you cannot tell anything about its two legs. Each of them may be of any length between (but not including) 0 and $2r$. For instance, here is one way that you may legitimately redraw the figure:

    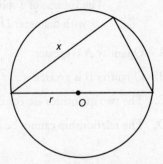

    So how do we compare the two quantities? First, consider Quantity A. The circumference of the circle is $2\pi r$, and since $\pi \approx 3.14$, the circumference is approximately equal to $6.28r$.

Next, examine a couple of different possibilities for Quantity B. If the triangle were isosceles, it would be a 45-45-90 right triangle, and x would equal $r\sqrt{2}$. $\sqrt{2}$ is somewhat smaller than 1.5, so $r\sqrt{2}$ is somewhat smaller than $1.5r$, and $4x$ is somewhat smaller than $6r$. In this scenario, Quantity A is greater. However, x can be almost as large as the diameter. Therefore, $4x$ can be almost as large as $4 \times 2r$, or $8r$—so Quantity B may be greater than Quantity A.

5. **The correct answer is A.** By looking at the graph, you can estimate the relationship of the three numbers to one another—and this estimate will be enough because you don't need to find exact values in order to answer the question correctly:

   b, the y-coordinate of point L, is greater than a, the y-coordinate of point K, because point L is farther up than point K. That is, $b > a$, so $b - a > 0$, and Quantity A is positive. a, the x-coordinate of point L, is greater than c, the x-coordinate of point K, because point L is farther to the right than point K. That is, $a > c$, so $c - a < 0$, and Quantity B is negative.

   Thus, Quantity A is larger than Quantity B.

6. **The correct answer is B.** The circumference of a circle with diameter d is πd. Since $\pi > 1$, $\pi d > d$. So Quantity B is greater.

7. **The correct answer is B.** The prime factorization of 88 is $2^3 \times 11$. So its largest prime factor is 11. The divisors of 90 are 2, 3, 5, 6, 9, 10, 15, 18, 30, and 45. The largest even divisor is 30. Quantity B is larger.

8. **The correct answer is D.** Observe that $\dfrac{x}{y} + \dfrac{y}{x} = \dfrac{x^2 + y^2}{xy} = \dfrac{1}{xy}$ (using the assumption that $x^2 + y^2 = 1$). It is not possible to determine if this is larger than xy without more information. If x and y are both between 0 and 1, then Quantity A is larger, while if both x and y are greater than 1, then Quantity B is larger.

9. **The correct answer is A.** On this question, you may use the calculator or estimate. If you estimate, you should recall that 225 is the square of 15, so Quantity A is slightly larger than 15. For Quantity B, list all the primes between 10 and 20: 11, 13, 17 and 19. The average of these four numbers is exactly 15. Thus, Quantity A is larger.

10. **The correct answer is C.** Simplifying the two quantities is the strategy to use here. First, work on Quantity A, the simpler one of the two: $\dfrac{14}{42} = \dfrac{1}{3}$, so $\left(\dfrac{14}{42}\right)^4 = \left(\dfrac{1}{3}\right)^4$. Don't calculate any further: you may not have to. If, after simplifying Quantity B, you still need to simplify Quantity A further, you can do so then. Move on to Quantity B and see what that simplifies to.

   First, cancel out the minus signs from the numerator and denominator:

   $$\frac{1}{3} \times \frac{2}{9} \times \frac{3}{6} \times \frac{1}{3}$$

   Then, rearrange the terms:

   $$\frac{1}{3} \times \frac{1}{3} \times \frac{2}{6} \times \frac{3}{9}$$

   Next, simplify the last two fractions:

   $$\frac{1}{3} \times \frac{1}{3} \times \frac{1}{3} \times \frac{1}{3}$$

   And finally, write the product as a power of the fraction $\dfrac{1}{3}$:

   $$\left(\frac{1}{3}\right)^4$$

   The two quantities are equal.

11. **The correct answer is C.** Simplify the quantities in order to compare them more easily. Start with Quantity B, which is more straightforward. The area of this triangle is given by:

$$A = \frac{1}{2}\frac{x}{y}y = \frac{1}{2}x$$

Next, simplify Quantity A. Notice that the two terms in parentheses on the numerator are the factored form of the special product $a^2 - b^2$, where $a = 5$ and $b = \sqrt{17}$:

$$\frac{x\left(5 - \sqrt{17}\right)\left(\sqrt{17} + 5\right)}{\sqrt{256}}$$

$$= \frac{\left(5^2 - \left(\sqrt{17}\right)^2\right)x}{\sqrt{256}}$$

$$= \frac{(25 - 17)x}{\sqrt{256}}$$

$$= \frac{8x}{\sqrt{256}}$$

As for the denominator, you should recognize that 256 is the square of 16. Thus, the fraction becomes:

$$\frac{8x}{16} = \frac{1}{2}x$$

Thus, Quantity A is equal to Quantity B.

12. **The correct answer is B.** Quantity A is the harder of the two to deal with, so start with Quantity B: 99 = 33 × 3, so there are 33 multiples of 3 between 1 and 100.

Returning to Quantity A, you now have an easier task. You don't have to find the exact number of primes between 1 and 100. You only need to determine whether there are fewer or more prime numbers than 33. In other words, estimate! There are 98 integers between 1 and 100. Forty-nine of them are even, and none of those, other than the number 2, is prime. Thus, you are already down to $98 - 48 = 50$ numbers remaining: The number 2 and all the odd numbers in the range.

Next, you can eliminate all the odd multiples of 3 (other than 3 itself) because these are

not prime. (Do not eliminate all multiples of 3 because the even ones are included in the 48 even numbers you eliminated in the previous step.) There are 33 multiples of 3 between 1 and 100, and both the first one (3) and the last one (99) are odd. Therefore, of these 33 multiples, 17 are odd and 16 are even. Subtract 16 of the 17 odd ones (that is, all of them other than 3) from the 50 remaining numbers: $50 - 16 = 34$.

At this point, if you can find at least two additional nonprime numbers, you are finished. Look for nonprime numbers that are neither even nor multiples of 3. The numbers 25 and 55 are two such numbers (not even, not multiples of 3, and not prime), so you can remove them from the list, as well. You are now left with, at most, 32 numbers; in other words, the number of primes between 1 and 100 is definitely smaller than 33. (The number is 25.)

13. **The correct answer is B.** If you dissect methodically the centered information using the properties of positives and negatives, as well as those of exponents, you'll be able to find the right answer.

First, examine the first inequality: $xy^2z^3 > 0$. y^2 is positive, so the product of x and z^3 must also be positive (if xz^3 were negative, then you'd have a negative number multiplied by a positive number to produce another positive number, which is impossible).

Now, for xz^3 to be positive, x and z have to be either both positive or both negative. That's as far as you can go with this inequality alone.

Next, examine the second inequality: $xyz < 0$. Because xz^3 is positive (based on the first inequality), xz must also be positive. Therefore, for xyz to be negative, y must be negative. You can now answer the question! You have proven that Quantity A is negative, while Quantity B is positive.

14. **The correct answer is A.** Start by interpreting the centered information. If points P and Q are symmetric about the origin, then their x- and y-coordinates are opposites of each other. In other words, $a = -m$ and $b = -n$. Also, since P lies in quadrant I, then a and b are positive numbers, while m and n are negative.

Next, examine Quantity A. Drawing a diagram helps:

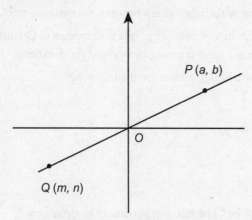

The distance between P and Q is equal to the length of line segment PO plus the length of line segment OQ. This sum is equal to two times the length of the segment PO, since $PO - OQ$.

PO is the hypotenuse of a right triangle with legs PR and OR (see the following figure). The length of PR is b (the y-coordinate of P), and the length of OR is a (the x-coordinate of R).

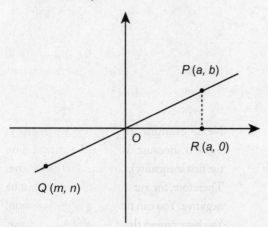

You can use the Pythagorean theorem to find the length of segment PO:

$$PO = \sqrt{a^2 + b^2}$$

Thus, the length of PQ is twice the length of PO: $PQ = 2\sqrt{a^2 + b^2}$.

Now, move on to Quantity B. First, tackle the absolute value signs so you can simplify the expression. Since a is positive, $|a| = a$. Additionally, since $b = -n$ and b is positive, $|n| = b$. Next, $|bm| = |b| \times |m|$, and since $m = -a$, $|bm| = |b| \times |a|$. Further, since a and b are both positive, $|bm| = a \times b$.

Now you're ready to transform the expression, so that $\left[\left(|a| + |n| \right)^2 - 2|bm| \right]^{\frac{1}{2}}$ becomes:

$$\sqrt{(a+b)^2 - 2ab}$$

Distribute the first term:

$$\sqrt{a^2 + b^2 + 2ab - 2ab}$$

Finally, cancel the two $2ab$:

$$\sqrt{a^2 + b^2}$$

Quantity B equals $\sqrt{a^2 + b^2}$, whereas Quantity A equals twice $\sqrt{a^2 + b^2}$. Since $\sqrt{a^2 + b^2}$ is a positive number (it's the length of a line segment), twice $\sqrt{a^2 + b^2}$ is larger than once $\sqrt{a^2 + b^2}$, so Quantity A is larger.

15. **The correct answer is A.** The volume of a sphere of diameter D, and hence radius $\frac{D}{2}$, is $\frac{4}{3}\pi \left(\frac{D}{2} \right)^3 = \frac{1}{6}\pi D^3$, while the volume of a right circular cone with the given dimensions is $\frac{1}{3}\pi \left(\frac{D}{2} \right)^2 D = \frac{1}{12}\pi D^3$. Since $\frac{1}{6}$ is larger than $\frac{1}{12}$, Quantity A is larger.

SUMMING IT UP

- Quantitative comparison questions present two quantities, A and B, that you must compare. To select an answer, you choose one answer from the following list:
  - Quantity A is greater.
  - Quantity B is greater.
  - The two quantities are equal.
  - The relationship cannot be determined from the information given.
- Some questions feature additional information centered above the two quantities. You should use this information to help you determine the relationship between the two quantities.
- Any symbol that appears more than once in a question (e.g., one that appears in Quantity A and in the centered information) has the same meaning throughout the question.
- Specific strategies for quantitative comparison questions are the following:
  - Pick and plug numbers.
  - Simplify the quantities.
  - Avoid unnecessary calculations.
  - Estimate.
  - Redraw the figure.
  - Recognize when the answer cannot be "The relationship cannot be determined."
- Data interpretation sets are not used for quantitative comparison questions.

PART VI

THREE PRACTICE TESTS

Practice Test 2

The test begins with general information about the number of sections on the test (six for the computer-delivered test, including the unidentified unscored section or an identified research section, and five for the paper-delivered test) and the timing of the test (approximately 3 hours and 45 minutes, including one 10-minute break after Section 3, 1-minute breaks after the other sections for the computer-delivered test, and 3 hours and 30 minutes for the paper-delivered test with similar breaks). The following practice test contains the five scored sections.

Each section has its own time allocation and, during that time period, you may work on only that section.

Next, you will read ETS's policy on scoring the Analytical Writing responses. Each essay is read by experienced readers, and ETS may cancel any test scores that show evidence of unacknowledged use of sources, unacknowledged collaboration with others, preparation of the response by another person, and language that is "substantially" similar to the language in one or more other test responses.

Each section has specific instructions for that section.

You will be told when to begin.

Practice Test 2

PRACTICE TEST 2 ANSWER SHEETS

Section 1: Analytical Writing

Analyze an Issue

FOR PLANNING

Analyze an Issue Response

Analyze an Issue Response

_____

_____

_____

_____

_____

_____

_____

_____

_____

_____

_____

_____

_____

_____

_____

_____

_____

_____

_____

_____

_____

_____

_____

Analyze an Issue Response

_____

_____

_____

_____

_____

_____

_____

_____

_____

_____

_____

_____

_____

_____

_____

_____

_____

_____

_____

_____

_____

_____

answer sheet

Analyze an Issue Response

_____

_____

_____

_____

_____

_____

_____

_____

_____

_____

_____

_____

_____

_____

_____

_____

_____

_____

_____

_____

_____

_____

Analyze an Argument

FOR PLANNING

Analyze an Argument Response

_____

_____

_____

_____

_____

_____

_____

_____

_____

_____

_____

_____

_____

_____

_____

_____

_____

_____

_____

_____

_____

_____

Analyze an Argument Response

_____

_____

_____

_____

_____

_____

_____

_____

_____

_____

_____

_____

_____

_____

_____

_____

_____

_____

_____

_____

answer sheet

Analyze an Argument Response

_____

_____

_____

_____

_____

_____

_____

_____

_____

_____

_____

_____

_____

_____

_____

_____

_____

_____

_____

_____

_____

_____

_____

_____

Analyze an Argument Response

_____

_____

_____

_____

_____

_____

_____

_____

_____

_____

_____

_____

_____

_____

_____

_____

_____

_____

_____

_____

_____

_____

_____

answer sheet

Section 2: Verbal Reasoning

1. Ⓐ Ⓑ Ⓒ Ⓓ Ⓔ
2. Ⓐ Ⓑ Ⓒ Ⓓ Ⓔ
3. Ⓐ Ⓑ Ⓒ Ⓓ Ⓔ Ⓕ
4. Ⓐ Ⓑ Ⓒ Ⓓ Ⓔ Ⓕ Ⓖ Ⓗ Ⓘ
5. Ⓐ Ⓑ Ⓒ Ⓓ Ⓔ Ⓕ Ⓖ Ⓗ Ⓘ
6. Ⓐ Ⓑ Ⓒ Ⓓ Ⓔ
7. Ⓐ Ⓑ Ⓒ Ⓓ Ⓔ

8. Ⓐ Ⓑ Ⓒ
9. Ⓐ Ⓑ Ⓒ Ⓓ Ⓔ
10. Ⓐ Ⓑ Ⓒ Ⓓ Ⓔ
11. Ⓐ Ⓑ Ⓒ Ⓓ Ⓔ
12. Ⓐ Ⓑ Ⓒ Ⓓ Ⓔ
13. Ⓐ Ⓑ Ⓒ Ⓓ Ⓔ
14. Ⓐ Ⓑ Ⓒ

15. Ⓐ Ⓑ Ⓒ Ⓓ Ⓔ
16. Ⓐ Ⓑ Ⓒ Ⓓ Ⓔ Ⓕ
17. Ⓐ Ⓑ Ⓒ Ⓓ Ⓔ Ⓕ
18. Ⓐ Ⓑ Ⓒ Ⓓ Ⓔ Ⓕ
19. Ⓐ Ⓑ Ⓒ Ⓓ Ⓔ Ⓕ
20. Ⓐ Ⓑ Ⓒ Ⓓ Ⓔ

Section 3: Verbal Reasoning

1. Ⓐ Ⓑ Ⓒ Ⓓ Ⓔ
2. Ⓐ Ⓑ Ⓒ Ⓓ Ⓔ
3. Ⓐ Ⓑ Ⓒ Ⓓ Ⓔ Ⓕ
4. Ⓐ Ⓑ Ⓒ Ⓓ Ⓔ Ⓕ Ⓖ Ⓗ Ⓘ
5. Ⓐ Ⓑ Ⓒ Ⓓ Ⓔ Ⓕ Ⓖ Ⓗ Ⓘ
6. Ⓐ Ⓑ Ⓒ Ⓓ Ⓔ
7. Ⓐ Ⓑ Ⓒ Ⓓ Ⓔ

8. Ⓐ Ⓑ Ⓒ Ⓓ Ⓔ
9. Ⓐ Ⓑ Ⓒ Ⓓ Ⓔ
10. Ⓐ Ⓑ Ⓒ Ⓓ Ⓔ
11. Ⓐ Ⓑ Ⓒ Ⓓ Ⓔ
12. Ⓐ Ⓑ Ⓒ
13. Ⓐ Ⓑ Ⓒ Ⓓ Ⓔ
14. Ⓐ Ⓑ Ⓒ Ⓓ Ⓔ

15. Ⓐ Ⓑ Ⓒ
16. Ⓐ Ⓑ Ⓒ Ⓓ Ⓔ Ⓕ
17. Ⓐ Ⓑ Ⓒ Ⓓ Ⓔ Ⓕ
18. Ⓐ Ⓑ Ⓒ Ⓓ Ⓔ Ⓕ
19. Ⓐ Ⓑ Ⓒ Ⓓ Ⓔ Ⓕ
20. Ⓐ Ⓑ Ⓒ Ⓓ Ⓔ

Section 4: Quantitative Reasoning

1. Ⓐ Ⓑ Ⓒ Ⓓ
2. Ⓐ Ⓑ Ⓒ Ⓓ
3. Ⓐ Ⓑ Ⓒ Ⓓ
4. Ⓐ Ⓑ Ⓒ Ⓓ
5. Ⓐ Ⓑ Ⓒ Ⓓ
6. Ⓐ Ⓑ Ⓒ Ⓓ
7. Ⓐ Ⓑ Ⓒ Ⓓ
8. Ⓐ Ⓑ Ⓒ Ⓓ
9. Ⓐ Ⓑ Ⓒ Ⓓ Ⓔ
10. Ⓐ Ⓑ Ⓒ Ⓓ Ⓔ

11. Ⓐ Ⓑ Ⓒ Ⓓ Ⓔ
12. Ⓐ Ⓑ Ⓒ Ⓓ Ⓔ
13. Ⓐ Ⓑ Ⓒ Ⓓ Ⓔ
14. Ⓐ Ⓑ Ⓒ Ⓓ Ⓔ
15. Ⓐ Ⓑ Ⓒ Ⓓ Ⓔ Ⓕ Ⓖ
16. Ⓐ Ⓑ Ⓒ Ⓓ Ⓔ Ⓕ Ⓖ Ⓗ
17.

18. ▭
    ▭
19. ▭
    ▭

20. Ⓐ Ⓑ Ⓒ Ⓓ Ⓔ

Section 5: Quantitative Reasoning

1. Ⓐ Ⓑ Ⓒ Ⓓ
2. Ⓐ Ⓑ Ⓒ Ⓓ
3. Ⓐ Ⓑ Ⓒ Ⓓ
4. Ⓐ Ⓑ Ⓒ Ⓓ
5. Ⓐ Ⓑ Ⓒ Ⓓ
6. Ⓐ Ⓑ Ⓒ Ⓓ
7. Ⓐ Ⓑ Ⓒ Ⓓ

8. Ⓐ Ⓑ Ⓒ Ⓓ
9. Ⓐ Ⓑ Ⓒ Ⓓ Ⓔ
10. Ⓐ Ⓑ Ⓒ Ⓓ Ⓔ
11. Ⓐ Ⓑ Ⓒ Ⓓ Ⓔ
12. Ⓐ Ⓑ Ⓒ Ⓓ Ⓔ
13. Ⓐ Ⓑ Ⓒ Ⓓ Ⓔ
14. Ⓐ Ⓑ Ⓒ Ⓓ Ⓔ

15. Ⓐ Ⓑ Ⓒ Ⓓ Ⓔ
16. Ⓐ Ⓑ Ⓒ
17. Ⓐ Ⓑ Ⓒ Ⓓ Ⓔ Ⓕ
18. Ⓐ Ⓑ Ⓒ Ⓓ Ⓔ Ⓕ Ⓖ Ⓗ
19. ▭
20. ▭

SECTION 1: ANALYTICAL WRITING

Analyze an Issue

30 minutes

The time for this task is 30 minutes. You must plan and draft a response that evaluates the issue given below. If you do not respond to the specific issue, your score will be zero. Your response must be based on the accompanying instructions, and you must provide evidence for your position. You may use support from reading, experience, observations, and/or course work.

Parents should be involved in the education of their young children, and it is reasonable for teachers to expect parents to help teach their children such essential skills as learning to read, write, and solve math problems.

Write a response that takes and explains the extent to which you agree or disagree with this statement. As you present, develop, and explain your position, discuss when and how the statement might or might not hold true. Explain how those possibilities provide support for your own point of view.

Your response will be read by experienced readers who will assess your ability to do the following:

* Follow the set of task instructions.

* Analyze the complexities involved.

* Organize, develop, and explain ideas.

* Use pertinent reasons and/or illustrations to support ideas.

* Adhere to the conventions of Standard Written English.

You will be advised to take some time to plan your response and to leave time to reread it before the time is over. Those taking the paper-delivered GRE® General Test will find a blank page in their answer booklet for making notes and then four ruled pages for writing their actual response. Those taking the computer-delivered test will be given scrap paper for making notes.

STOP!
IF YOU FINISH BEFORE THE TIME IS UP,
YOU MAY CHECK YOUR WORK IN THIS SECTION ONLY.

Analyze an Argument

30 minutes

The time for this task is 30 minutes. You must plan and draft a response that evaluates the argument given below. If you do not respond to the given argument, your score will be zero. Your response must be based on the accompanying instructions, and you must provide evidence in support of your analysis.

You should not present your views on the subject of the argument, but on the strength or weakness of the argument.

In the downtown area, buildings in a state of disrepair are rapidly being demolished to make way for new construction. These new luxury condominiums are raising home values in the neighborhood, which is great for homeowners, but the situation is also making it difficult for lower-income families to find affordable places to live downtown. So what initially seemed like a boon for downtown is actually a highly unfortunate situation for the people who can no longer afford to live there. Therefore, the only moral thing to do is halt all projects involving buildings in the downtown area.

Write a response that identifies and explains the specific evidence required to determine whether the argument is reasonable. Discuss how that evidence would weaken or strengthen the argument.

Your response will be read by experienced readers who will assess your ability to do the following:

- Follow the set of task instructions.
- Analyze the complexities involved.
- Organize, develop, and explain ideas.
- Use pertinent reasons and/or illustrations to support ideas.
- Adhere to the conventions of Standard Written English.

You will be advised to take some time to plan your response and to leave time to reread it before the time is over. Those taking the paper-delivered GRE® General Test will find a blank page in their answer booklet for making notes and then four ruled pages for writing their actual response. Those taking the computer-delivered test will be given scrap paper for making notes.

STOP!
IF YOU FINISH BEFORE THE TIME IS UP,
YOU MAY CHECK YOUR WORK IN THIS SECTION ONLY.

INSTRUCTIONS FOR THE VERBAL REASONING AND QUANTITATIVE REASONING SECTIONS

You will find information here on the question formats for the Verbal Reasoning and Quantitative Reasoning sections, as well as information about how to use the software program, or, if you're taking the paper-delivered test, how to mark your answers in the answer booklet.

Perhaps the most important information is a reminder about how these two sections are scored. Every correct answer earns a point, but points are not subtracted for incorrect answers. The advice from ETS is to guess if you aren't sure of an answer. ETS says that this is better than not answering a question.

All multiple-choice questions on the computer-delivered test will have answer options preceded by either blank ovals or blank squares, depending on the question type. The paper-delivered test will follow the same format for answer choices, but it will use letters instead of ovals or squares for answer choices.

For your convenience in answering questions and checking answers, this book uses letter designations (A, B, C, etc.) for answer choices. Having these letters to refer to will make it easier for you to check your answers against the answer key and explanation sections.

SECTION 2: VERBAL REASONING

30 minutes • 20 questions

(The paper-delivered test will have 25 questions to be completed in 35 minutes.)

For each question, follow the specific directions and choose the best answer.

For Questions 1–5, choose <u>one</u> answer for each blank. Select from the appropriate column for each blank. Choose the answer that best completes the sense of the text.

1. With its colorful name coined in 1921, a Yellow Dog Contract _____ that workers must be members of trade unions in order to remain employed.

A. etched
B. stipulated
C. declared
D. intended
E. exacted

2. In 1988, U.N. Secretary-General Javier Perez de Cuellar was responsible for a much-needed _____ in the border war between Iran and Iraq.

A. armistice
B. bombardment
C. trust
D. resignation
E. document

3. Humanism is the philosophical term used to emphasize the place of we as human beings in the (i) _____ of life. It (ii) _____ our value, our agency, and the fact that all we know is rooted in our rational observations, experiments, and analyses.

Blank (i)	Blank (ii)
A. catastrophe	D. accentuates
B. scheme	E. darkens
C. concept	F. flashes

4. The modern orchestra and symphony have their roots in the work of a(n) (i) _____ of composers from the mid-18th century. Led by the (ii) _____ composer Johann Stamitz, they were (iii) _____ in the southwestern German city of Mannheim.

Blank (i)	Blank (ii)	Blank (iii)
A. marriage	D. preeminent	G. put
B. fraternity	E. popular	H. situated
C. antagonism	F. beloved	I. shoved

5. Pennsylvania and Mississippi are not just the names of U.S. states. They are also the (i) _____ of periods on the geologic (ii) _____ that sit between the Devonian and Permian Periods. The Pennsylvania and Mississippi are sometimes (iii) _____ subperiods of a Carboniferous Period.

Blank (i)	Blank (ii)	Blank (iii)
A. designations	D. chronicle	G. seared
B. trademarks	E. timescale	H. sculpted
C. countenances	F. distance	I. branded

For Questions 6–20, choose only <u>one</u> answer choice unless otherwise indicated.

Questions 6–8 are based on the following passage.

The child, it has often been said, is the most imitative of beings. This is only another way of saying that childhood is the most suggestible period of life. Precisely because the critical faculty is then undeveloped the child readily accepts and translates into some form of action

Line the suggestions impinging on his mind from the external world. Necessarily some impres-
5 sions are experienced by him more frequently than others, and by the very fact of repetition these tend to induce in him a more or less fixed mode of reaction. Thus, without the slightest awareness, he acquires good or bad "habits" of thinking and acting, and displays moods and tendencies which, often regarded by parents as quite inexplicable, are the logical and inevitable product of suggestions with which he has been bombarded since his life began.

10   In this way are to be explained many personal characteristics often mistakenly attributed to the influence of heredity. If a man is a "grouch," and his young son also displays unmistakable signs of grouchiness, it would indeed be rash to jump to the conclusion that the son had been born grouchy. It may well be—the chances are, it is—that he has acquired a grouchy turn of mind simply through imitation of his father's habitual attitude.

—Excerpt from *Psychology and Parenthood* by H. Addington Bruce

6. Based on the passage, the author evidently believes that

  A. all children develop their personalities by imitating their parents.

  B. children are born with personalities that rarely change significantly.

  C. adults need to be on their best behavior if they want to raise respectful children.

  D. environment is more influential on children than heredity is.

  E. grouchiness is a personality flaw that can be eliminated with a proper upbringing.

7. In this passage, "faculty" (line 3) means

  A. staff.

  B. gift.

  C. facility.

  D. talent.

  E. personnel.

For Question 8, consider each answer individually and select <u>all</u> choices that apply.

8. Which of the following ideas are clearly supported in this passage?

  A. A child is more imitative than an adult is.

  B. Children are not born with any individual traits.

  C. Fathers have a greater influence on their children than mothers do.

Questions 9 and 10 are based on the following passage.

Cheerfulness and equanimity are about the only traits that have invariably marked the life of those who have lived to extreme old age. Nothing is more clearly settled by experience, than that grief acts as a slow poison, not only in the immediate infliction of pain, but in gradually
Line impairing the powers of life, and in subtracting from the sum of our days.
5   If, then, by any process of instruction, discipline and mental force, we can influence our circumstances, banish grief and create cheerfulness, we can, in the same degree, reduce rules, for the pursuit of happiness, to a system; and make that system a matter of science. Can we not do this? The very million who deride the idea of seeking for enjoyment through the medium of instruction, unconsciously exercise the power in question to a certain extent—though not
10 to the extent, of which they are capable. All those wise individuals, who have travelled with equanimity and cheerfulness through the diversified scenes of life, making the most of its good, and the least of its evils, bear a general testimony to the truth of this fact. We find in them a conviction that they had such power, and a force of character that enabled them to act according to their convictions.

—Excerpt from *Art of Being Happy* by Timothy Flint

9. Which of the following statements expresses the author's opinion about aging?

    A. Everyone must do a lot of work to develop a cheerful personality.

    B. Having a positive attitude helps one live longer.

    C. Cheerfulness is interchangeable with wisdom.

    D. There is a scientific basis for cheerfulness.

    E. Grief is the most common cause of early death.

10. All of the following are stated or implied in the passage EXCEPT:

    A. Experiencing grief is painful.

    B. People can train themselves to be happy.

    C. Experience makes the fact that grief is unhealthy obvious.

    D. Every extremely old person is happy.

    E. There can be no scientific system for ensuring happiness.

Questions 11 and 12 are based on the following passage.

The year 1860 may be regarded as a landmark of importance in the history of plant physiology, for it was in that year that Sachs discovered that the bringing together of water and carbon-dioxide, in the green chlorophyll-corpuscles of the plant exposed to sunlight, results in the formation of the grains of starch found in these corpuscles.

Previous to this date Dutrochet (1826-37) had introduced the then crude idea of osmosis into physiology; vegetable anatomy had improved, and the modern conceptions of the living cell, protoplasm, nucleus, etc., were slowly looming; sieve-tubes had been discovered, and the proteids and starch in various parts of the plant examined; and the suggestion was abroad, replacing Liebig's idea that plant acids were the first products of carbon-assimilation, that some substance, of a slimy nature, was manufactured in the cells of the leaves and thence distributed as the formative material from which the plant constructed its parts. Davy and Boussingault had even surmised that a carbohydrate might be the first-formed product in assimilation.

—Excerpt from *Disease in Plants* by H. Marshall Ward

11. Select the sentence that supports the author's opinion that 1860 was a significant year.

   A. Sachs discovered that water and carbon-dioxide form grains of starch in corpuscles.

   B. Dutrochet introduced the idea of osmosis into vegetable physiology.

   C. Dutrochet's idea that osmosis affects vegetable physiology was deemed a crude one.

   D. The concept of osmosis improved scientific knowledge of vegetable anatomy.

   E. Modern conceptions of living cells, proplasm, and starch in plants were examined.

12. Which of the following, if it were true, would weaken the author's conclusion?

   A. Dutrochet is considered a great pioneer in the science of plant life.

   B. A carbohydrate is not the first-formed product in assimilation.

   C. Liebig was wrong to believe that plant acids were the first products of carbon-assimilation.

   D. Scientific understanding of plant life continues to improve to this very day.

   E. Dutrochet did not yet understand everything there is to know about plants.

Questions 13–15 are based on the following passage.

   At the beginning of the Seventeenth century colonial expansion had become for England an economic necessity. Because of the depletion of her forests, which constituted perhaps the most important of her natural resources, she could no longer look for prosperity from the old
Line industries that for centuries had been her mainstay. In the days when the Norman conquerors
   5 first set foot upon English soil the virgin woods, broken occasionally by fields and villages, had stretched in dense formation from the Scottish border to Sussex and Devonshire. But with the passage of five centuries a great change had been wrought. The growing population, the expansion of agriculture, the increasing use of wood for fuel, for shipbuilding, and for the construction of houses, had by the end of the Tudor period so denuded the forests that
   10 they no longer sufficed for the most pressing needs of the country.

   —Excerpt from *The Planters of Colonial Virginia* by Thomas Jefferson Wertenbaker

13. Which is the most significant detail about the depletion of forests in England?

   A. It occurred in the seventeenth century.

   B. It deprived England of natural resources.

   C. It forced England to look beyond natural resources for prosperity.

   D. It caused a population explosion in England.

   E. It completely stopped the English shipbuilding industry.

For Question 14, consider each answer individually and select <u>all</u> choices that apply.

14. What does the author suggest about the depletion of forests in England?

   A. Attacks by the Normans contributed to it.

   B. The need for fuel contributed to it.

   C. The growing population contributed to it.

15. "Denuded" (line 9) most nearly means

   A. concealed.

   B. disrobed.

   C. exposed.

   D. peeled.

   E. stripped.

For Questions 16–19, choose the <u>two</u> answers that best fit the meaning of the sentence as a whole and result in two completed sentences that are alike in meaning.

16. Roald Amundsen and Robert Falcon Scott are the men for whom the United States' Amundsen–Scott South Pole Station is _____.

   A. titled

   B. alleged

   C. instructed

   D. apprehended

   E. named

   F. issued

17. While most people are _____ of the terms *tartar* and *plaque* for the build up of bacterial coating on teeth, dental professionals use the more technical term *calculus*.

   A. cognizant

   B. awake

   C. knowledgeable

   D. aware

   E. expert

   F. abreast

18. Barely thirteen years after his father had done the same, Prime Minister of Lebanon Saad Hariri _____ his position on November 4, 2017.

    A. handed

    B. surrendered

    C. absolved

    D. upended

    E. abated

    F. relinquished

19. Just an hour's drive from the capital city of Brisbane sits Gold Coast, an Australian city that has become a significant attraction for tourists for its _____ beauty and surfer-friendly waters.

    A. rural

    B. picturesque

    C. scenic

    D. ambient

    E. cerebral

    F. plentiful

Question 20 is based on the following passage.

Demoralization, like the black plague of the middle ages, spread in every direction immediately following the first overt acts of war. Men who were millionaires at nightfall awoke the next morning to find themselves bankrupt through depreciation of their stock-holdings.
Line Prosperous firms of importers were put out of business. International commerce was dislocated
5 to an extent unprecedented in history.

The greatest of hardships immediately following the war, however, were visited upon those who unhappily were caught on their vacations or on their business trips within the area affected by the war. Not only men, but women and children, were subjected to privations of the severest character. Notes which had been negotiable, paper money of every description,
10 and even silver currency suddenly became of little value. Americans living in hotels and pensions facing this sudden shrinkage in their money, were compelled to leave the roofs that had sheltered them. That which was true of Americans was true of all other nationalities, so that every embassy and the office of every consul became a miniature Babel of excited, distressed humanity.

—Excerpt from *History of the World War: An Authentic Narrative of the World's Greatest War* by Richard Joseph Beamish

20. Select the sentence that best explains how war was like a plague.

   A. Demoralization, like the black plague of the middle ages, spread in every direction immediately following the first overt acts of war.

   B. Men who were millionaires at nightfall awoke the next morning to find themselves bankrupt through depreciation of their stock-holdings.

   C. The greatest of hardships immediately following the war, however, were visited upon those who unhappily were caught on their vacations or on their business trips within the area affected by the war.

   D. Not only men, but women and children, were subjected to privations of the severest character.

   E. That which was true of Americans was true of all other nationalities, so that every embassy and the office of every consul became a miniature Babel of excited, distressed humanity.

STOP!
IF YOU FINISH BEFORE THE TIME IS UP,
YOU MAY CHECK YOUR WORK IN THIS SECTION ONLY.

SECTION 3: VERBAL REASONING

30 minutes • 20 questions

(The paper-delivered test will have 25 questions to be completed in 35 minutes.)

For each question, follow the specific directions and choose the best answer.

For Questions 1–5, choose <u>one</u> answer for each blank. Select from the appropriate column for each blank. Choose the answer that best completes the sense of the text.

1. In June 2015, Misty Copeland became the first African-American woman to become a(n) _____ performer in the 75-year-old American Ballet Theater.

A. signature
B. abundant
C. obsequious
D. principal
E. inconsequential

2. Beloved by children for his fanciful illustrations and _____ characters, Dr. Seuss also intended to appeal to the adult intellect with stories that served as cagey examinations of such serious topics as the evils of nuclear war, environmental destruction, and fascism.

A. baleful
B. banal
C. whimsical
D. ridiculous
E. nonsensical

3. There are twelve cities along Lake Ontario that (i) _____ 100,000 residents. However, only one of these cities has more than 210,000 people. That highly (ii) _____ city is Rochester, New York.

Blank (i)	Blank (ii)
A. enlarge	D. famous
B. exceed	E. lively
C. swell	F. populous

4. While the name of the Canary Islands may (i) _____ images of singing birds, it is actually (ii) _____ from the Latin word canis meaning dog. Historian Pliny the Elder gave the archipelago its (iii) _____ name after noting the great number of dogs living there.

Blank (i)	Blank (ii)	Blank (iii)
A. appear	D. torn	G. handsome
B. recall	E. derived	H. bizarre
C. respond	F. bequeathed	I. distinctive

5. On June 17, 1972, five men were arrested for burglarizing the Democratic National Committee at the Watergate Hotel. The following September 15, a federal grand jury (i) _____ the burglars, as well as (ii) _____ G. Gordon Liddy and E. Howard Hunt, in a move that (iii) _____ the end of Richard Milhouse Nixon's career as President of the United States of America.

Blank (i)	Blank (ii)	Blank (iii)
A. arrested	**D.** operatives	**G.** expedited
B. indicted	**E.** executives	**H.** trotted
C. penalized	**F.** foes	**I.** hastily

For Questions 6–20, choose only <u>one</u> answer choice unless otherwise indicated.

Questions 6–8 are based on the following passage.

    The first newspaper supposed to have been published in England appeared in the reign of Queen Elizabeth during the Spanish Armada panic. This journal was called the *English Mercurie*, and was by authority "imprinted at London by Christopher Barker, Her Highnesses
Line printer, 1583." This paper was said to be started for the prevention of the fulmination of false
5 reports, but it was more like a succession of extraordinary gazettes, and had by no means the appearance of a regular journal, as we understand the term. It was promoted by Burleigh, and used by him to soothe, inform, or exasperate the people as occasion required. Periodicals and papers really first came into general use during the civil wars in the reign of Charles I., and in the time of the Commonwealth; in fact, each party had its organs, to disseminate senti-
10 ments of loyalty, or to foster a spirit of resistance against the inroads of power. The country was accordingly overflowed with tracts of every size and of various denominations, many of them displaying great courage, and being written with uncommon ability.

    —Excerpt from *A History of Advertising* by Henry Sampson

6. Select the sentence that most likely states the author's opinion.

    A. The first newspaper supposed to have been published in England appeared in the reign of Queen Elizabeth during the Spanish Armada panic.

    B. This journal was called the *English Mercurie*, and was by authority "imprinted at London by Christopher Barker, Her Highnesses printer, 1583."

    C. This paper was said to be started for the prevention of the fulmination of false reports, but it was more like a succession of extraordinary gazettes, and had by no means the appearance of a regular journal, as we understand the term.

    D. It was promoted by Burleigh, and used by him to soothe, inform, or exasperate the people as occasion required.

    E. The country was accordingly overflowed with tracts of every size and of various denominations, many of them displaying great courage, and being written with uncommon ability.

7. Which of the following sentences would serve as the most logical and relevant addition to the paragraph?

   A. Most of these newspapers were contemptible rags full of the prattling of amateur journalists.

   B. At this time, England was flooded with all varieties of newspapers containing eloquent and timely pieces of journalism.

   C. It was during the time of Queen Elizabeth that the first newspaper was published in Great Britain.

   D. Newspapers not only contain news items describing current events, but they also include editorials, cartoons, and advertisements.

   E. The newspapers of the period included *the Dutch Spye*, *the Scots Dove*, and *the Parliament Kyte*.

8. What would the author most likely advise on the subject of England's earliest newspapers?

   A. They were too unsophisticated and should have been replaced by better publications.

   B. Their titles should have been less quirky so that readers would take them more seriously.

   C. Studying them is all one needs to do to understand sixteenth-century England.

   D. They should be brought back to replace the inferior newspapers being published today.

   E. They would serve as fine role models for contemporary newspapers.

Questions 9–11 are based on the following passage.

These bodies of ours are built somewhat like automobiles. An automobile is made up of a framework, wheels, body, gasoline tank, engine, and steering-gear. The human body has much the same form of construction. We have a frame, which is made of the bones of the
Line body. We have arms and legs, which correspond to the wheels of the automobile. We have
5 many little pockets in our bodies in which fat is stored, and these little pockets answer to the gasoline tank of the automobile. We have an engine which, like the automobile engine, is made up of many parts; and we have a head or brain, that plays the same part as the steering-gear of the automobile.

The automobile has a tank in which is carried the gasoline necessary to develop power for
10 the machine. If the gasoline gives out, the engine will not run, and before the owner starts on a trip, he is always careful to see that the tank is well filled. In the same way, if we do not provide new fat for the pockets in our bodies in which the fat is stored, our supply will soon give out and our bodies will refuse to work, just as the engine of the automobile will refuse to work when the gasoline is used up.

—Excerpt from *Principles of Public Health* by Thos. D. Tuttle

9. The author's primary purpose in this passage is to

   A. describe the parts of an automobile.

   B. amuse the reader with an absurd comparison.

   C. make the human body easier to understand.

   D. explain the purposes of human bones and limbs.

   E. argue that the human body is mechanical.

10. Based on the passage, what is the purpose of fat?

    A. To energize the body

    B. To fill pockets in the body

    C. To stop the body from working

    D. To maintain the body's shape

    E. To insulate the body

11. According to the passage, what is the main reason the automobile is similar to the human body?

    A. They both have essential parts that mobilize them.

    B. They both stop working without fuel.

    C. They are both extremely common things one sees every day.

    D. They both consist of numerous parts essential for functioning.

    E. They both have parts that help them to steer.

Questions 12 and 13 are based on the following passage.

"What shall I do?" exclaims the young student who expects soon to face public audiences. "Shall I write out what I have to say, polish it as highly as possible, and then utter this finished product? Or must I take the risk of being able to say nothing at all, in hope of gaining the *Line* ease and naturalness of spontaneous speech?"

5   It must be admitted that the first course indicated above has many advantages, and seems in harmony with the marked tendency of civilization toward division of labor. It is hard to perform several different operations at the same moment. Look how heavily the extempore speaker is burdened. He must think of his subject; arrange his ideas, sentences, and words; remember quotations; originate proper tones and gestures; and keep his attention closely 10 fixed upon his audience. All this he must do with the utmost promptness and regularity, or incur a fearful penalty—that of embarrassment and failure. Few men have the courage to stand long before an audience, waiting for a missing word or idea. To avoid this danger the mind of an extempore speaker must be accustomed to work with the rapidity and precision of a printing-press; otherwise, the appalling danger of failure and ridicule will constantly 15 stare him in the face. It is not wonderful that such perils have made many speakers perpetual slaves of the pen.

—Excerpt from *How to Become a Public Speaker* by William Pittenger

For Question 12, consider each answer individually and select <u>all</u> choices that apply.

12. What does the phrase "must I take the risk of being able to say nothing at all, in hope of gaining the ease and naturalness of spontaneous speech?" suggest?

    A. That not planning a speech might result in a failure to convey a message

    B. That not planning a speech might result in a clear and understandable message

    C. That not planning a speech might result in a more sincere performance

13. What function do the quotations in the first paragraph serve in this passage?

    A. They flesh out the main character of the passage.

    B. They summarize the main conclusion of the passage.

    C. They voice concerns that the reader probably has.

    D. They make the passage more realistic.

    E. They introduce the mystery the passage intends to solve.

Questions 14 and 15 are based on the following passage.

Too much importance is attached to what is believed to be inspiration, but obviously if inspired, design is rather in the nature of an accident than of the deliberate intention it should be and cannot be credited to the individual exponent. What at first sight suggests
Line inspired thought may be accounted for by sub-consciousness, which is really responsible for
5 the evolution of an idea or the solution of some problem.

It would be beneficial to reject once and for all the idea of inspiration with its tendency to encourage the "artistic temperament" in the belief that it "does not feel like it."

The designer must be ready to respond at any time, and this implies a logical and balanced mind, capable of grasping essentials, and conditions, and of evolving some desirable solution.

10 Another superstition is that a design is a drawing, and it only requires a facility in this form of expression to produce a design. This is a fallacy, as though many designs are for convenience expressed through this medium, any such drawing must be made with a knowledge of the technical details of the final method of production, to be a practical design.

—Excerpt from *Design and Tradition* by Amor Fenn

14. "Nature" (line 2) most nearly means

    A. scenery.

    B. type.

    C. environment.

    D. personality.

    E. disposition.

For Question 15, consider each answer individually and select all choices that apply.

15. The author of the passage implies that artists often make the same excuses for relying on inspiration by

    A. quoting such excuses in the second paragraph.

    B. stating that too much importance is placed on inspiration.

    C. referring to the idea that a design is a drawing as a "superstition."

For Questions 16–19, choose the two answers that best fit the meaning of the sentence as a whole and result in two completed sentences that are alike in meaning.

16. While the violent _____ that occurred from June 5, 1967, through June 10 of that same year is known as the "War of 1967" in the Arab World, much of the rest of the world refers to it as the "Six-Day War."

    A. defense

    B. campaign

    C. operation

    D. annihilation

    E. bustle

    F. gaff

17. The nine largest companies in Europe earned their status by earning the most _____ per year, not by employing the most employees or occupying the most real estate.

    A. invest

    B. spending

    C. revenue

    D. value

    E. monetary

    F. income

18. Ergonomics is a(n) _____ of engineering science focused on the physical relationship between humans and machinery.

    A. entreaty

    B. subsidiary

    C. tributary

    D. offshoot

    E. stream

    F. finger

19. In France, French toast is known as *pain perdu*, which translates as "lost bread" because it was originally a method of _____ stale bread.

   A. reviving

   B. conjuring

   C. creation

   D. sowing

   E. cultivating

   F. resuscitating

Question 20 is based on the following passage.

It is usually admitted that states of consciousness, sensations, feelings, passions, efforts, are capable of growth and diminution; we are even told that a sensation can be said to be twice, thrice, four times as intense as another sensation of the same kind. This latter thesis, which
Line is maintained by psychophysicists, we shall examine later; but even the opponents of psycho-
5 physics do not see any harm in speaking of one sensation as being more intense than another, of one effort as being greater than another, and in thus setting up differences of quantity between purely internal states. Common sense, moreover, has not the slightest hesitation in giving its verdict on this point; people say they are more or less warm, or more or less sad, and this distinction of more and less, even when it is carried over to the region of subjective
10 facts and unextended objects, surprises nobody. But this involves a very obscure point and a much more important problem than is usually supposed.

—Excerpt from *Time and Free Will* by Henri Bergson

20. Which of the following can be inferred from the passage?

   A. People have an uncanny ability to measure the degrees of their own feelings.

   B. A sensation can be twice, thrice, or four times as intense as another sensation of the same kind.

   C. People never actually experience the sensations they claim to experience.

   D. If people made more of an effort to interpret obscure points they would do a better job of measuring their feelings.

   E. The author is skeptical of people's ability to measure the variations in their feelings.

STOP!
IF YOU FINISH BEFORE THE TIME IS UP,
YOU MAY CHECK YOUR WORK IN THIS SECTION ONLY.

SECTION 4: QUANTITATIVE REASONING

35 minutes • 20 questions

(The paper-delivered test will have 25 questions to be completed in 40 minutes.)

For each question, follow the specific directions and choose the best answer.

The test maker provides the following information that applies to all questions in the Quantitative Reasoning section of the GRE® General Test:

- All numbers used are real numbers.

- All figures are assumed to lie in a plane unless otherwise indicated.

- Geometric figures, such as lines, circles, triangles, and quadrilaterals, *are not necessarily* drawn to scale. That is, you should *not* assume that quantities such as lengths and angle measures are as they appear in a figure. You should assume, however, that lines shown as straight are actually straight, points on a line are in the order shown, and more generally, all geometric objects are in the relative positions shown. For questions with geometric figures, you should base your answers on geometric reasoning, not on estimating or comparing quantities by sight or by measurement.

- Coordinate systems, such as *xy*-planes and number lines, *are* drawn to scale. Therefore, you can read, estimate, or compare quantities in such figures by sight or by measurement.

- Graphical data presentations, such as bar graphs, circle graphs, and line graphs, *are* drawn to scale. Therefore, you can read, estimate, or compare data values by sight or by measurement.

For Questions 1–8, compare Quantity A and Quantity B. Some questions will have additional information above the two quantities to use in determining your answer.

1.

Quantity A	Quantity B
$3^{-1} \bullet \sqrt{\dfrac{16}{25}}$	$2^2 \bullet (3 \bullet 5)^{-1}$

- **A.** Quantity A is greater.
- **B.** Quantity B is greater.
- **C.** The two quantities are equal.
- **D.** The relationship cannot be determined from the information given.

2. $a - b = 3$

Quantity A	Quantity B
$-2a$	$-2b$

A. Quantity A is greater.

B. Quantity B is greater.

C. The two quantities are equal.

D. The relationship cannot be determined from the information given.

3.

Quantity A	Quantity B
75% of $\frac{4}{5}$	90% of $\frac{3}{5}$

A. Quantity A is greater.

B. Quantity B is greater.

C. The two quantities are equal.

D. The relationship cannot be determined from the information given.

4. $x < 0 < y$

Quantity A	Quantity B
xy	x^2

A. Quantity A is greater.

B. Quantity B is greater.

C. The two quantities are equal.

D. The relationship cannot be determined from the information given.

5. $m = -2m + 1$

$n + 1 = 2n - 5$

Quantity A	Quantity B
$18m$	n

A. Quantity A is greater.

B. Quantity B is greater.

C. The two quantities are equal.

D. The relationship cannot be determined from the information given.

6.

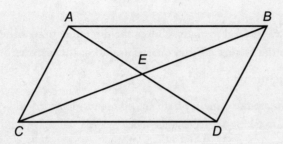

Quantity A	Quantity B
The length *AE*	The length *EC*

A. Quantity A is greater.

B. Quantity B is greater.

C. The two quantities are equal.

D. The relationship cannot be determined from the information given.

7.

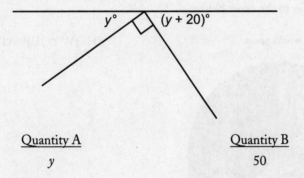

Quantity A	Quantity B
y	50

A. Quantity A is greater.

B. Quantity B is greater.

C. The two quantities are equal.

D. The relationship cannot be determined from the information given.

8.   A car is sold for $29,000. The salesperson earns a 2% commission.

Quantity A	Quantity B
The salesperson's commission	$700

A. Quantity A is greater.

B. Quantity B is greater.

C. The two quantities are equal.

D. The relationship cannot be determined from the information given.

Questions 9–20 have several formats. Unless the directions state otherwise, choose one answer choice. For the Numeric Entry questions, follow the instructions below.

Numeric Entry Questions

The following items are the same for both the computer-delivered and the paper-delivered tests. However, those taking the computer-delivered test will have additional information about entering answers in decimal and fraction boxes on the computer screen. Those taking the paper-delivered test will have information about entering answers on answer grids.

- Your answer may be an integer, a decimal, or a fraction, and it may be negative.

- If a question asks for a fraction, there will be two boxes. One box will be for the numerator and one will be for the denominator.

- Equivalent forms of the correct answer, such as 2.5 and 2.50, are all correct.

- Enter the exact answer unless the question asks you to round your answers.

Questions 9–11 refer to the chart below.

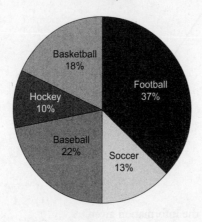

Favorite Sport

SHOW YOUR WORK HERE

9. The two most popular sports represent what percentage of the respondents?

    A. 10%

    B. 30%

    C. 40%

    D. 45%

    E. 59%

10. What percentage of respondents do NOT prefer football or soccer?

  A. 13%

  B. 40%

  C. 41%

  D. 50%

  E. 63%

11. If the total number of people surveyed was 9,860, how many people prefer the least popular sport?

  A. 986

  B. 1,282

  C. 1,775

  D. 8,874

  E. 9,860

12. A circle has a radius of 6, and a square has a perimeter of 48. What is the difference in the area between the two?

  A. 10.32

  B. 18.96

  C. 30.96

  D. 108

  E. 125.16

13. The expression $(a+b)^2 - (a-b)^2$ is equivalent to

  A. $4ab$

  B. $a^2 - b^2$

  C. $2a^2 + 2b^2$

  D. $a^4 - 2ab$

  E. $a^2 - 4ab + b^2$

SHOW YOUR WORK HERE

14. Whitney bought new tires for her car. The tires were on sale for 12% off, and she paid a 6.5% sales tax on the discounted amount. If she paid a total of $786.11, what was the original price of the tires?

A. $541.40

B. $649.56

C. $736.74

D. $838.79

E. $1,387.69

SHOW YOUR WORK HERE

For Questions 15 and 16, indicate <u>all</u> the answers that apply.

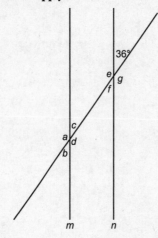

15. If lines *m* and *n* are parallel, which angles measure 144°?

A. *a*

B. *b*

C. *c*

D. *d*

E. *e*

F. *f*

G. *g*

16. A sequence begins with the terms

$\frac{1}{2}, \frac{3}{4}, \frac{5}{8}, \frac{7}{16}, \ldots$. What are the next

three terms?

A. $\frac{8}{17}$

B. $\frac{9}{32}$

C. $\frac{9}{18}$

D. $\frac{8}{32}$

E. $\frac{11}{64}$

F. $\frac{7}{64}$

G. $\frac{11}{128}$

H. $\frac{13}{128}$

SHOW YOUR WORK HERE

For Questions 17–19, enter your answers in the boxes.

17. Suppose j and k are different positive numbers. If $p = \dfrac{6jk - 6k^2}{-5k^2 + 5jk}$, what does p equal?

Give your answer as a fraction.

18. $\frac{1}{3} \cdot \frac{3}{5} \cdot \frac{5}{7} \cdot \frac{7}{9} =$

Give your answer as a fraction.

19. In a biology class consisting of freshman and sophomores, the ratio of freshmen to sophomores is $\frac{5}{2}$. What is the ratio of freshman to the total number of students?

Give your answer as a fraction.

SHOW YOUR WORK HERE

20. If there are 3,785 milliliters per gallon, how many gallons are there in 27,252 milliliters?

A. 0.14

B. 5.2

C. 6.2

D. 7.2

E. 8.2

STOP!
IF YOU FINISH BEFORE THE TIME IS UP,
YOU MAY CHECK YOUR WORK IN THIS SECTION ONLY.

SECTION 5: QUANTITATIVE REASONING

35 minutes • 20 questions

(The paper-delivered test will have 25 questions to be completed in 40 minutes.)

For each question, follow the specific directions and choose the best answer.

The test maker provides the following information that applies to all questions in the Quantitative Reasoning section of the GRE® General Test:

- All numbers used are real numbers.
- All figures are assumed to lie in a plane unless otherwise indicated.
- Geometric figures, such as lines, circles, triangles, and quadrilaterals, *are not necessarily* drawn to scale. That is, you should *not* assume that quantities such as lengths and angle measures are as they appear in a figure. You should assume, however, that lines shown as straight are actually straight, points on a line are in the order shown, and more generally, all geometric objects are in the relative positions shown. For questions with geometric figures, you should base your answers on geometric reasoning, not on estimating or comparing quantities by sight or by measurement.
- Coordinate systems, such as *xy*-planes and number lines, *are* drawn to scale. Therefore, you can read, estimate, or compare quantities in such figures by sight or by measurement.
- Graphical data presentations, such as bar graphs, circle graphs, and line graphs, *are* drawn to scale. Therefore, you can read, estimate, or compare data values by sight or by measurement.

For Questions 1–8, compare Quantity A and Quantity B. Some questions will have additional information above the two quantities to use in determining your answer.

1.

$$-\frac{3}{4}p = -\frac{9}{8}$$

Quantity A	Quantity B
p	$\frac{3}{2}$

A. Quantity A is greater.

B. Quantity B is greater.

C. The two quantities are equal.

D. The relationship cannot be determined from the information given.

2.

Quantity A	Quantity B
$\dfrac{(4,000)(3,000)}{600}$	2×10^5

A. Quantity A is greater.
B. Quantity B is greater.
C. The two quantities are equal.
D. The relationship cannot be determined from the information given.

3.   A circle has a radius of 7.

Quantity A	Quantity B
The area of the circle	147

A. Quantity A is greater.
B. Quantity B is greater.
C. The two quantities are equal.
D. The relationship cannot be determined from the information given.

4.

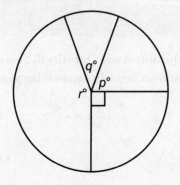

Quantity A	Quantity B
The average of angles p, q, r	80

A. Quantity A is greater.
B. Quantity B is greater.
C. The two quantities are equal.
D. The relationship cannot be determined from the information given.

5.

Quantity A	Quantity B
$\left(6^{1.9}\right)\left(3^{2.8}\right)$	$(36)(27)$

A. Quantity A is greater.

B. Quantity B is greater.

C. The two quantities are equal.

D. The relationship cannot be determined from the information given.

6.

$$t^2 = 5$$

Quantity A	Quantity B
$-3t(-2t)$	30

A. Quantity A is greater.

B. Quantity B is greater.

C. The two quantities are equal.

D. The relationship cannot be determined from the information given.

7.

x and y are positive numbers

Quantity A	Quantity B
x% of y	y% of x

A. Quantity A is greater.

B. Quantity B is greater.

C. The two quantities are equal.

D. The relationship cannot be determined from the information given.

8.

Jar A contains 7 red marbles and Jar B contains 19 red marbles.

Quantity A	Quantity B
The probability of randomly choosing a red marble from Jar A	The probability of randomly choosing a red marble from Jar B

A. Quantity A is greater.

B. Quantity B is greater.

C. The two quantities are equal.

D. The relationship cannot be determined from the information given.

Questions 9–20 have several formats. Unless the directions state otherwise, choose one answer choice. For the Numeric Entry questions, follow the instructions below.

Numeric Entry Questions

The following items are the same for both the computer-delivered version and paper-delivered tests. However, those taking the computer-delivered test will have additional information about entering answers in decimal and fraction boxes on the computer screen. Those taking the paper-delivered test will have information about entering answers on answer grids.

- Your answer may be an integer, a decimal, or a fraction, and it may be negative.
- If a question asks for a fraction, there will be two boxes. One box will be for the numerator and one will be for the denominator.
- Equivalent forms of the correct answer, such as 2.5 and 2.50, are all correct.
- Enter the exact answer unless the question asks you to round your answers.

9. Two standard six-sided dice are rolled. What is the probability that at least one die shows a 4?

    SHOW YOUR WORK HERE

  A. $\dfrac{1}{36}$

  B. $\dfrac{1}{6}$

  C. $\dfrac{11}{36}$

  D. $\dfrac{1}{3}$

  E. 1

10. Solve the inequality $3\left(x - \dfrac{1}{2}\right) > 4 + x$.

  A. $x < \dfrac{11}{4}$

  B. $x > \dfrac{9}{4}$

  C. $x < -\dfrac{11}{4}$

  D. $x > \dfrac{11}{4}$

  E. $x > \dfrac{11}{2}$

Questions 11–13 refer to the graph below.

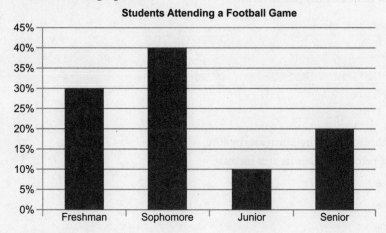

11. What percentage of the students attending
    the game are seniors?

    A. 5%
    B. 10%
    C. 15%
    D. 20%
    E. 25%

12. What percentage of the students attending
    the game are NOT juniors?

    A. 60%
    B. 70%
    C. 80%
    D. 90%
    E. 100%

13. If all of the freshmen left the game, and a new
    graph was created to show the percentages of
    students still at the game, what percentage
    would the sophomores be?

    A. 14%
    B. 29%
    C. 30%
    D. 40%
    E. 57%

SHOW YOUR WORK HERE

14. A student had scores of 78, 82, 89, 85, and 91 on five exams. What is the difference between the mean and median scores?

   A. 0

   B. 3

   C. 4

   D. 6

   E. 8

15. When the radius of a circle increases by 40%, by what percentage does its area increase?

   A. 18%

   B. 40%

   C. 62%

   D. 80%

   E. 96%

For Questions 16–18, indicate <u>all</u> answers that apply.

16. Suppose x and y are integers. If n is a prime number that is a factor of both x^2 and y, then n is also a factor of which of the following?

   A. x

   B. $\dfrac{x^2}{n}$

   C. $\dfrac{y}{n}$

   D. $x + y$

17. On a trip to the store, Shanna buys twice as many apples as oranges, and never more than seven pieces of fruit altogether. If apples cost $0.50 each, oranges cost $0.75 each, and she buys at least one of each, which of the following are possible amounts of money for Shanna to spend on apples and oranges?

   A. $1.75

   B. $2.75

   C. $3.50

   D. $4.25

   E. $5.00

   F. $5.50

SHOW YOUR WORK HERE

18. Which of the following are multiples of 9?

SHOW YOUR WORK HERE

   A. 3

   B. 6

   C. 18

   D. 27

   E. 81

   F. 126

   G. 4,000

   H. 8,199

For Questions 19–20, enter your answers in the boxes.

19. If $\left(\dfrac{x^3 x^{-2}}{\left(x^4\right)^2} \right)^{-1} = x^k$, then $k =$ ☐

20. In an isosceles triangle, the vertex angle is twice the size of one of the base angles. What is the measure of the largest angle, in degrees?

☐

STOP!
IF YOU FINISH BEFORE THE TIME IS UP,
YOU MAY CHECK YOUR WORK IN THIS SECTION ONLY.

ANSWER KEY AND EXPLANATIONS

Section 1: Analytical Writing

Analyze an Issue

Model: 6 points out of 6

Whether most people realize it or not, education begins at home. When parents play with their children, the children are learning to develop their motor skills and to interact with others. When parents sing the "Alphabet Song" with their children, the children are learning their ABCs. When parents merely speak to their children, the children are learning new words and how to construct sentences. So it is not unreasonable for teachers to require parents to continue such activities once the child reaches school age. However, teachers need to provide reasonable guidelines for parents who have no background in education.

In today's competitive education environment, some teachers are expecting more and more of parents. Teachers are looking to dads and moms to assist when it comes to the famed "three Rs": reading, writing, and arithmetic. These skills are so essential, that it should not be too difficult for most parents to assist in teaching them. Simply reading a book to a child helps foster a love of reading and a desire to read. So spending a little time with a book is a great and educational way for a parent and child to bond. Mathematical skills such as adding and subtracting are easy enough for the parent who received straight Ds in math to teach.

However, many parents simply might not know where to start when expected to teach such subjects. So any teacher who wants parents to be more involved in the educational process needs to assist parents as much as those teachers expect parents to assist them. Teachers cannot simply dump a homework assignment that tests skills unfamiliar to children in parents' laps and expect the parents to introduce their kids to multiplication or the difference between verbs and nouns. Such concepts must be introduced in the classroom so that the parents are only expected to build upon or clarify such now familiar concepts at home.

If teachers have something more involved in mind for parents, they should provide parents with clear written instructions for teaching their children at home. For example, teachers can give parents directions for constructive projects or lessons that will help their children to learn essential skills. Simply sending kids home with a page of unfamiliar math problems to solve and expecting parents to guide their children through such an assignment is less reasonable.

Involving parents more in the educational process has a number of benefits. It not only relieves some of the pressure on teachers, but it strengthens both a child's education and the bond between child and parent. It also keeps parents on top of the things their children are learning during those hours a parent and child spend apart. So I believe that expecting parents to help out with teaching basic skills is a fair expectation for teachers to have—those teachers just need to make sure the specifics of those expectations are equally fair and well explained.

This response scores 6 out of 6 for the following reasons:

- **It answer the task.** It follows specific instructions by analyzing the issue of whether or not parents should be involved in their children's educations and it reveals some of the complexities of the issue, such as the need for teachers to provide parents with clear instructions.

- **It is well supported.** The complex approach to the issue is best reflected in the clear and satisfying support, which draws on issues related to children's educations, such as the multiple benefits of parents assisting in the educational process.

- **It is well organized.** The introduction creates interest and uses repetition to intriguing effect; the body paragraphs provide thoughtful support and each paragraph is focused on a specific subtopic; and the conclusion restates the writer's position clearly and thoughtfully. The writer uses transitions such as *However* and *So* to connect ideas.

- **It is fluid.** Sentences range from simple sentences to complex sentences. Vocabulary is mature and appropriate for the given audience.

- **It observes the conventions of Standard Written English.**

Model: 3 points out of 6

Parents should be involved in their children's education. I agree with that point. I think that one way parents can be more involved is to help their children learn basic skills like math, English, and writing. Teachers should require them to do that.

Parents are usually pretty smart and they are adults so they have the math skills and reading skills and writing skills they acquired when they were students as younger people. They have the ability to do these things, and we are talking about younger children here, so they won't be expected to do anything too complex. Some adults don't know, for example, logarhythms. It would not be fair for teachers to accept parents to teach that unless teachers teach them that first. But it is also unreasonable to expect teachers to teach parents formally, so I don't know.

Parents can definitely help out with simpler assignments though. They can do adding and subtraction no problem. They can teach about the alphabet if children are extremely young and don't know that yet. That should not be a problem and adults have no excuse for not knowing such things and getting involved in their children's educations. They have time to do it.

If I were a teacher, I would think it was very helpful if parents took some of the burden and helped with homework or even lessons at home. If I were a parent I'd be more than willing to help out at the teacher's requirement. In fact, I'd do it even if I wasn't told to.

This response scores 3 out of 6 for the following reasons:

- **It answers the task in a limited way.** This response makes its position very clear but doesn't develop that idea in a meaningful way.

- **It offers inadequate support.** Support is present, especially in the second paragraph, but the writer makes too many assumptions about parents' ability to teach and the available time they have to assist with educating their children.

- **It lacks organization.** The structure rambles, and each paragraph does not focus on a very specific subtopic.

- **It is only moderately fluid and is not precise.** Most sentences are relatively fluid, but it is difficult to determine what the writer is referring to at times. However, there are no egregious run-ons or fragments.

- **It contains errors in the conventions of Standard Written English.** There are several consistent flaws, some of which interfere with meaning.

Model: 1 point out of 6

Parents arent qualified to teach period. Moms and dads already have enough to do. Now they're supposed to be teachers? What do they know about teaching? They already jobs. Teachers should do there jobs and leave the parents to the parenting. I would never want to become a parent if I thought I'd have to teach math to. I am terribel at math. The idea of teaching math to some kid even my own kid is terribel. I will not do it.

This response scores 1 out of 6 for the following reasons:

- **It barely answers the task.** Although the writer takes a position on the prompt, disagreeing with the idea that parents should help out with the educational process, he or she fails to even consider the other side of the argument and approaches the task from a simplistic point of view.

- **It is not supported.** The writer barely provides any support for the argument, only stating that parents are too busy and too unqualified to help teach their children basic skills.

- **It has no sense of sentence construction.** The opening sentence is a run-on. The fifth sentence is a fragment. The author's complete sentence are all simple sentences, and the entire essay is too short. The wording is too informal.

- **It contains major errors in the conventions of Standard Written English.**

Analyze an Argument

Model: 6 points out of 6

Progress is not always a good thing. For those who will profit from them, and those who can afford to live in them, the new luxury condominiums springing up like weeds in the downtown area surely qualify as positive progress. The many less fortunate people who will be displaced amidst these rapid changes will likely disagree. However, halting all construction projects in the downtown area, as the writer of this argument suggests, may not actually be the most moral approach to a serious and complex problem.

No one likes to look at crumbling buildings, and it is surely considerably worse to live in them. Living in the kind of derelict buildings in the downtown area can be so downright dangerous, so it is understandable that the city wants to give its landscape a makeover. Renovating the downtown area is a project that few citizens would likely protest. The problem is that luxury condominiums are completely beyond the budgets of the lower-income people who currently live in the area. Indeed, it is immoral to displace these people, as the writer of the argument insists. However, I also believe that these people deserve better places to live than those that are currently available to them.

The author makes a moral argument while expecting lower-income people to continue living in dilapidated homes. I do not see the morality in that. Perhaps the most moral solution would be to take such projects out of the hands of real estate companies that merely expect to profit from the sale of high-priced condominiums and place them solely in the hands of the city and use tax dollars to repair the buildings currently barely standing.

Giving the lower-income residents of the downtown area better homes to live in is the truly moral solution to the problem described in this argument. I agree that it is immoral to allow profiteers to displace people from their homes, but I also contend that it is immoral to expect people to continue living in unlivable situations just because they do have little money. Therefore, the argument would be stronger if the author had taken more time to consider an alternate solution to the rather extreme one of simply halting all projects in the downtown area. Perhaps if the author specified halting demolition and construction projects only, the argument would be more reasonable.

The point of a society is to help each other. The situation described in this argument is a perfect opportunity to put this concept into action. While there are flaws in this argument, its most basic stance can be a springboard for enacting real and positive change that will benefit the people who most need a bit of assistance.

This response scores 6 out of 6 for the following reasons:

- **It answers the task.** The author thoughtfully analyzes the argument, acknowledges where she or he agrees with it and how it can be strengthened.

- **It is well supported.** The evidence the author uses to support the analysis is strong, and the author even offers an alternate solution to the problem he or she feels the writer of the argument failed to solve successfully.

- **It is well organized.** The opening paragraph introduces the topic effectively and concludes by stating the author's complex evaluation of the argument clearly. The supporting paragraphs remain on topic and feature strong transitions. The entire essay is coherent and well organized.

- **It is fluid.** The author uses a variety of sentences. There are no fragments or run-ons. The first-person point of view is used effectively and consistently without lapsing into informality.

- **It observes the conventions of Standard Written English.**

Model: 3 points out of 6

Yes, yes, yes. I firmly agree with this argument. And it is well argued indeed. Who would be so cruel to displace lower income people from there homes? Yet, there are those who would. And they are the villains of this scenario that most definitely deserves the support of any moral thinking person.

So, to be extremely clear I agree and think the argument is a strong one. First of all, it says that the buildings are in disrepair not totally destroyed. It is extremely wasteful to demolish something that is only in a state of disrepair. In other words, it can be salvaged. I bet the people who live in it think it can be. They'd probably rather live in a building that is in a state of disrepair then lose their homes completely anyway!

So in conclusion…great argument! I see no problems here. I opt for the moral solution. Let them stay!

The second good thing that writer does is admit that there are good things about the construction project for lower income people. They are good for the neighborhood. If you just criticize criticize and more criticize, it weakens your argument because it makes you look biased. That was a very clever thing for the writer to do.

This response scores 3 out of 6 for the following reasons:

- **It answers the task in a limited way.** This response makes its position very clear. In fact, it's almost too clear as the writer has a tendency to repeat her- or himself.

- **It offers passable support.** Support is passable. The writer makes a somewhat interesting point about the author's use of the term *disrepair*; however the writer misinterprets the detail about how luxury condominiums raise home values in a neighborhood as a positive thing for lower income people. The response is also too brief.

- **It lacks organization.** Phrases such as *First of all*, *The second good thing*, and *in conclusion* give the impression of organization, but the paragraphs they introduce are out of order. The conclusion should appear at the end of the response, not in the middle of it.

- **It is fluid, but not precise.** Ideas flow in a variety of sentence structures, but the fragment that begins the response is too informal. The third paragraph is very choppy. Although the writer occasionally utilizes strong vocabulary (*scenario, opt, salvaged, biased*), at other times the lack of clear references makes it difficult to understand the writer's meaning.

- **It contains errors in the conventions of Standard Written English.** There are several consistent flaws, some of which interfere with meaning.

Model: 1 point out of 6

Out with the old in with the new I say. Some people cant live in places because they're not repaired why would someone want to stay in a place like that. Building new buildings is a good thing to do, and anyone who would complain about something like that is someone who does not pay attention to issues, who would complain about that kind thing. I do. I think it's a good idea.

This response scores 1 out of 6 for the following reasons:

- **It does not answer the task.** While the writer seems to take a stance on the issue in the argument, there is no actual acknowledgement of the argument itself.

- **It lacks organization.** This single paragraph is completely unfocused. Supporting paragraphs and a concluding paragraph are missing. There are no transitions to link the scant ideas in this paragraph.

- **It offers no support.** While the writer takes a position on the issue, she or he fails to provide any strong logical support for that position.

- **It has poorly constructed sentences.** There are run-on sentences and convoluted constructions with redundant ideas that render the writer's message incoherent.

- **It contains major errors in the conventions of Standard Written English.**

Section 2: Verbal Reasoning

1. B	**6.** D	**11.** A	**16.** A, E
2. A	**7.** C	**12.** B	**17.** A, D
3. B, D	**8.** A	**13.** C	**18.** B, F
4. B, D, H	**9.** B	**14.** B, C	**19.** B, C
5. A, E, I	**10.** E	**15.** E	**20.** B

1. **The correct answer is B.** When discussing a formal document such as a contract, *stipulated* is the most appropriate word to use to describe what the contract determined. *Etched* (choice A) describes the physical way something is written, and one would not etch into a paper contract in any event. *Declared* (choice C) is more associated with verbal speech. *Intended* (choice D) is not precise enough. *Exacted* (choice E) is too strong a word to describe what a contract determined.

2. **The correct answer is A.** Since the sentence explains that something is needed to resolve a war, the missing word must be a positive resolution such as an armistice. *Bombardment* (choice B) describes a violent action that might not necessarily bring a war to an end. The words *trust* (choice C), *resignation* (choice D), and *document* (choice E) do not make much sense if used to fill in the blank.

3. **The correct answers are B and D.** Answer Blank (i): *Scheme* makes the most sense in this context, since *catastrophe* (choice A) has negative connotations not implied in the sentence and *concept* (choice C) is not as specific of a way to describe the "design" of life as *scheme* is.

Answer Blank (ii): Since the second sentence implies that the ideas that follow the blank are tenets of humanism, *accentuates* is the best answer. *Darkens* (choice E) does not make as much sense and has negative connotations. *Flashes* (choice F) does not make much sense either.

4. **The correct answers are B, D, and H.** Answer Blank (i): A *fraternity* is a group of men, so it is the best answer for this context. *Marriage* (choice A) is usually used to describe a couple, not a larger group. *Antagonism* (choice C) has negative connotations and describes feelings within a group, not a group, itself.

Answer Blank (ii): The leader of the composers is probably the best of the group, and that is what *preeminent* suggests. All members might be popular or beloved in their own right, so choices E and F are not as strong of an answer as choice D is.

Answer Blank (iii): The final word should indicate the fact that the composers were located in Mannheim, and *situated* is a synonym for *located*. One puts an object, not a person, somewhere, so choice G is not the best answer. *Shoved* (choice I) has violent connotations that do not suit this sentence.

5. **The correct answers are A, E, and I.** Answer Blank (i): Pennsylvania and Mississippi are names, and *designations* is a synonym for *names*. *Trademarks* (choice B) suggests companies or products, and Pennsylvania and Mississippi are not companies or products. *Countenances* (choice C) are facial appearances, not names.

   Answer Blank (ii): This sentence discusses a timeline or *timescale* on which eras sit. *Chronicle* (choice D) is a story told in time order. The distance of time is what a timescale measures, but one would not call a timescale a *distance*, so choice F does not make sense in this context.

   Answer Blank (iii): The word on the blank should imply that Pennsylvania and Mississippi are labeled subperiods, and *branded* is a synonym for *labeled*. *Seared* (choice G) is a synonym for a different meaning of *branded* than the one used in this sentence. *Sculpted* (choice H) is not a clear synonym of *labeled*.

6. **The correct answer is D.** The main idea of the passage is that the environment in which a child is raised is more influential on that child than whatever the child biologically inherits from her or his parents. Choice A seems to support that conclusion, but it does so with an extreme generalization that the author never really suggests. Choice B makes the opposite point of the author's argument. Choices C and E draw conclusions based on the author's opinion, but they do not exactly reflect the argument in this particular passage.

7. **The correct answer is C.** Each answer choice listed could be used as a synonym for *faculty*, but *facility* makes the most sense in this context. *Staff* (choice A) and *personnel* (choice E) refer to a group of people, not a facility such as the ability to be critical. *Gift* (choice B) and *talent* (choice D) are better suited to an ability much more unique than the ability to be critical.

8. **The correct answer is A.** The opening sentence of the passage serves as strong support for the idea that a child is more imitative than an adult. Choice B is an extreme interpretation of a passage that really only discusses personality traits. Choice C places too much importance on the particular example used in the passage to illustrate the author's point; there is no reason to believe a mother would not be just as influential as a father would.

9. **The correct answer is B.** The statement that "having a positive attitude helps one live longer," sums up the author's main point very well. Choice A makes the extreme suggestion that *everyone* must do a lot of work to develop a cheerful personality. While the author does imply that it is wise to be cheerful since cheerfulness prolongs life, he never actually suggests that cheerfulness and wisdom are interchangeable (choice C). There is also no implication that the author believes there is a scientific basis for cheerfulness (choice D) as he only says that there is a scientific basis for making a cheerful attitude a goal. While he suggests that grief is bad for one's health, he never implies that grief is the most common cause of early death (choice E).

10. **The correct answer is E.** The author states that the opposite of choice E is possible. Choices A, B, and C are all ideas the author introduces in the passage. While extreme conclusions should usually be avoided, the author does draw an extreme conclusion in the first sentence of this passage, so choice D is not the correct answer.

11. **The correct answer is A.** Only choice A describes the significant event that occurred in 1860 that supports the author's opinion that "The year 1860 may be regarded as a landmark of importance in the history of plant physiology." Choices B, C, D, and E describe things that happened before 1860.

12. **The correct answer is B.** The author describes significant findings that helped build scientific understanding of plants and ends with the detail about how Davy and Boussingault surmised that a carbohydrate might be the first-formed product in assimilation. If this were not true, it would weaken the author's main idea. Choice A supports the author's description of the development of scientific understanding of plant life. Choice C reflects a fact stated in the passage explicitly. The passage discusses only the earliest days of scientific knowledge of plant life, so neither choice D nor choice E clashes with the conclusion of this passage.

13. **The correct answer is C.** Most significantly, the depletion of forest in England forced the country to look beyond natural resources for prosperity. While choices A and B describe ideas that the passage supports, these ideas are not as significant than the one in choice C. Choice D suggests that the depletion of forest somehow caused a population explosion in England, which the passage does not support. Choice E is an extreme conclusion that the passage does not clearly support either.

14. **The correct answers are B and C.** The author mentions both the need for fuel (choice B) and the growing population (choice C) as causes for the depletion of English forests. Norman conquerors are only discussed in terms of history before the depletion of those forests, so choice A does not apply.

15. **The correct answer is E.** The word *denuded* is used to describe how various factors had stripped English forests of their trees. *Disrobed* (choice B), *exposed* (choice C), and *peeled* (choice D) could all be used as synonyms for *denuded* in other contexts, but none could really be used to describe anything that might happen to forests. *Concealed* (choice A) is the opposite of *denuded*.

16. **The correct answers are A and E.** The station is named (choice E) after Amundsen and Scott, and *titled* (choice A) is a synonym for *named*. The other answer choices would not make any sense in this context.

17. **The correct answers are A and D.** This sentence deals with people knowing particular terms, and *cognizant* (choice A) and *aware* (choice D) are synonyms that mean "knowing." One would not say that a person is *awake* (choice B) or *expert* (choice E) of something. *Knowledgeable* (choice C) implies a deeper understanding than merely being cognizant or aware of something.

18. **The correct answers are B and F.** In this context, *surrendered* (choice B) or *relinquished* (choice F) make sense. One would not have *handed* (choice A), *absolved* (choice C), or *upended* (choice D) a position.

19. **The correct answers are B and C.** The sentence describes an area of land, and *picturesque* (choice B) and *scenic* (choice C) are terms that specifically describe how areas of land look. An area of land may be rural, and it may even look rural, but choice A lacks the specifically positive connotations this sentence requires to suggest that the area is attractive to tourists. *Ambient* (choice D), *cerebral* (choice E), and *plentiful* (choice F) would not be used to describe how an area of land looks.

20. **The correct answer is B.** The author compares war to the Black Plague to suggest that war is devastating. Choice B provides the most specific example of that devastation. Choice A only introduces the comparison; it does not support it with a specific example. Choice C is not as specific as choice B. Choices D and E provide no specifics regarding the nature of war's devastating effects; they only explain who was affected by those effects.

Section 3: Verbal Reasoning

1. D	**6.** E	**11.** D	**16.** B, C
2. C	**7.** E	**12.** A, C	**17.** C, F
3. B, F	**8.** E	**13.** C	**18.** B, D
4. B, E, I	**9.** C	**14.** B	**19.** A, F
5. B, D, G	**10.** A	**15.** A	**20.** E

1. **The correct answer is D.** The word *principal* (choice D) makes sense in this context because it means "main." *Signature* (choice A) has a similar meaning, but it does not make as much sense in this particular context since one does not usually refer to a person as being "signature." A single person also cannot be *abundant* (choice B), which means "plentiful." While a person can be *obsequious* (choice C), which means "fawning" or "submissive," that particular word does not suit this context. This sentence is clearly discussing an important achievement, and becoming an *inconsequential* (choice E), or unimportant, performer is not a very important achievement.

2. **The correct answers are C.** The needed word must have positive connotations and be descriptive of the kinds of characters who appear in children's stories. *Whimsical* accomplishes this because it means "quirky" or "unusual." *Baleful* (choice A) means "threatening," and while some characters in children's books might be baleful, it is unlikely that such characters would cause a story to be beloved by children. *Banal* (choice B) means "predictable" and "simplistic," which does not have positive connotations either. *Ridiculous* (choice D) and *nonsensical* (choice E) are closer to the mark, but neither word has as positive connotations as *whimsical* does.

3. **The correct answers are B and F.** Answer Blank (i): While *enlarge*, *exceed*, and *swell* all have similar meanings, only *exceed* makes complete grammatical sense in this particular context.

    Answer Blank (ii): An area that is home to a lot of people is described as populous. A city can be *famous* (choice D) or *lively* (choice E), but this sentence is concerned with the fact that a lot of people live in an area.

4. **The correct answers are B, E, and I.** Answer Blank (i): The word to fill in the blank should mean "bring to mind," and that is what *recall* means. *Appear* (choice A) and *respond* (choice C) do not mean "bring to mind."

    Answer Blank (ii): According to the sentence, *canis* is a root word of *Canary*, and a word is derived from its root. One does not say that a word is *torn* (choice D) or *bequeathed* (choice F), meaning "donated," from a root word.

    Answer Blank (iii): The correct word describes a name, and it is not commonplace to describe a name as "handsome" (choice G). While a name can be bizarre (choice H), or extremely strange, there is nothing particularly *bizarre* about the name Canary Islands. However, that name is fairly distinctive, so choice I is the best answer.

5. **The correct answers are B, D, and G.** Answer Blank (i): It is not the job of a jury to arrest or penalize anyone. However, a jury is capable of indicting someone accused of a crime.

Answer Blank (ii): This part of the paragraph deals with people who worked with burglars to commit an involved crime, and *operatives* (choice D) best describes such people. The word *executives* (choice E) describes business people and is not a word usually used to describe people who play a part in executing a scheme. *Foes* (choice F) means "enemies," and one probably would not help his enemies commit a crime.

Answer Blank (iii): A past tense verb that means "made something happen quicker," such as *expedited* (choice G), fits on this line. *Trotted* (choice H) means "moved quickly," not "made something happen quicker." *Hastily* (choice I) is an adverb meaning "quickly"; it is not a past tense verb.

6. **The correct answer is E.** This is the only sentence that expresses the author's opinion, and the opinion in question is that the writing in early English newspapers was courageous and ably written. Since not everyone may agree with those assessments, it is an opinion, not a fact. The sentences in choices A, B, C, and D only contain facts based in observation, not disputable opinions.

7. **The correct answer is E.** Choice E is the best additional sentence because it provides more details about an idea introduced in the final sentence of the paragraph: all of the newspapers published in England. Choice A is a poor addition because its opinions contradict the opinions in the final sentence of the paragraph. Choice B is redundant since it basically just rewords that final sentence. Choice C rewords the first sentence of the paragraph. Choice D would be jarring, since it just gives very basic details about

newspapers that the reader probably already knows; it is not unique to the particular newspapers discussed in this paragraph.

8. **The correct answer is E.** In the author's opinion, the early English newspapers displayed "great courage" and were "written with uncommon ability," so it makes sense that he would think they'd be fine role models for contemporary newspapers. That high opinion contradicts the one in choice A. The author never implies that the titles of early English newspapers were particularly quirky in this excerpt, so choice B is not a strong conclusion. Choices C and D are extreme conclusions that the passage does not support well.

9. **The correct answer is C.** The author attempts to make the human body easier to understand by comparing it to a common object: an automobile. Choice A is not the best answer because the automobile is used for comparison purposes and is not the most important thing in the passage. While comparing human bodies to automobiles might strike some as absurd, amusing readers (choice B) is not this passage's main purpose. Choice D hones in on a few details in the passage and fails to capture the purpose of the passage as a whole. While the author does compare the human body to a machine, he is not actually arguing that the body is mechanical (choice E).

10. **The correct answer is A.** The author compares fat in the human body to gasoline in an automobile, and gas powers or energizes an automobile the way that fat energizes the body. Choice B does not describe the purpose of fat; it merely describes where fat is stored. Choice C is the opposite of the correct answer. Choice D is never suggested in the passage. Choice E is actually true, but it is never mentioned in the passage either, so it cannot be correct.

11. **The correct answer is D.** The correct answer should draw a general conclusion about the entire passage, and that is what choice D does. The other answer choices are all true in and of themselves, but none of them are general enough to answer this particular question successfully.

12. **The correct answers are A and C.** With this quotation, the author imagines a student weighing the pros and cons of not planning a speech: the con is that it may result in a failure to convey the intended message effectively (choice A), and the pro is that it may result in a more natural, sincere performance (choice C). While the student does consider that it will result in a performance with greater ease, the student does not suggest that failing to plan the speech will make his or her message easier for the audience to understand, so choice B is incorrect.

13. **The correct answer is C.** The most likely reader of this passage is a person who needs to make a speech, and by voicing such a person with the quotations in the opening paragraph, the author voices some of the concerns the reader might have. This is an informational passage, and informational passages do not generally have well fleshed-out characters (choice A). While the quotations introduce the main idea of the passage, no conclusion is reached in them, so choice B is incorrect. The author is not particularly concerned with establishing an air of realism in an informational passage such as this, so choice D is not the best answer. There is no mystery in this passage either, so choice E is incorrect.

14. **The correct answer is B.** While each answer choice can be used as a synonym for *nature* in a different context, only choice B makes sense in this particular context. Choices A and C refer to nature in the sense of the natural landscape or outdoor environment. Choices D and E refer to a person's nature.

15. **The correct answer is A.** Only the quotations in the second paragraph really illustrate the idea that artists often make the same excuses for relying on inspiration. Choice B does not illustrate that exact idea as clearly because it makes no reference to excuses. Choice C refers to a completely different issue with artists: that many confuse designs with drawings.

16. **The correct answers are B and C.** The sentence describes a particular event in a war, which must be some type of battle or military scheme. The only words that describe such a thing are *campaign* (choice B) and *operation* (choice C). One would not describe a defense (choice A) as violent. Use of the word *annihilation* (choice A) is more fitting, but it still fits awkwardly into this context. *Bustle* (choice E) and *gaff* (choice F) are far too mild and unspecific.

17. **The correct answers are C and F.** A company's earnings or money are called *revenue* (choice C) or *income* (choice F). *Invest* (choice A) and *spending* (choice B) are things one does with income; it does not mean income. *Value* (choice D) is the worth of money; it does not mean "money." *Monetary* is anything that has to do with money, but it is not a synonym for *money* as *income* and *revenue* are.

18. The correct answers are B and D. Based on the sentence, it is reasonable to deduce that ergonomics is a branch of engineering science, and such a branch can be referred to as a *subsidiary* (choice B) or *offshoot* (choice D). *Entreaty* (choice A) means "appeal," and it makes no sense in this context. A *tributary* (choice C) is a sort of branch, but it is usually used to describe a body of water that branches off from a river. *Stream* (choice E) and *finger* (choice F) are not usually used to describe something like a branch of a particular science.

19. The correct answers are A and F. Stale bread is usually the kind of thing someone would throw in the garbage, but if it can be made into something as tasty such as French toast, it can be brought back to life so to speak, and *reviving* (choice A) and *resuscitating* (choice F) mean "bringing back to life." None of the other answer choices have this specific meaning.

20. The correct answer is E. Throughout the passage, the author discusses how people have no problem discussing their feelings in measurable terms, but indicating that there is a "problem" with this in the final sentence implies that the author is skeptical of people's ability to measure the variations in their feelings. Choice A describes the very thing the author does not seem to believe. Choice B is an example of the idea of which the author is skeptical. Choice C is a very extreme interpretation of the author's main point and the passage does not support it well. Choice D takes various ideas in the passage and jumbles them into an inference never made in the passage.

answers practice test 2

Section 4: Quantitative Reasoning

1. C	7. B	13. A	
2. B	8. B	14. D	18. $\frac{1}{9}$
3. A	9. E	15. A, D, E, G	
4. B	10. D	16. B, E, H	19. $\frac{5}{7}$
5. C	11. A	17. $\frac{6}{5}$	20. D
6. D	12. C		

1. **The correct answer is C.**
   Simplify each quantity.
   $3^{-1} \cdot \sqrt{\frac{16}{25}} = \frac{1}{3} \cdot \frac{4}{5} = \frac{4}{15}$ and
   $2^2 \cdot (3 \cdot 5)^{-1} = 4 \cdot \frac{1}{15} = \frac{4}{15}$

   The two quantities are equal.

2. **The correct answer is B.** Since $a - b = 3$, a is greater than b. Both a and b are multiplied by -2, and multiplying by a negative value reverses the relative order of numbers. Therefore, $-2b > -2a$, so Quantity B is greater.

3. **The correct answer is A.** 75% of $\frac{4}{5}$ is $\frac{3}{4} \cdot \frac{4}{5} = \frac{3}{5}$, and 90% of $\frac{3}{5}$ is less than $\frac{3}{5}$, so Quantity A is greater.

4. **The correct answer is B.** x is negative and y is positive. As the product of a positive number and a negative number, xy is negative, while x^2 is positive since it is the square of a non-zero number. Therefore, Quantity B is greater.

5. **The correct answer is C.** Solve the equations:
   $$m = -2m + 1$$
   $$3m = 1$$
   $$m = \frac{1}{3}$$
   $$n + 1 = 2n - 5$$
   $$-n = -6$$
   $$n = 6$$

Therefore $18m$ is $18\left(\frac{1}{3}\right) = 6$, which is the same as n. The two quantities are equal.

6. **The correct answer is D.** Because there are no parameters given for the shape $ABCD$, the lengths can't be determined.

7. **The correct answer is B.** The three angles shown form a straight line, so you can solve for y:
   $$90 + y + (y + 20) = 180$$
   $$2y + 110 = 180$$
   $$2y = 70$$
   $$y = 35$$

8. **The correct answer is B.** Compute the commission. 2% of $29,000 equals $580. Therefore, Quantity B is greater.

9. **The correct answer is E.** The two most popular sports represent 37% and 22% of the respondents, respectively, for a sum of 59%.

10. **The correct answer is D.** Football and soccer are preferred by 37% and 13% of the respondents, respectively, for a total of 50% (37 + 13 = 50). Therefore, 50% of the respondents do not prefer them.

11. **The correct answer is A.** The least popular sport was hockey, with 10% of respondents choosing it. 10% of 9,860 is 986.

12. **The correct answer is C.** The area of the circle is $\pi r^2 = 3.14(6)^2 = 3.14(36) = 113.04$. The perimeter of the square is 48, so each side has length 12. Its area is then $12 \cdot 12 = 144$. The difference of the areas is $144 - 113.04 = 30.96$. Choice A is the difference in perimeters, not the difference in areas. Choice B is incorrect because you mistakenly calculated the area of the square as 132 rather than 144. Choice D is incorrect because you did not use the factor of π when calculating the area of the circle. Choice E is incorrect because you forgot to square the radius when calculating the area of the circle.

13. **The correct answer is A.** Expand and simplify:

$$(a + b)^2 - (a - b)^2$$
$$= (a^2 + 2ab + b^2) - (a^2 - 2ab + b^2)$$
$$= 2ab - (-2ab)$$
$$= 4ab$$

Choices B, C, and E are incorrect since both quadratic terms cancel after expanding. Choice D is incorrect because a quartic term cannot appear in the expression, which is at most quadratic.

14. **The correct answer is D.** $786.11 is 106.5% of the discounted price, so the discounted price is $\frac{\$786.11}{1.065} = \$738.13$. But this reflects a 12% discount, so it is 88% of the original price. The original price was therefore $\frac{\$738.13}{0.88} = \$838.79$.

Choice A is incorrect because you divided by 1.65 rather than 1.065. Choice B is incorrect because you multiplied by 88% instead of dividing by it. Choice C is incorrect because you multiplied by both percentages rather than dividing by them. Choice E is incorrect because you multiplied by 1.88 rather than dividing by 0.88.

15. **The correct answers are A, D, E, and G.** When parallel lines are crossed by a transversal, all of the acute angles are congruent, all of the obtuse angles are congruent, and the measurements of these sum to 180°. Since $180 - 36 = 144$, all of the obtuse angles are 144°. Choices B, C, and F are all incorrect because they are 36° like the angle shown.

16. **The correct answers are B, E, and H.** The nth term of the sequence is $\frac{2n - 1}{2^n}$. The next three terms of the sequence are

$$\frac{2(5) - 1}{2^5} = \frac{9}{32}, \quad \frac{2(6) - 1}{2^6} = \frac{11}{64}, \quad \text{and}$$

$$\frac{2(7) - 1}{2^7} = \frac{13}{128}.$$

The other answers are incorrect because although they all have powers of 2 in their denominators, their numerators do not match the formula in the numerator.

17. **The correct answer is $\frac{6}{5}$.** Factor and simplify the expression:

$$p = \frac{6jk - 6k^2}{-5k^2 + 5jk}$$
$$= \frac{6k(j - k)}{5k(-k + j)}$$
$$= \frac{6}{5}$$

18. **The correct answer is $\frac{1}{9}$.** The 3, 5, and 7 all appear in both the numerator and denominator, so they can be canceled, leaving $\frac{1}{9}$.

19. **The correct answer is $\frac{5}{7}$.** There are 5 freshmen for every 2 sophomores, so 5 out of every 7 students are freshmen.

20. **The correct answer is D.** Divide:

$$27{,}252 \div 3{,}785 = 7.2$$

Choice A is incorrect because you divided 3,785 by 27,252. Choices B, C, and E are incorrect because you made an arithmetic mistake when performing the division.

Section 5: Quantitative Reasoning

1. C	**6.** C	**11.** D	**16.** A, D
2. B	**7.** C	**12.** D	**17.** A, C
3. A	**8.** D	**13.** E	**18.** C, D, E, F, H
4. A	**9.** C	**14.** A	**19.** 7
5. B	**10.** D	**15.** E	**20.** 90

1. **The correct answer is C.** The two quantities are equal. Multiply both sides of the equation by $-\frac{4}{3}$ to solve for p:

$$-\frac{4}{3}\left(-\frac{3}{4}p\right) = -\frac{4}{3}\left(-\frac{9}{8}\right) \Rightarrow p = \frac{3}{2}$$

2. **The correct answer is B.** Quantity A contains 6 factors of 10 in the numerator, and 2 in the denominator, so the quotient has 4 factors of 10, and is $\frac{4 \cdot 3}{6} \times 10^4 = 2 \times 10^4$.

   Quantity B has an extra factor of 10. Therefore, Quantity B is greater.

3. **The correct answer is A.** The area of the circle is $\pi r^2 = \pi(7)^2 = 49\pi$. Since π is greater than 3, this value (Quantity A) is greater than $(49)(3) = 147$.

4. **The correct answer is A.** Angles that form a full circle have to sum to 360°. One angle of 90° is shown, so the remaining angles must have a sum of $360 - 90 = 270°$. Their average is therefore $\frac{p + q + r}{3} = \frac{270}{3} = 90$, which is larger than Quantity B.

5. **The correct answer is B.** $6^{1.9}$ is less than 6^2, which equals 36, and $3^{2.8}$ is less than 3^3, which equals 27. Thus, the product of the two factors in Quantity A must be less than the product of the two factors in Quantity B.

6. **The correct answer is C.** $-3t(-2t) = 6t^2 = 30$ so the two quantities are equal.

7. **The correct answer is C.** Even though the values of x and y are unknown, the relationship can still be determined. $x\%$ of y is numerically equal to $\frac{x}{100} \cdot y$, and $y\%$ of x is $\frac{y}{100} \cdot x$. These are both the same as $\frac{xy}{100}$, so the two quantities are equal.

8. **The correct answer is D.** Even though Jar B contains more than twice as many red marbles as Jar A, the probabilities remain completely unknown. They do not necessarily have any relationship to each other since their relative values depend on how many marbles are in each jar altogether.

9. **The correct answer is C.** First, find the probability of the complement; that is, that neither die shows a 4. This is $\frac{5}{6} \cdot \frac{5}{6} = \frac{25}{36}$, since the probability of each die not showing a 4 is $1 - \frac{25}{36} = \frac{11}{36}$. Therefore, the probability that at least one die does show a 4 is $1 - \frac{25}{36} = \frac{11}{36}$.

   Choice A is incorrect since it is the probability that both dice show a 4, but the question only required that at least one of the dice show a 4. Choice B is incorrect since it is simply the probability that an individual die shows a 4, but does not take the combination of both dice into account. Choice D is incorrect because you added the probabilities of the individual dice showing 4, but in doing so, you overcounted the possibilities for at least one showing a 4.

10. **The correct answer is D.** Distribute the 3: $3x - \frac{3}{2} > 4 + x$. Subtract x and add $\frac{3}{2}$: $2x > \frac{11}{2}$. Finally, divide by 2: $x > \frac{11}{4}$.

Choice A is incorrect because you flipped the inequality, but that should be done only when multiplying or dividing by a negative number. Choice B is incorrect because you did not distribute the 3 to the $\frac{1}{2}$. Choice C is incorrect since you solved for $-x$, not x. Choice E is incorrect because you did not divide by 2 to isolate x.

11. **The correct answer is D.** The "Senior" bar extends up to 20%.

12. **The correct answer is D.** According to the bar graph, the juniors represent 10% of the students. Therefore, 90% of the students attending the game are not juniors.

13. **The correct answer is E.** The sophomores are 40% of the entire student body initially at the game. Once the freshmen leave, only 70% of the students remain. The sophomores represent $\frac{40}{70} \approx 57\%$ of these students. Choice A would be the percentage of juniors in the new graph. Choice B would be the percentage of seniors in the new graph. Choice C is the percentage of students that left, not the percentage of sophomores among those that remain. Choice D is the percentage of sophomores in the initial crowd, not the percentage after the freshmen have left.

14. **The correct answer is A.** The sum of the numbers is 425, so the mean is $\frac{425}{5} = 85$. The median is also 85, since if the numbers are put in order, 85 is in the middle. Therefore, the difference between the mean and median is 0. Choice B is incorrect because you used 82 as the median, instead of 85. Choice C is incorrect because you did not put the numbers in order before finding the median. Choices D and E are incorrect because of an arithmetic error in calculating the mean.

15. **The correct answer is E.** If the original radius was r, then the original area was πr^2. The new radius is $1.4r$, and the new area is $\pi(1.4r)^2 = 1.96(\pi r^2)$, which is 96% greater than the original area. Choice A is incorrect because you took the square root of 1.4 instead of squaring it. Choice B is incorrect because the area does not increase at the same rate as the radius. Choice C is incorrect because you divided 1.4 by π rather than squaring it. Choice D is incorrect because you doubled the percent increase of the radius rather than squaring the proportion.

16. **The correct answers are A and D.** If n is a factor of x^2, and n is prime, then n must also be a factor of x. But then x^2 must have at least two factors of n, so $\frac{x^2}{n}$ still has at least one factor of n. On the other hand, y may have only one factor of n, so $\frac{y}{n}$ may not have any factors of n. Finally, if n is a factor of both x and y, then it must also be a factor of their sum, $x + y$.

answers practice test 2

17. **The correct answers are A and C.** The only possible combinations she can buy are 2 apples/1 orange or 4 apples/2 oranges. The first combination costs $1.50, and the second combination $3.50. The other choices are all attainable with a combination of apples and oranges, but they all violate either the condition that there needs to be twice as many apples as oranges, or the condition that limits the total number of fruits to seven.

18. **The correct answers are C, D, E, F, and H.** A number is divisible by 9 if the sum of its digits is divisible by 9. This is true of 18, 27, 81, 126, and 8,199. It is not true of 3, 6, and 4,000.

19. **The correct answer is 7.** Use the rules of exponents: the numerator is $x^3 x^{-2} = x^1$, and the denominator is $\left(x^4\right)^2 = x^8$, so the fraction simplifies to x^{-7}. This is raised to the -1 power, leaving $\left(x^{-7}\right)^{-1} = x^7$, so $k = 7$.

20. **The correct answer is 90.** If the measure of one of the base angles is x, then the vertex angle has measure $2x$. The sum of the three angles is $x + x + 2x = 4x$, and this must be equal to 180, so $x = 45$. The angles are 45, 45, and 90, so the largest angle is 90.

Practice Test 3

The test begins with general information about the number of sections on the test (six for the computer-delivered test, including the unidentified unscored section or an identified research section, and five for the paper-delivered test) and the timing of the test (approximately 3 hours and 45 minutes, including one 10-minute break after Section 3, 1-minute breaks after the other sections for the computer-delivered test, and 3 hours and 30 minutes for the paper-delivered test with similar breaks). The following practice test contains the five scored sections.

Each section has its own time allocation and, during that time period, you may work on only that section.

Next, you will read ETS's policy on scoring the Analytical Writing responses. Each essay is read by experienced readers, and ETS may cancel any test scores that show evidence of unacknowledged use of sources, unacknowledged collaboration with others, preparation of the response by another person, and language that is "substantially" similar to the language in one or more other test responses.

Each section has specific instructions for that section.

You will be told when to begin.

PRACTICE TEST 3 ANSWER SHEETS

Section 1: Analytical Writing

Analyze an Issue

FOR PLANNING

Analyze an Issue Response

_____
_____
_____
_____
_____
_____
_____
_____
_____
_____
_____
_____
_____
_____
_____
_____
_____
_____
_____
_____
_____

answer sheet

Analyze an Issue Response

_____

_____

_____

_____

_____

_____

_____

_____

_____

_____

_____

_____

_____

_____

_____

_____

_____

_____

_____

_____

_____

_____

Analyze an Issue Response

_____

_____

_____

_____

_____

_____

_____

_____

_____

_____

_____

_____

_____

_____

_____

_____

_____

_____

_____

_____

answer sheet

Analyze an Issue Response

_____

_____

_____

_____

_____

_____

_____

_____

_____

_____

_____

_____

_____

_____

_____

_____

_____

_____

_____

_____

_____

_____

Analyze an Argument

FOR PLANNING

Analyze an Argument Response

_____

_____

_____

_____

_____

_____

_____

_____

_____

_____

_____

_____

_____

_____

_____

_____

_____

_____

_____

_____

_____

_____

_____

_____

_____

_____

Analyze an Argument Response

_____

_____

_____

_____

_____

_____

_____

_____

_____

_____

_____

_____

_____

_____

_____

_____

_____

_____

_____

_____

_____

_____

answer sheet

Analyze an Argument Response

_____

_____

_____

_____

_____

_____

_____

_____

_____

_____

_____

_____

_____

_____

_____

_____

_____

_____

_____

_____

_____

_____

_____

_____

_____

Analyze an Argument Response

_____

_____

_____

_____

_____

_____

_____

_____

_____

_____

_____

_____

_____

_____

_____

_____

_____

_____

_____

_____

_____

answer sheet

Section 2: Verbal Reasoning

1. Ⓐ Ⓑ Ⓒ Ⓓ Ⓔ
2. Ⓐ Ⓑ Ⓒ Ⓓ Ⓔ
3. Ⓐ Ⓑ Ⓒ Ⓓ Ⓔ Ⓕ
4. Ⓐ Ⓑ Ⓒ Ⓓ Ⓔ Ⓕ Ⓖ Ⓗ Ⓘ
5. Ⓐ Ⓑ Ⓒ Ⓓ Ⓔ Ⓕ Ⓖ Ⓗ Ⓘ
6. Ⓐ Ⓑ Ⓒ Ⓓ Ⓔ
7. Ⓐ Ⓑ Ⓒ Ⓓ Ⓔ

8. Ⓐ Ⓑ Ⓒ
9. Ⓐ Ⓑ Ⓒ Ⓓ Ⓔ
10. Ⓐ Ⓑ Ⓒ Ⓓ Ⓔ
11. Ⓐ Ⓑ Ⓒ Ⓓ Ⓔ
12. Ⓐ Ⓑ Ⓒ Ⓓ Ⓔ
13. Ⓐ Ⓑ Ⓒ Ⓓ Ⓔ
14. Ⓐ Ⓑ Ⓒ

15. Ⓐ Ⓑ Ⓒ Ⓓ Ⓔ
16. Ⓐ Ⓑ Ⓒ Ⓓ Ⓔ Ⓕ
17. Ⓐ Ⓑ Ⓒ Ⓓ Ⓔ Ⓕ
18. Ⓐ Ⓑ Ⓒ Ⓓ Ⓔ Ⓕ
19. Ⓐ Ⓑ Ⓒ Ⓓ Ⓔ Ⓕ
20. Ⓐ Ⓑ Ⓒ Ⓓ Ⓔ

Section 3: Verbal Reasoning

1. Ⓐ Ⓑ Ⓒ Ⓓ Ⓔ
2. Ⓐ Ⓑ Ⓒ Ⓓ Ⓔ
3. Ⓐ Ⓑ Ⓒ Ⓓ Ⓔ Ⓕ
4. Ⓐ Ⓑ Ⓒ Ⓓ Ⓔ Ⓕ Ⓖ Ⓗ Ⓘ
5. Ⓐ Ⓑ Ⓒ Ⓓ Ⓔ Ⓕ Ⓖ Ⓗ Ⓘ
6. Ⓐ Ⓑ Ⓒ Ⓓ Ⓔ
7. Ⓐ Ⓑ Ⓒ Ⓓ Ⓔ

8. Ⓐ Ⓑ Ⓒ Ⓓ Ⓔ
9. Ⓐ Ⓑ Ⓒ Ⓓ Ⓔ
10. Ⓐ Ⓑ Ⓒ Ⓓ Ⓔ
11. Ⓐ Ⓑ Ⓒ Ⓓ Ⓔ
12. Ⓐ Ⓑ Ⓒ
13. Ⓐ Ⓑ Ⓒ Ⓓ Ⓔ
14. Ⓐ Ⓑ Ⓒ Ⓓ Ⓔ

15. Ⓐ Ⓑ Ⓒ
16. Ⓐ Ⓑ Ⓒ Ⓓ Ⓔ Ⓕ
17. Ⓐ Ⓑ Ⓒ Ⓓ Ⓔ Ⓕ
18. Ⓐ Ⓑ Ⓒ Ⓓ Ⓔ Ⓕ
19. Ⓐ Ⓑ Ⓒ Ⓓ Ⓔ Ⓕ
20. Ⓐ Ⓑ Ⓒ Ⓓ Ⓔ

Section 4: Quantitative Reasoning

1. Ⓐ Ⓑ Ⓒ Ⓓ
2. Ⓐ Ⓑ Ⓒ Ⓓ
3. Ⓐ Ⓑ Ⓒ Ⓓ
4. Ⓐ Ⓑ Ⓒ Ⓓ
5. Ⓐ Ⓑ Ⓒ Ⓓ
6. Ⓐ Ⓑ Ⓒ Ⓓ
7. Ⓐ Ⓑ Ⓒ Ⓓ
8. Ⓐ Ⓑ Ⓒ Ⓓ

9. Ⓐ Ⓑ Ⓒ Ⓓ Ⓔ
10. Ⓐ Ⓑ Ⓒ Ⓓ Ⓔ
11. Ⓐ Ⓑ Ⓒ Ⓓ Ⓔ
12. Ⓐ Ⓑ Ⓒ Ⓓ Ⓔ
13. Ⓐ Ⓑ Ⓒ Ⓓ Ⓔ
14. Ⓐ Ⓑ Ⓒ Ⓓ Ⓔ
15. Ⓐ Ⓑ Ⓒ Ⓓ Ⓔ

16. Ⓐ Ⓑ Ⓒ Ⓓ Ⓔ
17. Ⓐ Ⓑ Ⓒ Ⓓ Ⓔ Ⓕ Ⓖ Ⓗ
18. Ⓐ Ⓑ Ⓒ Ⓓ Ⓔ
19. ☐
20. ☐

Section 5: Quantitative Reasoning

1. Ⓐ Ⓑ Ⓒ Ⓓ
2. Ⓐ Ⓑ Ⓒ Ⓓ
3. Ⓐ Ⓑ Ⓒ Ⓓ
4. Ⓐ Ⓑ Ⓒ Ⓓ
5. Ⓐ Ⓑ Ⓒ Ⓓ
6. Ⓐ Ⓑ Ⓒ Ⓓ
7. Ⓐ Ⓑ Ⓒ Ⓓ
8. Ⓐ Ⓑ Ⓒ Ⓓ

9. Ⓐ Ⓑ Ⓒ Ⓓ Ⓔ
10. Ⓐ Ⓑ Ⓒ Ⓓ Ⓔ
11. Ⓐ Ⓑ Ⓒ Ⓓ Ⓔ
12. Ⓐ Ⓑ Ⓒ Ⓓ Ⓔ
13. Ⓐ Ⓑ Ⓒ Ⓓ Ⓔ
14. Ⓐ Ⓑ Ⓒ Ⓓ Ⓔ
15. Ⓐ Ⓑ Ⓒ Ⓓ Ⓔ

16. Ⓐ Ⓑ Ⓒ Ⓓ Ⓔ
17. Ⓐ Ⓑ Ⓒ Ⓓ Ⓔ
18. Ⓐ Ⓑ Ⓒ Ⓓ Ⓔ Ⓕ Ⓖ Ⓗ
19. ☐
20. ☐

SECTION 1: ANALYTICAL WRITING

Analyze an Issue

30 minutes

The time for this task is 30 minutes. You must plan and draft a response that evaluates the issue given below. If you do not respond to the specific issue, your score will be zero. Your response must be based on the accompanying instructions, and you must provide evidence for your position. You may use support from reading, experience, observations, and/or course work.

Private schools offer children opportunities that public schools do not, and all parents who can afford to send their children to private schools should do so.

Write a response that takes and explains the extent to which you agree or disagree with this statement. As you present, develop, and explain your position, discuss when and how the statement might or might not hold true. Explain how those possibilities provide support for your own point of view.

Your response will be read by experienced readers who will assess your ability to do the following:

- Follow the set of task instructions.
- Analyze the complexities involved.
- Organize, develop, and explain ideas.
- Use pertinent reasons and/or illustrations to support ideas.
- Adhere to the conventions of Standard Written English.

You will be advised to take some time to plan your response and to leave time to reread it before the time is over. Those taking the paper-delivered GRE® General Test will find a blank page in their answer booklet for making notes and then four ruled pages for writing their actual response. Those taking the computer-delivered test will be given scrap paper for making notes.

STOP!
IF YOU FINISH BEFORE THE TIME IS UP,
YOU MAY CHECK YOUR WORK IN THIS SECTION ONLY.

Analyze an Argument

30 minutes

The time for this task is 30 minutes. You must plan and draft a response that evaluates the argument given below. If you do not respond to the given argument, your score will be zero. Your response must be based on the accompanying instructions, and you must provide evidence in support of your analysis.

You should not present your views on the subject of the argument, but on the strength or weakness of the argument.

Casual dress impedes an atmosphere of professionalism in the workplace. Business people tend to not take their jobs as seriously when they come into work looking slovenly in T-shirts and jeans. This is especially problematic when clients come to the office expecting to deal with professional-looking employees. Therefore, all offices should require employees to dress appropriately in business suits. It is the ultimate key in running a professional and successful business.

Write a response that identifies and explains the specific evidence required to determine whether the argument is reasonable. Discuss how that evidence would weaken or strengthen the argument.

Your response will be read by experienced readers who will assess your ability to do the following:

- Follow the set of task instructions.
- Analyze the complexities involved.
- Organize, develop, and explain ideas.
- Use pertinent reasons and/or illustrations to support ideas.
- Adhere to the conventions of Standard Written English.

You will be advised to take some time to plan your response and to leave time to reread it before the time is over. Those taking the paper-delivered GRE® General Test will find a blank page in their answer booklet for making notes and then four ruled pages for writing their actual response. Those taking the computer-delivered test will be given scrap paper for making notes.

STOP!
IF YOU FINISH BEFORE THE TIME IS UP,
YOU MAY CHECK YOUR WORK IN THIS SECTION ONLY.

INSTRUCTIONS FOR THE VERBAL REASONING AND QUANTITATIVE REASONING SECTIONS

You will find information here on the question formats for the Verbal Reasoning and Quantitative Reasoning sections, as well as information about how to use the software program, or, if you're taking the paper-delivered test, how to mark your answers in the answer booklet.

Perhaps the most important information is a reminder about how these two sections are scored. Every correct answer earns a point, but points are not subtracted for incorrect answers. The advice from ETS is to guess if you aren't sure of an answer. ETS says that this is better than not answering a question.

All multiple-choice questions on the computer-delivered test will have answer options preceded by either blank ovals or blank squares, depending on the question type. The paper-delivered test will follow the same format for answer choices, but it will use letters instead of ovals or squares for answer choices.

For your convenience in answering questions and checking answers, this book uses letter designations (A, B, C, etc.) for answer choices. Having these letters to refer to will make it easier for you to check your answers against the answer key and explanation sections.

practice test 3

SECTION 2: VERBAL REASONING

30 minutes • 20 questions

(The paper-delivered test will have 25 questions to be completed in 35 minutes.)

For each question, follow the specific directions and choose the best answer.

For Questions 1–5, choose <u>one</u> answer for each blank. Select from the appropriate column for each blank. Choose the answer that best completes the sense of the text.

1. In discussing the appendix, Charles Darwin once described this organ as a(n) "_____ of evolution" that had served a purpose in earlier humans but was now obsolete.

A. indication
B. hint
C. vestige
D. reflection
E. remaining

2. The _____ in which the private information of 50 million Facebook users was stolen for political purposes had very negative consequences for the popular website.

A. debacle
B. confusion
C. botch
D. error
E. boon

3. The brains of all mammals are (i) _____ in three membranes known as the meninges. These membranes (ii) _____ the arachnoid mater, the dura mater, and the pia mater.

Blank (i)	Blank (ii)
A. coated	**D.** involve
B. enveloped	**E.** comprise
C. paralleled	**F.** contain

4. In 1944, a huge (i) _____ construction project involved the (ii) _____ of a small hamlet known as Heathrow. Heathrow had been located on the western side of London. Today, the area that Heathrow once (iii) _____ sits in the borough of Hillingdon.

Blank (i)	Blank (ii)	Blank (iii)
A. civil	**D.** demolition	**G.** occupied
B. mechanical	**E.** ruin	**H.** visited
C. excruciating	**F.** sullying	**I.** burrowed

5. Zydeco is a musical genre (i) _____ from Louisiana. This lively form (ii) _____ such other musical modes as jazz, blues, country and western, and rhythm and blues. Among the instruments most closely (iii) _____ with Zydeco are the accordion and the *vest frottoir* or rub board.

Blank (i)	Blank (ii)	Blank (iii)
A. growing	**D.** electrifies	**G.** met
B. emanating	**E.** synthesizes	**H.** joined
C. departing	**F.** designs	**I.** linked

For Questions 6–20, choose only <u>one</u> answer choice unless otherwise indicated.

Questions 6–8 are based on the following passage.

In the year 1885, the Eiffel firm, which also had an extensive background of experience in structural engineering, undertook a series of investigations of tall metallic piers based upon its recent experiences with several lofty railway viaducts and bridges. The most spectacular
Line of these was the famous Garabit Viaduct (1880–1884), which carries a railroad some 400
5 feet above the valley of the Truyere in southern France. While the 200-foot height of the viaduct's two greatest piers was not startling even at that period, the studies proved that piers of far greater height were entirely feasible in iron construction. This led to the design of a 395-foot pier, which, although never incorporated into a bridge, may be said to have been the direct basis for the Eiffel Tower.
10 Preliminary studies for a 300-meter tower were made with the 1889 fair immediately in mind. With an assurance born of positive knowledge, Eiffel in June of 1886 approached the Exposition commissioners with the project. There can be no doubt that only the singular respect with which Eiffel was regarded not only by his profession but by the entire nation motivated the Commission to approve a plan which, in the hands of a figure of less stature,
15 would have been considered grossly impractical.

—Excerpt from *Elevator Systems of the Eiffel Tower 1889* by Robert M. Vogel

6. The passage implies that if the Eiffel firm had wanted to build the Garabit Viaduct piers 400 feet above the ground, then they

   A. could have done so before the end of 1884.

   B. would have to wait for technology to catch up with their ambitions.

   C. might have built a highly unstable structure.

   D. would have amazed people with their construction feat.

   E. would have been the most famous engineers firm in the world.

7. In this passage, "greatest" (line 6) most nearly means

   A. best.

   B. most famous.

   C. tallest.

   D. strongest.

   E. nicest.

For Question 8, consider each answer individually and select <u>all</u> choices that apply.

8. Which of the following ideas are clearly supported in this passage?

   A. The Exposition Commission might not have approved the 300-foot tower if someone other than Eiffel had proposed it.

   B. The Exposition Commission was skeptical that Eiffel was capable of building a 300-foot tower.

   C. Eiffel intended his 300-foot tower to be part of the 1889 Exposition.

Questions 9 and 10 are based on the following passage.

In undertaking a study of insects it is well first of all to know something about what they are, their general nature, appearance, habits and development. The insects comprise the largest group of animals on the globe. There are about four times as many different kinds
Line of insects as all other kinds of animals combined. Insects vary greatly in size. Some are as
5 large as small birds, while others are so small that a thousand placed in one pile would not equal the size of a pea.

Insects are commonly spoken of as "bugs." This term, however, is properly used only when referring to the one order of insects which includes the sap and blood-sucking insects such as the chinch bug, bed-bug, squash bug, and the like. Then too, there are many so-called
10 "bugs" which are not insects at all. Spiders, thousand-legs, crawfishes and even earthworms are often spoken of as bugs.

Insects are variously formed, but as a rule the mature ones have three and only three pairs of legs, one pair of feelers, one pair of large eyes, and one or two pairs of wings. The body is divided into a head, thorax and abdomen. The head bears the eyes, feelers and mouth,
15 the thorax bears the legs and wings, and the abdomen is made up of a number of segments. The presence of wings at once decides whether or not it is an insect, for, aside from bats and birds, insects alone have true wings.

—Excerpt from *Elementary Study of Insects* by Leonard Haseman

9. As used in the passage, "order" (line 8) most likely means

   A. command.

   B. instruction.

   C. stability.

   D. class.

   E. arrange.

10. In the context of this passage, what is significant about the number of legs a mature insect has?

    A. It helps insects to move quickly.

    B. It makes insects more stable when climbing.

    C. It is the most distinctive part of the insect's anatomy.

    D. It helps one tell the difference between birds and insects.

    E. It distinguishes insects from other creatures.

Questions 11 and 12 are based on the following passage.

    Why do people go to the movies? Because their caged souls seek forgetfulness and joy as insistently as blind eyes yearn for light. But joy is such a stranger to them that they ignorantly mistake this owl-eyed Monster of Darkness for the Blue Bird of Happiness. I have asked *Line* many why they go to the movies, and have heard many reasons—most of them bad—but 5 one answer recurs like a refrain: "There isn't any thing else to do." It reminds me of John Russel's reason why Eliza (of *Uncle Tom's Cabin*) crossed the river on the ice. "The poor girl had no other place to go—all the saloons were closed."…

    The priests of the temple of the Movie Momus do not know that they are offering a form of amusement which stifles the mind and hardens the heart. Doubtless they believe the contrary, 10 but it is a case of the blind led by the blind: Neither know where they are going, and each depends upon the other to lead the way. Producers, impresarios, scenario-writers have always their ears to the ground to catch the first faint rumble of condemnation or approval. Their business is frankly to assimilate the popular taste in order to reproduce it. But this taste is fickle, being that of a child with a digestion impaired by too much of the wrong kind of food. 15 The movie public is like the Athenian populace always eager for "some new thing," and like the Roman mob it shows an insatiable greed for danger (to others) cruelty and destruction.

    —Excerpt from "The Movies" by Claude Bragdon

11. The author of the passage would most likely agree with which view?

    A. Reading a novel is a worthwhile use of one's time.

    B. Not every movie is completely worthless.

    C. Movies would be better if they were made with more care.

    D. There is at least one valuable reason for watching movies.

    E. Movies are terrible because they do not take public tastes into consideration.

12. "Fickle" (line 14) most nearly means

    A. irritable.

    B. changeable.

    C. constant.

    D. economic.

    E. altered.

Questions 13–15 are based on the following passage.

It is commonly said that everybody can sing in the bathroom; and this is true. Singing is very easy. Drawing, though, is much more difficult. I have devoted a good deal of time to Drawing, one way and another; I have to attend a great many committees and public meetings, and at such functions I find that Drawing is almost the only Art one can satisfactorily pursue during the speeches. One really cannot sing during the speeches; so as a rule I draw. I do not say that I am an expert yet, but after a few more meetings I calculate that I shall know Drawing as well as it can be known.

The first thing, of course, is to get on to a really good committee; and by a good committee I mean a committee that provides decent materials. An ordinary departmental committee is no use: generally they only give you a couple of pages of lined foolscap and no white blotting-paper, and very often the pencils are quite soft. White blotting-paper is essential. I know of no material the spoiling of which gives so much artistic pleasure—except perhaps snow. Indeed, if I was asked to choose between making pencil-marks on a sheet of white blotting-paper and making foot-marks on a sheet of white snow I should be in a thingummy.

—Excerpt from "On Drawing" by A.P. Herbert

13. The point of the first paragraph of the passage is to

    A. prove that singing is very easy.

    B. explain that one needs to practice a lot to draw well.

    C. describe the materials one needs to draw.

    D. argue that singing during speeches is difficult.

    E. entertain the reader with a silly story about drawing during speeches.

For Question 14, consider each answer individually and select all choices that apply.

14. Select the sentence in the passage that does NOT directly add support to the main idea.

    A. It is commonly said that everybody can sing in the bathroom; and this is true.

    B. One really cannot sing during the speeches; so as a rule I draw.

    C. White blotting-paper is essential.

15. Which of the following, if it were true, would weaken the author's argument?

    A. While one may be born with the ability to draw, it takes education to sharpen that skill.

    B. Attendees at meetings rarely pay attention to what others are doing.

    C. The author of the passage is not a famous artist.

    D. The author of the passage is both a great singer and a great artist.

    E. Some people train for years to become great singers.

For Questions 16–19, choose the <u>two</u> answers that best fit the meaning of the sentence as a whole and result in two completed sentences that are alike in meaning.

16. An area with "wilderness character" is legally defined as land that is _____ and affords the opportunity for solitude.

    A. eradicated

    B. natural

    C. cleared

    D. untrammeled

    E. razed

    F. gashed

17. Italy's election of 2018 was particularly _____, with three viable candidates representing the severely different ideologies of a highly divided country.

    A. fractious

    B. unified

    C. shattered

    D. heated

    E. unfazed

    F. bland

18. Although the character originated in comic books, Batman has been depicted in so many media—from numerous print forms to numerous television series to numerous films—that there is no one _____ depiction of the superhero.

    A. primary

    B. original

    C. representation

    D. definitive

    E. consequential

    F. ultimate

19. Irving Stone's novel *The Agony and the Ecstasy* told the story of artist Michelangelo, whose crowning achievement was the complex painting that _____ the ceiling of the Sistine Chapel.

    A. decorates

    B. shields

    C. adorns

    D. masks

    E. blankets

    F. infiltrates

Question 20 is based on the following passage.

Most people think of school matters from the pupil's point of view. When they learned arithmetic and grammar, or later when they studied algebra and Latin, each course was presented to them as though it were a perfect system. The teacher did not confide in them that
Line arithmetic probably ought to be revised by the omission of many of its topics, that formal
5 grammar is a very doubtful subject, and that both algebra and Latin are on the point of losing their places as required subjects. The pupil sees the front of the school scenery; the machinery behind is known only to those who conduct the performance.

It would be possible to multiply indefinitely examples which show that the pupil's view of the school is very limited. What pupil understands the duties of the principal or the
10 superintendent, or of the still more remote and mysterious board of education? Where does the daily program come from? Who decides about textbooks? Why are school buildings commonly planned with large study-rooms? Most of these questions are never thought of by pupils. Everything in school life seems to have a kind of inevitableness which raises it above question or even consideration.

—Excerpt from *The Scientific Study of Education* by Charles Hubbard Judd

20. What is the author's opinion about education?

   A. More people have the perspectives of students than teachers.

   B. Grammar is not a very worthwhile subject.

   C. Teachers usually do not explain to students how they are being taught.

   D. Students must know more about how they are being taught.

   E. Textbooks should be altered to fit the student's perspective more accurately.

STOP!
IF YOU FINISH BEFORE THE TIME IS UP,
YOU MAY CHECK YOUR WORK IN THIS SECTION ONLY.

SECTION 3: VERBAL REASONING

30 minutes • 20 questions

(The paper-delivered test will have 25 questions to be completed in 35 minutes.)

For each question, follow the specific directions and choose the best answer.

For Questions 1–5, choose <u>one</u> answer for each blank. Select from the appropriate column for each blank. Choose the answer that best completes the sense of the text.

1. Thousands of species are categorized in the _____ *Annelida*, and most of these creatures are worms.

A. slot
B. company
C. association
D. classroom
E. phylum

2. The area of the brain called the hippocampus earned its unusual name due to its _____ to the mythical creature of the same name: a sea horse that pulled Poseidon's chariot in the epic poem *The Iliad*.

A. appearance
B. feature
C. identical
D. similitude
E. repetitive

3. Sweep is a particular form of the competitive sport of rowing. It (i) _____ each rower using both hands to pull a single oar. Sculling is the (ii) _____ in which a rower pulls two oars, holding one in each hand.

Blank (i)	Blank (ii)
A. entails	**D.** variant
B. exemplifies	**E.** difference
C. affixes	**F.** feature

4. The popular simile "mad as a hatter" has its origins in a nervous disease that (i) _____ haberdashers. Exposure to the high levels of mercury in the felt used to make hats was the source of the disease. (ii) _____, author Lewis Carroll was inspired to create the (iii) _____ character of the Mad Hatter in his beloved book *Alice's Adventures in Wonderland.*

Blank (i)	Blank (ii)	Blank (iii)
A. disabled	D. Resulting	G. contemporary
B. afflicted	E. Consequently	H. obscure
C. ailed	F. Ultimately	I. timeless

5. Of the six pyramids in Giza, the Great Pyramid is the oldest. While its (i) _____ is difficult to pinpoint precisely, the most popular theory is that Fourth Dynasty ruler Khufu (ii) _____ its creation. In the Western world, Khufu is better known by the (iii) _____ Cheops.

Blank (i)	Blank (ii)	Blank (iii)
A. birth	D. commissioned	G. moniker
B. primeval	E. purchased	H. entitle
C. genesis	F. constructed	I. nominal

For Questions 6–20, choose only <u>one</u> answer choice unless otherwise indicated.

Questions 6–8 are based on the following passage.

Science is knowledge; it is what we know. But mere knowledge is not science. For a bit of knowledge to become a part of science, its relation to other bits of knowledge must be found. In botany, for example, bits of knowledge about plants do not make a science of botany. To

Line have a science of botany, we must not only know about leaves, roots, flowers, seeds, etc., but

5 we must know the relations of these parts and of all the parts of a plant to one another. In other words, in science, we must not only *know*, we must not only have *knowledge*, but we must know the significance of the knowledge, must know its *meaning*. This is only another way of saying that we must have knowledge and know its relation to other knowledge.

A scientist is one who has learned to organize his knowledge. The main difference between

10 a scientist and one who is not a scientist is that the scientist sees the significance of facts, while the non-scientific man sees facts as more or less unrelated things. As one comes to hunt for causes and inquire into the significance of things, one becomes a scientist. A thing or an event always points beyond itself to something else. This something else is what goes before it or comes after it—is its cause or its effect. This causal relationship that exists between

15 events enables a scientist to prophesy.

—Excerpt from *The Science of Human Nature* by William Henry Pyle

6. The point of the passage is to

    A. explain what constitutes science and scientists.

    B. prove that science is knowledge.

    C. define the term *scientist*.

    D. contrast the term *knowledge* with *meaning*.

    E. show what the science of botany requires.

7. Which of the following, if it were true, would weaken the author's argument?

    A. A scientist must have knowledge of facts.

    B. A botanist is a scientist who studies plant life.

    C. Sometimes non-scientific jobs require one to see the significance of facts.

    D. A police detective is technically not a scientist.

    E. Scientists are often fascinated by puzzles.

8. The passage implies that the ways scientists use their knowledge

    A. are incomprehensible to non-scientists.

    B. seem almost mystical.

    C. are more important than their ability to deduce meaning.

    D. appear to be more complex than they really are.

    E. can be learned by any non-scientist.

Questions 9–11 are based on the following passage.

    Nothing in our educational history is more striking than the steady pressure of democracy upon its universities to adapt them to the requirements of all the people. From the State Universities of the Middle West, shaped under pioneer ideals, have come the fuller recognition
Line of scientific studies, and especially those of applied science devoted to the conquest of nature;
   5 the breaking down of the traditional required curriculum; the union of vocational and college work in the same institution; the development of agricultural and engineering colleges and business courses; the training of lawyers, administrators, public men, and journalists—all under the ideal of service to democracy rather than of individual advancement alone. Other universities do the same thing; but the head springs and the main current of this great stream
  10 of tendency come from the land of the pioneers, the democratic states of the Middle West. And the people themselves, through their boards of trustees and the legislature, are in the last resort the court of appeal as to the directions and conditions of growth, as well as have the fountain of income from which these universities derive their existence.

    The State University has thus both a peculiar power in the directness of its influence upon
  15 the whole people and a peculiar limitation in its dependence upon the people. The ideals

of the people constitute the atmosphere in which it moves, though it can itself affect this atmosphere. Herein is the source of its strength and the direction of its difficulties. For to fulfill its mission of uplifting the state to continuously higher levels the University must, in
Line the words of Mr. Bryce, "serve the time without yielding to it;" it must recognize new needs
20 without becoming subordinate to the immediately practical, to the short-sightedly expedient. It must not sacrifice the higher efficiency for the more obvious but lower efficiency. It must have the wisdom to make expenditures for results which pay manifold in the enrichment of civilization, but which are not immediate and palpable.

—Excerpt from *The Frontier in American History* by Frederick Jackson Turner

9. Based on the passage, the author evidently believes that

   A. capitalism will eventually have a more profound effect on education than democracy will.

   B. the influence of democracy on state universities is not a completely positive thing for universities.

   C. democracy has a more profound effect on business colleges than it does on agricultural colleges.

   D. democracy is more influential on education in the Middle Western colleges than it is in universities outside of that area.

   E. pioneer ideals have not had a significant effect on state universities.

10. What function does the quotation in the second paragraph serve in this argument?

   A. It supports the main argument with details from an expert witness.

   B. It provides a counterargument to the author's main point.

   C. It states a significant point with simple eloquence.

   D. It summarizes the main idea of the passage.

   E. It defines a term the author introduced.

11. In the passage, "conquest" (line 4) means

   A. mastering.

   B. defeat.

   C. destruction.

   D. victory.

   E. capture.

Questions 12 and 13 are based on the following passage.

The economic theory of profit-sharing is that by inducing greater care and diligence on the part of the employee he will himself create the fund from which he is paid. It is claimed by its advocates that it increases both the quantity and the quality of the product and that it *Line* promotes greater care of implements and materials, thus reducing the cost at the same time 5 that it increases the output. The classic example of this is the case of the original profit-sharing scheme, the Maison Leclaire, in Paris; the result of the first six years' experiment was a dividend on wages of $3,753 a year, derived entirely from the increased economy and care of the workers. In some cases, however, the object of the employers is to secure immunity from strikes and other labor disturbances and a greater permanence of the labor force; and 10 participation in profits is conditioned on the men abstaining from joining a trade union, or on uninterrupted service. In these cases the deferred participation plan is used. The advantages claimed for the system are not merely the increase in product already spoken of and the greatest efficiency of the worker, but also the improvement in his material and moral standards, and the promotion of industrial peace by lessening discontent and friction. The 15 main basis for the system, since it is economic and not philanthropic in its nature, must of course be the increase in production brought about by its adoption.

—Excerpt from *Business Administration*, edited by Walter Dwight Moody and Samuel MacClintock

For Question 12, consider each answer individually and select all choices that apply.

12. Select the sentence from the passage that best exemplifies the main point of the passage.

   A. The economic theory of profit-sharing is that by inducing greater care and diligence on the part of the employee he will himself create the fund from which he is paid.

   B. It is claimed by its advocates that it increases both the quantity and the quality of the product and that it promotes greater care of implements and materials, thus reducing the cost at the same time that it increases the output.

   C. The advantages claimed for the system are not merely the increase in product already spoken of and the greatest efficiency of the worker, but also the improvement in his material and moral standards, and the promotion of industrial peace by lessening discontent and friction.

13. Based on the passage, what should a company do if it wants to reduce the risk of its workers going on strike?

   A. It should implement a standard profit-sharing plan.

   B. It should eliminate its profit-sharing plan.

   C. It should reduce the hours that employees have to work.

   D. It should implement a deferred participation plan.

   E. It should explain the purpose of profit-sharing to employees.

Questions 14 and 15 are based on the following passage.

The desire to make money is common to most men. Stronger or weaker, in some degree it is present in the mind of nearly every one. Now, how far does this desire grow to be an aim or object in our lives, and to what extent is such an aim a worthy one?

Line
5   The typical money-maker as commonly pictured in our imagination is a narrow, grasping, selfish individual who has chosen to follow lower rather than higher ideals and who often is tempted, and always may be tempted, to employ illegitimate means for the attainment of his ends. The aims he has adopted are made to stand in opposition to the practice of certain virtues. Thus we contrast profits and patriotism; enriching one's self and philanthropy; getting all the law allows and justice; taking advantage of the other fellow and honesty; becoming
10   engrossed in acquisition and love of family. Now, such contrasts obviously prove nothing more than that money-making is and would be a vicious aim if pursued regardless of these virtues, and it could well be replied that consideration of patriotism, philanthropy, love of family, etc., must in themselves impel one to earn and to save. "The love of money is the root of all evil" implies an exclusive devotion to acquisition that may well be criticized. But aside from this
15   there is no doubt that amid the confused ideas held on the subject, aiming to make money is commonly regarded as in some sort of antagonism to the social virtues.

—Excerpt from *Creating Capital: Money-Making as an Aim in Business* by Frederick L. Lipman

14. Without the desire to make money, which of the following would most people likely believe to be true?

    A. More people would be antagonistic toward social virtues.

    B. More people would be free to live lives of perfect virtue.

    C. More people would be inclined toward patriotism.

    D. More people would be inclined to make money for virtuous reasons.

    E. More people would be considered to be wealthy.

For Question 15, consider each answer individually and select <u>all</u> choices that apply.

15. In the passage, "typical" (line 4) means

    A. symbolic.

    B. usual.

    C. characteristic.

For Questions 16–19, choose the <u>two</u> answers that best fit the meaning of the sentence as a whole and result in two completed sentences that are alike in meaning.

16. *The Twilight Zone* is among the most _____ of fantastical television series; it inspired other series such as *Tales from the Crypt* and *Black Mirror* to adopt both its anthology format and its shocking, twist endings.

 A. seminal

 B. worn

 C. constant

 D. ubiquitous

 E. acclaimed

 F. influential

17. Drupes include such _____ treats as cherries, peaches, and plums, as well as more savory items such as olives and almonds.

 A. succulent

 B. scrumptious

 C. cloying

 D. savory

 E. putrid

 F. delectable

18. Honky Tonk is a _____ of country music that originated in saloons.

 A. segment

 B. strain

 C. subgenre

 D. link

 E. compartment

 F. division

19. Shawnee National Forest in southern Illinois is approximately 280,000 acres wide, which is _____ enough to place areas of it in nine different counties.

 A. sprawling

 B. large

 C. expansive

 D. lengthy

 E. stretched

 F. elastic

Question 20 is based on the following passage.

The group of birds usually known as the *Raptores*, or Rapacious Birds, embraces three well-marked divisions, namely, the Owls, the Hawks, and the Vultures. In former classifications they headed the Class of Birds, being honored with this position in consequence of
Line their powerful organization, large size, and predatory habits. But it being now known that
5 in structure they are less perfectly organized than the *Passeres* and *Strisores*, birds generally far more delicate in organization, as well as smaller in size, they occupy a place in the more recent arrangements nearly at the end of the Terrestrial forms.

The complete definition of the order *Raptores*, and of its subdivisions, requires the enumeration of a great many characters; and that their distinguishing features may be more easily
10 recognized by the student, I give first a brief diagnosis, including their simplest characters, to be followed by a more detailed account hereafter.

—Excerpt from *A History of North American Birds; Land Birds; Vol. 3 of 3* by Baird et al.

20. Based on the passage, what will be the most significant result of the author giving the distinguishing features of certain birds?

   A. The author will help the reader to be more imaginative.

   B. The author will help the reader to know which birds are dangerous.

   C. The author will have explained the meaning of the term *Raptores*.

   D. The author will have explained the simplest features of rapacious birds.

   E. The author will help students to identify rapacious birds.

STOP!
IF YOU FINISH BEFORE THE TIME IS UP,
YOU MAY CHECK YOUR WORK IN THIS SECTION ONLY.

SECTION 4: QUANTITATIVE REASONING

35 minutes • 20 questions

(The paper-delivered test will have 25 questions to be completed in 40 minutes.)

For each question, follow the specific directions and choose the best answer.

The test maker provides the following information that applies to all questions in the Quantitative Reasoning section of the GRE® General Test:

- All numbers used are real numbers.

- All figures are assumed to lie in a plane unless otherwise indicated.

- Geometric figures, such as lines, circles, triangles, and quadrilaterals, *are not necessarily* drawn to scale. That is, you should *not* assume that quantities such as lengths and angle measures are as they appear in a figure. You should assume, however, that lines shown as straight are actually straight, points on a line are in the order shown, and more generally, all geometric objects are in the relative positions shown. For questions with geometric figures, you should base your answers on geometric reasoning, not on estimating or comparing quantities by sight or by measurement.

- Coordinate systems, such as *xy*-planes and number lines, *are* drawn to scale. Therefore, you can read, estimate, or compare quantities in such figures by sight or by measurement.

- Graphical data presentations, such as bar graphs, circle graphs, and line graphs, *are* drawn to scale. Therefore, you can read, estimate, or compare data values by sight or by measurement.

For Questions 1–8, compare Quantity A and Quantity B. Some questions will have additional information above the two quantities to use in determining your answer.

1.

Quantity A	Quantity B
$\dfrac{\frac{1}{2}}{\frac{1}{4^2}}$	8

- **A.** Quantity A is greater.
- **B.** Quantity B is greater.
- **C.** The two quantities are equal.
- **D.** The relationship cannot be determined from the information given.

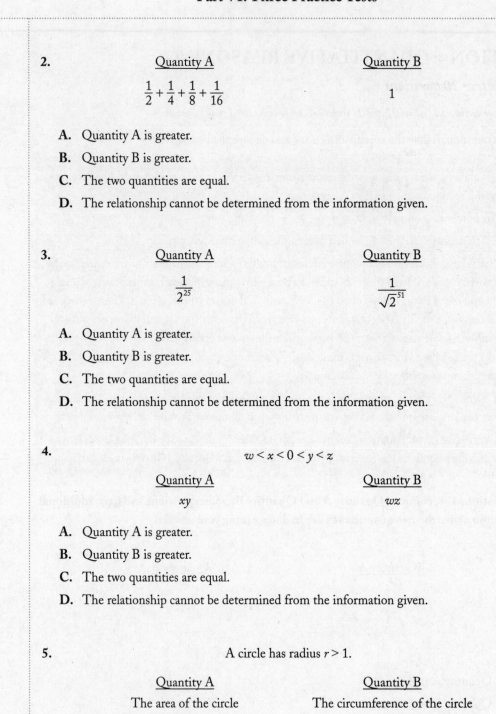

2.

Quantity A	Quantity B

$\frac{1}{2} + \frac{1}{4} + \frac{1}{8} + \frac{1}{16}$ 1

A. Quantity A is greater.

B. Quantity B is greater.

C. The two quantities are equal.

D. The relationship cannot be determined from the information given.

3.

Quantity A	Quantity B

$\frac{1}{2^{25}}$ $\frac{1}{\sqrt{2}^{51}}$

A. Quantity A is greater.

B. Quantity B is greater.

C. The two quantities are equal.

D. The relationship cannot be determined from the information given.

4.

$$w < x < 0 < y < z$$

Quantity A	Quantity B

xy wz

A. Quantity A is greater.

B. Quantity B is greater.

C. The two quantities are equal.

D. The relationship cannot be determined from the information given.

5.

A circle has radius $r > 1$.

Quantity A	Quantity B

The area of the circle   The circumference of the circle

A. Quantity A is greater.

B. Quantity B is greater.

C. The two quantities are equal.

D. The relationship cannot be determined from the information given.

6.

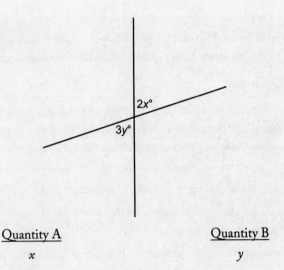

Quantity A	Quantity B
x	y

A. Quantity A is greater.

B. Quantity B is greater.

C. The two quantities are equal.

D. The relationship cannot be determined from the information given.

7. $$x = 0, y > 0$$

Quantity A	Quantity B
$xy(x + 3)^2$	$x^3(y + x)^3$

A. Quantity A is greater.

B. Quantity B is greater.

C. The two quantities are equal.

D. The relationship cannot be determined from the information given.

8. Fran is older than John, John is younger than Beth, and Beth is younger than Tabitha.

Quantity A	Quantity B
Fran's age	Tabitha's age

A. Quantity A is greater.

B. Quantity B is greater.

C. The two quantities are equal.

D. The relationship cannot be determined from the information given.

Questions 9–20 have several formats. Unless the directions state otherwise, choose one answer choice. For the Numeric Entry questions, follow the instructions below.

Numeric Entry Questions

The following items are the same for both the computer-delivered and paper-delivered tests. However, those taking the computer-delivered test will have additional information about entering answers in decimal and fraction boxes on the computer screen. Those taking the paper-delivered test will have information about entering answers on answer grids.

- Your answer may be an integer, a decimal, or a fraction, and it may be negative.

- If a question asks for a fraction, there will be two boxes. One box will be for the numerator and one will be for the denominator.

- Equivalent forms of the correct answer, such as 2.5 and 2.50, are all correct.

- Enter the exact answer unless the question asks you to round your answers.

Questions 9–10 refer to the graph below.

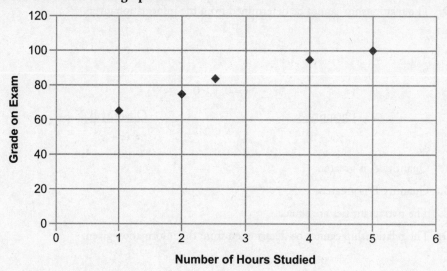

9. What kind of correlation exists between the number of hours studied and a grade on an exam?

    A. positive

    B. negative

    C. none

    D. quadratic

    E. exponential

SHOW YOUR WORK HERE

10. Which of the following is the best estimate for the grade a student would receive if she studied for 3 hours?

   A. 60

   B. 70

   C. 80

   D. 90

   E. 100

11. A rectangle has a perimeter of 34 and a length of 15. What is its area?

   A. 2

   B. 17

   C. 30

   D. 34

   E. 68

12. A rectangular garden measures 12 feet by 16 feet. If it is enlarged on all sides by 2 feet, what is the area of the new garden?

   A. 192 square feet

   B. 240 square feet

   C. 252 square feet

   D. 256 square feet

   E. 320 square feet

13. What is the volume of the cylinder shown?

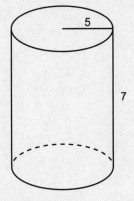

   A. 35π cubic feet

   B. 70π cubic feet

   C. 175π cubic feet

   D. 245π cubic feet

   E. $1,225\pi$ cubic feet

SHOW YOUR WORK HERE

practice test 3

14. Find the area of the rectangle shown.

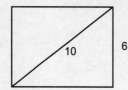

A. 28

B. 48

C. 60

D. 80

E. 480

15. The wholesale price of a laptop is $600. A retailer marks it up by 15% but then puts it on sale for 10% off. What percentage of the wholesale price does it sell for?

A. 76.5%

B. 90%

C. 93.5%

D. 103.5%

E. 126.5%

16. There are eight stacks of coins. Three of the stacks have $1.75, four of them have $2.25, and one of them has $3.27. What is the mean value of the eight stacks?

A. $2.19

B. $2.42

C. $5.84

D. $7.27

E. $17.52

SHOW YOUR WORK HERE

For Questions 17 and 18, choose <u>all</u> the answers that apply.

17. The first term of a sequence is given by $a_1 = 2$, and for $n > 1$, the nth term of the sequence is given by $a_n = 2a_{n-1} - 1$. Which of the following are terms of the sequence?

   A. 3
   B. 4
   C. 5
   D. 9
   E. 12
   F. 17
   G. 33
   H. 60

18. If $3x^3 - 5x^2 - 2x = 0$, what are the possible values for x?

   A. $-\dfrac{1}{3}$
   B. 0
   C. $\dfrac{1}{3}$
   D. -1
   E. 2

For Questions 19 and 20, enter your answers in the boxes.

SHOW YOUR WORK HERE

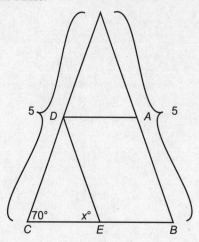

19. If $\overline{AB}$ is parallel to $\overline{DE}$, what is the value of x?

20. A recording artist rents a studio for a week to record an album. If the rental fee was $5,400, and she sells albums for $12.50, how many must she sell to cover the cost of the rental?

STOP!
IF YOU FINISH BEFORE THE TIME IS UP,
YOU MAY CHECK YOUR WORK IN THIS SECTION ONLY.

SECTION 5: QUANTITATIVE REASONING

35 minutes • 20 questions

(The paper-delivered test will have 25 questions to be completed in 40 minutes.)

For each question, follow the specific directions and choose the best answer.

The test maker provides the following information that applies to all questions in the Quantitative Reasoning section of the GRE® General Test:

- All numbers used are real numbers.
- All figures are assumed to lie in a plane unless otherwise indicated.
- Geometric figures, such as lines, circles, triangles, and quadrilaterals, *are not necessarily* drawn to scale. That is, you should *not* assume that quantities such as lengths and angle measures are as they appear in a figure. You should assume, however, that lines shown as straight are actually straight, points on a line are in the order shown, and more generally, all geometric objects are in the relative positions shown. For questions with geometric figures, you should base your answers on geometric reasoning, not on estimating or comparing quantities by sight or by measurement.
- Coordinate systems, such as *xy*-planes and number lines, *are* drawn to scale. Therefore, you can read, estimate, or compare quantities in such figures by sight or by measurement.
- Graphical data presentations, such as bar graphs, circle graphs, and line graphs, *are* drawn to scale. Therefore, you can read, estimate, or compare data values by sight or by measurement.

For Questions 1–8, compare Quantity A and Quantity B. Some questions will have additional information above the two quantities to use in determining your answer.

1. $d < e < f < g$

Quantity A	Quantity B
$g - f$	$e - d$

A. Quantity A is greater.

B. Quantity B is greater.

C. The two quantities are equal.

D. The relationship cannot be determined from the information given.

2.

Quantity A	Quantity B
The number of quarters in $8.00	The number of nickels in $2.00

A. Quantity A is greater.

B. Quantity B is greater.

C. The two quantities are equal.

D. The relationship cannot be determined from the information given.

3.

Quantity A	Quantity B
$\left(\frac{4}{21}\right)\left(\frac{4}{2}\right)\left(\frac{14}{8}\right)$	$\left(\frac{2}{3}\right)\left(\frac{2}{1}\right)\left(\frac{2}{4}\right)$

A. Quantity A is greater.

B. Quantity B is greater.

C. The two quantities are equal.

D. The relationship cannot be determined from the information given.

4.

$$a > b > 1$$

Quantity A	Quantity B
ab	$\frac{a}{b}$

A. Quantity A is greater.

B. Quantity B is greater.

C. The two quantities are equal.

D. The relationship cannot be determined from the information given.

5.

$$ABC \text{ is a triangle.}$$

Quantity A	Quantity B
The average degree value of angles A, B, and C	60

A. Quantity A is greater.

B. Quantity B is greater.

C. The two quantities are equal.

D. The relationship cannot be determined from the information given.

6.

$$x + y = 3$$
$$x - y = 1$$

Quantity A	Quantity B
x	y

A. Quantity A is greater.

B. Quantity B is greater.

C. The two quantities are equal.

D. The relationship cannot be determined from the information given.

7. A circle has a circumference of 8π, and a square has perimeter of 30.

Quantity A	Quantity B
The area of the circle	The area of the square

A. Quantity A is greater.

B. Quantity B is greater.

C. The two quantities are equal.

D. The relationship cannot be determined from the information given.

8.

Quantity A	Quantity B
$\dfrac{1}{100}\%$ of 100	10^{-2}

A. Quantity A is greater.

B. Quantity B is greater.

C. The two quantities are equal.

D. The relationship cannot be determined from the information given.

Questions 9–20 have several formats. Unless the directions state otherwise, choose one answer choice. For the Numeric Entry questions, follow the instructions below.

Numeric Entry Questions

The following items are the same for both the computer-delivered and paper-delivered tests. However, those taking the computer-delivered test will have additional information about entering answers in decimal and fraction boxes on the computer screen. Those taking the paper-delivered test will have information about entering answers on answer grids.

- Your answer may be an integer, a decimal, or a fraction, and it may be negative.

- If a question asks for a fraction, there will be two boxes. One box will be for the numerator and one will be for the denominator.

- Equivalent forms of the correct answer, such as 2.5 and 2.50, are all correct.

- Enter the exact answer unless the question asks you to round your answers.

9. A salesperson received a commission of $340 on the sale of a car. If the commission rate is 1.7%, how much did the car sell for?

   A. $5.78
   B. $2,000
   C. $19,660
   D. $20,000
   E. $200,000

SHOW YOUR WORK HERE

10. Payal can shovel the snow from a driveway in 12 minutes, and Shreya can shovel the snow from the same driveway in 18 minutes. Working together, how long will it take for them to shovel the driveway? Round to the nearest minute.

    A. 6 minutes
    B. 7 minutes
    C. 12 minutes
    D. 15 minutes
    E. 30 minutes

11. 12 miles per hour is equivalent to how many feet per second?

A. 1.47

B. 8.18

C. 12

D. 17.6

E. 1,056

SHOW YOUR WORK HERE

12. Evaluate $9^{\frac{3}{2}}$.

A. 3

B. 6

C. 9

D. 13.5

E. 27

Questions 13 and 14 refer to the figure below.

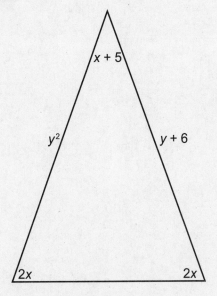

13. What is the value of *x*?

A. 5

B. 19

C. 35

D. 36

E. 45

practice test 3

14. What is the value of y?

   A. 0

   B. 1

   C. 2

   D. 3

   E. 3 or −2

SHOW YOUR WORK HERE

15. If A = {7, 9, 11, 13} and B = {6, 8, 12, 14}, which of the following are true?

   A. A and B have the same mean and the same standard deviation.

   B. A and B have different means but the same standard deviation.

   C. A and B have different means and different standard deviations.

   D. A and B have the same mean, but A has a larger standard deviation.

   E. A and B have the same mean, but B has a larger standard deviation.

16. $4,500 is invested in an account earning 3.5% annual interest, compounded monthly. What is the value of the account after 2 months?

   A. $4,513.13

   B. $4,526.25

   C. $4,526.29

   D. $4,657.50

   E. $4,766.33

For Questions 17 and 18, choose <u>all</u> the answers that apply.

17. If a is even and b is odd, which of the following are even?

   A. $a + b$

   B. $a - b$

   C. ab

   D. a^b

   E. b^a

18. Suppose $a_n = 3$ and for $n > 1$, $a_n = 2 - a_{n-1}$.

    Which of the following numbers will appear as terms of this sequence?

    A. −1
    B. 1
    C. −2
    D. 2
    E. −3
    F. 3
    G. −4
    H. 4

For Questions 19 and 20, enter your answers in the boxes.

19. If $x = 2a$, $a = 3b$, $b = 7y$, and $x = ky$, find k.

20. The surface area and volume of a cube are numerically equal. What is the length of a side of the cube?

STOP!
IF YOU FINISH BEFORE THE TIME IS UP,
YOU MAY CHECK YOUR WORK IN THIS SECTION ONLY.

practice test 3

ANSWER KEYS AND EXPLANATIONS

Section 1: Analytical Writing

Analyze an Issue

Model: 6 points out of 6

The quandary of whether or not to send one's children to private or public school is one with which most people will not have to contend. That's because it is an issue that solely affects those who have the financial resources to send their children to expensive private schools. It is a "problem" that excludes the less privileged in more ways than one, and that fact relates to my reasoning behind arguing against the position that "parents who can afford to send their children to private schools should do so."

Attending school is not just about the topics taught in class. Children also learn to socialize, and ideally, learn about the people with whom they are socializing. A well-to-do child will learn far less in a classroom populated with similarly privileged kids than she or he would in a room with a variety of peers from a variety of social and cultural backgrounds. Children are more likely to encounter such diverse peers in a public school. While concepts of tolerance and the divide between the financially fortunate and the less fortunate can be taught in the abstract in private schools, they become more "real" in an environment in which children from all backgrounds are forced to interact.

Furthermore, the exorbitant tuition fees of private schools set unfair goals for parents who cannot afford to send their children to private schools. It creates a system in which less fortunate people overextend themselves in order to compete and that is simply a system I cannot support.

Granted, there are benefits to private schools that public schools cannot match. Smaller class sizes and less strict curriculums are highly beneficial to more effective learning. These are not minor considerations, and for many parents, they will be the ultimate deciding factors in the choice between private and public schools. However, the "deprivations" associated with public schooling can also be viewed in a more positive light as challenges that can be overcome and have been by all of the successful people who've passed through the public education system. They can be viewed as yet another aspect of that system that builds stronger human beings than the cushy private system does.

Consequently, I choose to not support a system that continually favors the rich over the poor, the privileged over the underprivileged. Success is not just measured in terms of how one performs in school but also in how one performs in society. I for one believe that public schools better prepare the children of today to be the conscientious adults who will shape the society of the future for the better.

This response scores 6 out of 6 for the following reasons:

- **It answers the task.** This response takes a thoughtful position that explains the position and addresses both sides of the issue in a way that does not undermine the writer's central point.

- **It is well supported.** Notice how the writer takes a particular position on the issue (the position of choosing public schooling for social and political reasons) and sticks to it through the variety of supporting details. Notice how the support is explained and elaborated upon logically, clearly, and convincingly. Part of this support appears in the acknowledgment and explanation of the issue's complexity.

- **It is well organized.** Paragraph 1 is a strong introduction that sharpens the focus on the larger economic and social implications of sending one's child to private school and expands on that through supporting paragraphs that deal with different aspects of this issue, before reaching a philosophical conclusion that sums up the position the writer expressed throughout the preceding paragraphs.

- **It is fluid, precise, and graceful.** Precise word choices include nouns such as *quandary* and *deprivations* and adjectives such as *exorbitant* and *conscientious*. Sentences are varied in their structure, type, length, and openings.

- **It observes the conventions of Standard Written English.**

Model: 3 points out of 6

Everyone knows how rough it is to go to public schools. Teachers are not as concerned and conditions can be very poor. Your education can be better under private circumstances, so that is definitely the way to go.

Private schools are very expensive so not everyone can go to them. So that won't be an issue for them. People with a lot of money are different. They can go. It's the only decision.

Better education. That's a plus. I don't know how much they cost. I guess that's not an issue in this case. We will assume you can afford to go there, so if you have the money to spend, why not spend it? It is your kids education after all and what is more important than that.

People who have money and value there kids choose private school. Simple as that. Uniforms are part of private school I believe. That teaches disiplin. Stronger disiplin makes for better behaved kids. And some kids are simply out of control. Send them to private school.

This is a recipe for a better society. More private schools. But maybe they should be less expensive so everyone can go.

This response scores 3 out of 6 for the following reasons:

- **It answers the task in a limited way.** This response makes its position very clear, but it does not deal with the problems of this particular issue in a realistic way. The author never acknowledges the exclusive nature of private schools directly while also offering an unrealistic solution (make private schools more affordable) in a roundabout way of dealing with this issue.

- **It offers inadequate support.** Support is limited to a few phrases about how private schools offer a "better education" and how people who can afford to should spend their money on their children's educations, but these ideas are not developed or supported in any meaningful way.

- **It lacks organization.** The introductory paragraph presents the writer's position fairly well, but the subsequent paragraphs lack focus. They tend to repeat the same idea (people who can afford to send their children to private school should do so) with slightly different wording.

- **It is fluid, but not precise.** Ideas are mostly organized in fluid sentences, though some of the fragments are ineffective and make the essay seem more unpolished than pithy. The writer's choice of words is often unclear and tends to cloud the meaning of his or her analysis.

- **It contains errors in the conventions of Standard Written English.** There are several consistent flaws, some of which interfere with meaning.

Model: 1 point out of 6

If I was still a student, I'd go to public school. I remember my public school days. It was a lot of fun. All my friends were there. Probably make friends in a private school too though. So maybe that wouldn't be so bad. Education is always the same so that's not part of the decision I'm making here. I don't see how that would change since teachers are teachers and they pretty much always do a good job as they can so far as I can tell.

This response scores 1 out of 6 for the following reasons:

- **It barely answers the task.** While the position (the writer essentially disagrees with the argument in favor of private school over public school) is ultimately clear, the response does not deal with the complexities of this issue at all and personalizes the response in a manner that makes it seem as though he or she did not really understand the task.

- **It lacks support.** The author's focus on how he or she prefers public school because of his or her own experiences with making friends in public school is neither convincing nor well-developed support.

- **It has major problems with the conventions of Standard Written English.** The problems with lack of sentence structure are not quite significant enough to obscure meaning, but they are too abundant to ignore.

Analyze an Argument

Model: 6 points out of 6

There are no strict rules when it comes to how the modern workplace should be managed. Some opt for a casual environment, while others take the more traditional and admittedly professional approach. The author of this argument clearly favors the latter approach, and makes a fairly convincing argument in favor of a more professional dress code in the office. However, there is a significant problem with this argument that needs to be addressed, and it is an issue of extremes.

The strongest point of the author's argument is the matter of dealing with clients in unprofessional attire. I can certainly see how doing so may not foster the kind of atmosphere of professionalism that would make a client feel as though she or he is in good hands. Even if the client comes into the office in street clothes, it is still imperative for the business people in question to greet that client with the utmost professionalism. That could decide the difference between the continuation of a professional relationship and the cessation of it.

The author also makes a fair point in suggesting that workers might not take their jobs as seriously if improperly attired. I agree that one's behavior does seem to change with the clothing he or she is wearing. Based on my own experience, I agree that one tends to slip into the casual attitude one adopts on the weekend when dressed in weekend attire. Business attire does go a certain way toward building a professional, business-like manner.

However, it only goes a certain way, and one either is or isn't prepared to do her or his job effectively. In essence, I think the author of this argument ultimately places too much emphasis on attire. To suggest that wearing any kind of clothing "is the ultimate key in running a professional and successful business" is almost laughably simplistic and naïve, and it undermines the stronger points the author makes. This is not the only extreme in the argument. I also take issue with the author's insistence that "all offices" should adopt strict dress codes. In making this statement, the author exposes his or her own failure to comprehend that all offices are not alike. Not all businesses greet clients on the premises. Some offices might even suffer from adopting a strict businesslike dress code, such as offices in which creative work is performed. More causal dress wear may help to stimulate the kind of atmosphere off of which a creative office feeds. After all, it's hard to be completely free to create when there's a tie tightened around your throat.

So while I agree with the author's position in essence, I think more nuance could have strengthened it considerably. The author's argument in favor of strict dress codes would certainly be beneficial for certain offices, but not all of them. The strength of an argument hinges on its wording, and the wording of this argument leaves it with somewhat rusty hinges.

This response scores 6 out of 6 for the following reasons:

- **It answers the task.** The writer analyses the argument with nuance and intelligence, acknowledging its strengths and even taking a position on its overall argument but also noting its flawed use of extremes.

- **It is well supported.** Descriptions of various kinds of offices that would benefit from or suffer from the situation the argument argues in favor of are thoughtful, logical, and effective. The reader clearly sees how the central problem with the argument devalues it central recommendation.

- **It is well organized.** All five substantial paragraphs are logically organized and lead smoothly one to the next. The essay concludes as sure-footedly as it begins. Transitions and other elements of coherence ease the reader's passage through the essay.

- **It is fluid and precise.** The writing is clear and direct; the tone is appropriate. Word choices are apt and sentences are varied. Colorful turns of phrase such as "it's hard to be completely free to create when there's a tie tightened around your throat" and "The strength of an argument hinges on its wording, and the wording of this argument leaves it with somewhat rusty hinges" really bring the writing to life.

- **It observes the conventions of Standard Written English.**

Model: 3 points out of 6

I get the writer's position. It's an obviously excellent argument. A business office that requires business dress code is going to seem more business like. I just don't think the argument is made as well as it could be.

I for one would not want to work in an office where I'd have to wear a suit and tie every single day. It isn't fair to employees. Suits are expensive. So I'd have to buy a new suit for every day of the week? That's five suits. But then everyone would see you wear the same five suits week after week. So you'd need at least ten suits to change them up every two weeks. That is a lot of money and a lot to expect of people in an office.

So the problem with this argument is that the author doesn't even say that. If the author said it, then at least he'd show he was thinking about this serious issue. But he doesn't. He just says that business suits make you look more professional or whatever. Well obviously. But what about the other side of this issue that he doesn't even mention at all.

So I totally agree with what the author is saying but I would agree more if he told me how people do this. Seriously? How do people afford new suits every day? Can anyone even answer that if they aren't rich? A lot of jobs don't even pay that well. Any your still supposed to have a new suit practically every day. It's unrealistic.

This response scores 3 out of 6 for the following reasons:

- **It answers the task in a limited way.** This response makes its position clear (the author's failure to mention the prohibitive costs of business attire undermines the argument), but it fails to consider any issues beyond this one oversight. The author also contradicts her or his own position with extreme statements such as "It's an obviously excellent argument " and "I totally agree with what the author is saying."

- **It offers inadequate support.** The writer focuses on just one perceived flaw in the argument, but does not support it well. The questions in the final paragraph go off track and turn what should be a formal analysis into a sort of informal plea.

- **It lacks organization.** The introductory paragraph is adequate but the supporting paragraphs lack variation. The concluding paragraph reiterates ideas in the previous paragraphs without wording them in a manner that brings the essay to a satisfying conclusion.

- **It is fluid, but not precise.** The ideas are generally fluidly worded in a variety of sentence structures, and fragments are not used in an overtly ungrammatical way, though they do give an essay that should be fairly formal an inappropriately informal tone. The lack of precise wording is a problem, particularly in the confusing third paragraph.

- **It contains errors in the conventions of Standard Written English.** There are several consistent flaws, some of which interfere with meaning.

Model: 1 point out of 6

No way you'll ever catch me in a business suit. I don't do it, not matter how much you argue that its better for the business. You can't tell people what to where. It's a dictatorship. This argument says you should but who says freedom has no place in business. Not me. I will wear what I want to wear al the time even at work. You cannot convince me that I am wrong even this argument can't.

This response scores 1 out of 6 for the following reasons:

- **It does not answer the task.** The task requires writers to analyze an argument, but this writer only discusses how he or she would not comply with the position in the argument. This is a rant, not an analysis.

- **It lacks organization.** The single paragraph lacks clear focus. It is a rambling stream of ideas expressing the writer's distaste for business suits.

- **It offers illogical support.** The writer's personal preferences and simplistic concepts of freedom do not constitute strong support for what should be an analytical essay.

- **It has poorly constructed sentences.** Run-on sentences, fragments, and convoluted sentences interfere with coherence.

- **It contains some errors in the conventions of Standard Written English.**

Section 2: Verbal Reasoning

1. C	**6.** A	**11.** A	**16.** B, D
2. A	**7.** C	**12.** B	**17.** A, D
3. B, E	**8.** A, C	**13.** B	**18.** D, F
4. A, D, G	**9.** D	**14.** A, B	**19.** A, C
5. B, E, I	**10.** E	**15.** E	**20.** B

1. **The correct answer is C.** Something that once served a purpose but no longer does is a leftover, and another word for leftover is *vestige* (choice C). While a vestige may be an *indication* (choice A), *hint* (choice B), or *reflection* (choice D) of something that occurred earlier, these words are not synonymous with *vestige*. *Remaining* (choice E) is an adjective, and in this context, the correct answer is a noun.

2. **The correct answer is A.** Something that has very negative consequences is a disaster, and *debacle* (choice A) means "disaster." While a debacle may cause confusion, *confusion* and *debacle* do not share the same meaning. The correct word should be a noun, but *botch* (choice C) is a verb. *Error* (choice D) is far too mild a word, and *boon* (choice E) means the opposite of *debacle*.

3. **The correct answers are B and E.** Answer Blank (i): The correct word is a verb that belongs with the preposition *in* and *enveloped* in this context means a "natural enclosing covering" such as a membrane. While something can be coated in a substance, *coated* (choice A) is used to indicate a covering that is viscous or powdery, and a membrane is not viscous or powdery. *Paralleled* (choice C) is incorrect because one does not say that something is paralleled *in* something else—it is paralleled *with* something else.

Answer Blank (ii): While the terms in the list are likely unfamiliar to you, the structure of the sentence indicates that these terms are included in a list of membranes. *Comprise* (choice E) means "include." *Involve* (choice D) is less concrete a synonym for *include* than *comprise* is. The word *contain* (choice F) makes it sound as though the membranes are a physical container that holds the arachnoid mater, the dura mater, and the pia mater, which does not make sense since the sentence already indicated that the brain is contained in these membranes.

4. **The correct answers are A, D, and G.** Answer Blank (i): The references to different parts of a city in the paragraph suggest that the construction project was not a private one—it was a city-wide one. *Civil* (choice A) means "relating to cities." While mechanical tools might be involved in such a project, one would not refer to the project, itself, as *mechanical* (choice B). *Excruciating* (choice C) has negative connotations, and there is nothing explicitly negative in this paragraph.

Answer Blank (ii): The second sentence of the paragraph refers to Heathrow in the past tense, so it clearly ceased to exist. Therefore, *demolition* (choice D) makes sense in this context. Something may be ruined without being completely gone, so choice E is not as strong of an answer. The correct answer should be a noun, and *sullying* (choice F) is a verb. *Sully* means "to soil" or "to defame" and does not make sense in any part of speech.

Answer Blank (iii): The correct answer should be a synonym of *located*, and that is what *occupied* is. A town such as Heathrow cannot visit anything, so choice H makes no sense. *Burrowed* (choice I) means "dug" and does not make sense either.

5. **The correct answers are B, E, and I.** Answer Blank (i): Specific types of music, such as Zydeco, originate from specific locations, such as Louisiana. *Emanating* (choice B) means "originating."

    Answer Blank (ii): The list of musical styles indicates that Zydeco is a combination of all these styles, and *synthesizes* (choice E) means "combines." Choices D and F suggest that Zydeco affected these other musical styles, which is the opposite of the truth.

    Answer Blank (iii): The final sentence of the paragraph refers to instruments used to play Zydeco, and such instruments would be *linked* (choice I) with the genre. It does not make sense to say that a musical style and instruments *met* (choice G) or *joined* (choice H).

6. **The correct answer is A.** The first paragraph indicates that even during the time of the Garabit Viaduct's construction, piers larger than its 200-foot tall ones could have been constructed, so choice A is the best answer. That fact also contradicts choices B and C, which imply that such a structure was not possible during that time. It also means that choice D is a conclusion that the passage does not really support. There is no strong support for choice E either.

7. **The correct answer is C.** While the word *greatest* could be used as a synonym for any of the answer choices, only choice C makes sense in this particular context. Mention of the piers' "200-foot height" is a clue that *greatest* refers to height in this context.

8. **The correct answers are A and C.** The second paragraph of the passage contains details that support choices A and C. The final sentence of the paragraph supports choice A and contradicts the conclusion in choice B. The first sentence supports choice C.

9. **The correct answer is D.** While the word *order* can be used as a synonym for any of the answer choices, only *class* (choice D) makes sense in this context. The term *bugs* is a type or class of insects. Choices A, B, and C simply do not make sense in this context. The correct answer also must be a noun, and *arrange* (choice E) is a verb.

10. **The correct answer is E.** The passage mentions the number of legs an insect has as a way to identify insects and distinguish them from other creatures. Choices A and B may be true, but these are not significant reasons the author mentions about the number of legs mature insects have in this passage. The number of legs a mature insect has is just one of the distinguishing features listed in this passage, so choice C is not the best answer. The author only mentions wings when comparing insects to birds, so choice D is not the best answer either.

11. The correct answer is A. While the author clearly hates movies, his uncritical reference to the novel *Uncle Tom's Cabin* suggests that he has no such problems with novels. The author is not critical of certain movies; he is critical of all movies, which eliminates choice B. His complete lack of constructive criticism also eliminates choices C and D. The line, "Their business is frankly to assimilate the popular taste in order to reproduce it" contradicts the conclusion in choice E.

12. The correct answer is B. When the author refers to taste as *fickle* when describing how what people want tends to change a lot, so choice B is the best answer. Choice C is the opposite of *fickle*. Choice D is a synonym for *fiscal*, not *fickle*. Choice E is a verb but *fickle* is an adjective.

13. The correct answer is B. Choice B best explains the point of the first paragraph of the passage. Choice A is just one detail in the paragraph, and it isn't a very important detail. Choice C is the point of the second paragraph, not the first one. Choice D is another individual detail from the first paragraph. While the passage is fairly humorous, there is a greater purpose than merely entertaining the reader, so choice E is not the best answer.

14. The correct answers are A and B. The passage is mainly about how one needs to learn how to draw, and the sentences in choices A and B do not support this main idea directly. Choice C is an instruction for obtaining the right materials for drawing, so it is relevant.

15. The correct answer is E. The author begins the passage by asserting that singing is easy, but choice E, which is a truthful statement, weakens that argument. Choice A supports the author's argument that one must work to sharpen his or her drawing skills. If attendees at meetings paid close attention to what other attendees were doing, the author would not be able to practice drawing at them, so choice B does not weaken the author's argument. One does not need to be a famous artist to be a good one, so choice C is wrong, and choice D would do nothing to weaken the author's argument.

16. The correct answers are B and D. By definition, wilderness land is *natural* (choice A) and *untrammeled* (choice D) by human development. *Eradicated* (choice A), *cleared* (choice C), and *razed* (choice E) would all refer to land that people have altered for development or other purposes, and such land would no longer be wilderness land. *Gashed* (choice F) is not a word one would use to describe an area of land in any event.

17. The correct answers are A and D. Phrases such as "severely different ideologies" and "highly divided" are clues that the election was one in which tempers were bad, and *fractious* (choice A) and *heated* (choice D) would indicate such a testy atmosphere. *Unified* (choice B) implies a peaceful atmosphere. *Shattered* (choice C) is not a word one would use to describe the atmosphere surrounding a political election. *Unfazed* (choice E) and *bland* (choice F) are neutral terms that do not suggest the testiness of the election in question.

18. **The correct answers are D and F.** *Definitive* (choice D) and *ultimate* (choice F) refer to the one main thing, and this sentence specifies that there was no one main depiction of Batman. Choice A would suggest the opposite of this since *primary* means "main." *Original* (choice B) just means "first," and it does not fit this context. The correct answer should be an adjective, but *representation* (choice C) is a noun. *Consequential* (choice E) means "effective," and it does not fit this context.

19. **The correct answers are A and C.** A painting might *decorate* (choice A) or cover a ceiling, and *adorns* (choice C) means "decorates." *Shields* (choice B) implies protection, but a painting cannot really protect anything. *Masks* (choice D) means "hides," and the purpose of a painting could be to mask something unsightly, but that purpose is never implied in the sentence. *Blankets* (choice E) means "covers," but one would use it more to describe a physical covering such a blanket or bed of snow rather than a painting. *Infiltrates* (choice F) means "invades," and one would not say that a painting invades anything.

20. **The correct answer is B.** When the author refers to grammar as "doubtful," he is implying that it is not a very worthwhile subject, which is only his personal opinion and not a fact about education. The author offers the idea in choice A in the opening sentence of the passage, but this is likely a fact since there will always be more students than teachers. It is true that teachers are generally more interested in teaching lessons than explaining how they planned those lessons, so choice C is more fact than opinion. One can conclude that the author is working toward the opinion in choice D, but this opinion is never actually expressed in this particular passage. The opinion in choice E is never expressed in this passage either.

Section 3: Verbal Reasoning

1. E	6. A	11. A	16. A, F
2. D	7. D	12. A, B, C	17. A, B, F
3. A, D	8. B	13. D	18. B, C
4. B, E, I	9. B	14. C	19. A, C
5. C, D, G	10. C	15. B, C	20. E

1. **The correct answer is E.** Use of the technical categorical name *Annelida* indicates that the sentence requires a technical term for a category of animals, and that is *phylum* (choice E). *Slot* (choice A), *company* (choice B), and *association* (choice D) are not sufficiently technical, and *classroom* (choice D) simply does not make sense.

2. **The correct answer is D.** This sentence deals with how a part of the brain looks like a mythical creature, and *similitude* (choice D) indicates that two things share some trait such as appearance. *Appearance* (choice A) and *feature* (choice B) do not indicate sameness at all. *Identical* (choice C) indicates too much similarity, and it is an adjective when this sentence requires a noun. *Repetitive* (choice E) is also an adjective.

3. **The correct answers are A and D.** Answer Blank (i): The second sentence of the paragraph explains what the sport of sweep involves, and *entails* means "involves." *Exemplifies* (choice B) means "represents," and *affixes* (choice C) means "attaches." Neither word makes sense in this context.

Answer Blank (ii): The third sentence describes a form of rowing slightly different from sweep, and *variant* (choice D) means "a different form." *Difference* (choice E) relates to *variant*, but it is not a synonym. *Feature* (choice F) indicates nothing about difference.

4. **The correct answers are B, E, and I.** Answer Blank (i): *Afflicted* (choice B) describes how one is affected by an illness. One who is affected by an illness may be disabled, but *disabled* (choice A) and *afflicted* are not synonyms. One is not *ailed* (choice C) by a disease.

Answer Blank (ii): This blank requires a word used to transition from an idea (exposure to the high levels of mercury in the felt used to make hats was the source of the disease) to its consequence (author Lewis Carroll was inspired). Therefore, the best word is *consequently* (choice E). *Resulting* (choice D) is not a transitional word. *Ultimately* (choice F) is used to transition to a final result, not a consequence.

Answer Blank (iii): The word *beloved* is a clue that the character in the book is as well-loved as the book is. *Timeless* (choice I) indicates something that is long lasting because it is so well loved. *Contemporary* (choice G) suggests timeliness rather than timelessness. *Obscure* (choice H) means "little known," and something beloved is not little known.

5. **The correct answers are C, D, and G.** Answer Blank (i): The paragraph discusses how the Great Pyramid of Giza was first created, and *genesis* (choice C) indicates the beginning of something. One would not describe a pyramid as being born, so *birth* (choice A) is an odd word for this context. *Primeval* (choice B) means "primitive," and something does not need to be primitive to have an origin or genesis.

    Answer Blank (ii): One can deduce from the context that Khufu was responsible for having the Great Pyramid built, and when one is responsible for such a thing, that person has *commissioned* (choice D) the thing's creation. It is strange to imply that someone has purchased something that has not been made yet, so choice E is not the best answer. It is unlikely that a ruler such as Khufu would personally construct a pyramid, so choice F is not the best answer either.

    Answer Blank (iii): The final sentence of the paragraph explains an alternate name by which Khufu is known, and *moniker* (choice G) means "name." *Entitle* (choice H) is a verb meaning "to title something," but the correct answer is a noun. *Nominal* (choice I) is an adjective meaning "in name only."

6. **The correct answer is A.** The first paragraph of the passage explains what constitutes a science and the second paragraph explains what constitutes a scientist. While the idea that "science is knowledge" is directly in the first words of the passage, the rest of the passage expands on this idea to the degree that choice B is an insufficient explanation of the passage's main point. Choice C makes the passage seem like a dictionary entry. The terms in choice D are not actually contrasted in the passage. Choice E focuses on just one supporting detail in the passage instead of explaining the point of the passage as a whole.

7. **The correct answer is D.** The author defines a scientist as one who hunts "for causes and inquire into the significance of things," which is what a police detective does. However, if a police detective is not technically a scientist, then this weakens the author's argument that a scientist is one who hunts "for causes and inquire into the significance of things." The author does state that scientists must have knowledge of facts, but he says that this not all that a scientist must do, so choice A is not the best answer. The idea that non-scientific jobs require one to see the significance of facts (choice C) is not specific enough to weaken the author's argument. The other answer choices are all things that would support the author's argument regarding science and scientists, not weaken it.

8. **The correct answer is B.** The ability to make prophesies, or see the future, is a mystical ability, so by stating that the way scientists use knowledge to comprehend causal relationship "enables a scientist to prophesy" supports choice B. While the author draws distinctions between scientists and non-scientists, he does not make the extreme implication that is in choice A. The author also stresses the important relationship between knowledge and meaning and does not necessarily indicate that one side of that relationship is more important than the other, so choice C is not the best answer. There is no strong support for the inferences in choices D or E either.

9. **The correct answer is B.** The author's statement that "peculiar limitation in its dependence upon the people" supports the conclusion in choice B. The author does not discuss capitalism in the passage at all, so there is no support for the conclusion in choice A. The author never makes any comparisons that might support the conclusion in choice C. While the author specifically stresses the influence of democracy on Middle Western universities, the fact that he does not discuss universities outside of this area deprives choice D of adequate support. The author states that the State Universities of the Middle West were "shaped under pioneer ideals," so choice E is incorrect.

10. **The correct answer is C.** The author uses the quotation from Mr. Bryce because it eloquently yet simply explains what is required for a university to fulfill its mission. No other answer choice explains the author's use of the quotation accurately. Choice A can be eliminated because there is no clue that Mr. Bryce is a witness to anything. The quotation supports the author's argument; it does not serve as a counterargument to the argument (choice B). The quotation supports the argument, but it does not summarize it (choice D). The quotation does not define a term either (choice E).

11. **The correct answer is A.** While the word *conquest* can be used as a synonym for any of the answer choices, only choice A makes sense in this particular context. It would not be industrious to defeat (choice B) or cause the destruction (choice C) of nature. Choice D implies the opposite of the author's intention. One cannot actually capture nature, so choice E does not make sense.

12. **The correct answers are A, B, and C.** The main point of the passage is to explain the benefits of profit sharing, and each of the sentences in choices A, B, and C support this purpose with relevant supporting information.

13. **The correct answer is D.** The author uses reduction of labor strikes as a reason to implement a deferred participation plan in the passage. Since such a plan is apparently distinct from a standard profit-sharing plan, choice A is not the best answer. Taking the action in choice B would not help this particular situation either. Choice C might be true in itself, but this particular passage does not support it. Merely explaining the meaning of a term is not likely to reduce the risk of a labor strike, so choice E does not make much sense.

14. **The correct answer is C.** According to the passage, people generally believe that the desire to make money is in opposition to the "virtue" of patriotism, so it is reasonable to conclude that most people would believe that others would be more inclined toward patriotism without that desire. The author indicates that the desire for money is in antagonism to the social virtues, which supports the opposite of choice A. Choice B, however, is too extreme a conclusion to draw from this particular passage. There is no support for choices D or E either.

15. **The correct answers are B and C.** While the word *typical* could be used to mean any of the answer choices, only choice B and C make sense in this particular context. As described in line 4, the money maker is more of a usual image or character than a more abstract symbol, so choice A is incorrect.

16. **The correct answers are A and F.** The sentence describes how *The Twilight Zone* affected other television series and something that is *seminal* (choice A) or *influential* (choice F) affects the things that follow it. *Worn* (choice B) has negative connotations and does not fit this context. *Constant* (choice C) is not specifically related to affecting other things. *Ubiquitous* (choice D) means "inescapable" and does not have much to do with being influential or seminal. Something can be acclaimed, or well loved, without necessarily affecting anything else, so choice E is not the best answer.

17. **The correct answers are A, B, and F.** The word *treats* is a clue that the needed adjective should indicate qualities that make a particular food taste good enough to be considered a treat. *Scrumptious* (choice B) and *delectable* (choice F) both mean "delicious" and are qualities that would make a food a treat. *Succulent* (choice A), meaning "full of juice" or "moist and tasty," is also a correct answer. *Cloying* (choice C) means "overly sweet" and has somewhat negative connotations. The sentence draws a contrast between two lists of foods, and since the second list is already defined as savory foods, a different term is needed to define the first list, so choice D can be eliminated. *Putrid* (choice E) means "disgusting," so it should be eliminated as well.

18. **The correct answers are B and C.** The correct answers should indicate that Honky Tonk is a kind of country music, and terms such as *strain* (choice B) and *subgenre* (choice C) are often used to mean "kind" when discussing music. *Segment* (choice A), *compartment* (choice E), and *division* (choice F) all have similar connotations, but these terms are not typically used when discussing music. One would not say that something is a link *of* anything else, so choice D should be eliminated.

19. **The correct answers are A and C.** Since this sentence describes the size of the park, the correct answer should refer to that size and its incredible hugeness. *Sprawling* (choice A) and *expansive* (choice C) convey the extreme size of something that is 280,000 acres wide. *Large* (choice B) is not as strong of a word as *sprawling* or *expansive*, so it is not as strong of answer choice for a context in which extreme largeness should be expressed. *Lengthy* (choice D), *stretched* (choice E), and *elastic* (choice F) would be more appropriate for describing something that is a bit elongated rather than something that is 280,000 acres wide.

20. **The correct answer is E.** In the second paragraph of the passage, the author indicates that giving the distinguishing features of certain birds will help define them as *Raptores*, or Rapacious Birds. Picturing something that actually exists would not really help anyone to be more imaginative, so choice A is not a very strong answer. While some rapacious birds may be dangerous, the author never implies that choice B is the purpose behind describing their appearances. The author already explained the meaning of the term *Raptores*, so choice C is incorrect. While choice D is true in itself, it is not the *most significant* result of giving the distinguishing features of certain birds.

Section 4: Quantitative Reasoning

1. C	6. A	11. C	16. A
2. B	7. C	12. E	17. A, C, D, F, G
3. A	8. D	13. C	18. A, B, E
4. A	9. A	14. B	19. 70
5. D	10. D	15. D	20. 432

1. **The correct answer is C.**

   Simplify Quantity A.

   $$\dfrac{\frac{1}{2}}{\frac{1}{4^2}} = \frac{1}{2}\cdot\frac{4^2}{1} = \frac{16}{2} = 8,$$

   so the two quantities are equal.

2. **The correct answer is B.** A common denominator for the terms in Quantity A is 16, and the expression becomes $\dfrac{8+4+2+1}{16} = \dfrac{15}{16}$, which is less than 1.

3. **The correct answer is A.**

   $$\frac{1}{\sqrt{2}^{51}} = \frac{1}{\sqrt{2}\cdot\left(\sqrt{2}^2\right)^{25}} = \frac{1}{\sqrt{2}}\cdot\frac{1}{2^{25}}.$$

   But $\dfrac{1}{\sqrt{2}} < 1$, so this is less than $\dfrac{1}{2^{25}}$.

4. **The correct answer is A.** Both xy and wz consist of a negative times a positive, so both are negative. However, wz has a larger absolute value, since its factors have greater absolute values than those of xy. Therefore, wz is farther to the left on a number line, so xy is greater.

5. **The correct answer is D.** The circumference of a circle is $2\pi r$, and the area is πr^2. These expressions are equal when $r = 2$. When $r < 2$, the circumference is greater. When $r > 2$, the area is greater. Therefore, if the information we have is just that $r > 1$, we cannot determine whether the area or circumference is greater.

6. **The correct answer is A.** The image shows that $2x = 3y$, so $x = \dfrac{3}{2}y$.

7. **The correct answer is C.** Both quantities have a factor of x, which is 0, so both quantities are in fact equal to 0.

8. **The correct answer is D.** The information given is consistent with any relationship between the ages of Fran and Tabitha. For example, if John is 5, Beth is 6, and Tabitha is 10, then Fran could be 7, 10, or 11 (along with other possibilities).

9. **The correct answer is A.** The points on the graph clearly approximate a line with a positive slope. Choice B is incorrect since the line rises to the right instead of falling to the right. Choice C is incorrect because there is, in fact, a clear pattern seen in the graph. Choices D and E are incorrect since the points approximately form a line, not another shape.

10. **The correct answer is D.** The graph shows a consistent increase in grade as the number of hours studied increases. Therefore, the estimated grade for studying 3 hours should be between the values associated with 2.5 and 4 hours. The only answer choice that satisfies this condition is 90.

11. The correct answer is C. If the length is 15, then the two lengths make up 30 of the perimeter. This means the two widths must account for the other 4, so the width is 2. The area is then $(2)(15) = 30$. Choice A is incorrect because you found the width but did not multiply by the length. Choice B is incorrect because you added the length and width instead of multiplying them. Choice D is incorrect since 34 is the perimeter, not the area. Choice D is incorrect because you multiplied the perimeter by the width, instead of the length by the width.

12. The correct answer is E. Each of the dimensions increases by 4, since the expansion applies on all sides. The new dimensions are 16 feet by 20 feet, so the area is $(16)(20) = 320$ square feet. Choice A is incorrect because 192 square feet is the area of the original garden, not the expanded one. Choices B and D are incorrect because you increased only one of the dimensions, not both. Choice C is incorrect because you increased each dimension by 2 instead of 4.

13. The correct answer is C. The volume of a cylinder is the area of the base times the height. The area of the base is $\pi r^2 = \pi (5)^2 = 25\pi$, so the volume is $25\pi(7) = 175\pi$. Choice A is incorrect because you forgot to square the radius. Choice B is incorrect because you used the perimeter of the base instead of the area. Choice D is incorrect because you squared the height instead of the radius. Choice E is incorrect because you squared both the height and the radius, instead of just the radius.

14. The correct answer is B. By the Pythagorean theorem, the length of the rectangle is $\sqrt{10^2 - 6^2} = \sqrt{64} = 8$. The area is therefore $(8)(6) = 48$. Choice A is the perimeter of the rectangle rather than the area. Choices C and D are incorrect because you multiplied the diagonal by one of the dimensions rather than the length by the width. In choice E, you multiplied the length, width, and diagonal, when you should have left out the diagonal.

15. The correct answer is D. The retail price is $(1.15)(600) = 690$, and the discount is $(0.10)(690) = 69$, so it sells for $690 - 69 = 621$. This is $\frac{621}{600} = 1.035 = 103.5\%$ of the wholesale price. Choice A is incorrect because you used the 15% as a discount, not as a markup. Choice B is incorrect because you did not markup the wholesale price before taking the discount. Choice C is incorrect because you switched the percentages for the markup and discount. Choice E is incorrect because you used the 10% as an additional markup rather than as a discount.

16. The correct answer is A. The total value of all eight stacks is $3 \times \$1.75 + 4 \times \$2.25 + 1 \times \$3.27 = \$17.52$, so the average is $\frac{\$17.52}{8} = \$2.19$. Choice B is incorrect because you took the average of the three values given without taking the weights into account. In choice C, you found the correct total but divided by 3 instead of 8. Choice D is incorrect because you simply added up the three values given. Choice E is incorrect because you found the total amount of money, but not the mean value per stack.

17. The correct answers are A, C, D, F, and G. Each term is one less than twice the previous term, so the sequence begins 2, 3, 5, 9, 17, 33, 65, 129. It always increases, so all of the other answers will never be part of the sequence.

18. The correct answers are A, B, and E. Factor and solve:

$$3x^3 - 5x^2 - 2x = 0$$
$$x(3x^2 - 5x - 2) = 0$$
$$x(3x + 1)(x - 2) = 0$$
$$x = 0, -\frac{1}{3}, 2$$

The other answers are incorrect since they do not show up as solutions when the polynomial is factored. You can also substitute those values for x to check; they will not result in an answer of 0.

19. The correct answer is 70. The large triangle is isosceles since two of its sides are equal. Therefore, angle ABE is equal to angle DCE, so it is 70°. Since $\overline{AB}$ and $\overline{DE}$ are parallel, their corresponding angles are congruent, so $x = 70$.

20. The correct answer is 432. Divide 5,400 by 12.50 to get 432.

Section 5: Quantitative Reasoning

1. D	**6.** A	**11.** D	**16.** C
2. B	**7.** B	**12.** E	**17.** C, D
3. C	**8.** C	**13.** C	**18.** A, F
4. A	**9.** D	**14.** E	**19.** 42
5. C	**10.** B	**15.** E	**20.** 6

1. **The correct answer is D.** The information given tells us only that both quantities are positive, since $f < g$ and $d < e$. It does not give any indication of how far apart these are from each other though, so there is no way to know which difference is greater, or if they are equal.

2. **The correct answer is B.** There are $8 \times 4 = 32$ quarters in \$8.00, and $2 \times 20 = 40$ nickels in \$2.00.

3. **The correct answer is C.**
$$\left(\frac{4}{21}\right)\left(\frac{4}{2}\right)\left(\frac{14}{8}\right) = \frac{224}{336} = \frac{2}{3}, \text{ and}$$
$$\left(\frac{2}{3}\right)\left(\frac{2}{1}\right)\left(\frac{2}{4}\right) = \frac{8}{12} = \frac{2}{3} \text{ as well.}$$

4. **The correct answer is A.** Since a is positive, multiplying by a number greater than 1 increases its value, while dividing by a number greater than 1 decreases its value.

5. **The correct answer is C.** The angles in a triangle always add up to 180°, so the average degree value of the angles is $\frac{180}{30} = 60$.

6. **The correct answer is A.** Add the two equations to get $2x = 4$, and $x = 2$. Now substitute $x = 2$ into the first equation to get $y = 1$.

7. **The correct answer is B.** Circumference is given by $2\pi r$, so the radius of the circle is 4, and its area is $\pi r^2 = 16\pi \approx 50.24$. If the perimeter of the square is 30, its side length is 7.5, so its area is $7.5^2 = 56.25$.

8. **The correct answer is C.** $\frac{1}{100}$% of 100 is $0.0001(100) = 0.01 = 10^{-2}$.

9. **The correct answer is D.** Divide the commission by the rate: $\frac{340}{0.017} = 20,000$.

Choice A is incorrect because you multiplied the commission by the rate. Choice B is incorrect because you used 0.17 as the rate instead of 0.017. Choice C is incorrect because you subtracted the commission amount from the sale price. Choice E is incorrect because you used 0.0017 as the rate instead of 0.017.

10. **The correct answer is B.** Payal completes $\frac{1}{12}$ of the driveway per minute, and Shreya completes $\frac{1}{18}$ of the driveway per minute. Together, then, they complete $\frac{1}{12} + \frac{1}{18} = \frac{5}{36}$ of the driveway per minute. The entire driveway will therefore take $\frac{36}{5} = 7.2$ minutes, rounded to 7. Choice A is incorrect because you subtracted their times. Choice C is incorrect since you just used the smaller time. Choice D is incorrect because you took the average of the times. Choice E is incorrect because you added the rates.

11. **The correct answer is D.**

$$\frac{12 \text{ miles}}{1 \text{ hour}} \cdot \frac{5280 \text{ feet}}{1 \text{ mile}} \cdot \frac{1 \text{ hour}}{60 \text{ minutes}} \cdot \frac{1 \text{ minute}}{60 \text{ seconds}} = \frac{17.6 \text{ feet}}{1 \text{ second}}$$

Choice A is incorrect because you started with 1 mile per hour instead of 12. Choice B is incorrect because you divided by 5,280 and multiplied by 3,600 instead of the opposite. Choice C is incorrect because you gave the answer in miles per hour, not feet per second. Choice E is incorrect since you converted to minutes, not to seconds.

12. **The correct answer is E.**

$9^{\frac{3}{2}} = \left(\sqrt{9}\right)^3 = 3^3 = 27$. Choice A is incorrect because you took the square root of 9 but did not cube it. In choice B, you multiplied 9 by $\frac{2}{3}$ instead of raising it to the $\frac{3}{2}$. In choice C, you divided 9 by 3 and then multiplied by 3. Choice D is incorrect because you multiplied 9 by $\frac{3}{2}$ instead of raising it to the $\frac{3}{2}$.

13. **The correct answer is C.** The angles in a triangle add up to 180, so:

$$2x + 2x + (x + 5) = 180$$

Solving the equation gives you $x = 35$. In choice A, you set $2x$ equal to $x + 5$ instead of making all the angles add up to 180. In choice B, you set the sum of the angles to 100 instead of 180. Choice D is incorrect since you forgot to include the $x + 5$ in your sum. Choice E is incorrect because you used x instead of $x + 5$ as the vertex angle.

14. **The correct answer is E.** Since two of the angles are equal, the triangle is isosceles, and therefore $y^2 = y + 6$, or $y^2 - y - 6 = 0$. This factors as $(y - 3)(y + 2) = 0$, so $y = 3$ or -2. Choosing $y = 3$ results in side lengths of 6, and choosing $y = -2$ results in a triangle with side lengths of 4. Choice A is incorrect since that would make the side length of the triangle 0, which is impossible. Choice B is incorrect because you set $y^2 = y$ but forgot the 6. In choice C, you solved $y^2 + y + 6 = 0$ instead of $y^2 - y - 6 = 0$. Choice D is incorrect because while you got a correct answer for y, you left out another correct answer.

15. **The correct answer is E.** A and B both have a sum of 40, so both have a mean of 10. The numbers in B are farther away from the mean of 10 compared to the numbers in A, so B has a larger standard deviation.

16. **The correct answer is C.** After the first month, the value is:

$$4,500\left(1 + \frac{.035}{12}\right) = 4,513.13$$

After the second month, it is

$$4,513.13\left(1 + \frac{.035}{12}\right) = 4,526.29$$

Choice A is incorrect, as this is the value after only one month. Choice B is incorrect because you did not account for the compounding that takes place after one month. Choice D is the value that the account would have after a year without any compounding. In choice E, you used 35% interest instead of 3.5%.

17. **The correct answers are C and D.** The product of an even number with any other number is even. The sum or difference of an even and an odd number is odd, so choices A and B are incorrect. The product of an odd number with an odd number is odd, so choice E is incorrect.

18. **The correct answers are A and F.**

$2 - 3 = -1$ and $2 - (-1) = 3$, so the sequence will always alternate between 3 and -1. These are the only numbers that will ever appear.

19. **The correct answer is 42.** $x = 2a = 2(3b) = 2(3(7y)) = 42y$. But $x = ky$, so $42y = ky$, and $k = 42$.

20. **The correct answer is 6.** The surface area of a cube with side length x is $6x^2$, and the volume is x^3. Therefore, we need to solve $6x^2 = x^3$. This is equivalent to $6x^2 - x^3 = 0$, which factors as $x^2(6 - x) = 0$, so $x = 0$ or $x = 6$. A cube cannot have sides of length 0, so the answer is 6.

Practice Test 4

The test begins with general information about the number of sections on the test (six for the computer-delivered test, including the unidentified unscored section or an identified research section, and five for the paper-delivered test) and the timing of the test (approximately 3 hours and 45 minutes, including one 10-minute break after Section 3, 1-minute breaks after the other sections for the computer-delivered test, and 3 hours and 30 minutes for the paper-delivered test with similar breaks). The following practice test contains the five scored sections.

Each section has its own time allocation and, during that time period, you may work on only that section.

Next, you will read ETS's policy on scoring the Analytical Writing responses. Each essay is read by experienced readers, and ETS may cancel any test scores that show evidence of unacknowledged use of sources, unacknowledged collaboration with others, preparation of the response by another person, and language that is "substantially" similar to the language in one or more other test responses.

Each section has specific instructions for that section.

You will be told when to begin.

PRACTICE TEST 4 ANSWER SHEETS

Section 1: Analytical Writing

Analyze an Issue

FOR PLANNING

Analyze an Issue Response

_____

_____

_____

_____

_____

_____

_____

_____

_____

_____

_____

_____

_____

_____

_____

_____

_____

_____

_____

_____

answer sheet

Analyze an Issue Response

_____

_____

_____

_____

_____

_____

_____

_____

_____

_____

_____

_____

_____

_____

_____

_____

_____

_____

_____

_____

_____

_____

_____

Analyze an Issue Response

_____

_____

_____

_____

_____

_____

_____

_____

_____

_____

_____

_____

_____

_____

_____

_____

_____

_____

_____

answer sheet

Analyze an Issue Response

_____

_____

_____

_____

_____

_____

_____

_____

_____

_____

_____

_____

_____

_____

_____

_____

_____

_____

_____

_____

_____

Analyze an Argument

FOR PLANNING

Analyze an Argument Response

_____

_____

_____

_____

_____

_____

_____

_____

_____

_____

_____

_____

_____

_____

_____

_____

_____

_____

_____

_____

_____

_____

_____

_____

Analyze an Argument Response

_____

_____

_____

_____

_____

_____

_____

_____

_____

_____

_____

_____

_____

_____

_____

_____

_____

_____

_____

_____

_____

_____

_____

answer sheet

Analyze an Argument Response

_____

_____

_____

_____

_____

_____

_____

_____

_____

_____

_____

_____

_____

_____

_____

_____

_____

_____

_____

_____

_____

_____

_____

Analyze an Argument Response

_____

_____

_____

_____

_____

_____

_____

_____

_____

_____

_____

_____

_____

_____

_____

_____

_____

_____

_____

_____

_____

_____

_____

_____

_____

_____

answer sheet

Section 2: Verbal Reasoning

1. Ⓐ Ⓑ Ⓒ Ⓓ Ⓔ
2. Ⓐ Ⓑ Ⓒ Ⓓ Ⓔ
3. Ⓐ Ⓑ Ⓒ Ⓓ Ⓔ Ⓕ
4. Ⓐ Ⓑ Ⓒ Ⓓ Ⓔ Ⓕ
5. Ⓐ Ⓑ Ⓒ Ⓓ Ⓔ Ⓕ Ⓖ Ⓗ Ⓘ
6. Ⓐ Ⓑ Ⓒ Ⓓ Ⓔ
7. Ⓐ Ⓑ Ⓒ Ⓓ Ⓔ

8. Ⓐ Ⓑ Ⓒ Ⓓ Ⓔ
9. Ⓐ Ⓑ Ⓒ Ⓓ Ⓔ
10. Ⓐ Ⓑ Ⓒ Ⓓ Ⓔ
11. Ⓐ Ⓑ Ⓒ Ⓓ Ⓔ
12. Ⓐ Ⓑ Ⓒ
13. Ⓐ Ⓑ Ⓒ Ⓓ Ⓔ
14. Ⓐ Ⓑ Ⓒ Ⓓ Ⓔ

15. Ⓐ Ⓑ Ⓒ
16. Ⓐ Ⓑ Ⓒ Ⓓ Ⓔ
17. Ⓐ Ⓑ Ⓒ Ⓓ Ⓔ
18. Ⓐ Ⓑ Ⓒ Ⓓ Ⓔ
19. Ⓐ Ⓑ Ⓒ Ⓓ Ⓔ
20. Ⓐ Ⓑ Ⓒ Ⓓ Ⓔ

Section 3: Verbal Reasoning

1. Ⓐ Ⓑ Ⓒ Ⓓ Ⓔ
2. Ⓐ Ⓑ Ⓒ Ⓓ Ⓔ
3. Ⓐ Ⓑ Ⓒ Ⓓ Ⓔ
4. Ⓐ Ⓑ Ⓒ Ⓓ Ⓔ Ⓕ
5. Ⓐ Ⓑ Ⓒ Ⓓ Ⓔ Ⓕ
6. Ⓐ Ⓑ Ⓒ Ⓓ Ⓔ
7. Ⓐ Ⓑ Ⓒ Ⓓ Ⓔ

8. Ⓐ Ⓑ Ⓒ Ⓓ Ⓔ
9. Ⓐ Ⓑ Ⓒ Ⓓ Ⓔ
10. Ⓐ Ⓑ Ⓒ Ⓓ Ⓔ
11. Ⓐ Ⓑ Ⓒ Ⓓ Ⓔ
12. Ⓐ Ⓑ Ⓒ
13. Ⓐ Ⓑ Ⓒ
14. Ⓐ Ⓑ Ⓒ Ⓓ Ⓔ

15. Ⓐ Ⓑ Ⓒ Ⓓ Ⓔ
16. Ⓐ Ⓑ Ⓒ Ⓓ Ⓔ
17. Ⓐ Ⓑ Ⓒ Ⓓ Ⓔ
18. Ⓐ Ⓑ Ⓒ Ⓓ Ⓔ
19. Ⓐ Ⓑ Ⓒ Ⓓ Ⓔ
20. Ⓐ Ⓑ Ⓒ Ⓓ Ⓔ

Section 4: Quantitative Reasoning

1. Ⓐ Ⓑ Ⓒ Ⓓ
2. Ⓐ Ⓑ Ⓒ Ⓓ
3. Ⓐ Ⓑ Ⓒ Ⓓ
4. Ⓐ Ⓑ Ⓒ Ⓓ
5. Ⓐ Ⓑ Ⓒ Ⓓ
6. Ⓐ Ⓑ Ⓒ Ⓓ
7. Ⓐ Ⓑ Ⓒ Ⓓ

8. Ⓐ Ⓑ Ⓒ Ⓓ
9. Ⓐ Ⓑ Ⓒ Ⓓ Ⓔ
10. Ⓐ Ⓑ Ⓒ Ⓓ Ⓔ
11. Ⓐ Ⓑ Ⓒ Ⓓ Ⓔ
12. Ⓐ Ⓑ Ⓒ Ⓓ Ⓔ
13. Ⓐ Ⓑ Ⓒ Ⓓ Ⓔ
14. Ⓐ Ⓑ Ⓒ Ⓓ Ⓔ

15. Ⓐ Ⓑ Ⓒ Ⓓ Ⓔ
16. Ⓐ Ⓑ Ⓒ Ⓓ Ⓔ
17. Ⓐ Ⓑ Ⓒ Ⓓ Ⓔ
18. Ⓐ Ⓑ Ⓒ Ⓓ Ⓔ Ⓕ Ⓖ Ⓗ
19. ▢
20. ▢

Section 5: Quantitative Reasoning

1. Ⓐ Ⓑ Ⓒ Ⓓ
2. Ⓐ Ⓑ Ⓒ Ⓓ
3. Ⓐ Ⓑ Ⓒ Ⓓ
4. Ⓐ Ⓑ Ⓒ Ⓓ
5. Ⓐ Ⓑ Ⓒ Ⓓ
6. Ⓐ Ⓑ Ⓒ Ⓓ
7. Ⓐ Ⓑ Ⓒ Ⓓ
8. Ⓐ Ⓑ Ⓒ Ⓓ

9. Ⓐ Ⓑ Ⓒ Ⓓ
10. Ⓐ Ⓑ Ⓒ Ⓓ Ⓔ
11. Ⓐ Ⓑ Ⓒ Ⓓ Ⓔ
12. Ⓐ Ⓑ Ⓒ Ⓓ Ⓔ
13. Ⓐ Ⓑ Ⓒ Ⓓ Ⓔ
14. Ⓐ Ⓑ Ⓒ Ⓓ Ⓔ
15. Ⓐ Ⓑ Ⓒ Ⓓ Ⓔ

16. Ⓐ Ⓑ Ⓒ Ⓓ Ⓔ Ⓕ
17. Ⓐ Ⓑ Ⓒ Ⓓ Ⓔ
18. ▢
19. ▢
20. ▢

SECTION 1: ANALYTICAL WRITING

Analyze an Issue

30 minutes

The time for this task is 30 minutes. You must plan and draft a response that evaluates the issue given below. If you do not respond to the specific issue, your score will be zero. Your response must be based on the accompanying instructions, and you must provide evidence for your position. You may use support from reading, experience, observations, and/or course work.

People who use free social media sites should not have any expectation of data privacy. When these companies receive personal data and information from their users in exchange for use of a free online service, it belongs to the companies, and they should be able to use it as they see fit.

Write a response that takes and explains the extent to which you agree or disagree with this statement. As you present, develop, and explain your position, discuss when and how the statement might or might not hold true. Explain how those possibilities provide support for your own point of view.

Your response will be read by experienced readers who will assess your ability to do the following:

- Follow the set of task instructions.

- Analyze the complexities involved.

- Organize, develop, and explain ideas.

- Use pertinent reasons and/or illustrations to support ideas.

- Adhere to the conventions of Standard Written English.

You will be advised to take some time to plan your response and to leave time to reread it before the time is over. Those taking the paper-delivered GRE® General Test will find a blank page in their answer booklet for making notes and then four ruled pages for writing their actual response. Those taking the computer-delivered test will be given scrap paper for making notes.

STOP!
IF YOU FINISH BEFORE THE TIME IS UP,
YOU MAY CHECK YOUR WORK IN THIS SECTION ONLY.

Analyze an Argument

30 minutes

The time for this task is 30 minutes. You must plan and draft a response that evaluates the argument given below. If you do not respond to the given argument, your score will be zero. Your response must be based on the accompanying instructions, and you must provide evidence in support of your analysis.

You should not present your views on the subject of the argument, but on the strength or weakness of the argument.

> As the world struggles with the issue of poverty and income inequality, some in the U.S. are calling for a universal minimum wage of $15. This sounds great in theory, but in reality it places financial pressure on business owners and does not necessarily have the intended effects on the lives of lower-income Americans. A more logical solution would be to invest money in community programs that support education and job training, to help ensure that people have the skills they'll need to compete in the job market as it is, rather than rely on low-skill jobs on a long-term basis.
>
> *Write a response that identifies and explains the specific evidence required to determine whether the argument is reasonable. Discuss how that evidence would weaken or strengthen the argument.*

Your response will be read by experienced readers who will assess your ability to do the following:

- Follow the set of task instructions.
- Analyze the complexities involved.
- Organize, develop, and explain ideas.
- Use pertinent reasons and/or illustrations to support ideas.
- Adhere to the conventions of Standard Written English.

You will be advised to take some time to plan your response and to leave time to reread it before the time is over. Those taking the paper-delivered GRE® General Test will find a blank page in their answer booklet for making notes and then four ruled pages for writing their actual response. Those taking the computer-delivered test will be given scrap paper for making notes.

STOP!
IF YOU FINISH BEFORE THE TIME IS UP,
YOU MAY CHECK YOUR WORK IN THIS SECTION ONLY.

INSTRUCTIONS FOR THE VERBAL REASONING AND QUANTITATIVE REASONING SECTIONS

You will find information here on the question formats for the Verbal Reasoning and Quantitative Reasoning sections, as well as information about how to use the software program, or, if you're taking the paper-delivered version, how to mark your answers in the answer booklet.

Perhaps the most important information is a reminder about how these two sections are scored. Every correct answer earns a point, but points are not subtracted for incorrect answers. The advice from ETS is to guess if you aren't sure of an answer. ETS says that this is better than not answering a question.

All multiple-choice questions on the computer-delivered test will have answer options preceded by either blank ovals or blank squares, depending on the question type. The paper-delivered test will follow the same format for answer choices, but it will use letters instead of ovals or squares for answer choices.

For your convenience in answering questions and checking answers, this book uses letter designations (A, B, C, etc.) for answer choices. Having these letters to refer to will make it easier for you to check your answers against the answer key and explanation sections.

SECTION 2: VERBAL REASONING

30 minutes • 20 questions

(The paper-delivered test will have 25 questions to be completed in 35 minutes.)

For each question, follow the specific directions and choose the best answer.

For Questions 1–5, choose <u>one</u> answer for each blank. Select from the appropriate column for each blank. Choose the answer that best completes the sense of the text.

1. Despite the controversy over "fake news" appearing in people's social media feeds, many people still believe that social media is the ideal way to stay _____ of current events and breaking news.

A. avoidant
B. apprehensive
C. abreast
D. compassionate
E. heedless

2. The victory proved to be _____, given that immediately afterward, the team was disqualified for having a player test positive for a banned substance.

A. ephemeral
B. procedural
C. epidural
D. epochal
E. unequivocal

3. The eyewitness was compelled to come to court by a (i) _____, but after she (ii) _____ her previous testimony about the defendant being at the party, the prosecution had no choice but to withdraw the charges against the defendant.

Blank (i)	Blank (ii)
A. recusal	**D.** recanted
B. whim	**E.** recalibrated
C. subpoena	**F.** reiterated

4. I enjoyed the lecture and thought that the visiting professor made some (i) _____ points about George Washington's leadership of the Continental Army. However, I have to (ii) _____ with his presenting of Washington's apocryphal childhood cherry tree story as fact.

Blank (i)	Blank (ii)
A. salient	**D.** remark
B. recalcitrant	**E.** quibble
C. nascent	**F.** concur

5. Hamlet's "to be or not to be" (i) _____ in Act 1 is one of the most famous scenes in all of theatre history. In it, the (ii) _____ Prince of Denmark asks himself whether he should continue on with life, despite the pain and agony. Gone is the playful, (iii) _____ prince he had been before his father's death.

Blank (i)	Blank (ii)	Blank (iii)
A. dialogue	D. sanguineous	G. candid
B. soliloquy	E. morose	H. fretful
C. manifesto	F. foolhardy	I. mirthful

For Questions 6–20, choose only <u>one</u> answer choice unless otherwise indicated.

Questions 6–8 are based on the following passage.

The stars awaken a certain reverence, because though always present, they are inaccessible; but all natural objects make a kindred impression, when the mind is open to their influence. Nature never wears a mean appearance. Neither does the wisest man extort her secret, and
Line lose his curiosity by finding out all her perfection. Nature never became a toy to a wise spirit.
5 The flowers, the animals, the mountains, reflected the wisdom of his best hour, as much as they had delighted the simplicity of his childhood.

When we speak of nature in this manner, we have a distinct but most poetical sense in the mind. We mean the integrity of impression made by manifold natural objects. It is this which distinguishes the stick of timber of the wood-cutter, from the tree of the poet. The
10 charming landscape which I saw this morning, is indubitably made up of some twenty or thirty farms. Miller owns this field, Locke that, and Manning the woodland beyond. But none of them owns the landscape. There is a property in the horizon which no man has but he whose eye can integrate all the parts, that is, the poet. This is the best part of these men's farms, yet to this their warranty-deeds give no title.

—excerpt from *Nature* by Ralph Waldo Emerson

6. It can be inferred from the passage that the author believes that

A. property is the most important thing a man can own.

B. landscapes should be controlled by the government to avoid property disputes among land owners.

C. natural ownership of land takes precedence over legal ownership.

D. ownership is unnecessary when one can enjoy the beauty of the land.

E. property owners have an obligation to preserve the natural beauty of their land.

7. The author refers to nature as a "toy to a wise spirit" in order to

A. illustrate that nature cannot be bought or kept.

B. suggest that nature is best appreciated by children.

C. undermine the idea that nature is valuable and lasting.

D. show that nature is easily broken.

E. imply that nature is trivial compared to adult concerns.

8. Which of the following is most similar in reasoning to the idea expressed in the final sentence?

    A. Poets have more integrity than farmers.

    B. True land ownership does not exist.

    C. It is impossible for land owners to appreciate nature.

    D. The most worthwhile parts of land are free.

    E. Nature can only be evaluated by poets.

Questions 9–11 are based on the following passage.

But it is in the new monarchy that difficulties really exist. Firstly, if it is not entirely new, but a member as it were of a mixed state, its disorders spring at first from a natural difficulty which exists in all new dominions, because men change masters willingly, hoping to better
Line themselves; and this belief makes them take arms against their rulers, in which they are
5   deceived, as experience shows them that they have gone from bad to worse. This is the result of another very natural cause, which is the necessary harm inflicted on those over whom the prince obtains dominion, both by his soldiers and by an infinite number of other injuries unavoidably caused by his occupation.

Thus you find enemies in all those whom you have injured by occupying that dominion,
10   and you cannot maintain the friendship of those who have helped you to obtain this possession, as you will not be able to fulfil their expectations, nor can you use strong measures with them, being under an obligation to them; for which reason, however strong your armies may be, you will always need the favour of the inhabitants to take possession of a province. It was from these causes that Louis XII of France, though able to occupy Milan without
15   trouble, immediately lost it, and the forces of Ludovico alone were sufficient to take it from him the first time, for the inhabitants who had willingly opened their gates to him, finding themselves deluded in the hopes they had cherished and not obtaining those benefits that they had anticipated, could not bear the vexatious rule of their new prince.

—excerpt from *The Prince* by Niccolo Machiavelli

9. Select the sentence that restates the premise of the author's argument.

    A. A prince can trust only his subjects after he takes over.

    B. A new ruler has very little support that he can rely upon.

    C. Supportive friends are the key to maintaining power.

    D. Inhabitants rarely change their minds about the leader they want.

    E. Once a ruler is in power, it is easy to maintain that role.

10. "Vexatious" (line 18) most nearly means

    A. well-liked.

    B. bothersome.

    C. frightening.

    D. lengthy.

    E. cruel.

11. The passage implies that a new prince's rule is

    A. natural.

    B. inherited.

    C. impossible.

    D. unstable.

    E. unhappy.

Questions 12 and 13 are based on the following passage.

Neither the purpose nor the effect of punishment has ever been definitely agreed upon, even by its most strenuous advocates. So long as punishment persists it will be a subject of discussion and dispute. No doubt the idea of punishment originated in the feeling of resentment *Line* and hatred and vengeance that, to some extent at least, is incident to life. The dog is hit with 5 a stick and turns and bites the stick. Animals repel attack and fight their enemies to death. The primitive man vented his hatred and vengeance on things animate and inanimate. In the tribes no injury was satisfied until some member of the offending tribe was killed. In more recent times family feuds have followed down the generations and were not forgotten until the last member of a family was destroyed. Biologically, anger and hatred follow fear and 10 injury, and punishment follows these in turn. Individuals, communities and whole peoples hate and swear vengeance for an injury, real or fancied. Punishments, even to the extent of death, are inflicted where there can be no possible object except revenge. Whether the victim is weak or strong, old or young, sane or insane, makes no difference; men and societies react to injury exactly as animals react.

—excerpt from *Crime: Its Cause and Treatment* by Clarence Darrow

For Question 12, consider each answer individually and select <u>all</u> choices that apply.

12. What does the author's comparison of humans and animals suggest?

    A. Punishment cannot overcome biological urges.

    B. Punishment is the only thing that separates humans and animals.

    C. Vengeance is a natural reaction to injury.

13. "Incident" (line 4) most nearly means

    A. an event.

    B. confrontation.

    C. unusual.

    D. natural.

    E. dependent.

Questions 14 and 15 are based on the following passage.

Of the worship of Diana at Nemi some leading features can still be made out. From the votive offerings which have been found on the site, it appears that she was conceived of especially as a huntress, and further as blessing men and women with offspring, and granting
Line expectant mothers an easy delivery. Again, fire seems to have played a foremost part in her
5 ritual. For during her annual festival, held on the thirteenth of August, at the hottest time of the year, her grove shone with a multitude of torches, whose ruddy glare was reflected by the lake; and throughout the length and breadth of Italy the day was kept with holy rites at every domestic hearth. Bronze statuettes found in her precinct represent the goddess herself holding a torch in her raised right hand; and women whose prayers had been heard by her
10 came crowned with wreaths and bearing lighted torches to the sanctuary in fulfilment of their vows. Some one unknown dedicated a perpetually burning lamp in a little shrine at Nemi for the safety of the Emperor Claudius and his family. The terra-cotta lamps which have been discovered in the grove may perhaps have served a like purpose for humbler persons. If so, the analogy of the custom to the Catholic practice of dedicating holy candles in churches would be
15 obvious. Further, the title of Vesta borne by Diana at Nemi points clearly to the maintenance of a perpetual holy fire in her sanctuary. A large circular basement at the north-east corner of the temple, raised on three steps and bearing traces of a mosaic pavement, probably supported a round temple of Diana in her character of Vesta, like the round temple of Vesta in the Roman Forum. Here the sacred fire would seem to have been tended by Vestal Virgins,
20 for the head of a Vestal in terra-cotta was found on the spot, and the worship of a perpetual fire, cared for by holy maidens, appears to have been common in Latium from the earliest to the latest times. Further, at the annual festival of the goddess, hunting dogs were crowned and wild beasts were not molested; young people went through a purificatory ceremony in her honour; wine was brought forth, and the feast consisted of a kid cakes served piping hot
25 on plates of leaves, and apples still hanging in clusters on the boughs.

—excerpt from *The Golden Bough* by Sir James George Frazier

14. What is the likely reason for perpetually burning lamps found at the shrine?
   A. Warding off animals
   B. Ensuring safety for specific people
   C. Purifying young people
   D. Representing Vestal Virgins
   E. Praying for fertility

For Question 15, consider each answer individually and select <u>all</u> choices that apply.

15. Which of the following are NOT listed as tributes to Diana?

    A. An animal sacrifice

    B. Dedications to the emperor

    C. Sacred fire tended by maidens

For Questions 16–19, choose the <u>two</u> answers that best fit the meaning of the sentence as a whole and result in two completed sentences that are alike in meaning.

16. The house was _____, but what it lacked in splendor it made up in homey charm.

    A. modest

    B. magnificent

    C. monstrous

    D. expensive

    E. unassuming

17. I had trouble following the lecture; the professor's _____ style led to her following one tangent after another for the entire hour.

    A. focused

    B. roundabout

    C. impressive

    D. oblique

    E. syllabus

18. The Peace of Westphalia is the collective name for a series of _____ that ended the Thirty Years' War and the Eighty Years' War.

    A. settling

    B. disputes

    C. treaties

    D. accords

    E. amity

19. As part of the tax audit, Mark was required to hand over all documents that _____ to his income for the past five years.

    A. pertained

    B. concerned

    C. related

    D. taxed

    E. align

Question 20 is based on the following passage.

The host always goes out into the front hall and shakes hands with every one who arrives. He asks the guests if they want to be shown to their rooms, and, if not, sees that the gentlemen who come without valets give their keys to the butler or footman, and that the ladies without *Line* maids of their own give theirs to the maid who is on duty for the purpose.

5   Should any of them feel dusty or otherwise "untidy" they naturally ask if they may be shown to their rooms so that they can make themselves presentable. They should not, however, linger longer than necessary, as their hostess may become uneasy at their delay. Ladies do not—in fashionable houses—make their first appearance without a hat. Gentlemen, needless to say, leave theirs in the hall when they come in.

—excerpt from *Etiquette* by Emily Post

20. It can be inferred from the passage that the author believes that

   A. a household staff is essential for receiving guests.

   B. the valet is responsible for greeting guests properly.

   C. guests should be able to amuse themselves upon arrival.

   D. untidy guests should feel ashamed for their appearance.

   E. everyone should wear hats while visiting.

STOP!
IF YOU FINISH BEFORE THE TIME IS UP,
YOU MAY CHECK YOUR WORK IN THIS SECTION ONLY.

SECTION 3: VERBAL REASONING

30 minutes • 20 questions

(The paper-delivered test will have 25 questions to be completed in 35 minutes.)

For each question, follow the specific directions and choose the best answer.

For Questions 1–5, choose <u>one</u> answer for each blank. Select from the appropriate column for each blank. Choose the answer that best completes the sense of the text.

1. Many blamed voter _____ for the low turnout in last November's special election to fill the departing senator's seat.

A. indignation
B. apathy
C. enthusiasm
D. puritanism
E. attendance

2. In the 1960s, there was a strong public _____ attached to couples who lived together before marriage. These days, however, studies have shown that more than 50% of couples live together before getting married.

A. stigma
B. stipulation
C. consequence
D. sustenance
E. attraction

3. Although it has been popular for more than 10 years, that reality dating show has long been criticized for its glorifying of _____ contestants mindlessly vying for the attention of a man they don't even know.

A. invested
B. fascinating
C. vapid
D. beguiling
E. ecstatic

4. A mysterious maple syrup smell that would occasionally (i) _____ over New York City was determined to be caused by a New Jersey fragrance processing plant. This knowledge (ii) _____ nervous New Yorkers, who worried it might be a chemical attack.

Blank (i)	Blank (ii)
A. migratory	D. assaulted
B. waft	E. assuaged
C. outbreak	F. asserted

5. During the (i) _____ at the funeral, the pastor spoke at length about the deceased, waxing (ii) _____ about her life although he had never even met her and had heard stories secondhand.

Blank (i)	Blank (ii)
A. trilogy	D. loquaciously
B. travelogue	E. gregariously
C. eulogy	F. mendaciously

For Questions 6–20, choose only <u>one</u> answer choice unless otherwise indicated.

Questions 6–8 are based on the following passage.

Often enough, staying in a hotel in a foreign town, I have wished to sally forth and to dine or breakfast at the typical restaurant of the place, should there be one. Almost invariably I have found great difficulty in obtaining any information regarding any such restaurant.
Line The proprietor of the caravanserai at which one is staying may admit vaguely that there
5 are eating-houses in the town, but asks why one should be anxious to seek for second-class establishments when the best restaurant in the country is to be found under his roof. The hall-porter has even less scruples, and stigmatizes every feeding-place outside the hotel as a den of thieves, where the stranger foolishly venturing is certain to be poisoned and then robbed. This book is an attempt to help the man who finds himself in such a position. His
10 guide-book may possibly give him the names of the restaurants, but it does no more. My co-author and myself attempt to give him some details—what his surroundings will be, what dishes are the specialties of the house, what wine a wise man will order, and what bill he is likely to be asked to pay.

—excerpt from *The Gourmet's Guide to Europe* by Algernon Bastard and Lieut.-Col. Newnham-Davis

6. It can be inferred from the passage that the author
   A. has had frustrating dining experiences while traveling to foreign places.
   B. is the proprietor of a caravanserai, and wants to attract travelers.
   C. is very picky when it comes to choosing restaurants when traveling.
   D. does not trust the opinions of hall-porters who recommend restaurants.
   E. has been both poisoned and robbed while traveling to foreign places.

7. Which of the following is likely to be the most reliable source for information, according to the author?
   A. Hotel staff
   B. Word-of-mouth recommendations
   C. Crime reports
   D. An impartial guidebook
   E. The author's travel memoir

8. What is the primary purpose of the phrase "wise man" in line 12?

   A. It insinuates the reader is unintelligent.

   B. It insults the hotel proprietor.

   C. It flatters the reader.

   D. It emphasizes the author's feeling of inferiority.

   E. It stigmatizes ordering wine.

Questions 9–11 are based on the following passage.

    The distinctive features of Millet's art are so marked that the most inexperienced observer easily identifies his work. As a painter of rustic subjects, he is unlike any other artists who have entered the same field, even those who have taken his own themes. We get at the heart of the matter when we say that Millet derived his art directly from nature. "If I could only do what I like," he said, "I would paint nothing that was not the result of an impression directly received from nature, whether in landscape or in figure." His pictures are convincing evidence that he acted upon this theory. They have a peculiar quality of genuineness beside which all other rustic art seems forced and artificial.

    The human side of life touched him most deeply, and in many of his earlier pictures, landscape was secondary. Gradually he grew into the larger conception of a perfect harmony between man and his environment. Henceforth landscape ceased to be a mere setting or background in a figure picture, and became an organic part of the composition. As a critic once wrote of the *Shepherdess*, "the earth and sky, the scene and the actors, all answer one another, all hold together, belong together." The description applies equally well to many other pictures and particularly to the *Angelus*, the *Sower*, and the *Gleaners*. In all these, landscape and figure are interdependent, fitting together in a perfect unity.

    As a painter of landscapes, Millet mastered a wide range of the effects of changing light during different hours of the day. The mists of early morning in *Filling the Water-Bottles*; the glare of noonday in the *Gleaners*; the sunset glow in the *Angelus* and the *Shepherdess*; the sombre twilight of the Sower; and the glimmering lamplight of the Woman Sewing, each found perfect interpretation. Though showing himself capable of representing powerfully the more violent aspects of nature, he preferred as a rule the normal and quiet.

    —Excerpt from *John Francois Millet* by Estelle M. Hurll

9. All of the following are stated or implied in the passage EXCEPT that Millet

   A. was primarily a landscape painter.

   B. had an affinity for nature.

   C. prioritized human subjects over nature.

   D. captured the rustic charm of his subjects.

   E. valued authenticity in his art.

10. Select the sentence that best summarizes the passage.

    A. Human subjects are insignificant compared to landscapes.

    B. Rustic art is boring and outdated.

    C. Even experienced critics underestimate Millet.

    D. Distinctive style can sometimes hide subtle touches.

    E. Millet's landscape work was stronger than his portraits.

11. "Impression" (line 5) most nearly means

    A. a difference.

    B. a feeling.

    C. an imitation.

    D. an indentation.

    E. a premonition.

Questions 12 and 13 are based on the following passage.

    Before the close of the following year, 1885, came what was known as the "Texas Famine." Thousands of miles of wild land, forming the Pan Handle, had been suddenly opened by the building of a Southern Railroad. In the speculative anxiety of the Road to people its newly
Line acquired territory, unwarranted inducements of climatic advantages had been unscrupulously
5 held out to the poor farmers of Mississippi, Alabama, and Georgia.

    Lured by the pictures presented them, some thousands of families had been induced to leave their old, worn-out farms, and with the little they could carry or drive, reach the new Eldorado, to find a new farm that needed only the planting to make them rich, prosperous, and happy, without labor. They planted. The first year brought some returns—the second
10 was a drought with no returns—the third the same. Hunger for themselves and starvation for their stock stared them in the face. They could not pick up and go back—the rivers were dry from the Rio Grande to the Brazos—the earth was iron, and the heavens brass; cattle wandered at will for water and feed, and their bones whitened the plains.

    —excerpt from *A Story of the Red Cross* by Clara Barton

For Questions 12–13, consider each answer individually and select <u>all</u> choices that apply.

12. The passage notes each of the following as contributing factors of the Texas Famine EXCEPT:

    A. farmers with unrealistic expectations.

    B. the opening of the Southern Railroad.

    C. flooded pastures.

13. Which of the following, if it were true, would weaken the author's description of the Texas Famine?

A. Some farmers were able to successfully plant crops and manage cattle during the Texas famine.

B. Land speculators were caught and punished for convincing people to move to the Texas panhandle.

C. The drought in the Texas panhandle actually lasted less than a year.

Questions 14 and 15 are based on the following passage.

Female suffrage is a reform demanded by the social conditions of our times, by the high culture of woman, and by the aspiration of all classes of society to organize and work for the interests they have in common. We can not detain the celestial bodies in their course; neither
Line can we check any of those moral movements that gravitate with irresistible force towards their
5 center of attraction: Justice. The moral world is governed by the same laws as the physical world, and all the power of man being impotent to suppress a single molecule of the spaces required for the gravitation of the universe, it is still less able to prevent the generation of the ideas that take shape in the mind and strive to attain to fruition in the field of life and reality.

It is an interesting phenomenon that whenever an attempt is made to introduce a social
10 reform, in accordance with modern ideas and tendencies and in contradiction with old beliefs and prejudices, there is never a lack of opposition, based on the maintenance of the status quo, which it is desired to preserve at any cost. As was to be expected, the eternal calamity howlers and false prophets of evil raise their fanatical voices on this present occasion, in protest against female suffrage, invoking the sanctity of the home and the necessity of perpetuating
15 customs that have been observed for many years.

—Excerpt from *The Woman and the Right to Vote* by Rafael Palma

14. "Generation" (line 7) most nearly means

A. group.

B. cohort.

C. creation.

D. era.

E. batch.

15. Which of the following is most similar in reasoning to the ideas expressed in the final sentence?

A. Allowing women to vote would have devastating consequences.

B. Arguments against suffrage are overdramatic and overblown.

C. Supporters of suffrage are afraid to change the status quo.

D. Protesters against suffrage are more realistic than supporters are.

E. Culture should be preserved, no matter what the cost.

For **Questions 16–19**, choose the <u>two</u> answers that best fit the meaning of the sentence as a whole and result in two completed sentences that are alike in meaning.

16. After the actress's foul-mouthed _____ against her assistant went viral, she was fired from her TV show.
    - **A.** confab
    - **B.** tirade
    - **C.** commendation
    - **D.** harangue
    - **E.** agitate

17. One of the most famous monarchs to _____ the throne was England's Edward VIII, whose marriage to American commoner and divorcee Wallis Simpson would not be sanctioned by the Church of England.
    - **A.** abdicate
    - **B.** postulate
    - **C.** abandoned
    - **D.** relinquishing
    - **E.** renounce

18. The late New York Yankees catcher Yogi Berra is famous for his slightly off-center _____ like, "If you come to a fork in the road, take it!"
    - **A.** aphids
    - **B.** apocrypha
    - **C.** maxims
    - **D.** dictations
    - **E.** dictums

19. After keeping passengers stuck on the tarmac for more than two hours, the airline attempted to _____ passengers with an extra round of free snacks.
    - **A.** mollify
    - **B.** mortify
    - **C.** prevaricate
    - **D.** placate
    - **E.** fabricate

Question 20 is based on the following passage.

The causes of hostility among nations are innumerable. There are some which have a general and almost constant operation upon the collective bodies of society. Of this description are the love of power or the desire of pre-eminence and dominion—the jealousy of power, or
Line the desire of equality and safety. There are others which have a more circumscribed though
5 an equally operative influence within their spheres. Such are the rivalships and competitions of commerce between commercial nations. And there are others, not less numerous than either of the former, which take their origin entirely in private passions; in the attachments, enmities, interests, hopes, and fears of leading individuals in the communities of which they are members. Men of this class, whether the favorites of a king or of a people, have in too
10 many instances abused the confidence they possessed; and assuming the pretext of some public motive, have not scrupled to sacrifice the national tranquillity to personal advantage or personal gratification.

—excerpt from *Federalist Paper #6* by Alexander Hamilton

20. All of the following are mentioned as causes of international hostility EXCEPT:

   A. lust for power.
   B. economic conflicts.
   C. personal gratification.
   D. abuse of power.
   E. public scruples.

STOP!
IF YOU FINISH BEFORE THE TIME IS UP,
YOU MAY CHECK YOUR WORK IN THIS SECTION ONLY.

SECTION 4: QUANTITATIVE REASONING

35 minutes • 20 questions

(The paper-delivered test will have 25 questions to be completed in 40 minutes.)

For each question, follow the specific directions and choose the best answer.

The test maker provides the following information that applies to all questions in the Quantitative Reasoning section of the GRE® General Test:

- All numbers used are real numbers.

- All figures are assumed to lie in a plane unless otherwise indicated.

- Geometric figures, such as lines, circles, triangles, and quadrilaterals, *are not necessarily* drawn to scale. That is, you should *not* assume that quantities such as lengths and angle measures are as they appear in a figure. You should assume, however, that lines shown as straight are actually straight, points on a line are in the order shown, and more generally, all geometric objects are in the relative positions shown. For questions with geometric figures, you should base your answers on geometric reasoning, not on estimating or comparing quantities by sight or by measurement.

- Coordinate systems, such as xy-planes and number lines, *are* drawn to scale. Therefore, you can read, estimate, or compare quantities in such figures by sight or by measurement.

- Graphical data presentations, such as bar graphs, circle graphs, and line graphs, *are* drawn to scale. Therefore, you can read, estimate, or compare data values by sight or by measurement.

For Questions 1–8, compare Quantity A and Quantity B. Some questions will have additional information above the two quantities to use in determining your answer.

1.
Quantity A	Quantity B
(400)(30)(2,000)	(300)(8,000)

   A. Quantity A is greater.

   B. Quantity B is greater.

   C. The two quantities are equal.

   D. The relationship cannot be determined from the information given.

2.

$$x \neq 0, \ x + y = 0$$

Quantity A	Quantity B
x	y

A. Quantity A is greater.

B. Quantity B is greater.

C. The two quantities are equal.

D. The relationship cannot be determined from the information given.

3.

Quantity A	Quantity B
$\dfrac{1}{17^{\frac{3}{2}}}$	$\dfrac{1}{64}$

A. Quantity A is greater.

B. Quantity B is greater.

C. The two quantities are equal.

D. The relationship cannot be determined from the information given.

4.   Bank A pays 3% simple annual interest. Bank B pays 4% simple annual interest.

Quantity A	Quantity B
$100 invested at Bank A for 4 years	$100 invested at Bank B for 3 years

A. Quantity A is greater.

B. Quantity B is greater.

C. The two quantities are equal.

D. The relationship cannot be determined from the information given.

5. x, y, and z are consecutive integers

Quantity A	Quantity B
xz	y^2

A. Quantity A is greater.

B. Quantity B is greater.

C. The two quantities are equal.

D. The relationship cannot be determined from the information given.

6.

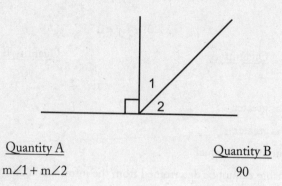

Quantity A	Quantity B
m∠1 + m∠2	90

A. Quantity A is greater.

B. Quantity B is greater.

C. The two quantities are equal.

D. The relationship cannot be determined from the information given.

7.

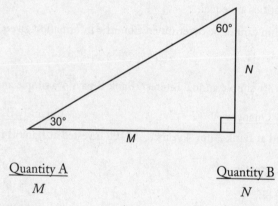

Quantity A	Quantity B
M	N

A. Quantity A is greater.

B. Quantity B is greater.

C. The two quantities are equal.

D. The relationship cannot be determined from the information given.

8.   Team A has 12 wins and has won 60% of its games.
Team B has 14 wins and has lost 30% of its games.

Quantity A	Quantity B
The number of games played by Team A	The number of games played by Team B

A. Quantity A is greater.

B. Quantity B is greater.

C. The two quantities are equal.

D. The relationship cannot be determined from the information given.

Questions 9–20 have several formats. Unless the directions state otherwise, choose one answer choice. For the Numeric Entry questions, follow the instructions below.

Numeric Entry Questions

The following items are the same for both the computer-delivered and the paper-delivered test. However, those taking the computer-delivered test will have additional information about entering answers in decimal and fraction boxes on the computer screen. Those taking the paper-delivered test will have information about entering answers on answer grids.

•   Your answer may be an integer, a decimal, or a fraction, and it may be negative.

•   If a question asks for a fraction, there will be two boxes. One box will be for the numerator and one will be for the denominator.

•   Equivalent forms of the correct answer, such as 2.5 and 2.50, are all correct.

•   Enter the exact answer unless the question asks you to round your answers.

9.   The diagonal of a square has length $5\sqrt{2}$.   **SHOW YOUR WORK HERE**

What is its perimeter?

A. 5

B. 20

C. $20\sqrt{2}$

D. 25

E. 40

10.   Avocados are sold at 3 for $5 and mangos are sold at 2 for $3. What is the cost of 7 avocados and 7 mangos?

A. $3.17

B. $8.00

C. $21.00

D. $22.17

E. $56.00

11. If x and y have a mean of 6, and u, v, and w have a mean of 9, what is the mean of u, v, w, x, and y?

   A. 7.2

   B. 7.5

   C. 7.8

   D. 15

   E. 19.5

12. Two fair six-sided dice with faces numbered 1, 2, 3, 4, 5, and 6 are rolled. What is the probability that at least one of the dice shows a 3?

   A. $\dfrac{1}{36}$

   B. $\dfrac{1}{6}$

   C. $\dfrac{5}{18}$

   D. $\dfrac{11}{36}$

   E. $\dfrac{1}{3}$

13. The two legs of a right triangle have lengths 12 and 16. What is the length of the hypotenuse?

   A. 5.3

   B. 14

   C. 20

   D. 28

   E. 400

SHOW YOUR WORK HERE

14. A car rental company charges $14 per day plus $0.25 per mile. Another company charges $40 per day but does not have an additional mileage charge. If you are renting a car for 6 days, how many miles would you have to drive for the costs of renting from the two companies to be equal?

   A. 39
   B. 104
   C. 208
   D. 624
   E. 904

15. Line A passes through the points $(3, 7)$ and $(-2, 1)$. Line B is perpendicular to Line A and passes through the origin. What of the following equations represents Line B?

   A. $y = -\dfrac{5}{6}x$

   B. $y = -\dfrac{6}{5}x$

   C. $y = \dfrac{6}{5}x$

   D. $y = \dfrac{5}{6}x$

   E. $y = \dfrac{5}{6}x + 1$

SHOW YOUR WORK HERE

Questions 16 and 17 refer to the table below.

x	$f(x)$	$g(x)$
−1	−4	−5
0	1	−1
1	8	0
2	3	2
3	2	1

16. Evaluate $f(g(0))$.

   A. −5

   B. −4

   C. −1

   D. 0

   E. 8

17. What is the average rate of change of $g(x)$ between $x = -1$ and $x = 3$?

   A. −5

   B. $-\dfrac{3}{2}$

   C. 1

   D. $\dfrac{3}{2}$

   E. 6

For Question 18, choose all that apply.

18. Which of the following values are NOT in the domain of $h(x) = \dfrac{\sqrt{x+5}}{x-1}$?

   A. −7

   B. −5

   C. −3

   D. −1

   E. 1

   F. 3

   G. 5

   H. 7

For Questions 19 and 20, enter your answers in the boxes.

19. What is the sum of the positive prime integers between 2 and 20, inclusive?

    ┌──────────┐
    │   │
    └──────────┘

20. The height of a ball thrown upwards from a height of 6 feet at a speed of 96 feet per second is given by the function

    $h(t) = -16t^2 + 96t + 6,$

    where t is the time in seconds since the ball was thrown and h is its height in feet. What is the maximum height reached by the ball, in feet?

    ┌──────────┐
    │   │
    └──────────┘

STOP!
IF YOU FINISH BEFORE THE TIME IS UP,
YOU MAY CHECK YOUR WORK IN THIS SECTION ONLY.

practice test 4

SECTION 5: QUANTITATIVE REASONING

35 minutes • 20 questions

(The paper-delivered version will have 25 questions to be completed in 40 minutes.)

For each question, follow the specific directions and choose the best answer.

> The test maker provides the following information that applies to all questions in the Quantitative Reasoning section of the GRE® General Test:
>
> - All numbers used are real numbers.
>
> - All figures are assumed to lie in a plane unless otherwise indicated.
>
> - Geometric figures, such as lines, circles, triangles, and quadrilaterals, *are not necessarily* drawn to scale. That is, you should *not* assume that quantities such as lengths and angle measures are as they appear in a figure. You should assume, however, that lines shown as straight are actually straight, points on a line are in the order shown, and more generally, all geometric objects are in the relative positions shown. For questions with geometric figures, you should base your answers on geometric reasoning, not on estimating or comparing quantities by sight or by measurement.
>
> - Coordinate systems, such as *xy*-planes and number lines, *are* drawn to scale. Therefore, you can read, estimate, or compare quantities in such figures by sight or by measurement.
>
> - Graphical data presentations, such as bar graphs, circle graphs, and line graphs, *are* drawn to scale. Therefore, you can read, estimate, or compare data values by sight or by measurement.

For Questions 1–9, compare Quantity A and Quantity B. Some questions will have additional information above the two quantities to use in determining your answer.

1.
Quantity A	Quantity B
$\dfrac{1}{2^{-3}}$	$\dfrac{1}{3^{-2}}$

A. Quantity A is greater.

B. Quantity B is greater.

C. The two quantities are equal.

D. The relationship cannot be determined from the information given.

2.
$$S = \{19, 21, 23, 25, 27\}$$

<u>Quantity A</u>

The mean of the numbers in S

<u>Quantity B</u>

The median of the numbers in S

A. Quantity A is greater.

B. Quantity B is greater.

C. The two quantities are equal.

D. The relationship cannot be determined from the information given.

3.
$$x > 20$$

<u>Quantity A</u>

$\sqrt[5]{32}$

<u>Quantity B</u>

$\sqrt[4]{x}$

A. Quantity A is greater.

B. Quantity B is greater.

C. The two quantities are equal.

D. The relationship cannot be determined from the information given.

4.
m and n are solutions to the equation $x^2 - 5x - 14 = 0$, and $m \neq n$

<u>Quantity A</u>

$m + n$

<u>Quantity B</u>

mn

A. Quantity A is greater.

B. Quantity B is greater.

C. The two quantities are equal.

D. The relationship cannot be determined from the information given.

5.
A fair coin is flipped twice.

<u>Quantity A</u>

The probability of getting heads twice

<u>Quantity B</u>

The probability of getting heads and then tails

A. Quantity A is greater.

B. Quantity B is greater.

C. The two quantities are equal.

D. The relationship cannot be determined from the information given.

6. $x < 0$, y is a positive odd integer.

Quantity A   Quantity B

$y - x$ x^y

A. Quantity A is greater.

B. Quantity B is greater.

C. The two quantities are equal.

D. The relationship cannot be determined from the information given.

7.   A circle has a radius of 12.

Quantity A   Quantity B

The area of a 60° sector of the circle   The perimeter of the circle

A. Quantity A is greater.

B. Quantity B is greater.

C. The two quantities are equal.

D. The relationship cannot be determined from the information given.

8.   A rectangle has a perimeter of 20.

Quantity A   Quantity B

The area of the rectangle   20

A. Quantity A is greater.

B. Quantity B is greater.

C. The two quantities are equal.

D. The relationship cannot be determined from the information given.

9.   Quantity A   Quantity B

$4^{\left(3^2\right)}$ $\left(4^3\right)^2$

A. Quantity A is greater.

B. Quantity B is greater.

C. The two quantities are equal.

D. The relationship cannot be determined from the information given.

Questions 10–20 have several formats. Unless the directions state otherwise, choose one answer choice. For the Numeric Entry questions, follow the instructions below.

Numeric Entry Questions

The following items are the same for both the computer-delivered and paper-delivered tests. However, those taking the computer-delivered test will have additional information about entering answers in decimal and fraction boxes on the computer screen. Those taking the paper-delivered test will have information about entering answers on answer grids.

- Your answer may be an integer, a decimal, or a fraction, and it may be negative.

- If a question asks for a fraction, there will be two boxes. One box will be for the numerator and one will be for the denominator.

- Equivalent forms of the correct answer, such as 2.5 and 2.50, are all correct.

- Enter the exact answer unless the question asks you to round your answers.

10. Starting from her house, Kendra walks 3 miles north, 6 miles east, 1 mile south, and 1 mile west. How far from her house is she?

   A. 5.39 miles

   B. 6.71 miles

   C. 7.00 miles

   D. 8.06 miles

   E. 29.00 miles

11. Among the 450 students in a high school senior class, 150 take AP Calculus, 78 take AP Chemistry, and 49 take both. How many students do not take either AP Calculus or AP Chemistry?

   A. 130

   B. 173

   C. 179

   D. 222

   E. 271

12. Solve for x: $\sqrt{x + 5} = x - 1$

   A. −1

   B. 2 or −3

   C. 4

   D. −1 or 4

   E. No solution

SHOW YOUR WORK HERE

Questions 13–15 refer to the chart below.   **SHOW YOUR WORK HERE**

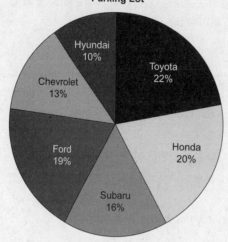

Cars Counted in a Large Parking Lot

13. If there were 48 Subaru cars in the parking lot, how many cars were there altogether?

     A.   48

     B.   100

     C.   252

     D.   300

     E.   3000

14. If there were 600 cars in the parking lot, how many Hyundai and Toyota cars were there?

     A.   60

     B.   132

     C.   192

     D.   408

     E.   600

15. What is the ratio of Hyundai cars to Honda cars?

   A. $\dfrac{1}{2}$

   B. $\dfrac{2}{1}$

   C. $\dfrac{1}{10}$

   D. $\dfrac{1}{5}$

   E. $\dfrac{5}{11}$

For Questions 16 and 17, choose <u>all</u> that apply.

16. Find the next three numbers in the sequence:
2, 6, 12, 20, 30, …

   A. 40

   B. 42

   C. 56

   D. 64

   E. 72

   F. 90

17. Which of the following equations are true for all real-number values of x and y?

   A. $x + y = y + x$

   B. $x - 2y = y - 2x$

   C. $xy + x + 1 = (x + 1)(y + 1) - y$

   D. $\sqrt{xy} = \sqrt{x}\sqrt{y}$

   E. $(x + y)^2 = x^2 + y^2$

SHOW YOUR WORK HERE

For Questions 18–20, enter your answers in the boxes.

18. Brittany is 5 years older than Marla. When the sum of their ages is 45, Marla will be twice as old as Brittany is now. How old is Marla now?

    ☐

19. If $(x + 3)^2 = 16$ and $x^3 < 0$, what is the value of x^2?

    ☐

20. Srikar can speed read 45 pages in 25 minutes. To the nearest minute, how long will it take him to read a 98-page book?

    ☐

STOP!
IF YOU FINISH BEFORE THE TIME IS UP,
YOU MAY CHECK YOUR WORK IN THIS SECTION ONLY.

ANSWER KEYS AND EXPLANATIONS

Section 1: Analytical Writing

Analyze an Issue

Model: 6 points out of 6

It's a data-driven world these days—we just live in it. People are often just a collection of data points, with retailers and websites having a clear picture of who we are and what we like, even if they never meet us face to face. And unfortunately, these data profiles that follow us around as we browse online or network with friends on social media are often created without us realizing it, and without us knowing who is using that data. Companies that collect extensive user data have an obligation to let people know how their personal information is being used, and also to allow people to opt out of this invasive harvesting.

The data may technically "belong" to the companies, but users should be able to see and understand the extent to which their personal information has been compromised. It's not such an innocent game. People lose millions of dollars to identity theft each year, and personal data stolen or misused from legitimate online sites is a major contributor to that problem.

On an individual basis, we may never know the extent of the information that is collected on sites like Facebook or Twitter. With our friends and our friends-of-friends contributing to this invisible profile as well, it seems like a Sisyphean task to get a handle on what information about each person is out there in the data world. The first step in helping people take control of their own data is holding companies accountable for more visibility.

Although the fine print in user agreements theoretically tells the consumer what they're signing up for, the reality is that very few people understand what is being collected, and how it will be used. Social media sites should be required make each user's collected personal data available for the user's review, even if the user ultimately has little control over what information is stored.

Additionally, companies should also disclose how this data is being used—whether that's internally for user metrics, or selling it to external parties. Again, the data may belong to the platform, given that users sign up on an entirely voluntary basis. However, the opacity of what the companies do with this information is extremely problematic.

A social media platform may be legally entitled to sell my information to the highest ad bidder, but when it's done without my knowledge, I feel betrayed and it's a poor business practice. I may be a "free" user who doesn't pay to use the site, but I'm still a customer, and have the ability to cancel my account and go elsewhere. Having ultimate power over users does not mean it's smart to use that power without regard for the people involved.

This response scores 6 out of 6 for the following reasons:

- **It answers the task.** The writer clearly and directly challenges the statement in the prompt by saying that although the social media sites may own the data, they have additional obligations to their users. It's a nuanced disagreement, instead of saying "I disagree, and here's why."

- **It is well supported.** The writer uses examples like identity theft and incomprehensible user agreements to support her disagreement with the prompt's thesis.

- **It is well organized.** The introduction clearly expresses the writer's opinion, and each paragraph contains a separate supporting point.

- **It is fluid and precise.** Sentences range in complexity. The vocabulary is sophisticated, and the tone is appropriate for the audience.

- **It observes the conventions of Standard Written English.** There are a few small grammatical errors, but none that interfere with the coherence or readability of the essay.

Model: 3 points out of 6

There's no such thing as a free lunch. That's something I learned from my grandmother, and it's something I carry with me always. When you sign up, you're signing up for whatever the site wants to do with your information. It's right there in the fine print. If you're not paying to use a social media site (a product), you are the product. I agree that user data belongs to whatever owns the social media platform.

Signing up for a Twitter account is easy for a reason. They want you do sign on the dotted line and not look back. It's on you to read on the fine print and see what they can do with your data. Once you've signed up, your data no longer belongs to you, because again…there's no such thing as a free lunch.

There's no expectation anymore of privacy online anymore. This isn't 1998 anymore. People aren't using dial-up to access their favorite websites. Tracking cookies follow us everywhere we go online, and they report back to their owners. We have no way of seeing what information is tracked, so why hold the social media sites responsible for what everyone else is doing?

This response scores 3 out of 6 for the following reasons:

- **It answers the task in a limited way.** The writer clearly agrees with the prompt, but the information is presented without a sophisticated argument as to why.

- **It offers inadequate support.** Although the writer uses specific examples like Twitter and the fine print in user agreements, these are not really developed into a coherent argument.

- **It lacks organization.** The essay rambles, and the supporting paragraphs contain very little information beyond generalizations.

- **It is only moderately fluid and is not precise.** Most of the sentences are readable, but some lack coherence. The writer tends to repeat words and phrases.

- **It contains errors in the conventions of Standard Written English.** There are a number of distracting errors, which make some of the writer's points difficult to understand.

Model: 1 point out of 6

People who use free social media sites SHOULD have an expectation of data piracy. When I sign up. I expect that my personnel information will be, secure. I mean what is this the Wild West? My information belongs to me, end of story. If I thought my personnel information would be used for bad things I would never sign up I would tell my friends to do the same. You're information belongs to you.

This response scores 1 out of 6 for the following reasons:

- **It barely answers the task.** The writer expresses an opinion, but starts by simply restating the prompt with one simple change. The argument presented is simplistic and unsophisticated.

- **It is not supported.** Very little support is provided for the writer's opinion.

- **It has no sense of sentence construction.** The second sentence has a misplaced comma. The third and fifth sentences are run-ons.

- **It contains major errors in the conventions of Standard Written English.** There are numerous spelling, word usage, and grammar errors that make the essay difficult to read.

Analyze an Argument

Model: 6 points out of 6

A universal basic income sounds like the solution to so many of the world's problems. People tend to get caught in cycles of poverty that become difficult to escape, leaving them working two or three part-time jobs just to make ends meet. However, as the author suggests, the unintended consequences of raising the minimum wage—without necessarily resolving underlying issues—mean that may not be the panacea we think it is.

A key assumption on which this argument rests is that more money does not automatically resolve the issues that cause and perpetuate poverty. Proponents of a universal minimum wage likely believe that more money in the pockets of workers means that there will be more economic growth. Yet what this counterargument ignores is that the cost of living is likely to keep growing as well, out-pacing even the comfort zone afforded by a $15 minimum wage as opposed, to, say $10. The author understands that economic growth isn't just fueled by having more money out there and being spent.

The author's point that investments in community-building, housing, and skill development would be money better spent is one that has roots in the American Dream. In that old concept, people take what resources they have, and use those to better themselves and move up in the world. Although the realities of day-to-day life, especially for low-income people, can make "moving up" difficult, the ideal should still be creating an environment where people can thrive. Supportive communities, and affordable housing can make long-term development easier for people trying to break the cycle of poverty.

The argument is on its most solid basis when advocating for a more social, rather than monetary, approach to resolving the issue. However, there should be more economic analysis around the direct impact of such a change to the minimum wage. For example, Norway recently implemented a policy that guaranteed its citizens a basic yearly income. Yet the program was recently rolled back due to the unforeseen economic impacts (and not in the direction they'd hoped). The author also assumes that business owners are impacted by a minimum wage, but with no details about how this can affect hiring or business practices, we're limited to the social perspective on a universal minimum wage.

Ultimately, I agree with the author's overall assessment that there is no such thing as a quick-fix for such an entrenched problem like poverty. "$15 for all" makes a great slogan, but as the author is quick to point out, it doesn't tell the whole story.

This response scores 6 out of 6 for the following reasons:

- **It answers the task.** The writer clearly understands the argument being conveyed, and acknowledges where he or she agrees with it.

- **It is well supported.** The writer brings in real-world examples to assess the strength of the argument and show what could be improved upon in the original argument.

- **It is well organized.** The analysis draws on strong evidence to support the original argument.

- **It is fluid and precise.** Sentences range in complexity. The vocabulary is sophisticated, and the tone is appropriate for the audience.

- **It observes the conventions of Standard Written English.** There are a few small grammatical errors, but none that interfere with the coherence or readability of the essay.

Model: 3 points out of 6

I just don't agree that a universal minimum wage in this country is a problem rather than a benefit. Has the author ever worked a minimum wage fast food job? I doubt it. It seems like he's sitting in an ivory tower, getting paid a nice salary to think of ways to help the corporate business owner and not the workers who actually get things done.

It mentions that money should be pored into the community to change poverty, not given to the people themselves. Wheres the trust here? Are people not smart enough to use their $15 hourly for what they need to better there lives? Quite frankly I found this argument insulting. $10,000 to a community center is nice, but it does very little for a specific person or family. A fair minimum wage does more by putting money into the hands of people who need it, and what are already working hard for it.

This response scores 3 out of 6 for the following reasons:

- **It answers the task in a limited way.** The writer is very clear in his or her disagreement with the premise of the argument, but it becomes more of a personal response to the topic itself rather than a response to the original argument.

- **It offers inadequate support.** There are very few supporting points given. The writer makes a good point about how the author assumes giving money to the community is automatically better than paying individuals more, but it gets lost.

- **It lacks organization.** There is very little rhyme or reason to the paragraphs, with no specific structure.

- **It is only moderately fluid and is not precise.** Most of the sentences are readable, but there's an overall lack of coherence that makes the essay difficult to follow.

- **It contains errors in the conventions of Standard Written English.** There are a number of distracting errors, which make some of the writer's points difficult to understand.

Model: 1 point out of 6

Could not a gree more! Everyone wants what they can't have. If you want a job that pay's more, get that job! You want to stay in a dead end job, then fine. Its not on me or anyone else to give you more money to do that. The author makes very good points on the subject. And I wouldn't change one of them.

This response scores 1 out of 6 for the following reasons:

- **It barely answers the task.** The writer expresses personal opinions on the topic and seems to agree with how the argument is presented, but never analyzes the original argument.

- **It is not supported.** Very little support is provided for the writer's opinion.

- **It has no sense of sentence construction.** This is written in a stream-of-consciousness kind of way, with little regard to how the sentences are written or arranged.

- **It contains major errors in the conventions of Standard Written English.** There are numerous spelling, word usage, and grammar errors that make the essay difficult to read.

Section 2: Verbal Reasoning

1. C	6. D	11. D	16. A, E
2. A	7. A	12. A, C	17. B, D
3. C, D	8. D	13. D	18. C, D
4. A, E	9. B	14. B	19. A, C
5. B, E, I	10. B	15. A, B	20. E

1. **The correct answer is C.** Based on the word *despite*, you know the word in the blank should have a meaning that is contrary to the implication of "fake news." In this case, the word *abreast* makes the most sense. *Avoidant* and *heedless* (choices A and E) suggest that people are not using social media to stay informed about the news. *Apprehensive* (choice B) would be more appropriate if it were made clear that the idea of fake news causes anxiety. *Compassionate* (choice D) does not make sense in this context.

2. **The correct answer is A.** *Ephemeral* means something that lasts for a very short time—which fits with the rest of the sentence. *Procedural* (choice B) describes the official way something is done, which doesn't really fit with the rest of the sentence. An *epidural* (choice C) is a medical pain relieving treatment, which doesn't relate to the context here. *Epochal* (choice D) describes a significant or momentous period of time, and the rest of the sentence does not support the idea that the victory was momentous—just temporary. *Unequivocal* (choice E) means that there is no doubt, which is untrue based on the information that comes later in the sentence.

3. **The correct answers are C and D.** Answer Blank (i): A *subpoena* is the only option that makes sense with the given word *compelled*. *Recusal* (choice A) means to "bow out," and *whim* (choice B) suggests that it was her own idea—not that she was "compelled" to come to court.

   Answer Blank (ii): *Recant* is a legal term that describes taking back a confession or testimony, which works with the context of the sentence. *Recalibrated* (choice E) typically means to make mechanical changes. *Reiterated* (choice F) means to restate, which does not make sense given that the prosecution has to withdraw the charges.

4. **The correct answers are A and E.** Answer Blank (i): From the context of the sentence, the writer appears to be largely agreeing with the professor's comments about George Washington. *Salient* means "important," which works in the sentence. *Recalcitrant* (choice B) usually has a negative connotation and suggests disagreement. *Nascent* means "emerging" or "beginning," which does not fit with the context of the sentence.

   Answer Blank (ii): *However* tells you that the writer is about to show a change from the previous statements. *Remark* (choice D) and *concur* (choice F) don't really work, because they both show either positive or neutral agreement, whereas *quibble* (choice E) means that the writer is going to show minor disagreement.

5. **The correct answers are B, E, and I.** Answer Blank (i): The context suggests that Hamlet is the only one speaking, which makes *dialogue* (choice A) unlikely. A *manifesto* (choice C) can be the work of a solo person, but given that *soliloquy* (choice B) means a monologue, it fits the theater context more fully.

Answer Blank (ii): Hamlet is considering a painful choice, so *morose* fits the tone best out of the options. *Sanguineous* (choice D) means "optimistic," and *foolhardy* (choice F) means "reckless," which both seem the opposite of Hamlet's mood.

Answer blank (iii): The writer is setting up a juxtaposition between what Hamlet was like before and who he is now, so *mirthful* (choice I) is the best option to illustrate how much Hamlet has changed.

6. **The correct answer is D.** The author clearly prioritizes the natural qualities of the land over the legal ownership of it. When he states that the poet is the one who can truly appreciate the land, he is suggesting that true appreciation transcends everyday concerns like ownership. Choice A is the opposite of what the author appears to be saying about the land, and choice B runs contrary to the idea that the "poet" is the true connoisseur of the land. Choice C is close to what the author is saying, but there's nothing in the passage that suggests the author wants to change the legal ownership of the land. Choice E doesn't quite work because the passage does not make any specific recommendations for land owners.

7. **The correct answer is A.** The author says that nature has *not* become a toy to a wise spirit, suggesting that nature isn't something that can be bought, played with, and owned like a toy could be. Although the author does mention childhood, he is not comparing childhood with adulthood (choices B and E). There is not enough information in the passage to infer that the author is talking about the fragility of nature (choice D).

8. **The correct answer is D.** While the author suggests that the poet is more able to appreciate the beauty of the land, the author does not seem to believe that *only* poets can appreciate the land (choices C and E), or that they're inherently better than farmers (choice A). Choice B disputes legal ownership, which is not an idea expressed in the passage.

9. **The correct answer is B.** The second paragraph outlines the ways in which enemies, former friends, and new subjects can't be trusted to help a new ruler maintain power. The sentence "A new ruler has very little support that he can rely upon" supports the premise of the author's argument in the first paragraph that "men change masters willingly."

10. **The correct answer is B.** The root verb *vex* means "to bother or irritate," so *vexatious* most nearly means "bothersome." *Well-liked* (choice A) has the opposite meaning, which doesn't fit if you look at the context of the sentence. The sentence describes how the inhabitants feel about the prince, and given that the passage talks about how fickle they can be, it is unlikely that the rule is lengthy (choice D). Choices C and E are unlikely given the context—the passage is more about the political issues than the personal qualities of the prince himself, and there is no information that suggests he is scary or cruel.

11. **The correct answer is D.** The passage talks about how a prince in a new monarchy is subject to pressure and dangers on virtually all sides, which destabilizes the role (choice D). Choice A is incorrect because the second sentence suggests that the natural state is chaos and change, rather than accepting of new leadership. Choices C and E are also incorrect because while the prince may feel unhappy with the challenges of his new monarchy, and the rule is difficult, the author does not discuss the prince's personal feelings or suggest that ruling is impossible.

12. **The correct answers are A and C.** Choices A and C emphasize the writer's idea that the reactions to punishment and injury are not necessarily rational, but are instinctual like an animal's. Choice B is incorrect because the author is using animals to highlight the nature of human reactions, not necessarily to judge or compare humans versus animals.

13. **The correct answer is D.** Although the usual definition of *incident* is an occurrence or event, you need to make sure you're considering the context of the passage. The author is using the word as an adjective, which eliminates choices A and B. Choice C means the opposite of what the author is saying (that resentment and vengeance are unavoidable in life). Choice E doesn't work because resentment and vengeance do not depend on life, they exist in it.

14. **The correct answer is B.** The author compares the torches to the candles in a Catholic Church that are meant to protect certain people. Choice A is not supported by the passage. Purifying young people (choice C) is mentioned as part of the festival, but it has nothing to do with the lamps. Choices D and E describe rituals related to Diana, but not necessarily the lamps found at the shrine.

15. **The correct answers are A and B.** The passage states that although Diana was considered the goddess of the hunt, "dogs were crowned and wild beasts were not molested," which suggests that there were no animal sacrifices. Choice B is correct as well because although there were torches dedicated to the emperor and his family at the shrine, this is not mentioned as a tribute specific to Diana.

16. **The correct answers are A and E.** The sentence contrasts the house with "splendor," which suggests that the house is not big or impressive-looking. *Modest* and *unassuming* both describe something that is lacking in dazzle. The sentence is describing how the house looks, so *expensive* (choice D) doesn't fit. Both *monstrous* (choice C) and *magnificent* (choice B) would be too similar to *splendor* to set up a proper contrast.

17. **The correct answers are B and D.** The word in the blank should be an adjective describing "style," and the words *roundabout* and *oblique* describe the less than direct lecture. Choice A means the opposite of what the writer is trying to convey about the professor's style. Choice C is unlikely because the writer does not seem to be especially impressed by the professor's lecture, so the tone is off. Choice E is incorrect because a syllabus implies that an outline was followed, and the professor followed one tangent after another instead.

18. **The correct answers are C and D.** *Treaties* and *accords* are synonyms that mean "peaceful agreements." *Settling* (choice A) does not make sense because the word in the blank needs to be a noun that represents a series of something such as an agreement. Choice B doesn't make sense because *disputes* are typically among the causes of wars. *Amity* (choice E), meaning "friendly relations between nations," is incorrect because it is not an agreement.

19. **The correct answers are A and C.** The documents Mark was required to hand over needed to pertain to or relate to his income. Since the sentence is written in past tense, *pertained* and *related* are correct. While tax documents can concern income items, the past tense form of *concerned* (choice B) is not used with the preposition to and thus does not fit into the sentence. *Taxed* (choice D) and *align* (choice E) do not make sense in the context of the sentence.

20. **The correct answer is E.** It can be inferred that the author believes that everyone should wear hats while visiting. The passage explicitly says that men should wear hats and leave them in the hall, and that women should wear a hat when they first arrive. Although the passage mentions staff members like maids, butlers, and footmen, it is clear that the host or hostess (not the valet) is most responsible for greeting guests and ensuring that they're received properly, so choices A and B are incorrect. There is no information that insinuates that guests are responsible for their own entertainment (choice C). While the passage does make suggestions directly to guests, there is no indication that the author thinks that "untidy" guests are a problem (choice D).

answers practice test 4

Section 3: Verbal Reasoning

1. B	**6.** A	**11.** B	**16.** B, D
2. A	**7.** D	**12.** C	**17.** A, E
3. C	**8.** C	**13.** A, C	**18.** C, E
4. B, E	**9.** A	**14.** C	**19.** A, D
5. C, D	**10.** D	**15.** B	**20.** E

1. **The correct answer is B.** The word in the blank is a noun that would cause people to stay away from the polls, so *apathy* is the best choice. *Indignation* (choice A) and *enthusiasm* (choice C) are unlikely to cause a low turnout. *Puritanism* (choice D) could work if there were specific details given about the election, but *apathy* works better given the context of the sentence. *Attendance* (choice E) does not make sense in the sentence.

2. **The correct answer is A.** A *stigma* is a negative reputation attached to something. *Stipulation* (choice B) is a condition. *Consequence* (choice C) is a result, which doesn't really work with the sentence. *Sustenance* (choice D) is nourishment, which doesn't fit with the sentence's meaning. *Attraction* (choice E) doesn't work because the word in the blank isn't talking about the couples themselves, but rather the public perception of them.

3. **The correct answer is C.** You can use the word *mindlessly* as the necessary context clue; the word in the blank is likely to support that imagery. *Vapid* is the best word choice, as it means "bland" or "uninspiring." *Invested* (choice A) doesn't make sense. *Fascinating* (choice B), *beguiling* (choice D), and *ecstatic* (choice E) don't make sense with the tone of the description of the contestants.

4. **The correct answers are B and E.** Answer Blank (i): All three options suggest movement, but *waft* (which means "to drift") fits the best, as it has the correct tense and the best approximate meaning given the context of the sentence. *Migratory* (choice A) is not a verb. *Outbreak* (choice C) is not usually used as a verb and is usually associated with diseases or medical issues.

Answer Blank (ii): *Assuaged* means "reassured," so choice E works best with the sentence. *Assaulted* (choice D) carries an aggressive tone that does not fit with the rest of the sentence. *Asserted* (choice F) doesn't work with the sentence, as smells are not usually associated with the verb "to assert."

5. **The correct answers are C and D.** Answer Blank (i): A *eulogy* is a speech given at a funeral, so that option matches the context of the sentence. A *trilogy* (choice A) is a series of three things, such as books or movies. A *travelogue* (choice B) is a story about one's travels.

Answer Blank (ii): "Spoke at length" is the key context phrase here. *Loquaciously* (choice D) means "highly verbal" or "talkative," which works best with the rest of the sentence. *Gregariously* (choice E) means "sociable," which doesn't fit as well with the funeral setting. *Mendaciously* (choice F) means "dishonest" and there is no information given that suggests the pastor was lying.

6. **The correct answer is A.** This question asks you to identify the author's perspective on the events described in the passage. The author uses humorous examples (possibly exaggerated) to show the need for a guidebook that gives useful information about local restaurants. Choice A is best supported by the passage, particularly the last three sentences. Choice B is untrue, as the proprietor is a person described by the author, not the author himself. Choice C is incorrect because while the passage is about finding the right restaurant, there is not enough information given about the author's own preferences. The passage uses exaggeration and humor to make the author's points, and choice E is more literal. There is nothing in the passage to suggest that these things actually happened to the author.

7. **The correct answer is D.** The author is describing the purpose of the book, and in lines 10–13 he states that "My co-author and myself attempt to give him some details—what his surroundings will be, what dishes are the specialties of the house, what wine a wise man will order, and what bill he is likely to be asked to pay." This suggests that the guidebook is the most valuable insight of all when it comes to recommending restaurants. Choices A and B are unlikely because much of the passage is spent describing how unreliable the personal recommendations can be. And although the author humorously mentions a "den of thieves" and being poisoned and robbed, it's clear that these are meant facetiously, not literally, so choice C doesn't work. The author does not give specific details about his own travels, which makes choice E not the best answer.

8. **The correct answer is C.** The author uses the phrase "wise man" to suggest that the book is offering savvy advice for a reader who wants to be that wise man. It's not a comparison between the author and the reader, so choice A is incorrect. It's not a judgment of the hotel proprietor, so choice B is also incorrect. The author is trying to present his book as a superior source of information, and there is nothing in the passage to suggest that he feels inferior (choice D). Choice E is incorrect because the author is suggesting that wise men order particular wines, while the usage of the word *stigmatizes* suggests a negative judgment.

9. **The correct answer is A.** The passage does not state or imply that Millet was primarily a landscape painter. To confirm this answer, though, you need to make sure you're looking deeper, because at several points in the passage Millet's work in landscaping is described. However, in paragraph 2, the author makes it clear that Millet was also a figure painter.

10. **The correct answer is D.** Although the passage starts with a discussion of Millet's distinctive style, most of the passage is about the subtle touches that elevate Millet's art. Choices A and E are incorrect because the passage describes Millet's figure painting as equivalent to his landscape painting. Choice B is incorrect because the author only describes rustic art in relation to Millet's rustic art versus everyone else's—there is no specific judgment about rustic art in general. Choice C is incorrect because the author is not judging other critics in this passage, simply mentioning them to show how easily identified Millet's work is.

11. **The correct answer is B.** The author is using the word *impression* to describe the feelings and inspiration Millet received from nature. While choices A, C, D, and E are all alternative meanings, none of these answer choices fit the context of the sentence.

12. **The correct answer is C.** Choice C is the opposite of what actually happened (drought). Choices A and B increased the number of farmers coming to the new land in Texas and later starving.

13. **The correct answers are A and C.** The passage focuses on the events of the famine itself. But if a number of farmers were not affected by the drought (choice A), or if the drought lasted less than a year (choice C), then the author's description would be significantly less dramatic. If the unscrupulous land speculators were punished for sending people into the famine zone (choice B), it wouldn't affect the description of what actually happened during the famine.

14. **The correct answer is C.** In this case, *generation* is used as a verb so it most nearly means "creation" rather than describing a group of people (choices A and B), a specific time period (choice D), or a single stage of development (choice E).

15. **The correct answer is B.** The author uses strong language ("calamity howlers and false prophets") to illustrate how intense the rhetoric is on the anti-sufferage side of the issue. Choices A and E are untrue, because the author is arguing the opposite. Choices C and D are not supported by any part of the passage.

16. **The correct answers are B and D.** The best context clue is "foul-mouthed," so the best word choices are unlikely to be positive. The words *tirade* (choice B) and *harangue* (choice D) are the best choices. *Confab* (choice A) means an informal meeting, which doesn't quite match the tone of the sentence. *Commendation* (choice C) is positive in tone and therefore not the best answer choice in this context. *Agitate* (choice E) could match tone-wise, but the word in the blank is a noun, not a verb.

17. **The correct answers are A and E.** *Abdicate* and *renounce* both mean "to step down," which fits with the context of the sentence. *Postulate* (choice B) has the opposite meaning of step down. Choices C and D are inappropriate because they have the incorrect tense; the infinitive *to* suggests that the verb in the blank will be a simple present-tense verb, not past tense or the present participle.

18. **The correct answers are C and E.** *Maxims* and *dictums* are short statements that represent truisms about life. *Aphids* (choice A) are insects. An *apocrypha* (choice B) is a statement of uncertain origin, which doesn't make sense with the sentence. *Dictations* (choice D) are writings based on speech, which also doesn't make sense with the sentence.

19. **The correct answers are A and D.** *Mollify* and *placate* both mean "to appease." *Mortify* (choice B) means "to embarrass," which doesn't make sense with the sentence. *Fabricate* (choice E) means "to create" or "to falsify," and neither of which works in the sentence.

20. **The correct answer is E.** Public scruples are not mentioned as a cause of international hostility, so choice E is correct. Choice A is mentioned in the third sentence. Choice B is mentioned in the fifth sentence. Choices C and D are described in the seventh sentence.

Section 4: Quantitative Reasoning

1. A	**6.** C	**11.** C	**16.** B
2. D	**7.** A	**12.** D	**17.** D
3. B	**8.** C	**13.** C	**18.** A, E
4. C	**9.** B	**14.** D	**19.** 77
5. B	**10.** D	**15.** A	**20.** 150

1. **The correct answer is A.** Quantity A is equal to 24,000,000, and Quantity B is equal to 2,400,000.

2. **The correct answer is D.** Since $x + y = 0$, x and y are opposites; one is positive, and one is negative. However, based on the information given, there is no way to know which one is positive, and that is the one that will be greater.

3. **The correct answer is B.** First note that $17^{\frac{3}{2}} = \left(\sqrt{17}\right)^3$. Now $\sqrt{17} > 4$, so this is greater than $4^3 = 64$. The denominator in Quantity A is greater, which makes the entire fraction smaller, so that Quantity B is greater.

4. **The correct answer is C.** At Bank A, a $100 investment earns $3 per year, so the investment will be worth $112 after 4 years. At Bank B, $100 earns $4 per year, so the investment will be worth $112 after 3 years.

5. **The correct answer is B.** Since x, y, and z are consecutive integers, $x = y - 1$ and $z = y + 1$. So $xz = (y - 1)(y + 1) = y^2 - 1$, which is less than y^2.

6. **The correct answer is C.** Angles 1 and 2 combined form a straight line along with the right angle shown, so their sum must be $180 - 90 = 90$.

7. **The correct answer is A.** M is the length of the side across from the larger angle, so it is the longer side.

8. **The correct answer is C.** For Team A, 12 represents 60% of their games, so they've played a total of $\frac{12}{0.6} = 20$ games. For Team B, 14 represents 70% of their games, so they've played a total of $\frac{14}{0.7} = 20$ games as well.

9. **The correct answer is B.** The diagonal of a square is always $\sqrt{2}$ times its side length, so the side length is $\frac{5\sqrt{2}}{\sqrt{2}} = 5$. Therefore, the perimeter is $4(5) = 20$. In choice A, you found the side length but did not multiply by 4 to find the perimeter. Choice C is incorrect because you multiplied the diagonal by 4 instead of first finding the side length. Choice D is the area of the square instead of the perimeter. Choice E is incorrect since in trying to find the side length you multiplied by $\sqrt{2}$ instead of dividing by it.

10. **The correct answer is D.** Each avocado costs $\frac{\$5}{3}$ and each mango costs $\frac{\$3}{2}$, so 7 avocados and 7 mangos will cost a total of $7\left(\frac{\$5}{3}\right)+7\left(\frac{\$3}{2}\right)=\$22.17$. Choice A is incorrect because you added the cost of 1 avocado and 1 mango. Choice B is incorrect because you added the costs given for avocados and mangos, but those were for 3 avocados and 2 mangos, respectively, not 7 of each. In choice C, you multiplied instead of divided \$5 by 3 and \$3 by 2. Choice E is incorrect because you did not first find the cost of each avocado and each mango before multiplying by 7.

11. **The correct answer is C.** If x and y have a mean of 6, their sum must be $2(6) = 12$. Similarly, u, v, and w have a sum of $3(9) = 27$. Therefore, the sum of all 5 values is $12 + 27 = 39$. Their mean is then $\frac{39}{5} = 7.8$.

    In choice A, you multiplied 6 by 3 and 9 by 2 instead of the other way around. Choice B is incorrect because you simply took the average of 6 and 9 but did not take the weights into account. Choice D is incorrect because you simply took the sum of the two averages given. Choice E is incorrect because you divided the sum of 39 by 2 instead of by 5.

12. **The correct answer is D.** There are $6 \times 6 = 36$ total possible outcomes when rolling the two dice. Of these, 6 have a 3 on the first die (since the second die can show any of 6 values), and 6 have a 3 on the second die. However, both of these sets include the possibility of 3 showing on both dice, so the total number of outcomes that satisfy the condition given is $6 + 6 - 1 = 11$. The probability is therefore $\frac{11}{36}$. Choice A is the probability that BOTH dice show a 3.

Choice B is is the probability of a single die showing a 3. Choice C is the probability that EXACTLY one die shows a 3. In choice E, you simply doubled the probability of a single die showing a 3.

13. **The correct answer is C.** Using the Pythagorean theorem, the length of the hypotenuse is the following:

$$\sqrt{12^2 + 16^2} = \sqrt{144 + 256} = \sqrt{400} = 20.$$

In choice A, you forgot to square the 12 and 16. Choice B is the average of 12 and 16. In choice D, you simply added 12 and 16. In choice E, you did not take the square root after summing the squares.

14. **The correct answer is D.** The cost of renting from the first company will be $6(14) + 0.25m = 84 + 0.25m$, where m is the number of miles you drive. The cost of renting from the second company will be $6(40) = 240$. Set these expressions equal to each other and solve:

$$84 + 0.25m = 240$$
$$0.25m = 156$$
$$m = 624$$

The cost will be the same when you drive 624 miles over the course of 6 days. Choice A is incorrect because you multiplied by 0.25 instead of dividing. Choice B is the number of miles per day, instead of for the entire rental. Choice C is the number of miles for a 2-day trip, not a 6-day trip. Choice E is incorrect because you forgot to multiply the daily cost of the first company by 6.

15. The correct answer is A. The slope of Line A is $\frac{7-1}{3-(-2)}=\frac{6}{5}$. The slope of a line perpendicular to this has the opposite reciprocal slope, or $-\frac{5}{6}$. Since Line B passes through the origin, its y-intercept is 0, so its equation is $y=-\frac{5}{6}x$. All of the other answer choices are incorrect as they have the wrong slope. Choice E additionally has an incorrect y-intercept.

16. The correct answer is B. $g(0)=-1$, so $f(g(0))=f(-1)=-4$. Choice A is incorrect since you found $g(g(0))$. In choice B, you found $g(0)$ but did not then find the value of f at that point. Choice D is incorrect because you found $g(f(0))$ instead of $f(g(0))$. Choice E is incorrect since you found $f(f(0))$.

17. The correct answer is D. The average rate of change of $g(x)$ between -1 and 3 is $\frac{g(3)-g(-1)}{3-(-1)}=\frac{1-(-5)}{3-(-1)}=\frac{6}{4}=\frac{3}{2}$. Choice A is incorrect since you just found $g(-1)$. Choice B is incorrect since you reversed the subtraction in either the numerator or denominator. Choice C is incorrect since you just found $g(3)$. Choice E is incorrect since you found $g(3)-g(-1)$ but did not divide by $3-(-1)$.

18. The correct answers are A and E. There are two unrelated restrictions to the domain of $h(x)$. First, since $x+5$ is in a square root, it must be greater than or equal to 0, so x must be at least -5. Choice A is the only value that does not satisfy this. Second, the denominator cannot be 0, so x cannot be 1. This means that choice E is also a correct answer.

19. The correct answer is 77. The prime numbers between 2 and 20 inclusive are 2, 3, 5, 7, 11, 13, 17, and 19. Their sum is 77.

20. The correct answer is 150. The vertex of the function ax^2+bx+c occurs when $x=-\frac{b}{2a}$. In this case, it occurs after $t=-\frac{96}{2(-16)}=\frac{-96}{-32}=3$ seconds.

Substitute $t=3$ into the function:

$$h(3)=-16(3)^2+96(3)+6=150$$

Section 5: Quantitative Reasoning

1. B	6. A	11. E	16. B, C, E
2. C	7. C	12. C	17. A, C
3. B	8. D	13. D	18. 5
4. A	9. A	14. C	19. 49
5. C	10. A	15. A	20. 54

1. **The correct answer is B.** Evaluate each expression. $\frac{1}{2^{-3}} = 2^3 = 8$, and $\frac{1}{3^{-2}} = 3^2 = 9$. Therefore, Quantity B is greater.

2. **The correct answer is C.** The mean of the numbers is $(19 + 21 + 23 + 25 + 27) \div 5 = 23$, and the median is also 23, since the list is in order and 23 is in the middle.

3. **The correct answer is B.** $\sqrt[5]{32} = 2$, since $2^5 = 32$. Also, $2^4 = 16$, and x is certainly greater than 16, so $\sqrt[4]{x} > 2$.

4. **The correct answer is A.** $x^2 - 5x - 14 = (x - 7)(x + 2)$, so the two solutions of the equation are 7 and -2. Their sum is 5, and their product is -14.

5. **The correct answer is C.** Since the probabilities for heads and tails on each flip are both 0.5, the probability of getting any particular sequence of two flips is $(0.5)(0.5) = 0.25$.

6. **The correct answer is A.** Since x is negative, $y - x$ is subtracting a negative number, which is the same as adding a positive number. Since y itself is positive, $y - x$ is still positive. Raising a negative number to an odd power results in a negative answer, so x^y is negative.

7. **The correct answer is C.** The area of the entire circle is $\pi(12)^2 = 144\pi$. A 60° sector is $\frac{1}{6}$ of the circle, so its area is $\frac{144\pi}{6} = 24\pi$. The perimeter of the circle is $2\pi(12) = 24\pi$.

8. **The correct answer is D.** The area of the rectangle might be greater than or less than 20. For example, the dimensions could be 9 by 1, in which case the area would be 9, or they could be 5 by 5, in which case the area is 25.

9. **The correct answer is A.**

$4^{\left(3^2\right)} = \left(2^2\right)^9 = 2^{18}$, and $\left(4^3\right)^2 = \left(2^2\right)^6 = 2^{12}$, so Quantity A is certainly greater.

10. **The correct answer is A.** After walking the distances described, Kendra is 2 miles north and 5 miles east of her house. By the Pythagorean Theorem, her distance is $\sqrt{2^2 + 5^2} = \sqrt{29} \approx 5.39$ miles. Choice B is incorrect because you did not account for the backtracking of 1 mile in each direction. In choice C, you added the 2 and 5 instead of using the Pythagorean theorem. Choice D is incorrect because you added 1 to the 3 and 6 instead of subtracting 1. In choice E, you did not take the square root of the sum of squares.

11. **The correct answer is E.** Since 49 students take both AP Calculus and AP Chemistry, there are 150 − 49 = 101 students who take ONLY AP Calculus, and 78 − 49 = 29 students who take ONLY AP Chemistry. Combined with the 49 students who take both, there are 101 + 29 + 49 = 179 students in these two classes combined. Therefore, there are 450 − 179 = 271 students who do not take either class. Choice A is the number of students who take exactly one of the two classes listed, not neither. Choice B is incorrect because you counted 49 an extra time instead of subtracting it. Choice C is the number of students who do take either Calculus or Chemistry. Choice D is incorrect because you did not subtract the 49 students who take both.

12. **The correct answer is C.** Begin solving by squaring both sides of the equation.

$$\sqrt{x+5}^2 = (x-1)^2$$
$$x + 5 = x^2 - 2x + 1$$
$$0 = x^2 - 3x - 4$$
$$0 = (x-4)(x+1)$$
$$x = 4, -1$$

However, $x = -1$ is an extraneous solution, since if you substitute it into the original equation, you get $\sqrt{4} = -2$, which is not true. The only solution is $x = 4$. Choice A is incorrect because −1 is an extraneous solution. Choice B is incorrect because you incorrectly squared the right side of the equation. Choice D is incorrect since you included −1, an extraneous solution. Choice E is incorrect since $x = 4$ is a solution.

13. **The correct answer is D.** 48 is 16% of the total, so the total number of cars is $\frac{48}{0.16} = 300$.

Choice A is the number of Subarus, not the number of cars altogether. Choice B is incorrect since 48 out of 100 would be 48%, not 16%. Choice C is the total of cars that are NOT Subaru. Choice E is incorrect because you divided by 0.016 instead of 0.16.

14. **The correct answer is C.** Hyundai and Toyota combine to account for 10 + 22 = 32% of the cars, and 0.32(600) = 192. Choice A accounts only for Hyundai, and not Toyota. Choice B accounts only for Toyota, and not Hyundai. Choice D is the number of cars that are NOT Hyundai or Toyota. Choice E is the total number of cars in the lot, not the number that are Hyundai or Toyota.

15. **The correct answer is A.** Hyundai accounts for 10% of the cars, and Honda for 20%, so the ratio is $\frac{10}{20} = \frac{1}{2}$. Choice B is the ratio of Honda cars to Hyundai cars. Choice C is the ratio of Hyundai cars to all cars. Choice D is the ratio of Honda cars to all cars. Choice E is the ratio of Hyundai cars to Toyota cars.

16. **The correct answers are B, C, and E.** The nth term of the sequence is given by $a_n = n(n+1)$. The next three terms are 6(7) = 42, 7(8) = 56, and 8(9) = 72. Choices A and D are not part of the sequence at all, while choice F is part of the sequence, but not one of the next three terms.

17. **The correct answers are A and C.** Choice A is correct since addition of real numbers is commutative. Choice C is also correct since $(x + 1)(y + 1)$ expands to $xy + x + y + 1$, so combined with the $-y$ it will give the expression on the left side. Choice B is only true when $x = y$. Choice D will only be true when both x and y are non-negative. Choice E is only true when either x or y is 0.

18. **The correct answer is 5.** Brittany is 5 years older than Marla, so when the sum of their ages is 45, Brittany will be 25 and Marla will be 20. If Marla will be twice as old as Brittany is now, then Brittany must be 10 now. Finally, Marla is 5 years younger than Brittany, so she must be 5 years old now.

19. **The correct answer is 49.** First solve for x:

$$(x+3)^2 = 16$$
$$x + 3 = \pm 4$$
$$x = -3 \pm 4 = 1, -7$$

However, x must be negative, since $x^3 < 0$. Therefore, $x = -7$, so $x^2 = (-7)^2 = 49$.

20. **The correct answer is 54.** Set up a proportion and solve:

$$\frac{45}{25} = \frac{98}{x}$$
$$45x = 2,450$$
$$x = \frac{2,450}{45} \approx 54$$

APPENDIXES

Common Errors in Grammar and Mechanics

The rubrics for both the Argument Task and the Issue Task have expectations in regard to both grammar and mechanics. One of the ways a writer can gain a score of 6 is to "demonstrate facility with the conventions of Standard English (i.e., grammar, usage, and mechanics), but [the response] may have minor errors." The question is: How "minor" are minor errors? The rubric goes on to indicate that errors "in grammar, usage, or mechanics … can interfere with meaning." That's the real problem with errors in grammar and mechanics—no matter how minor, they can hinder the reader's understanding of your ideas. Certain errors can stop a reader and interrupt the flow of the ideas that you want to get across. Certain "minor errors" can force the reader to reread the sentence or even a couple of sentences to try to figure out what you mean.

"Common Errors in Grammar and Mechanics" is neither extensive nor exhaustive, but it focuses on the common problems with sentence construction that trip up many writers—occasionally, even the best of writers. This information should help you avoid some of the errors that can throw your meaning into question and detract from your analysis. It also highlights some problems with pronouns that, if consistently present, may detract from your score. You won't have much time to edit your response, so concentrate on possible problems in the order that you see here:

- Sentence Faults
- Misplaced Modifiers
- Subject-Verb Agreement
- Pronoun Problems
- A Few Additional Words of Advice

SENTENCE FAULTS

The most important idea to take away from this section on sentence faults is that fixing these problems is not just a matter of cleaning up grammar; it's a matter of making decisions that will make it easier for your reader to understand your ideas. There are three sentence faults, or problems with sentence constructions, that you should be aware of as you write and proofread your responses. You won't have time to do much editing, so concentrate on finding and correcting these three problems first as you review your responses. They can seriously detract from meaning and hinder your reader's understanding of your thesis.

Comma Splice

A comma splice occurs when two or more independent clauses are joined only by a comma.

> Sam decided to go back for his **umbrella, Jack** thought he would get his, too.

You can fix a comma fault by separating the two clauses completely with a period, or by separating them less completely with a semicolon. In the example sentence, the ideas are so closely related that a semicolon could be considered the better choice.

> Sam decided to go back for his **umbrella; Jack** thought he would get his, too.

You can also fix a comma splice by using a coordinating or a subordinating conjunction to join the two clauses.

- With a coordinating conjunction, the two clauses remain equal in importance.
- With a subordinating conjunction, one clause becomes subordinate to the other.

This decision isn't just a matter of grammar; it's a matter of meaning. It's a choice that you, as the writer, need to make. Are the ideas equally important? Is there one idea that you want to emphasize over the other? Perhaps you decide that the two ideas are equally important, and you choose to use a coordinating conjunction to connect the two ideas/clauses.

Coordinating Conjunctions

The coordinating conjunctions are as follows:

and	for	so
but	nor	yet
or		

With a coordinating conjunction:

> Sam decided to go back for his umbrella, **and** Jack thought he would get his, too.

If you decide that one idea is more important than the other, then you need to emphasize that idea. That idea becomes the main clause of the new sentence, and the second idea becomes the dependent, or subordinate, clause. Then you need to use a subordinating conjunction to fix the comma fault.

Subordinating Conjunctions

The following are commonly used subordinating conjunctions:

after	even if	once	when
although	even though	provided that	whenever
as far as	how	rather than	where
as soon as	if	since	whereas
as if	in case that	so that	wherever
as though	in order that	though	whether
because	no matter how	until	while
before	now that	unless	why

With subordinating conjunction:

> **When** Sam decided to go back for his umbrella, Jack thought he would get his, too.

Run-on Sentence

A run-on sentence has two or more independent clauses that are not connected by either punctuation or a conjunction.

> Sam took his wife's yellow ***umbrella he*** couldn't find his when he left for work.

As with comma splices, you can fix a run-on sentence by separating the two clauses with a period if the ideas are equal in importance. If the ideas are equal in importance and closely related, then use a semicolon between the two clauses.

> Sam took his wife's yellow ***umbrella; he*** couldn't find his when he left for work.

If the sentences are not equal in importance, the easiest way to correct the problem is with a subordinating conjunction.

> Sam took his wife's yellow umbrella ***because*** he couldn't find his when he left for work.

However, there are additional ways to solve the problem with a run-on sentence. You could use a conjunctive adverb or a transitional phrase. Both may require some rewriting of the original sentence.

With a conjunctive adverb:

> Sam couldn't find his umbrella when he left for work; ***consequently***, he took his wife's yellow umbrella.

With a transitional phrase:

> Sam couldn't find his umbrella when he left for work. ***As a result***, he took his wife's yellow umbrella.

There are a variety of conjunctive adverbs and transitional phrases you can use to solve run-on sentence problems.

TIP

Often in trying to get thoughts down in a timed situation like answering the Analytical Writing tasks, some writers tend to write a series of simple sentences. As you review your responses, if you have a number of simpler sentences in a row, try to combine some of them into a variety of sentences such as compound (using coordinating conjunctions), complex (using subordinating conjunctions, conjunctive adverbs, and transitional phrases), and compound-complex sentences (using both coordinating conjunctions and the other connectors listed in this section).

Conjunctive Adverbs

also	incidentally	now
anyhow	indeed	otherwise
anyway	likewise	similarly
besides	meanwhile	still
consequently	moreover	then
finally	nevertheless	therefore
furthermore	next	thus
however	nonetheless	

Transitional Phrases

after all	by the way	in other words
as a consequence	even so	in the first place, in the
as a result	for example	second place, etc.
at any rate	in addition	on the contrary
at the same time	in fact	on the other hand

Like fixing comma splices, fixing run-on sentences is not just a matter of cleaning up a grammar problem. It's a matter of deciding what you want to say—what's important—and choosing the best solution to make your meaning clear.

Sentence Fragment

A sentence fragment is a group of words that has a period at the end, but does not express a complete thought. It may have a verb form, that is, a verbal such as a participle, but that's not the same as a verb.

> Sam *carrying* a yellow umbrella to the office.

The following are possible corrections of the problem, depending on time:

> Sam *is carrying* a yellow umbrella to the office.

> Sam *carries* a yellow umbrella to the office.

> Sam *was carrying* a yellow umbrella to the office.

> Sam *carried* a yellow umbrella to the office.

There are several types of sentence fragments in addition to the example above and several ways to correct them.

A subordinate clause alone:

> *Because he thought it would rain.* Sam was carrying his umbrella.

Rewritten as a subordinate clause:

> *Because he thought it would rain,* Sam was carrying his umbrella.

A phrase:

> Sam was ready for rain. *First, his umbrella and then his raincoat.*

Rewritten as a sentence:

> Sam was ready for rain. ***First, he took out his umbrella and then his raincoat.***

A verbal phrase:

> Sam was impatient for the bus to come. *Kept looking up the street for it.*

Combined and rewritten as a single new sentence:

> ***Sam, impatient for the bus to come, kept looking up the street for it.***

This is an example of a writer's judgment. The writer decided that being impatient was less important to the context of what he or she wanted to say than looking up the street for the bus.

About Using Dashes

Use dashes sparingly. They often mark the work of writers who don't have a command of standard English, don't know how to develop ideas clearly, or have little to say. Use dashes if you want to show a break in thought, or to emphasize a parenthetical idea, for example, ". . . would be a sufficient reason—unless you are a dog owner."

Misplaced Modifiers

A misplaced modifier is any word, phrase, or clause that does not refer clearly and logically to other words or phrases in the sentence. There are two problems involving misplaced modifiers.

The first occurs when a word, phrase, or clause is not close to the part of the sentence that it refers to, thus confusing the reader. Let's look at a few examples:

Example 1

> Sam ***wrote*** that he was taking her umbrella ***in the note he left his wife***.

A clearer version is:

> Sam ***wrote in the note*** he left his wife that he was taking her umbrella.

Example 2

> Sam's ***wife*** was annoyed because now she didn't have an umbrella ***who is usually very easy-going***.

A clearer version is:

> Sam's ***wife, who is usually very easy-going,*** was annoyed because now she didn't have an umbrella.

Example 3

> At the bus stop, Sam didn't see the ***bus trying to stay dry under his umbrella***.

The bus was trying to stay dry under the umbrella? Interesting mental picture, but try this:

> At the bus stop, ***Sam, trying to stay dry under his umbrella,*** didn't see the bus.

NOTE

It's worth repeating that the names of the parts of speech are irrelevant. What you need to remember are the different problems you might run into in your writing and how to solve them.

TIP

An easy way to rec-
ognize a participle is
by the *-ing* ending.
Not all participles end
in *-ing* in English, but
many do.

The second and more serious problem with misplaced modifiers occurs when a phrase introduced by a verbal (a word formed from a verb but functioning as a different part of speech) such as a participle doesn't relate clearly to another word or phrase in the sentence. The problem is often the lack of a clear relationship between the subject of the sentence and the phrase.

Example 1

Holding the umbrella sideways, the car splashed him anyway.

In this sentence, the true subject is missing. It seems that the car was holding the umbrella sideways when the writer meant:

Holding the umbrella sideways, Sam was splashed by the car anyway.

Example 2

On entering the bus, there were no seats.

Who entered the bus?

On entering the bus, Sam saw there were no seats.

Example 3

Hot and tired, that was the perfect end to a perfect day, thought Sam ironically.

What? Try instead:

Hot and tired, Sam thought ironically that it was the perfect end to a perfect day.

The above examples are all simple so that you can easily see the problem and the correction. But the following example shows what can happen when a writer writes quickly to get thoughts down. See if you can spot the errors in this excerpt from a response to an Issue Task and how you think they should be fixed.

The arts make an important contribution to the economy of communities across the nation this is true. Even when the economy is in trouble. Governments should fund arts programs. When arts programs thrive, tax receipts flow into government coffers. It's not just the artists who make money. But people who work in allied businesses. For example, my small city has a live theater company that produces three plays a year plus has several concerts and dance programs. Having no other theater for a 75-mile radius, it brings in people from the region. These people go to dinner at local restaurants they park in a garage near the theater if they come early, they shop in local stores. All this brings in money to stores and restaurants that have to hire people to serve these theatergoers. Every sale means sales tax for the city and for the state, jobs and income taxes for the state and the federal government.

A revised version might read like this:

The arts make an important contribution to the economy of <u>communities.</u> <u>Across</u> the nation this is true. Even when the economy is in <u>trouble,</u> <u>governments</u> should fund arts programs. When arts programs thrive, tax receipts flow into government coffers. It's not just the artists who make money, but also people who work in allied businesses. For example, my small city has a live theater company that produces three plays a year plus has several concerts and dance programs. Having no other theater for a 75-mile radius, people come to my city from across the region. These people go to dinner at local restaurants and park in a garage near the theater. If they come early, they shop in local stores. All this brings in money to stores and restaurants that have to hire people to serve these theatergoers. Every sale means sales tax for the city and the state, and jobs and income taxes for the state and the federal government.

As you can see from the examples in this section, it is often necessary to rework sentences to establish the clear relationship between the misplaced word, phrase, or clause and the word it modifies. Keep this in mind as you revise your practice drafts so that on test day, you'll be able to spot problems quickly and know a range of options for correcting them.

Subject-Verb Agreement Problems

The following are probably two rules that you've heard a thousand times:

- A singular subject takes a singular verb.
- A plural subject takes a plural verb.

However, the correct subject-verb agreement can still elude a writer when several words, phrases, or even a subordinate clause comes between the subject and the verb. This is especially true when the subject is singular, but a plural noun ends a prepositional phrase just before the verb, or vice versa. Such an error usually doesn't impede understanding and one or two won't hurt your score, but try for as few of these problems as possible.

> Sam's *umbrella* along with his briefcase and gym shoes *were* under his desk.

The correct version may sound odd to your ear, but the verb should be *was*.

> Sam's *umbrella* along with his briefcase and gym shoes *was* under his desk.

Here's a plural subject-verb agreement problem:

> The *umbrellas*, which belonged to Sam and Jack and were a riot of color, *was* a welcome sight on the gray day.

In this example, the comma after *color* should clue you that *color* can't be the subject of the verb.

> The *umbrellas*, which belonged to Sam and Jack and were a riot of color, *were* a welcome sight on the gray day.

Pronoun Problems

There are a variety of pronouns and a variety of problems you can get into when using them. The most common problems involve using incorrect forms, having unclear antecedents, and confusing pronouns with other words. One or two or even three mistakes with pronouns shouldn't be reflected in your score, but consistent mistakes throughout your response could cause you to lose a point.

Unclear antecedents are a meaning issue; if the reader can't tell to whom or to what you're referring, that can affect meaning.

Unclear Antecedents for Pronouns

The antecedent is the word that the pronoun refers to, or stands in for, in the sentence. When you review your essays, check for any problems with clarity so that the reader will have no difficulty in telling to whom or to what pronouns refer.

> Jack and Sam went back to their offices to get their umbrellas because it was starting to rain. They were gone for a few minutes because *theirs* were across the floor from the elevator.

A clearer version is:

> Jack and Sam went back to their offices to get their umbrellas because it was starting to rain. They were gone for a few minutes because *their offices* were across the floor from the elevator.

Incorrect Forms

Is it *I* or *me*, *she* or *her*, *he* or *him*, *we* or *them*? Most people don't have trouble figuring out which pronoun to use when the subject of a sentence or clause is singular. The trouble comes when the subject is plural.

> *Her* and I went. *Him* and I went. We and *them* went, or even, *us* and *them* went.

The sentences should read:

> *She* and I went. *He* and I went. *We* and *they* went.

Objects of verbs and prepositions (*of, for, in, on*, etc.) are another problem area for pronoun forms.

> The umbrellas belong to *him* and **I** (or to *he* and *I*).

> The umbrellas belong to *her* and **I**, (or to *she* and *I*).

> The umbrellas belong to *them* and **I** (or to *they* and *I*).

The correct sentences are:

> The umbrellas belong to *him* and *me*.

> The umbrellas belong to *her* and *me*.

> The umbrellas belong to *them* and *me*.

Confusing Pronoun Forms with Other Words

You've probably heard these rules in every English/language arts class you've ever taken, but they're worth repeating because many writers still make these errors.

- **it's or its**

  It's is a contraction that stands for *it is*: *It's* raining. (*It is* raining.)

  Its is an adjective that modifies a noun: The dog got *its* coat wet because *it's* raining.

An easy way to test which word you should use is to substitute *it is* in the sentence: The dog got *it is* coat wet because *it is* raining. "It is coat" doesn't make sense, so it must be "*its* coat."

- **who's or whose**

This pair of often confused words is similar to the problem—and the solution—with *it's* and *its*. *Who's* is a contraction that stands for *who is*: *Who's* going to take an umbrella? (*Who is* going to take an umbrella?)

Whose is an interrogative pronoun that shows possession: *Whose* umbrella will we take?

Like testing out *it's* and *its*, substitute *who* and *whose* into the sentence: *Who is* going to take *who is* umbrella? "Who is umbrella" doesn't make sense, so it must be "*whose* umbrella."

- **they're, their, or there**

They're is a contraction that stands for *they are*: *They're* going to take umbrellas. (*They are* going to take umbrellas.)

Their is a possessive adjective that shows possession or ownership: Jack and Sam are taking *their* own umbrellas.

There is a pronoun that is used to introduce a clause or a sentence when the subject comes after the verb: *There* were no umbrellas in the closet.

Substitute *they are* in a sentence to see if the substitution makes sense: *They are* looking in *they are* desks for umbrellas. "They are desks" makes no sense, so it must be "*their* desks."

Knowing the difference between *there* and the other two forms is something you must learn; there's no easy solution, which brings up the issue of *there's* and *theirs*.

Theirs is a form of the personal pronoun that shows ownership in the third person (as opposed to the first person [*mine, ours*] or the second person [*yours*]): Those umbrellas are *theirs*. (The umbrellas belong to certain people.)

There's is a contraction that stands for *there is*: *There's* no umbrella in the closet. (*There is* no umbrella in the closet.)

Substitute *there is* in the sentence: *There is* one umbrella, but I doubt that it's either one of *there is*. "There is" at the end of the sentence doesn't make sense, so it must be *theirs*, meaning something belonging to two or more.

A Few Additional Words of Advice

Please keep these ideas in mind as you write and revise your responses:

- **Use Active Voice Whenever Possible.** Passive voice (the parts of the verb *to be*) can weaken your writing. Instead of "Ticket sales were underwritten by a grant," try "a grant underwrote ticket sales."

- **Get Rid of Redundancies.** Avoid wordiness and redundancies that just fill up space. It's the quality of your thoughts that counts toward your score, not the length. Repetition and wordiness can mask a good analysis.

- **Don't Use Jargon, Clichés, and Slang.** Jargon (words and phrases used by a certain group of people, usually in a specific profession) doesn't fit the tone and style required to answer either an issue or an argument task. The use of clichés (trite or overused expressions or ideas) can indicate that the writer is (1) not a very original thinker or (2) trying to fill up space. Slang doesn't fit the tone or style either.

FOUR STEPS TO HELP YOU PRACTICE YOUR GRAMMAR SKILLS

1. To practice what you've learned about correcting common errors that can affect your comprehension, choose four pieces of writing that you've done recently that are about the same length as the Analytical Writing tasks on the GRE® General Test. Review each one to see if you have any of the errors that are described in this section. Revise any errors that you find.

2. Review the two tasks on the Diagnostic Test and any of the Practice Tests (if you have already taken them). Correct any errors that you find.

3. Keep the concepts from this review in mind as you write any of the remaining writing tasks on the Practice Tests. After you evaluate and score each one, go back and correct any errors. The fewer the errors in Standard English, the better the chance of a score of 5 or 6 on the GRE® General Test and the better presentation you'll make in any written document in your professional life.

4. **Remember:** Errors like the ones described in these pages can make it difficult for the reader to understand your ideas, and that can affect your score.

Often Confused and Confusing Words

The confusion with these words may not come from a misunderstanding of their meaning, but rather from a problem of misspelling. As you review the word pairs in this section, pay special attention to the spelling of each word as well as its meaning.

A

accept: (verb) to receive

except: (preposition) excluding or omitting

(conjunction) other than, but

He bought all the tulips *except* the white ones.

He would have *accepted* the award in person *except* he was in Hong Kong.

accuse: (verb) to blame

allege: (verb) to state as a fact something that has yet to be proven

He was *accused* of white collar theft and was *alleged* to have stolen $5 million.

adopt: (verb) to take as one's own

adapt: (verb) to change

adept: (adjective) very skilled

Adept at organizational design, she *adopted* the plan and then *adapted* it to her unit's needs.

advice: (noun) opinion

advise: (verb) to guide or recommend concerning future action

He *advised* the accused on his rights, but his *advice* was ignored.

affect: (verb) to influence; to pretend

effect: (noun) result or outcome

(verb) to bring about (less common usage)

He was able to *affect* her decision, but the *effect* was minimal.

Her arrogance *effected* her downfall.

aggregate: (noun) collection of separate parts into a whole

(verb) to combine into one

total: (noun) a whole without regard to its parts

(verb) to add up

The *aggregate* budget deficits for the five largest cities *totaled* more than $100 billion; the *total* was staggering.

alternate: (adjective) happening in turns, first one and then the other

(verb) to take turns

alternative: (noun) choice between two mutually exclusive options

Rather than always meeting on the third Thursday of the month, the *alternative* was to *alternate* between third Thursdays and Tuesdays.

allude: (verb) to refer indirectly to a person, object, or event

elude: (verb) to evade or slip away from

The candidate *alluded* to her opponent by mimicking his answer that "the nuances of the Iran policy *elude*" some who would serve on the foreign affairs committee.

allusion: (noun) reference or mention of something or someone

illusion: (noun) mistaken perception of reality

In an effort to create the *illusion* of erudition in his paper, the student used many *allusions* to Shakespearian characters and themes.

ambivalent: (adjective) holding conflicting wishes, unable to decide, unsure

ambiguous: (adjective) difficult to understand, having more than one interpretation

He was *ambivalent* about the promotion because the new job description was *ambiguous* about to whom he actually reported: the CFO or the COO.

anachronism: (noun) person or object placed in the wrong time

anomaly: (noun) departure from the norm; peculiar, irregular, abnormal

The play had a number of *anachronisms*, but the worst was the presence of a telephone in an 1850s parlor; then there was the greatest *anomaly:* a zombie as the house maid.

arbitrate: (verb) to settle a dispute in a legal sense

mediate: (verb) to act as a go-between, to negotiate between parties

Jack was called in to *arbitrate* between management and the union when the judge ordered an injunction against the strikers.

Will had to *mediate* a dispute between his sons over whose turn it was to have the car.

authoritarian: (adjective) having complete power, expecting complete obedience

authoritative: (adjective) official, very reliable; exercising power

The president was *authoritarian* in his manner because the military backed him up.

The president had a very *authoritative* manner in dealing with his ministers.

This edition of the play is the *authoritative* version; no scholar questions that it represents the author's complete changes.

C

condemn: (verb) to express disapproval

condone: (verb) to excuse, to overlook; to forgive

The dictator *condemned* the protesters as criminals, but he *condoned* the methods his soldiers used to suppress the protesters.

complaisant: (adjective) tending to consent to others' wishes

complacent: (adjective) pleased with one's self

The members up for re-election were *complacent,* thinking their record in office was sufficient for re-election. They saw no need to be *complaisant* toward the voters and were soundly defeated as a result.

complement: (noun) completing a whole, satisfying a need

              (verb) to complete a whole, to satisfy a need

compliment: (noun) praise

             (verb) to praise

The full *complement* of engineers who worked on the project was *complimented* on their diligence. The work of the engineers *complemented* the work of the programmers—all of whom received *compliments* on their work.

contention: (noun) point made in an argument; dispute, controversy, quarrel

contentious: (adjective) quarrelsome, always ready to argue

The board meeting turned *contentious* with the *contention* by the new member that the director was out of order.

continual: (adjective) recurring regularly or frequently

continuous: (adjective) occurring without interruption

constantly: (adverb) regularly recurring

The faucet was leaking *constantly,* and I couldn't stand the *continual* drip-drip; it was worse than the sound of a *continuous* stream of water would have been.

credible: (adjective) believable, plausible

credulous: (adjective) too ready to believe, gullible

The plaintiff's testimony that she had bought drugs on the street thinking they were incense was *credible* only to the *credulous* member of the jury who had recently moved to the city.

D

defective: (adjective) faulty, flawed

deficient: (adjective) lacking some essential part, inadequate

The *defective* part didn't work; it was *deficient.*

deterrent: (noun) something that keeps another from doing something

detriment: (noun) something that causes harm or loss

Star Wars was supposed to be a *deterrent* to war with the Soviet Union, but it was considered by many to be a *detriment* to increased funding for the conventional army.

disinterested: (adjective) impartial

uninterested: (adjective) bored

The mediator was a *disinterested* party to the dispute between the couple, one of whom yawned constantly and seemed *uninterested* in the proceedings.

distinct: (adjective) unmistakable, clear

distinctive: (adjective) something that sets a person or thing apart from everything else, characteristic

I had the *distinct* impression that she wore a red scarf with every outfit so she would be *distinctive* in a roomful of her peers.

discrete: (adjective) separate, distinct, unconnected

discreet: (adjective) prudent, unobtrusive, diplomatic

The scientist was examining *discrete* bits of evidence and finding that they did not support his colleague's theory, but he was *discreet* about his findings until he was sure.

E

elicit: (verb) to draw out, to call forth

illicit: (adjective) unlawful

The lawyer was able to *elicit* from the witness information about the *illicit* bank transactions.

endemic: (adjective) prevalent in a particular area or among a particular group or region

epidemic: (adjective) spreading rapidly

　　　　　(noun) outbreak of a contagious disease

With the availability of air travel, an *epidemic* has the potential to spread quickly from being *endemic* to a country to being global.

energize: (verb) to give energy to, to invigorate

enervate: (verb) to weaken

I find that exercise *energizes* me rather than *enervates* me; I find that I am more alert and ready to tackle work after a good run.

expatiate: (verb) to enlarge on, to speak or write at length

expiate: (verb) to make amends for, to make up for

The professor *expatiated* on his favorite poet oblivious to the growing restlessness in his class. In an effort to *expiate* for his digression, the professor dismissed the class early.

expedient: (adjective) suitable, appropriate

　　　　　(noun) means to an end

expeditiously: (adjective) acting quickly and efficiently

The *expedient* thing to do was to process the woman's visa request as *expeditiously* as possible so she could visit her ill mother.

F

fortuitous: (adjective) occurring by chance or accident; happening by a lucky chance

fortunate: (adjective) being lucky, having good luck

Jack's winning the lottery was *fortuitous* because it means he'll be *fortunate* enough to begin his career with no debt.

H

humane: (adjective) marked by mercy, kindness, or compassion
humanitarian: (adjective) having the best interests of humankind at heart
         (noun) philanthropist
Mother Theresa was a great *humanitarian*; she believed that everyone, even the poorest of the poor, deserved *humane* care.

hypercritical: (adjective) excessively critical, overcritical
hypocritical: (adjective) insincere, expressing feelings or virtues that one doesn't have
The review panel's analysis was *hypercritical*, finding fault even with the feeding times used. The chief reviewer expressed sympathy with the lead researcher who thought him *hypocritical* because the two often competed for the same grants.

I

imply: (verb) to suggest indirectly
infer: (verb) to draw a conclusion from
The report *implied* that the deal was fraudulent, and I *inferred* from the details that the executive was the culprit.

incipient: (adjective) beginning to appear, emergent
insipid: (adjective) lacking spirit, dull boring; lacking taste or flavor
The *incipient* revolt was quashed by the army before it could attract many followers.
Lacking in flavor, the tea was as *insipid* as the dull host's conversation was boring.

ingenious: (adjective) inventive, skillful; clever; shrewd
ingenuous: (adjective) candid, frank, straightforward; showing a childlike innocence or simplicity
ingénue: (noun) naïve young woman or girl
Casting the college student as the *ingénue* was *ingenious*; she is perfect for the part of an *ingenuous* newcomer to Broadway.

insoluble: (adjective) unable to dissolve; unable to solve
insolvent: (adjective) unable to pay debts, bankrupt
Why two chemicals when mixed together were *insoluble* in water was an *insoluble* (also spelled *unsolvable*) problem for the chemistry class.
The company was *insolvent* and filed for Chapter 11 bankruptcy.

intense: (adjective) extreme, using great effort
intensive: (adjective) concentrated, making heavy use of something
The six-week immersion course in Spanish was *intensive* and was a very *intense* experience.

J

judicial: (adjective) relating to the courts

judicious: (adjective) showing good judgment

Certain *judicial* appointments below the Supreme Court require Senate confirmation, and presidents attempt to be *judicious* in selecting nominees who will win confirmation without heated debate.

M

marshal: (verb) to arrange in order; to solicit, to guide

martial: (adjective) relating to war or a fighter

Before applying for a license, the businessman *marshaled* support for his *martial* arts studio from the other storefront businesses.

N

negligible: (adjective) insignificant, unimportant

negligent: (adjective) lacking attention to something, careless

The attorney was *negligent* in not telling his witness of the change in court dates. However, the effect on the case was *negligible*.

P

populace: (noun) general public, population

populous: (adjective) having a large population

Much of the *populace* lived in the *populous* suburbs of the three major cities.

precede: (verb) to go before

proceed: (verb) to continue

He waved for the woman to *precede* him through the door, and then they *proceeded* down the hall together.

precipitate: (verb) to cause to happen sooner than expected

precipitous: (adjective) hasty, acting without thinking

The prime minister's refusal to fire his cabinet secretary *precipitated* a call for elections in June rather than September. The opposition may find that the move was *precipitous* because its poll numbers are falling steadily.

prescribe: (verb) to establish a rule or guide; to order medicine

proscribe: (verb) to forbid, to prohibit

The doctor *prescribed* an antibiotic for the infection.

The judge *proscribed* any further contact between the two parties to the lawsuit.

proceeding: (noun) course of action, sequence of events, legal action
preceding: (adjective) coming before
The juvenile *proceeding* took place in the judge's chamber, *preceding* the regular court cases for the day.

R

reversal: (noun) turning around
reversion: (noun) turning back
The *reversal* of the appeal required a *reversion* of the patent to the company's former employee.

S

simple: (adjective) not involved or complicated; unpretentious; humble
simplistic: (adjective) making complex problems overly simple
The explanation of the motivations of the antagonist was *simplistic*, but then the critic tended to look at most motivations as *simple* issues of right and wrong.

stultify: (verb) to make useless or worthless; to take away strength or efficiency
stupefy: (verb) to make dull or stupid; to confuse or astound
Many experts fear that the hours of television that children watch every day *stultifies* their brains. A woman born in 1900 would be *stupefied* by the gadgets available today in most U.S. kitchens.

subtitle: (noun) second part of a title, often an explanation of the title
subtle: (adjective) not obvious, difficult to detect or understand
The *subtitle* of the report was not *subtle* in describing the author's opinion.

PRACTICE

After you finish reading the list once, go back and check off each word that you have difficulty with or are unfamiliar with. Write a sentence of your own that will help you remember the word.

NOTES

NOTES

NOTES

NOTES

NOTES